DATE DUE

DEMCO 38-296

East Central European politics today

East Central European Politics Today is the first truly comparative volume to be written about the problems faced by the former East European bloc countries during the first six years of their transition from centrally planned, one-party communist states within the Soviet sphere of interest to free-market, liberal democracies on the verge of joining both NATO and the European Union. Keith Crawford chronicles and explains the chaos of those years and the emergence of a type of post-communist stability by the mid-1990s, based on his personal experience of living and working in the region during the whole period of that transition. A lucid and enlightening introduction to a region that is little understood in Western Europe and the USA, Keith Crawford's volume is essential reading for students and researchers of East Central Europe.

Keith Crawford is Visiting Professor of Political Science at Charles University, Prague, Czech Republic.

Politics Today

Series Editor: Bill Jones

East Central European politics today

From chaos to stability?

Keith Crawford

Manchester University Press
Manchester and New York

Distributed exclusively in the USA by St. Martin's Press

Copyright © Keith Crawford 1996

), USA

k,

British Library Cataloguing-in-Publication Data
A catalogue record for this book is available from the British Library

Library of Congress Cataloging-in-Publication Data

Crawford, Keith
    East Central European politics today / Keith Crawford.
      p. cm. – (Politics today)
    Includes bibliographical references.
    ISBN 0-7190-4621-1 (hardcover: alk. paper). – ISBN 0-7190-4622-X
(pbk.: alk. paper)
      1. Post-communism–Europe, Eastern.   2. Democracy–Europe,
Eastern.   3. Europe, Eastern–Politics and government–1989–
4. Europe, Eastern–Social conditions–1989–   I. Title.
II. Series: Politics today (Manchester, England)
JN96.A91C72 1996
943'.0009717–dc20   96-27172
                                                                 CIP

ISBN   0 7190 4621 1   *hardback*
        0 7190 4622 X   *paperback*

First published 1996

01 00 99 98 97   10 9 8 7 6 5 4 3 2 1

Printed by Biddles Ltd, Guildford and King's Lynn

Contents

Preface

The theme of the book

This book was begun in the autumn of 1994, on the fifth anniversary of the 'revolutions' in East Central Europe (ECE); it was completed in early 1996 and so is an attempt to analyse the six years of post-communist government within the region since January 1990. Thus, the book examines a period of chaotic, post-revolutionary confusion in which ECE is searching for its own model of democracy and a new geo-political role in the world.

During this period, Poland had five different governments and six premiers, while Bulgaria went full circle from an ex-communist, to a dissident, to a technocratic and back again to an ex-communist government. Yet the situation in both countries seems to have stabilised with the return to power of the ex-communists since 1993 (the so-called 'velvet restoration').

The purpose of this book is to analyse this period of instability and to question whether ECE will be able to make a successful transition to democracy, based on what has happened during the first six years since the 'revolutions'.

The present situation

The revolutions that occurred in the late 1980s throughout the former Soviet bloc represent some of the most dramatic and far-reaching changes in the history of Europe during the twentieth century. Stephen Heintz has likened them to a twentieth-century fall of the Roman Empire.

After the collapse of post-war communism, all ECE polities are undergoing a transition to democracy and a transformation of their formerly centrally planned economies. This is occurring at different speeds and to various extents throughout the region. The overriding question is where the transitional process will lead to: (1) the consolidation of democracy, (2) the establishment of ethnocracies, (3) the return to a sort of socialism or (4) the reversion to a more authoritarian-type regime.

One of the main purposes of this volume of the 'Politics Today' series is to help readers grasp the enormity of those changes and to place them in the context of the post-war development of the European continent.

ECE is very different

The division between East and West in Europe goes back to the eleventh-century schism between Roman Catholicism, predominantly in Western Europe, and Orthodox Christianity within the Eastern Byzantine Church. That dividing line met in ECE: the Poles, Czechs, Slovaks, Hungarians, Slovenes and Croats were mainly tied to the Roman Catholic Church, while the Russians, Ukrainians, Serbs, Bulgarians and Romanians remained Orthodox Christians.

The more recent, post-war, East–West divide was of a totally political nature and quite nonsensical geographically speaking. Within the context of the Cold War, the 'West' was defined by membership of the North Atlantic Treaty Organisation (NATO), the European Union or the Organisation for Economic Co-operation and Development (OECD). This meant that Ankara and Athens were both effectively part of Western Europe, while Budapest and Warsaw were not. Likewise, Vienna was automatically considered 'Western' via OECD membership, and yet the city lies further to the east than Prague, in post-war 'Eastern' Europe.

Furthermore, during most post-war history, the Communist, one-party dictatorships and centrally planned economies of the Soviet Union and Eastern Europe were known as the *Second World* (in comparison with the *First World* free-market economies and liberal democracies of Western Europe and North America and the *Third World* developing nations in parts of South America, Africa and Asia).

Although this Second World has disappeared, strictly speaking, ECE countries are still very different from the First World and will probably remain so for many decades. In general the region is considerably poorer, much less democratic in attitudes, less developed socially speaking and is only just beginning to introduce something resembling a market economy – which is why M. G. Roskin calls it 'World 1.5'.

In fact, the whole region has been 'backward' in comparison with Western Europe for centuries, economically, socially and politically speaking. Over forty years of Communist rule re-inforced that position of 'backwardness' during a time of quite incredible innovation and expansion in Western Europe. ECE's politics and economics in the 1990s, therefore, resemble those of Western European in the immediate post-1945 period – but without the cushioning effect of Marshall aid.

Politically speaking, today's situation in ECE also recalls the conditions immediately after the First World War. The fear is that the political development of the area could once again lead to the collapse of democracy and to a revival of the sorts of authoritarian regimes which characterised almost all of the region in the inter-war period before the rise of fascism.

What is in a name?

In the autumn of 1994 Richard Holbrooke, US Assistant Secretary of State, let it be known that henceforth, as far as US foreign policy is concerned, Hungary, the Czech and Slovak Republics, Poland, Slovenia and Croatia are to be called *Central Europe*, while Bulgaria, Romania, the rest of former Yugoslavia and Albania are still part of *Eastern Europe*.

It is true that the former East European region cannot be seen as one entity, being divided into those more central lands formerly ruled over by the Austrian Habsburgs, and those Balkan countries which previously fell under the influence of the Ottoman Turks. Each occupying empire left behind varying traditions and politico-economic structures, so that the post-war political, social and economic differences between former Czechoslovakia and Albania within COMECON were just as great as those between West Germany and Greece within the European Union.

For the inhabitants of the region, however, *Eastern Europe* is a loaded term and carries with it all the connotations of Soviet control. In any case, if Europe is taken to mean the land mass between the Atlantic and Urals, then there are many newly independent nations that could rightly be called Eastern Europe (e.g. Belarus, Lithuania, Latvia, Estonia, Moldova and Ukraine), which would mean that the area studied in this volume falls somewhere else, somewhere 'in-between'.

Furthermore, using the term *Central Europe* re-opens a debate that started shortly after the Napoleonic Wars and the 1815 Congress of Vienna. Since then, a whole host of writers and academics have attempted to define the concept. Depending on one's viewpoint, such far-flung places as southern Greece, British East Anglia and north-east Spain have all been called part of Central Europe at some time or other. In any case, Central Europe should not refer just to the region that was once under Communist control, but should also include other parts of *Western Europe*, in particular Austria, Germany, Liechtenstein, Switzerland and maybe northern Italy.

East Central Europe, on the other hand, is a term that has been used since 1989 specifically to distinguish the post-revolutionary regimes from the former Communist states of Eastern Europe. These countries can also be distinguished from *West Central Europe*, which would include those countries mentioned at the end of the preceding paragraph.

The term East Central Europe was first used by the historian Joseph Rothschild in a series of books about the region, published from the mid-1970s onwards. It has also been used by several authors to describe the region since 1989. For the purposes of this volume, Rothschild's example will be followed and reference made to the whole region during its entire history by its more recent title of East Central Europe. Furthermore, for the sake of brevity, the abbreviations 'ECE' or 'ECE countries' will be used throughout the book.

The countries chosen as constituting ECE are the same (originally) eight countries which feature in Rothschild's books – those countries which served as the *cordon sanitaire* between the former USSR and Western Europe: Poland, Czechoslovakia (after 1992 the Czech and Slovak Republics), Hungary, Romania, Bulgaria, East Germany, Albania and Yugoslavia (after 1990 dividing into the following independent nations – Slovenia, Croatia, Bosnia-Hercegovina, Macedonia and the Federal Republic of Yugoslavia – i.e. Serbia and Montenegro). The Baltic countries of Estonia, Latvia and Lithuania have been excluded, as they were part of the USSR itself and therefore had a very specific post-war history.

As with Western Europe, a single term will never be able to convey the differences among such a wide variety of cultures and political experiences (such as the differences between northern Western Europe – i.e. Scandinavia, Britain and Germany – and southern Western Europe – i.e. the Mediterranean countries like Spain, Portugal, southern France and Italy).

Structure of the book

It is the democratic transition that is central to the book, not the transformation of the previously centrally planned economies to the free market – although aspects of the latter are discussed throughout. Furthermore, there is no comprehensive analysis here of the new international relations and security issues that have arisen since the end of the Cold War. These two topics merit their own books and are just too lengthy to examine in any great depth in this volume.

The book is more or less divided into three parts:

(1) The first three chapters look at what preceded the post-communist period. Chapter 1 provides the background to the geography, history, cultural and political traditions of the region up to the Communist takeovers after 1945. Chapter 2 examines ECE under communism and in particular the effect of prevailing totalitarian or post-totalitarian attitudes on post-war ECE societies. Chapter 3 discusses the actual revolutions within each of the countries concerned.

(2) The second part of the book examines what these countries are moving towards, that is, democracy and nationhood. Chapter 4 defines 'democracy' and looks at much of the theory of transition, in order to compare ECE since 1989 with transitions to democracy elsewhere in the world. Chapter 5 attempts to chronicle many of the specific 'obstacles' to the transition process within ECE. Chapter 6 examines the special type of 'ethnic' nationalism which predominates within ECE. Chapter 7 looks at two case studies in terms of the break-up of the nation state in ECE since 1989 – former Czechoslovakia and Yugoslavia.

(3) The third and longest part of the book concentrates on the institutionalisation of democracy over the first six years of the post-revolutionary period. Chapter 8 looks at existing social cleavages; Chapter 9 analyses the elections that have taken place since 1989; Chapter 10 describes the elections in each of the thirteen countries individually and comments on political events between 1990 and 1995; Chapter 11 attempts to categorise the political parties and party systems that are emerging; Chapter 12 examines the effectiveness of the post-1990 parliaments; Chapter 13 looks at the choice made of parliamentary or presidential regimes.

Finally, the conclusion (Chapter 14) analyses whether a type of 'post-communist' society actually exists as something 'in-between' capitalism and communism and also poses the question 'Whither ECE?' in terms of international relations.

Each chapter first discusses the various theoretical concepts involved in everyday language and looks at the inter-war and communist periods, before attempting to examine what is happening today in terms of both theory and previous practice, often using Western Europe as a point of contrast.

A list of further reading is given at the end of each chapter, and the Appendix at the end of the book is a chronological history of each of the countries within the region, including a month-by-month account of events in Yugoslavia since 1990.

Three afterthoughts

(1) Throughout the book all ECE names have been printed without accents, as is common practice in many books and journals meant primarily for English speakers.

(2) The abbreviations for political parties used throughout the book are those currently used within the country itself. These are given on pages xviii–xxi.

(3) Since many of the citations made have come from lectures and personal interviews in Prague, it was decided not to provide a comprehensive list of the few references mentioned in the text. Where the citation has appeared in written form, the book or conference paper concerned is always listed in the 'Further reading' at the end of the chapter.

Keith Crawford
Prague
July 1996

Acknowledgements

It remains for me to thank some of the scores of people who have offered me insight or advice on both the structure and content of the book. Such people are almost too numerous to mention, but my particular thanks go to: Professor George Schöpflin of London University's School of Slavonic and East European Studies, for his invaluable comments on the first draft of this volume; Dr Bill Jones, the series editor, without whose constant encouragement the book would never have been finished; Dr Emil Kirchner of the University of Essex, who first suggested I attempt such a project; Karen Henderson of Leicester University, who helped me with the initial structuring of the book and provided me with some early ideas; Dr Jan Sokol of Prague's Charles University, Jan Urban, former leading Czech dissident, Christopher Storck of Köln University, Germany, Jan Herzmann of the Prague-based FACTUM Institute of Public Opinion Research, Abby Innes of the London School of Economics, and Steven Heintz of the Prague branch of the East–West Studies Institute, all of whom provided me with invaluable comments on the content of individual chapters; students Wendy Newman, Magdalena Andersonova and Jiri Hosek, who helped me with research in Prague; Stuart Horsburgh of Manchester Metropolitan University and Radka Kocumova, who provided me with access to a computer in order physically to complete the work; Richard Purslow, former Assistant Editor of Manchester University Press; and, finally, all analysts and co-workers at the Prague-based Open Media Research Institute.

It goes without saying that any inconsistencies or errors made in the final draft are entirely my own.

Notes on sources

It is still very difficult to obtain readable comparative studies of the ECE societies emerging from the collapse of communism. Even though six to ten titles for further reading are provided at the end of each chapter, it is worth mentioning a few authors and periodicals which cover the period 1989–95 and could be mentioned at the end of several chapters.

Background history

Michael G. Roskin's *The Rebirth of East Europe* (Prentice Hall, 1991) is a useful quick read and Joseph Rothschild's *East Central Europe between the Two World Wars* (University of Washington Press, 1992) is an excellent, more detailed account on a country-by-country basis. Anything written on this period by Hugh Seton-Watson, Jacques Rupnik, George Schöpflin or Vladimir Tismaneanu is also worth perusal.

ECE under communism

Four books of particular merit on this period are: Joseph Rothschild's *Return to Diversity: A Political History of East Central Europe Since World War II* (Harvest, 1975), Jacques Rupnik's *The Other Europe* (Weiden and Nicholson, 1989), George Schöpflin's *Politics in Eastern Europe* (Blackwell, 1993) and Vladimir Tismaneanu's *Reinventing Politics: Eastern Europe from Stalin to Havel* (The Free Press, 1992).

Details of the revolutions in 1989–90

Timothy Garton Ash's eyewitness reports *The Magic Lantern: The Revolution of '89 Witnessed in Warsaw, Budapest and Prague* (Random House, 1990) and *We The People* (Granta Books, 1990) and Misha Glenny's *The Rebirth of History: Eastern Europe in the Age of Democracy* (Penguin Books, 1990) are still probably among the best accounts of the revolutions themselves, although John Simpson's *Despatches from the Barricades* (Hutchinson, 1990) also provides interesting insights into the revolutionary process. Roger East's *Revolutions in Eastern Europe* (Printer Publishers, 1992) and J. F. Brown's *Surge to Freedom: The End of Communist Rule in Eastern Europe* (Duke University Press, 1991) are more academic in their approach.

Transition from Communist rule

Ralf Dahrendorf's *Reflections on the Revolution in Europe* (Chatto and Windus, 1990) is an excellent introduction to most of the themes involved. Otherwise two edited volumes providing useful background information are: Stephen White, Judy Batt and Paul Lewis (eds), *Developments in East European Politics* (Macmillan, 1993), and Stephen Whitefield (ed.), *The New Institutional Architecture of Eastern Europe* (St Martin's Press, 1993). Geoffrey Pridham and Paul Lewis have co-edited *Stabilising Fragile Democracies* (Routledge, 1995), which makes some interesting comparisons between ECE and southern Europe (Spain, Portugal and Greece).

The Institute of East–West Studies in both Prague and New York has also produced several papers analysing the post-1989 transition process, although their more recent studies have concentrated on economic transformation.

The *Budapest Papers on Democratic Transition* (published by the Budapest University of Economics) has several papers on comparative themes, although they usually concentrate on Hungary.

Political parties, party systems and social cleavages

This is more or less an undeveloped field at present, although Sten Berglund and Jan Ake Dellenbrant (eds), *The New Democracies in Eastern Europe. Party Systems and Party Cleavages* (Edward Elgar, 1991) and Gordon Wightman (ed.), *Party Formation in East Central Europe* (Edward Elgar, 1995), have produced two very useful comparative studies.

Parliaments

The *Budapest Papers on Democratic Transition* (published by the Budapest University of Economics) has included a whole series on ECE post-communist parliaments.

The Research Committee of Legislative Specialists (IPSA) has also published various papers on the development of ECE parliaments.

Journals/periodicals

The following journals specialise in ECE:

> *Communist and Post-Communist Studies* (USA)
> *East European Constitutional Review* (USA)
> *East European Politics and Societies* (USA)
> *East European Quarterly* (USA)
> *Journal of Communist Studies and Transition Politics* (UK)
> *Transition* (Open Media Research Institute, Prague)

Other journals have frequent articles on ECE:

> *Daedalus* (USA)
> *Europe–Asia Studies, Party Politics* (UK)
> *Journal of Democracy* (USA)
> *Political Quarterly* (UK)

Current information

For all up-to-date information and analysis on most recent events, the Open Media Research Institute's (OMRI) bi-weekly publication *Transition* is an invaluable source. OMRI also publishes a *Daily Digest*, which is available on e-mail.

For the January 1990–August 1994 period, the *Radio Free Europe/Radio Liberty* weekly journal provides clear-cut analysis of events.

Abbreviations and glossary

Below are given abbreviations for the main post-1989 political groupings of each ECE country, for the different Communist parties, and for relevant international organisations (with short descriptions of their roles), plus explanations of some of the terms used for government and Party structures within the post-war Communist regimes.

Post-war Communist parties

BKP	Bulgarian Communist Party
KSC	Communist Party of Czechoslovakia
MSZMP	Hungarian Socialist Workers' Party
PCR	Communist Party of Romania
PSS	Party of Labour of Albania
PZPR	Polish United Workers' Party
SD	Democratic Party (Poland)
SED	Socialist Unity Party of Germany
SKJ	League of Communists of Yugoslavia
ZSL	United Peasants' Party (Poland)

Main post-1989 political parties

AD	Democratic Alliance (Albania)
BBWR	Non-Party Bloc to Support Reform (Poland)
BSP	Bulgarian Socialist Party (communist successor party)

BZNS	Bulgarian Agrarian National Union
CDR	Democratic Convention (Romania)
CDU	Christian Democratic Union (East Germany)
CSSD	Czech Social Democratic Party
DEMOS	Democratic Opposition of Slovenia
DEPOS	Serbian Democratic Movement
DP–FSN	Democratic Party – National Salvation Front (communist successor party in Romania)
DPS	Movement for Rights and Freedoms (Turkish party in Bulgaria)
DPSCG	Democratic Party of Socialists of Montenegro
DS	Democratic Party (Serbia)
DS	Democratic Party (Slovenia)
DSS	Democratic Party of Serbia
FDP	Federal Democratic Party (East Germany)
FDSN	Democratic National Salvation Front (communist successor party in Romania)
FIDESZ	Federation of Young Democrats (Hungary)
FKGP	Independent Smallholders' Party (Hungary)
FSN	National Salvation Front (communist successor party in Romania)
HDZ	Croatian Democratic Community
HDZ BiH	Croatian Democratic Community of Bosnia-Herce-govina
HKDU	Croatian Christian Democratic Union
HNS	Croatian National Party
HSD–SMS	Movement for a Self-Governing Democracy – Society for Moravia and Silesia
HSLS	Croatian Social-Liberal Party
HSP	Croatian Party of Rights
HSS	Croatian Peasants' Party
HZDS	Movement for a Democratic Slovakia
KCSM	Communist Party of Bohemia and Moravia (communist successor party)
KDH	Christian Democratic Movement (Slovakia)
KDNP	Christian Democratic People's Party (Hungary)
KDS	Christian Democratic Party (Czech Republic)
KDU/CSL	Christian Democratic Union/People's Party (Czech Republic)
KLD	Liberal Democratic Congress (Poland)

KPN	Confederation for an Independent Poland
LB	Left Bloc (some Communists, Socialists and Agrarians) (Czechoslovakia)
LDS	Liberal Democratic Party (Slovenia)
MDF	Hungarian Democratic Forum (Hungary)
MSZDP	Hungarian Social Democratic Party
MSZP	Hungarian Socialist Party (communist successor party)
NDP	Democratic People's Party (Albanian Party in Macedonia)
NZSS	Solidarity Trade Unions Party (Poland)
ODA	Civic Democratic Alliance (Czech Republic)
ODS	Civic Democratic Party (Czech Republic)
OF	Civic Forum (Czechoslovakia)
OH	Civic Movement (Czech Republic)
OMONIA	Democratic Union of the Greek Minority (Albania)
PBDNJ	Party for the Defence of Human Rights (Greek party in Albania)
PC	Centre Alliance (Poland)
PD	Democratic Party (Albania)
PD–FSN	Democratic Party – National Salvation Front (communist successor party in Romania)
PDP	Party for Democratic Prosperity (Albanian party in Macedonia)
PDS	Party for Democratic Socialism (communist successor party in East Germany)
PDSR	Party of Social Democracy of Romania
PNL	National Liberal Party (Romania)
PR	Republican Party (Albania)
PRM	Greater Romanian Party
PS	Socialist Party of Albania (communist successor party)
PSD	Social Democratic Party (Albania)
PSL	Polish Peasants' Party (communist successor party)
PSM	Socialist Party of Labour (Romania)
PUNR	Party of Romanian National Unity
SDA	Party for Democratic Action (Muslim party in Bosnia)
SDL	Party of the Democratic Left (communist successor party in Slovakia)
SDS	Union of Democratic Forces (Bulgaria)

SDSM	Social Democratic Union of Macedonia (communist successor party)
SDS BiH	Serbian Democratic Party of Bosnia-Hercegovina
SK BiH–SDP	League of Communists – Party of Democratic Changes (communist successor party in Bosnia)
SLD	Democratic Left Alliance (communist successor party in Poland)
SM	Alliance for Macedonia (communist successor coalition)
SNS	Slovak National Party
SPD	Social Democratic Party (East Germany)
SPM	Socialist Party of Macedonia (communist successor party)
SPO	Serbian Renewal Movement
SPR–RSC	Republican Party (Czech Republic)
SPS	Socialist Party of Serbia (communist successor party)
SRS	Serbian Radical Party
SRSJ BiH	Alliance of Reform Forces of Bosnia-Hercegovina
SZDSZ	Alliance of Free Democrats (Hungary)
UD	Democratic Union (Poland)
UDMR	Hungarian Democratic Union of Romania
VMRO–DPMNE	Internal Macedonian Revolutionary Organisation – Democratic Party for Macedonian National Unity
VPN	Public Against Violence (Czechoslovakia)
ZCHN	Christian National Union (Poland)
ZLSD	Associate List of Social Democrats (communist successor party in Slovenia)
ZRS	Association of Slovak Workers

International organisations

CEI	Central European Initiative (originally called the Pentagonal group, it was founded in 1989 among Hungary, Poland, Czechoslovakia, Italy and Austria, and later extended to Slovenia, Croatia and Macedonia. This was the first attempt to create a regional economic bloc, including West European countries, which aimed at economic cooperation between the member states within the CSCE).

CEFTA	Central European Free Trade Area, established on 21 December 1992 by the so-called Visegrad countries – Hungary, Poland and Czechoslovakia (subsequently the Czech and Slovak Republics) – to stimulate trade among ECE members by mutually agreed tariff reductions.
EBRD	European Bank of Reconstruction and Development, founded in 1990 by the EU, USA and Japan to provide investment, advice on privatisation and global competition in the former Soviet bloc
ECE	East-Central Europe
EU	European Union, founded in 1957 as the European Economic Community (EEC), then known as the European Community (EC) 1965–94
IMF	International Monetary Fund, a UN organisation that helps countries worldwide with balance-of-payments difficulties and generally attempts to bring about stability of the world money supply
NATO	North Atlantic Treaty Organisation, established in 1949 by North American and West European countries as a military and defence alliance to guard against the threat of Soviet expansionism
OECD	Organisation for Economic Cooperation and Development, founded as the OEEC (Organisation for European Economic Cooperation) 1948–61 to co-ordinate the Marshall Plan aid programme; since 1961 under its new name it encourages economic growth within its mainly European member states and helps underdeveloped countries. The Czech Republic became the first ex-communist country to become a full member in November 1995
OSCE	Organisation on Security and Cooperation in Europe – known as the Conference of Security and Cooperation in Europe (CSCE) until 1995 (composed of those states that signed the Helsinki Accords in 1975–76 and the Charter for a New Europe in 1990)
WTO	World Trade Organisation, formally known as GATT (General Agreement on Tariffs and Trade) and founded in 1947 to encourage the expansion of free trade throughout the world

Glossary of communist terminology

Central Committee. One of the most important decision-making bodies of ECE Communist parties, usually composed of a few hundred members.

CMEA (COMECON). Council for Mutual Economic Assistance, founded in 1949 to develop trade and economic policies throughout the Soviet bloc, abolished in 1991.

Council of Ministers. Effectively the cabinet, as it included the heads of the most important government ministries, but was simply an administrative body to implement policies decided by the Party organisations.

First or General Secretary. 'First among equals' within the Politburo and leader of the Communist Party in each country, and not usually a dictator.

Nomenklatura. Colloquially refers to the (Communist) political elite throughout ECE Communist states, but originally used to describe the list of positions within the Communist governments for which the appointees needed Party approval.

Politburo. The top decision-making body in Communist states, usually composed of ten to fifteen government or Party leaders and formally appointed by the Central Committee.

Map of East Central Europe

Denmark

BALTIC SEA

Estonia

Riga

Russia

Latvia

Lithunaia

Vilnius

Kaliningrad

Gdansk

Pomoronia

Belarus

Berlin

Warsaw

Poland

Poznania

Germany

Cracow

Prague

Czech Rep.

Galicia

Bohemia

Silesia

Ukraine

Münich

Moravia

Slovak Rep.

Vienna

Bratislava

Ruthenia

Moldova

Budapest

Austria

Hungary

Transylvania

Bessarabia

Ljubljana

Romania

Trieste

Slovenia

Zagreb

Timisoara

Croatia

Vojvodina

Bosnia-Hercegovina

Southern Dobruja

Belgrade

Bucharest

BLACK SEA

ADRIATIC SEA

Sarajevo

Serbia

Yugoslavia

Rome

Monte-negro

Pristina

Bulgaria

Kosovo

Sofia

Podgorica

Italy

Skopje

Istanbul

Tirana

Macedonia

Albania

Greece

AEGEAN SEA

Turkey

Athens

MEDITERRANEAN SEA

0   300 km

1
East Central Europe

Central Europe as a family of small nations has its own vision of the world, a vision based on a deep distrust of history. (Milan Kundera)

For them [the Central Europeans] history had been a slaughter-house, a stage for continuous injustice and defeats. (Vladimir Tismaneanu)

Identifying the region

Perceptions from the West

During most of the post-1945 Cold War period until 1989, Europe was very conveniently divided into the capitalist, Catholic/Protestant democratic West and the Communist, supposedly atheistic, non-democratic East. From the Western viewpoint, there was little difference between the various countries of Soviet-dominated 'Eastern Europe': they were all part of what former US President Ronald Reagan once called the 'evil empire'.

Little attempt was made to distinguish ECE states – Poland, East Germany, Czechoslovakia, Hungary, Yugoslavia, Bulgaria, Romania and Albania – from the Soviet model. Each was led by a single Communist Party that adhered to Marxist-Leninist ideology, practised state ownership of all industry and agriculture, and did not tolerate any meaningful opposition to the regime. All were usually dubbed 'totalitarian' and compared with Nazi Germany.

The ECE peoples themselves, however, had always perceived Soviet Russia as yet another oppressive colonial power, quite alien in terms of culture and political traditions. So once they were freed from the yoke of Soviet occupation, they sought to distance themselves quickly from the idea of 'Eastern Europe', with all its previous, mostly negative connotations.

The post-1989 need to invent a new name for the region reflects a desire by the nations concerned to establish a cultural and historical identity distinct from the one imposed by the Soviets over four decades, and to rejoin Western Europe, which many inhabitants of the region regard as their rightful home.

Our parameters of 'East Central Europe'

In 1989 there were eight East European states within the Soviet sphere of influence. Four years later, three of those states no longer existed: the (East) German Democratic Republic had been absorbed into the (West) German Federal Republic, Yugoslavia had split into five separate ethnic republics and Czechoslovakia had divided into its two constituent 'nations'.

As explained in the Preface, this book focuses on the thirteen countries which, since 1989, have usually been known as East Central Europe: Poland, East Germany, the Czech and Slovak Republics, Hungary, Romania, Bulgaria, Albania and the states emerging from the split in Yugoslavia since 1991 – Slovenia, Croatia, Bosnia-Hercegovina, Macedonia and the rump Federal Republic of Yugoslavia (Serbia and Montenegro).

The former German Democratic Republic (GDR) (1949–90) is included within our understanding of ECE and figures in some sections of the book. This is because the area covered by the GDR was both historically part of Central Europe and since 1945 intrinsically tied to the Soviet bloc. On the other hand, the Baltic States of Lithuania, Latvia and Estonia, plus the other republics of the former Soviet Union – Belarus, Ukraine, Moldova and Russia – have been specifically excluded, owing to their very particular development inside the Russian and Soviet Empires for several centuries.

Characteristics of the region

The histories, cultures, languages, political traditions and levels of economic development of ECE countries are highly varied. During the nineteenth century, for example, there was very little in common between these countries, except that for most of the period they were all under imperial occupation. Moreover, for all the common features of the region's various countries, there are always exceptions to the rule.

With this proviso in mind, we will attempt to define the region in terms of its geography, history, culture and political traditions.

Geography

East Central Europe: a land of 'in-between'

Geographically speaking, during the past two centuries ECE was a band of countries that lay between Germany and Russia. From the beginning of inter-imperial rivalries within Europe, these lands were well aware of their 'in-betweenness'.

The region we are examining continually vacillated between West and East Europe in terms of its political and economic development. From the tenth to the fifteenth centuries the Poles, Czechs and Hungarians were very much part of Western Europe and they prospered. From the beginning of the fifteenth century onwards, however, came the 'second serfdom' (see below), which halted the advances made and pushed the region back into the East. At the same time the Turkish invasions began in the Balkans, thereby stunting economic and political development even further.

In a similar vein, in 1983, the exiled Czech writer Milan Kundera wrote his famous article entitled 'The Tragedy of Central Europe'. In this essay, Kundera argued that, culturally and spiritually, Central Europe more properly belonged to the West than to the East, and that it was only because the region had been 'kidnapped, displaced and brainwashed' after the Second World War that it became 'Eastern Europe'.

Geographical variety

East Central Europe is composed of four clearly distinct regions:

1   the extensive north European plain between the Baltic Sea
     and the northern Carpathian Mountains (about 500 kilo-
     metres in depth and exposed to both the east and west);
2   the Carpathian mountain range, which tends to run in a
     west–east direction in southern Poland and northern
     Romania, and the Tatra Mountains in northern Slovakia;
3   the broad Danube plain, which traverses the whole region
     to the south of these mountains;
4   the mountainous regions of the Balkan peninsula, south of
     the Danube plain and enclosed by the Adriatic, Aegean and
     Black Seas.

Small populations

The ECE states are small. Poland's is the largest population with
38 million, followed by Romania and East Germany with 23 and
16 million people respectively. The Czech Republic and Hungary
have 10.5 million each and Bulgaria 8.5 million. Albania, Bosnia,
Croatia, Macedonia, Slovakia and Slovenia are all mini-states with
only 2–5 million each. These sorts of figures put most of ECE on
the same level as Scandinavia in terms of population size.

The Bulgarians, Croats, Romanians, Slovenes, and Slovaks
have been losing population steadily throughout the twentieth
century, partly through the emigration of unemployed (mostly
rural) masses to the USA and elsewhere. The main population
changes, however, were due to the emigration and extermination
of sizeable Jewish communities during the Holocaust and to the
German expulsions after 1945. For example, the repatriation of
the Sudeten Germans after 1945, combined with war victims and
pre-war emigration of Jews, left the Czech lands in 1945 with
fewer people than in the 1890s.

Geographical vulnerability to invasion

Since ECE constitutes an area of extensive, undulating plain
broken by only the occasional mountain ranges – which run in a

mainly east–west direction – and with few sea coasts and large rivers, there were always very few barriers to invasion, especially from the east (Mongols, Russians and Turks) or the north (Swedes).

In particular, the region represented an exposed front line to the destructive Mongol invasions of the thirteenth century, or to the repeated incursions by the Ottoman Turks from the late fourteenth century onwards. Whereas the former were after booty, the latter imposed their own social and political system on their conquered territories, effectively cutting the region off from the dynamic economic and political developments within the rest of Europe.

Even in the sixteenth and seventeenth centuries, when Western Europe was in full expansion after the collapse of feudalism, ECE inhabitants were still fighting the Turks – defending Vienna in 1529 and 1683, while the rest of Western Europe sat back and watched.

It is therefore not surprising that most ECE countries became subject nations within various empires, although parts of Yugoslavia are exceptions – Montenegro, for example, was never conquered by the Ottoman Turks.

Geographically speaking, the boundaries of ECE were always difficult to determine precisely, let alone defend. The eastern boundary, in particular, has varied enormously, according to shifting empires. Perhaps only the Czech Republic has clearly defined borders, with a ring of hills on its northern, western and southern frontiers.

Lack of waterways as trading routes

Over centuries, waterways – both seas and large rivers – were crucial for commercial and industrial development and particularly important for the economic expansion of Western Europe. In comparison, ECE had very little accessible seacoast. For example, ice restricted the use of the Baltic Sea during the winter; the Dalmatian coast had very few large natural harbours and bad links with its hinterland; and the Black Sea lay under the control of the Ottoman Turks for centuries.

The region also lacks navigable rivers to serve as important trading corridors (whereas the Rhine in Western Europe connects five countries to the Atlantic Ocean). The region's large river, the Danube, was navigable for much of its length, but suffered from ice during the winter and its lowest reaches were always in the hands of the Ottoman Turks. In any case, the Danube did not flow westwards to the fast-growing West European commercial and industrial markets. Other rivers in ECE were navigable for only very short distances and those flowing north into the Baltic Sea were also invariably blocked by ice in winter.

Lack of raw materials

Compared with Western Europe, ECE lacked many of the essential raw materials needed for basic industry, such as iron ore, coking coal and other fuels. Those areas which were close to raw materials – northern Bohemia and southern Poland – or which benefited from good transport links – like Budapest – did, indeed, experience significant industrial development. Otherwise most of the region was deficient in most raw materials with only isolated exceptions, like the concentration of bauxite in areas of Yugoslavia, the Serbian coal fields or the Romanian oil fields.

History

Pre-modern history

During the Middle Ages, some ECE kingdoms were just as advanced as any in Western Europe. Mediaeval Poland, Bohemia, Serbia and Bulgaria all achieved great power and status, before much of the region fell under the rule of the Ottoman Empire from the fourteenth to sixteenth centuries. The subject nations then became little more than a source of loot for their imperial overlords.

Most ECE countries can look back on glorious periods in their pasts and to leading national figures. For Hungary there was the period of cultural expansion under their first king, St Stephen, in the early 1000s. For Poles the golden age was the period 1386–1572, when the Polish and Lithuanian Kingdom was one of the greatest powers in Europe, extending from the Baltic to the Black Sea and absorbing most of the Ukraine and Belarus.

The Czech lands had a period of incredible economic and cultural expansion under the Premysl dynasty, particularly Charles IV (1346–78). Before the rise of the Ottoman Empire, Bulgaria was also a powerful empire in the tenth century – encompassing Serbia, Romania, Macedonia, Albania and northern Greece.

Serbia too had a mediaeval empire, reaching its height under Stefan Dusan (1331–55), when it included all Serbian lands, Macedonia, Bulgaria, Albania and northern Greece. Croatia had a period of independence in the tenth and eleventh centuries, but was joined to Hungary in 1091. Albanians idolise their national hero Skanderbeg for driving the Ottoman Turks out of Albania for twenty-five years, from 1443 to 1468.

Otherwise, this was an area under frequent invasion, from the mid-fifteenth century onwards: continuously changing kingdoms and principalities with borders in a constant state of flux. Only the borders of the Czech lands have been stable throughout history – even so, Czechs still spent almost 400 years under Austrian rule.

Imperial occupation, 1526–1918

In the sixteenth and seventeenth centuries, while Western Europe was engaged in colonial expansion and increasing trade, ECE was still defending itself against repeated invasions by the Ottoman Turks, who conquered Hungary in 1526 and even besieged Vienna twice.

During this period up to the end of the First World War, there were four main imperial powers: the Habsburg (Austrian), Russian and Ottoman (Turkish) Empires and the Prussian (German) Kingdom. The key features of the region's history were the steady rise in power of the Habsburg Empire and the slow decline of the Ottoman Empire, which for 500 years until the 1850s extended over all of Bulgaria, Macedonia and Albania, most of Romania and Serbia and, at times, absorbed parts of Poland, Hungary and Austria.

Poland was, at the beginning of this period, the only other independent power. However, the partitions of Poland, in 1772, 1793 and 1795, among the Russian and Austrian Empires and the Prussian Kingdom ended the country's independent existence for almost 150 years. Of all ECE states, only Poland had a history of direct Russian occupation during this period.

Serbia revolted first against the Turks in the late 1790s, achieving limited autonomy in 1830 and full independence in 1878. Thereafter the Serbs endeavoured to expel all foreign rulers from the region, hoping to form a southern Slav state under Serbian leadership, that is, a Greater Serbia.

The provinces of Moldavia and Walachia also gained autonomy from the Turks in 1856, were unified in 1861, declared their independence in 1877 during the Russo-Turkish War, and were recognised as independent Romania in the 1878 Treaty of Berlin.

Bulgaria was under more direct Ottoman rule, but the Russian victory in the Russo-Turkish War 1877–78 helped them to establish a 'Greater Bulgaria' from the Danube to the Aegean, only for the country to lose these gains at the Treaty of Berlin in 1878. Bulgaria achieved full independence in 1908 and was dominated by the ambition of restoring its earlier frontiers, leading to its involvement in the Balkan Wars of 1912–13.

By defeating the Turks at the siege of Vienna in 1683, the Habsburgs reconquered Hungary, adding Transylvania and Hungarian northern Serbia to their empire after 1699. Hungary, with its powerful aristocracy and nationalist, urban middle class, acquired significant autonomy under the Habsburg Empire, culminating in equal status with Austria in the Dual Monarchy from 1867.

It was Hungary which exercised the Habsburg dominion over Transylvania, Slovakia and Croatia. Dissatisfied with limited autonomy from 1868, Croatian nationalism was anti-Hungarian and oriented towards the Serbian 'southern Slav state'.

The Habsburgs had acceded to the throne of the Czech lands (Bohemia and Moravia) in 1526 and crushed the rebellion by Czech nobles in 1620. The rise of a mostly urban, middle-class Czech nationalism was held in check by the Austrians, often by force.

The 'springtime of nations': 1848 in Budapest and Prague

The rebellions in 1848 were directed against both the economic and the political restrictions of the Habsburgs. Middle-class intellectuals and nationalists, inspired by events in France and Germany, demanded independence and parliamentary democracy. But these revolts were also aimed against recession, increasing unemployment, food shortages and other economic grievances.

In Budapest in March 1848, revolutionaries demanded a government responsible to the Hungarian parliament. The Habsburg Emperor Ferdinand at first gave into their demands, but then had the Croatians fight against the Hungarian rebels, promising the former autonomy under the Habsburgs. In the end, however, it was the Russian army (invited by the Habsburgs) that put down the rebellion, in August 1849. In Prague the Austrian armies crushed the 1848 rebellion, which had been sparked off by a congress of all the Slavic nations within the Habsburg Empire.

Involvement in the First World War

Many ECE countries entered the First World War in order to regain lost territory. Romania joined the Allies in 1916, hoping to retrieve Hungarian Transylvania. Bulgaria entered the war on the side of the Germans in the hope of restoring 'Greater Bulgaria'. The Hungarians fought with the Austrians in order to retain their territories of Croatia, Slovakia and Transylvania.

Albania was occupied by five different armies during the course of the war. King Alexander of Serbia used the wartime situation to persuade the other nationalities to found the South Slav 'Kingdom of Serbs, Croats and Slovenes' (renamed

Yugoslavia in 1929 and extended to Macedonia, Montenegro and Bosnia-Hercegovina).

Among the winners in the post-war peace treaties, Romania received much of its desired territory and doubled its size, but, in the process, inherited large Jewish, Hungarian and German minorities. Albania kept its independence, although its boundaries were not firmly fixed until 1921. The new state of Czechoslovakia was created from two quite different nations: the Czech lands of Bohemia and Moravia, and Slovakia. Poland was restored after 150 years of occupation, but with only a Polish corridor leading to the Baltic Sea.

As for the defeated nations, Hungary lost over two-thirds of its pre-war lands and population to neighbouring states (Transylvania to Romania, Croatia to the new Yugoslavian state and Slovakia to Czechoslovakia). Bulgaria re-lost the territories it had regained by conquest during the 1914–18 conflict.

The inter-war period: the collapse of democracy

Experiments in Western-style democracy were extremely short lived in most of inter-war ECE. In Hungary the democratic interlude under Count Karolyi lasted a matter of months, before the 1919 Communist revolution led by Bela Kun was followed by the establishment of an authoritarian regime under Admiral Horthy. In Bulgaria the quasi-democratic regime collapsed in 1924 when the leader of the Peasant Party, Alexander Stamboliski, was killed in a military coup. In Poland Marshal Jozef Pilsudski, a Polish war hero, staged a coup d'état in 1926 after a period of acute parliamentary immobilism. Romania, Yugoslavia and Albania were all under royal dictatorships by the mid-1930s. Czechoslovakia was the only exception, with democratic institutions lasting until 1939, after the Czech Sudetenland had been surrendered to Hitler without Czech consent at the so-called 'Munich Protocol' of 30 September 1938 (an agreement between Germany, Italy, France and Great Britain).

It should be mentioned, by way of comparison, that numerous other democracies failed during the inter-war period, such as

Spain, Italy, Portugal, Germany, Brazil, Japan and Greece. It should also be emphasised that the character of these military and royal dictatorships was specifically authoritarian, not totalitarian.

Why did democracy fail?

Following the Paris Peace Settlements and the 'triumph of democracy' in 1918, ECE countries simply copied their democratic structures from the West, usually choosing France's Third Republic as their role model. These Western parliamentary institutions and democratic political practices were imposed on predominantly peasant countries, where there was hardly any democratic tradition, and where, in the absence of genuine land reform, liberal democracy and free speech meant little to the peasant farmer.

The persistence of a strong bureaucratic tradition also undermined new democratic structures. Throughout much of the region administration was essentially arbitrary, dictatorial, inefficient and often corrupt, following the traditions and methods of the Ottoman Empire.

Unresolved national problems persisted with territorial claims over new borders. For example, Hungary had territorial claims against all its neighbours except Austria; Poland quarrelled with Czechoslovakia over Tesin; Bulgaria claimed the territory of South Dobrudzha from Romania; Yugoslavia contested Macedonia with both Bulgaria and Greece. This added to their problems in the inter-war period, as Hitler played one country against the other, in order to bind them to the Axis alliance. For instance, after invading Czechoslovakia, Hitler returned southern Slovakia and southern Ruthenia to Hungary, which joined the Axis powers by way of gratitude.

After 1918 Czechoslovakia, Poland and Romania, not to mention Yugoslavia, were just as ethnically diverse as the preceding empires: their minorities made up around a third of their respective populations. (Under the Austro-Hungarian Empire, half the population had been non-German-speaking.) Most minorities felt alienated in the new nation states, such as the

Sudeten Germans and Hungarians in Czechoslovakia, Hungarians in Serbia and Romanian Transylvania, or Ukrainians and Germans within Poland. The Sudeten Germans, in particular, wished to be united with Austria after 1918.

This was a period of excessive political pluralism. In Poland in the mid-1920s there were ninety-two registered political parties, with thirty-two represented in parliament; in Czechoslovakia in 1929 the figures were nineteen and sixteen, respectively. In Poland the legislative chaos and non-functioning parliament were factors leading to the military coup in 1926.

Political extremism was also common in the inter-war years. During the 1920s and 1930s right-wing, fascist movements grew in influence, such as the Iron Guard in Romania or the Arrow Cross in Hungary, although they were prevented from actually assuming power by the royal or military authoritarian regimes. Terrorist acts of violence and clashes between right-wing and left-wing paramilitary groups also characterised Bulgaria's unstable politics after 1924.

In elections during the 1920s, Communist parties won 10 per cent or so for the region as a whole, with a high of 20 per cent in Bulgaria in 1920. Much of the Communist and fascist electoral support was a protest vote, cast by people who knew little about Communists or fascists, but who disliked the existing democratic system and wanted strong leadership instead.

The Great Depression that started in 1929 affected ECE very badly because of its dependency on agriculture. Industrial growth stopped, farm prices collapsed, and so poor peasants became even poorer. As a result, many East Central Europeans were either indifferent to democracy or looked to a 'strong man' to end the recession. During this period, Germany was the only country willing to work by barter, exchanging ECE agricultural produce (at high prices) for German machinery and industrial goods. This 'saved' the agriculturally based economies, but it also tied them economically to Nazi Germany.

The abdication by the Western powers of their role in ECE affairs was also a factor in the collapse of democracy, since democracy and independence had been bestowed on ECE nations by the Western powers at the 1919 Paris Peace Conferences. Western indifference encouraged both Nazi Germany and, later, Soviet Russia to revise the 1919 treaties by force. Clearly the betrayal of Czechoslovakia by France and Britain at Munich in 1938 was the most outstanding example of such Western in-difference.

Finally, ECE political culture possesses a distinctly auth-oritarian nature, which militates against democratic practice (see below).

Overall, inter-war democracy throughout the region scarcely had a chance. After the destruction of the First World War, burgeoning problems with minorities and the disaster of the Great Depression, new democratic institutions and procedures quickly gave way to various types of authoritarianism.

However, it is worth repeating that the conservative and authoritarian regimes that ruled almost all of the new nations within ECE during the 1930s were never 'totalitarian' in the sense of Hitler's Germany or Stalin's Russia.

Involvement in the Second World War

The Second World War, like the First, started in ECE, when Germany demanded the return of territories lost in the Versailles Treaty to the re-established Poland. The 1939 Ribbentrop–Molotov Non-Aggression Pact and its secret clauses constituted a rejection of the Versailles Treaty. The Pact allowed Hitler to invade Poland and enabled Stalin to incorporate eastern Poland, the Baltic republics and other previously Russian territories back into the USSR.

Once Hitler invaded the USSR, most of the Second World War in Europe was fought on the Soviet–German front, where 90 per cent of the German forces were deployed. The Soviets lost some twenty million citizens during the war. (In comparison, the USA lost half a million service personnel in both its European and Pacific campaigns.)

However, the Soviet Red Army made a bad impression in its liberation of the region; looting and rape by Soviet soldiers were very common. Many ECE inhabitants feared and disliked the Russians – traditionally seen as a primitive and backward people.

After the war many Communists claimed to have played a key role in defeating the Germans, but much of the area's anti-German resistance was actually led by non-communist nationalists, for example in Poland. In Slovakia, Bulgaria, Poland, Yugoslavia and Albania Communists did organise uprisings or guerrilla warfare to combat the Germans, but often spent much of their time and energy fighting their other compatriots, rather than the Germans. Many of the post-war Communist leaders, however, spent most of the war in Moscow, where they were trained to set up the post-war Communist governments.

Immediate post-war activity

According to the 1944 Yalta agreement between Britain, the USA and the USSR (represented by Churchill, Roosevelt and Stalin, respectively), the post-war spheres of influence corresponded to the zones of occupation of the respective armies. The USSR, for example, was also allowed to retain the Polish territory it had acquired in 1939, while Poland received a large portion of eastern Germany in compensation.

At Yalta the Soviets also committed themselves to respect democracy and free elections within the occupied nations. But the Soviets understood 'democracy' to mean 'people's democracy' (i.e. controlled by the Communist Party) and interpreted 'freedom' as the freedom of ECE peoples to choose the political institutions recommended by the Soviets. (From the outset Stalin had intended to keep the region as a defensive shield for the USSR, which meant implanting friendly, reliable Communist regimes.)

The incorporation of ECE countries into the Soviet sphere of influence after 1945 was just as dramatic as any of the previous occupations. The imposition of the Soviet system kept the region underdeveloped, economically, politically and socially speaking, in comparison with the West for over forty years.

Culture

The cultural melting pot

The culture of ECE is the outcome of centuries of intermingling of different cultural traditions, generally via Germany and Austria. Exceptions were Romania, where cultural values remained from Roman times and were heavily influenced by France, and Albania, which had much closer links with Mediterranean countries, especially Italy.

Basically, though, ECE encompasses the region where Germanic peoples intermixed with Slavs. The German/Polish city of Danzig/Gdansk serves as a classic example in this respect: in the inter-war period the city was a sort of ECE melting pot of Poles, Germans, Jews and local Kashubs.

Therefore, the enforced repatriation of up to 12 million Germans into West and East Germany after 1945 considerably diluted the cultural mix of the area. In Czechoslovakia, in particular, the 1946 expulsion of the Sudeten Germans (25 per cent of the pre-war population) represented a radical rupture with the past.

Re-introduction of serfdom

Most of ECE suffered from the effective reintroduction of serfdom – that is, a re-entrenchment of the power of the nobility – during the fifteenth and sixteenth centuries. With the whole region being predominantly agricultural and with feudal structures remaining in place, the aristocracy was able to increase its power and exert an authoritarian, conservative and reactionary influence on the region's politics – particularly against the waves of liberalism penetrating the area after the 1789 French Revolution.

There was a particularly strong nobility in Poland, which bore full responsibility for the partition of the country in the late eighteenth century. East Germany, too, had a tradition of powerful, *Junker* nobility, which remained highly influential up to the Nazi era. In the Balkans the swift decline of the Ottoman Empire gave the local landlords much more power and freedom than before to exploit the landless peasantry.

The culture of dependency

With the advent of the industrial revolution, only northern Bohemia, plus isolated areas in Poland and Hungary, actually became industrialised. Otherwise, the principal role of ECE was to supply the expanding markets in Western Europe with agricultural produce, unprocessed minerals and fossil fuels, while serving as an easily penetrated market for manufactured goods from the West.

East–West trade increased throughout the nineteenth century, but did little to alter the relationship of dependency already described. Foreign investment was concentrated in those areas that would most benefit Western Europe: in agricultural and mining sectors, and in transportation (to enable quicker delivery of goods in both directions). Very little investment went into local manufacturing and industrial units, as they represented potential competition for Western firms.

Division between rural and urban societies

Very large differences, particularly before 1918, can be observed between those areas with large urban populations which experienced the nineteenth-century European industrial revolution (Germany, northern Bohemia, parts of Poland and some Hungarian cities) and those which remained primarily rural and largely untouched by the industrial revolution (Albania, Bulgaria, most of Yugoslavia, most of Slovakia and almost all of Romania).

For example, about two-thirds of the Bulgarian population still lived on the land in the 1930s – a percentage which was considerably higher in Romania, Yugoslavia and Albania. This was despite the fact that northern Bulgaria had a significant textile industry, Romania its oil fields and Serbia large resources of coal.

Weak middle classes

During the nineteenth century the region's middle class remained numerically small, powerless and often connected to the government bureaucracy. The concept of 'going into business' was quite rare and a young person with university education usually entered the civil service. (In addition, the entrepreneurial and commercial classes in ECE were often of German or Jewish origin, and thus were perceived as 'foreign'.)

The one exception to this scenario was the Czech lands, where the entrepreneurial middle classes played a key role in the political development of the state, in what was the most industrialised region of the entire Habsburg Empire. (Note that the indigenous Czech nobility had been dispossessed after 1620.)

Importance of intellectuals

In the more backward and underdeveloped societies of ECE, intellectuals developed a very special role, which was accentuated because of the lack of a normal bourgeois elite. They constituted a very small, ambitious grouping, which came mostly from the churches, army and the bureaucracy, but also from the nobility and gentry in Poland and Hungary. The predominance of the intelligentsia was particularly striking during times of change or revolution, as they tended to be the main substitute for the missing bourgeoisie.

There were basically two types of intellectual:

1   the 'supportive' intellectual, who served the traditional elite of the ruling empires;
2   the 'revolutionary' intellectual (a minority), who had utopian and messianic ideas about totally transforming society and the political system.

This latter group developed into a radical opposition, hostile to the existing order, but, at the same time, remaining extremely elitist and not especially attached to democracy as a concept. Being so small in number, they were also very isolationist – great individualists who did not want to be bound to organisations. There was always, therefore, a wide gap between intellectuals and normal citizens, based initially on the former's superior intelligence.

They played an important part in the building of national consciousness and in the promotion of Western political ideas during the nineteenth century. Generally, they were enamoured with the 'state', which they regarded as the main means of modernisation. During the twentieth century they adopted left and right political extremism, being particularly attracted to communism as a utopian, messianic ideology of total change. Actual power, of course, remained in the hands of the traditional elite, which was hostile to the ideas of the intelligentsia, as the latter represented a challenge to their privileged position.

Tremendous religious diversity

East Central Europe is an area where religion played a key and symbolic role among the mainly conservative peasantry, but where religion was quite diverse, ranging from predominantly Catholic Poland, Slovenia, Slovakia and parts of Hungary, through Orthodox Romania, Bulgaria, Macedonia and Serbia, and predominantly Lutheran East Germany, to Islamic Albania, Kosova and Bosnia-Hercegovina, not forgetting the sizeable Muslim Turkish minority in Bulgaria.

Catholics formed a majority in Hungary (and Transylvania), but practised alongside numerous Protestants. The Czechs lands were mainly Protestant (Hussite), but there was a significant Catholic minority (about 25 per cent). Only East Germany was predominantly Protestant (Evangelical).

The highest concentration of Jews within the region was in southern Poland, in Galicia. Jews also congregated in capital cities like Warsaw and Budapest, where they constituted 25 per cent of the urban populations and played key roles in the cities' commercial and intellectual life. Before and after the Second World War, vast numbers of Jews left for the New World – especially the USA – thereby seriously draining the economies of the region. All together about 6 million Jews were murdered in the Holocaust and a large proportion of that number came from ECE. Before the Second World War, Poland had the largest Jewish community in Europe – 3.3 million. Today Polish Jews number 5–7,000.

Strong link between Church and state

There was also a strong linkage between the Church and the state. The upper echelons of Church hierarchy were usually linked to power positions within the state, while the lower levels of clergy found their support among the peasantry.

In Poland the Roman Catholic Church played a crucial role in preserving the country's language and culture during the nineteenth century when the county did not officially exist. To a certain extent the Church was also the focal point of Polish nationalism during the post-war Communist regime.

Linguistic diversity

The language groups of ECE are Slavonic, Romance and Finno-Ugric. As a language group, the Slavonic languages – Polish, Czech, Serbo-Croat, Slovak, Bulgarian – are more or less mutually understandable. Hungarian, however, is incomprehensible to any Slav. Many gypsies throughout the region speak a dialect of Romanian, which also has a different linguistic base.

Ethnic divisions

The area has been characterised over time by a multitude of very distinct ethnic groups which have remained deeply antagonistic to each other over successive centuries. The frequent invasions and subordination by foreign powers prevented any national assimilation from taking place until the beginning of the twentieth century – by which time ethnic hostilities were deeply entrenched, especially in the Yugoslavian region.

Moreover, very large historical minorities of Jews, Germans and gypsies established themselves throughout ECE after the fourteenth century. The Holocaust reduced the Jewish communities significantly, so that now there is a sizeable Jewish community only in Budapest. Gypsies were also victims of the Nazi's ethnic cleansing, but large concentrations of gypsies can still be found throughout the area, for example in Bulgaria, Romania, Slovakia, Hungary and northern Bohemia. Some of these suffer acute racial problems in an area which has traditionally cared little for minority rights. The vast majority of the 13.5 million Germans living in the region were repatriated after 1945.

Special role of Germany within the region

It is difficult to escape the influence that Germany has had upon this region – in terms of religion, economy and culture. In the past, Germany was always looking east: this *Drang nach Osten* by Germany was seen as the main problem facing the future of Europe and played a major role in both world wars. Moreover, the numerous German minorities throughout ECE really gave the region its particular identity, as the place where Germans and Slavs intermixed.

Hence the enforced migrations at the end of the Second World War brought about a distinct change in the cultural make-up of the area, with up to 12 million Germans being expelled from the region after 1945. Most were expatriated into what remained of Germany. Half a million moved into Austria and some remained in their traditional communities but changed nationality.

Germans have always traded with and in ECE, and the last decade of the twentieth century has been no exception. But, trade breeds interdependence and the traditional relationship of the region to Germany has always been one of unequal dependency.

Existence of strong anti-Semitism

Traditional anti-Semitism (i.e. anti-Jewish attitudes because of their different religion, lifestyle and former money-lending activities) has a long history in ECE, but between the wars it generally became more ideological, owing predominantly to the Nazi influence. Although Jews were rarely more than a small fraction of the population, they were regionally concentrated, especially in the large towns and cities, where Jews were often leading professionals – intellectuals, lawyers, economists, surgeons, and so on.

During the inter-war period throughout the region, new countries with unstable regimes, suffering economic hardship (especially in the 1930s) and following the German Nazi example, tended to pick on the Jews as the perfect scapegoats. Many Jews were small traders and were noticeably better off than the average Slav. This second type of anti-Semitism fed the growth of local fascist movements and often led to an alignment with Nazi Germany. Even so, there were degrees of anti-Semitism within ECE: anti-Jewish feeling was particularly strong in Romania, Poland and Hungary. There was moderate anti-Semitism in Croatia and Slovakia, very slight in Serbia and Bohemia, and none at all in Bulgaria and Albania.

Political traditions

Between East and West

Feudal structures and the power of the nobles continued for longer than in Western Europe, so that ECE was characterised by the absolutist state, well into the twentieth century in some cases. In terms of political traditions, therefore, the region occupies a position between Russian patriarchal despotism and Western liberal democracy. George Schöpflin has described the region's prevailing political system as 'failed liberalism, moderate authoritarianism or enlightened despotism'.

Economic, political and cultural backwardness

On the whole, the region was poor, much poorer than Western Europe. The majority of East Central Europeans were peasants, some landless, others only smallholders, if not 'dwarfholders'. Yields per acre were much lower than in West Europe. Population increases and subdivisions of holdings reduced most peasants to subsistence farmers. There were very few market towns and even fewer industrial centres of any size, right up to the beginning of the twentieth century. Ninety per cent of the population of Yugoslavia at the time of the First World War, for example, were still living at subsistence level.

Late industrial revolution

Before 1918, only Germany, the Czech lands, parts of Poland and some Hungarian cities experienced the nineteenth-century European industrial revolution. The rest of the region remained primarily rural and largely untouched by industrialisation and urbanisation until the post-1945 Communist regimes. This applies to Bulgaria, Slovakia, Albania, most of Yugoslavia and almost all of Romania.

As a result, except in the Czech lands, a Western-type entrepreneurial class and a modern bureaucracy did not emerge and the land-owning gentry retained its dominant position well into the twentieth century. In addition, the entrepreneurial and commercial classes in ECE were often of German or Jewish origin, and thus were perceived as alien.

Late nations

The ECE nation states share a similar pattern of nation building, in the sense that they are late nations, even later than Italy and Germany. Most of the region's nation states were a result of the 1919 Paris Peace Conferences and of US President Wilson Woodrow's insistence on the idea of 'self-determination' for many ethnic minorities. Such attempts to make national and ethnic borders coincide were suspect from the beginning. Wherever the frontiers were drawn in the inter-war period, dissatisfied and disgruntled minorities were left under the rule of some national majority with little hope of self-rule or autonomy.

In contrast, in Western Europe nation building was much more of an evolutionary process over decades (Germany and Italy) if not centuries (Great Britain and France), and ethnic and political boundaries had a greater tendency to coincide.

Predominance of ethnic nationalism

In ECE nationalism was strongly influenced by a feeling of insecurity about national identity and there was a marked tendency to stress ethnic differentiation (based on language, religion or culture, or a mixture of all three). As a result, 'ethnic nationalism' permeated social and cultural life in a way that was almost unknown in Western Europe, emerging as a predominant political cleavage for most of the twentieth century (see Chapter 6).

Since such nationalism was suppressed for so long under imperial rule, it became most intolerant and quite exclusive. So, for example, when the Hungarian nationalists claimed their right to be independent in the 1848–49 revolution, they had no intention of granting the same rights to their own subject 'nations' – the Romanians, Croats and Slovaks.

Often this nationalism became quite radical, turning to fascism, anti-Semitism (hostility toward Jews) and racism (dislike of gypsies and foreigners). It also tended to divide East Central Europeans from each other and did not facilitate regional cooperation, for example against the growing Nazi threat in the 1930s.

Similarly, the continued suppression of nationalist aspirations under forty years of post-war Soviet occupation led to the explosion of very aggressive, exclusive and divisive nationalism after 1989, for example in the former Yugoslavia and Czecho-slovakia.

Lack of a civil society in the past

In stark contrast to Western traditions, ECE developed a typical 'subject' political culture, that is, the citizens saw themselves as apathetic servants to the state, rather than a collection of interactive and participating individuals. (See Chapter 4 for a lengthier discussion of this issue.)

Messianic concept of change

This was a passive, backward political culture which was prone to 'messianic ideas' and 'easy solutions' which would not entail any great deal of rational thought or debate. In other words, there was what George Schöpflin calls a 'messianic concept of political change', when political or economic ideas were accepted because of their novelty and because of their promise to bring about far-reaching social change – hence the faith usually placed in the 'strong leader' and the initial attraction of communism in the immediate post-war period.

Deep hostility towards politics by the peasantry

Among the peasants a very noticeable 'them' versus 'us' attitude developed over time and manifested itself in a deep animosity towards the state. This demonstrated itself in the overwhelming apathy many ordinary peasants felt towards state institutions, including the various parliamentary assemblies which seemed to serve the interests of the small number of landed gentry. The overwhelming majority of the peasantry were also more or less totally excluded from all corridors of power.

This was even more marked in the Balkans, where the countries were more predominantly of a peasant nature (90 per cent of their populations). Still the states were run in the interests of the bureaucracy (chosen from the military, nobility or entrepreneurial elites), and again the peasantry was excluded, but this time viewed the bureaucracy with antagonism, as it was seen as foreign and manipulative.

Habituation to arbitrary methods and authoritarianism

The most striking aspect of the ECE political culture is the dominance of the state and the concomitant weakness of society.

This dominance of the state (i.e. of the bureaucracy) originated in the royal prerogatives of the divine monarch, whereby the king or emperor took decisions unchallenged by representatives of the 'people'. The state bureaucracy continued this tradition even in the absence of the king. It ruled in a most arbitrary manner and expected its judgements to be accepted like the royal decrees of the past, without being questioned. This made the whole concept of parliamentary sovereignty quite meaningless and resulted in the transformation of legislatures into powerless institutions. It also demonstrates how the traditional primacy of today's ECE bureaucracy is deeply rooted in the past.

The peasant populations of ECE – whose main contact with the state was limited to paying taxes or joining the army – tended to accept the dictates that were handed down to them and rarely banded together to contest unpopular laws or taxes. This passivity, combined with the yearning for 'easy solutions' and 'messianic change', meant that the peasantry was more prone to strong leadership from the top rather than collective leadership via consensus. Authoritarianism was more acceptable than democratic parliamentarianism as a way of government.

Top-down modernisation

Owing to the late (or non-existent) industrialisation and to the non-development of Western-type entrepreneurial classes, the state had to take a leading role in society, becoming a substitute for the underdeveloped private sector. Hence, there arose a much more statist economic development than was common in other European countries at the time, with the state taking a leading role in society. Accordingly, the state in ECE became the key instrument of modernisation in the nineteenth century, involved in building up the economic infrastructure (roads, canals, railways) and in expanding the army. But top-down modernisation was seen primarily as a means of extending the power of the state (e.g. by creating a greater tax base and increasing the size of the armed forces) rather than of augmenting the welfare of society.

The dominant state

Modernisation imposed from above gradually reduced the power of the nobility during the nineteenth century, but it was the state administration, not the bourgeoisie, that played the role of leading entrepreneur. The only change possible was via the state, and there was the general acceptance of the power of the state to regulate society over a wide area of life. As a result, the state expanded enormously, while the institutions of an embryonic civil society remained underdeveloped and could do little to contain the growing power of the state's bureaucracy.

Power elites varied in their composition, but were usually an alliance between the bureaucracy and other elites, such as large landowners, big business, the military and the Church. The bureaucracy was recruited from these other elites, so the whole administrative elite was self-perpetuating, with the total exclusion of workers and peasants. Only in the Czech lands (where the native aristocracy had been dispossessed in 1620) was the political elite more broadly based, with the bourgeoisie, financiers, peasants and workers also represented.

Summary of the traditional model of the dominant state

The political traditions of ECE can be summarised as follows:

- acceptance of the power of the state to regulate society over a wide area of life;
- a habituation to arbitrary methods and authoritarianism;
- hostility towards the state by the (peasant) majority;
- a messianic concept of political change;
- a feeling among many of the intelligentsia that change could be affected only from above through massive state action.

Conclusion

By the beginning of the twentieth century, there was a very clear demarcation line in Europe for all sorts of cultural, economic and political reasons. Western Europe could be described as urbanised, industrialised, commercial and international. ECE could be viewed as rural, predominantly agricultural, backward and provincial. Farmers in the West participated in well organised markets, supplying urban centres; peasant farmers in ECE still existed mainly at subsistence levels.

Politically speaking, the West had experienced a steady evolution of democratic structures based on stable nation states throughout the nineteenth century – a process in which a dynamic entrepreneurial class had played a crucial role. The 1800s throughout ECE, on the other hand, had seen the continuation of the power of the land-owning nobles, the lack of any entrepreneurial class and a growth in the power of the state bureaucracies as the main agents of modernisation.

By the time of the First World War, the frequent invasions, the position of 'in-betweenness', the late industrialisation, the late arrival of nationhood and the predominance of 'backwardness' over centuries had given ECE countries a very particular type of retarded economic and political development.

The final Soviet occupation of the four decades from 1945 onwards and the enforced imposition of the Russian-made Communist model of society reinforced that position of backwardness and stunted the region's potential – again during a period of particularly dynamic expansion within Western Europe.

Further reading

Daniel Chirot, ed., *The Origins of Backwardness in Eastern Europe: Economics and Politics from the Middle Ages until the early Twentieth Century*, University of California Press, 1989.

On the subject of Central Europe and 'Mittleleuropa', see *Daedalus*, 119 (1), winter 1990 (articles by T. Garton Ash, E. Gellner, T. Judt, J. Rupnik, and G. Schöpflin, *inter alia*).

Stephen R. Graubard, ed., *Eastern Europe ... Central Europe ... Europe*, Westview Press, 1991.

Milan Kundera, 'The Tragedy of Central Europe', *New York Review of Books*, 26 April 1984.

Michael G. Roskin, *The Rebirth of East Europe*, Prentice Hall, 1991.

Joseph Rothschild, *East Central Europe between the Two World Wars*, University of Washington Press, 1992.

George Schöpflin, 'The Political Traditions of Eastern Europe', in *Eastern Europe ... Central Europe ... Europe*, Stephen R. Graubard (ed.), Westview Press, 1991.

Hugh Seton-Watson, *Eastern Europe between the Wars 1918–41*, Harper and Row, 1967.

Jeno Szucs, 'The Historical Regions of Europe', in *Civil Society and the State* (John Keane, ed.), Verso, 1988.

E. Garrison Walters, *The Other Europe: Eastern Europe to 1945*, Syracuse University Press, 1988.

2

Communism and totalitarianism

There is no such thing as non-totalitarian ruling communism. It either becomes totalitarian or it ceases to be communism. (Adam Michnik)

The object of a totalitarian system is to destroy all forms of communal life that are not imposed by the state and closely controlled by it, so that individuals are isolated from one another and become mere instruments in the hands of the state. (Leszek Kolakowski)

Communism in ECE in the inter-war period

In 1919, just two years after the 1917 Russian Revolution and a few months after the end of the First World War, Hungary experienced a Marxist-type revolution and a Bolshevik republic under Bela Kun for 133 days. Four years later the Communists were strong enough to attempt a coup in Bulgaria. (The former was ended by the invasion of the Romanian army, the latter easily put down by internal forces of law and order.)

Generally, though, during most of the inter-war period, the region's Communist parties were very small and very weak. There was limited electoral success: in Yugoslavia in the 1920 elections (12.4 per cent), in Czechoslovakia, where the Communists emerged as the strongest party on the left (second largest party overall in 1925), and in Bulgaria, where they attained 20 per cent of the vote in 1920.

Even before the arrival of the authoritarian, royal or military dictatorships of the 1930s, the Communist parties had been banned everywhere in ECE except Czechoslovakia. In Bulgaria it was after their ill-fated coup in September 1923, in Yugoslavia after a spate of Communist-led assassination attempts in 1920–21 and in Romania in 1924. In Hungary the Communist Party was destroyed (5,000 were executed and 75,000 imprisoned) during the 'White Terror' after the Bela Kun 1919 Marxist revolution. In Albania the Communist Party was not founded until 1941: to begin with there was just no support for such a party, and after 1924 all political parties were banned. In Poland all influence the Party might have had disappeared with the 1920–21 Polish–Soviet war: Communists were persecuted, but not outlawed.

As a result, the ECE Communist parties became increasingly dependent on Moscow for material and financial support. With the Nazi takeovers, most top Communist Party leaders escaped to the Soviet Union, where many of them were killed during some of Stalin's purges in the late 1930s – almost the entire leadership of the Polish and Yugoslav Communist parties, Bela Kun and other leaders of the 1919 Marxist revolution, the 'Trotskyite' members of the Bulgarian Communist Party and most of the founders of the Romanian Communist Party, for example. Consequently, a new generation of leaders, totally subservient to the Soviets, was then trained for developing the Communist movement after the war.

The inter-war Communist parties had no working class on which to build their support. The parties' leaders were predominantly middle class, intellectuals and often Jewish. Supporters of and voters for the Communist parties tended to be seasonal workers, refugees, students and particularly minorities – both national minorities, like Hungarians in Slovakia and Ukrainians in Poland, and region-wide ethnic minorities like the Jews. On the whole, this was a protest vote from among all social groups disliking the existing system.

How ECE became Communist

In general, the Communists did not immediately take over the governments of the newly liberated ECE countries, except in

Yugoslavia, Bulgaria and Albania, where local Communist partisans had fought both the German occupiers and local non-communist groups. In other countries, however, Stalin ordered his Communist cohorts to engage in what the Hungarian Communist leader Matyas Rakosi later referred to as 'salami tactics' – taking over slowly and gradually, one slice at a time. But, with the one possible exception of Czechoslovakia, no ECE Communist Party would ever have won a free election in the immediate post-war period.

The various stages of takeover

The Communist takeovers took place in four stages: popular-front tactics, facade coalitions, one-party dictatorships and finally full-blooded Stalinism. It is also imperative to take into account the original backdrop against which the Communists assumed control: immediate post-war chaos.

Backdrop to the takeovers: coping with chaos

To begin with, as the one organised political grouping with financial resources at their disposal, Communists were highly active in post-war restoration and, in particular, in setting up local government. They were usually the first group on the scene after the German departure and normally played a key role in the distribution of much-needed food, clothing, and so on. They then helped to set up the local administration, which ensured that they gained control of the police. In short, they generally maintained a highly visible profile and were perceived in a very positive light by the local populations.

The key role played by the Communists during this crucial period was greatly facilitated by several factors.

- Many 'national communists' had a good public image as wartime heroes or martyrs, since many had been imprisoned, tortured or even murdered by fascist governments.
- The early administrations were under the protection of the

> Red Army, which was an army of occupation throughout the region.
- The returning Communists, especially the younger members of the Party, were fanatical about the new society they wished to create.
- Many people responded to the sort of 'messianic' utopia the Communists were promising – although less so in Poland and East Germany.
- On the international scene, there was still considerable good faith in the Soviet Union as a wartime ally.

The first stage: popular-front organisations

National Front coalitions first emerged during the war as a consequence of the anti-Nazi resistance. The Communists usually played the leading role in bringing these coalitions together.

At first the Communists established coalition governments with other political groupings that had remained untouched by fascism or collaboration with the Germans. Very often, the presidents or leading ministers of such governments were leaders of re-established, pre-war peasant or liberal parties.

Sometimes such governments were formed after perfectly free elections, as in Hungary in late 1945, when the Smallholders' Party obtained 57 per cent of votes to the Communists' 17 per cent, or Czechoslovakia in 1946 when the Communists won the elections with 38 per cent of votes. In both countries there were National Front governments composed of several parties.

Elsewhere the Communists did not perform so well, but were still included in all coalitions: in the multi-party Fatherland Front in Bulgaria, in the National Democratic Front in Romania, and in the 1945 Polish government. Within all of these governments, the Communists usually managed to gain control of the interior and defence ministries, thereby acquiring responsibility for the police and army. In Czechoslovakia, almost all the most important posts went to Communists after the 1946 elections.

Communists also endeavoured to be in charge of land reform, that is, dispossessing the collaborating landowners and nobility of their estates and redistributing the land to the peasants in the immediate post-war period. In Poland and Yugoslavia this also entailed redistributing the land and property of the Germans expelled after 1945 (7 million from Poland) – a policy that was immensely popular with local peasants. (In Czechoslovakia, German expulsions were carried out mainly by the 1945–46 non-communist provisional government.)

Throughout this period, all Communist parties continually declared their commitment to democratic elections and respect for human rights. On the surface, they seemed like any normal political group wishing to restore government to the region.

The second stage: facade coalitions

The second phase was characterised by a consolidation of power by the Communist parties within the front organisations. Non-communist parties would face severe restrictions in publishing their material, holding public meetings or gaining access to the state media. Many of their leaders, including leading ministers, would often be exposed as Western agents or former collaborators and be compelled to resign.

Charges of collaboration were most often directed against leaders and members of the various peasants' parties: for example, the Hungarian Smallholders' Party, the Polish Peasants' Party, the Romanian Agrarian Union, and the Slovak Democratic Party. (The Czechoslovak Agrarians were prevented from re-establishing themselves after 1945 by the non-communist government in exile under President Benes.) In addition, the Communists would attempt to cause splits in the opposition parties by founding fake socialist or peasant parties to attract members away from established opposition parties; for example, Communists organised a bogus Peasant Party in Poland and a fake 'Ploughmen's Front' in Romania.

Finally, mass recruitment was also a key policy of the Communists during this period; for example, the Romanian Communist Party, which had perhaps 1,000 members in August 1944, grew to around 1 million within four years, the Czechoslovak Communist

Party from 40,000 to 2.67 million between July 1945 and October 1948, and the Hungarian Communist Party from 2,000 in November 1944 to 884,000 in May 1948.

The third stage: one-party dictatorship

In the third stage the Communists used rigged elections or other tactics of pressure to gain complete dominance within the government. (Note that rigged elections had been the norm during the inter-war period throughout ECE, especially in Bulgaria, Romania and Poland.) Afterwards, no political opposition of any kind was permitted, non-communists were dismissed from the cabinets, and only satellite parties which supported the leading role of the Communists were allowed to exist. All leading positions in society were filled by Communists. The various countries could now more or less be called 'socialist'.

Communists rigged elections:

- by ensuring that no other parties fielded candidates (e.g. in Yugoslavia in late 1945);
- by allotting each party a guaranteed number of seats in advance of the election (e.g. in Poland in 1947);
- by tampering with the electoral list to exclude any 'undesirable' persons (e.g. in Romania in 1946 and Hungary in 1947);
- by multiple balloting by Communists (e.g. in Hungary in 1947);
- by instilling an all-pervading atmosphere of fear and intimidation (e.g. in Romania in 1947).

In this way, the Communists and their satellite parties dominated the elected parliaments. In Poland, for example, they gained 382 out of 444 seats (compare the paltry 28 seats for the Peasant Party, which would quite probably have won a free election), in Yugoslavia they claimed 96 per cent support, in Romania most of the vote was 'won' by the National Democratic Front, and in Hungary the vote for the Peasant Party fell from 57 per cent in

1945 to 14 per cent two years later. Only in Czechoslovakia in 1946 could the Communist Party (KSC) be said to have won the first elections fairly.

Finally, socialist or social democratic parties were induced or coerced into merging with the Communist parties. The resulting parties – such as the Polish United Workers' Party (PZPR), the Hungarian Socialist Workers' Party (MSZMP) and the East German Socialist Unity Party (SED) – all introduced one-party rule, and claimed to represent the majority of the workers and peasants in each of the countries concerned.

Overall though, in contrast to the pre-war Nazi or fascist takeovers, it is worth emphasising that relatively small numbers of people were actually arrested or killed by the Communists. Bulgaria represented an exception, since the guerrilla forces of Todor Zhivkov organised people's tribunals which had close to 3,000 leading political personalities executed, including Nikola Petkov, leader of the large and influential Agrarian Union. In Albania, too, the National Liberation Movement, led by Enver Hoxha, had the members of the rival opposition National Front shot and killed.

The fourth and final stage: Stalinisation

The one-party governments then introduced the main features of the Soviet model of society: industries were nationalised and farms collectivised; education and the media fell under state (i.e. Communist Party) control; new constitutions were written, basically copying the 1936 Soviet constitution; officially each country became known as a 'People's Republic'; parliaments became rubber-stamps for Party dictates; finally, all ministerial appointments were made only among Communists.

The last stage was reached when the 'national communist leaders', whom Moscow rightly or wrongly mistrusted, were persecuted, humiliated in show trials, tortured or killed. In Albania Koci Xoxe, former Minister of the Interior, was sentenced to death as a Titoist in mid-1949; in Hungary, Laszlo Rajk, former Minister of the Interior and top Communist Party member, was executed for being a Western agent and American imperialist, in September 1949; in the same month Polish Communist leader Wladyslaw Gomulka was put under house arrest, as was Lucretiu Patranscanu, former Romanian Minister of Justice, who remained imprisoned until April 1954, when he was shot; finally, in Bulgaria, Traicho Kostov, an influential economist, was executed for Titoism and collaboration with the pre-war secret police in December 1949. This is to mention just a few examples of a region-wide phenomenon.

The last of Stalin's planned purges also took place in the satellites, with the instigation of a blatant anti-Jewish campaign among the Communist Party leadership. In 1952, in the Slansky trials (Czechoslovakia) and the Ana Pauker affair (Romania), high Party officials were singled out because of their 'Jewish origin' and accused of Zionism. Slansky and several others were all condemned to death and hanged. This fed on the widespread anti-Jewish feeling still prevalent within the region.

Reasons for the ease of the Communist takeovers after 1945

The two questions of real importance here are:

1   why there was so little resistance to the Communists, internally or externally;
2   why the non-communist forces, which always represented the majority in ECE, were unable to resist Communist pressure and conspiratorial activities.

Several factors interacted to give the Communists the upper hand:

The Soviet Union had been victorious in the Second World War and had gained prestige as the liberator of the region.

Certain 'national communists' had a good reputation because of their activities in the resistance against the fascist regimes.

There was a permanent and intimidating Soviet military presence – in all ECE countries except Czechoslovakia –

supported by Stalin's insistence on the region's total dependence on the USSR.

There were already widespread expectations of massive change and of a more just society, based on a more equal distribution of income and wealth. The Communists built on these expectations in the immediate post-war reconstruction.

The prevailing political culture in ECE was one in which the population as a whole had become habituated to statist and authoritarian practices.

The old elites had been demoralised or annihilated by the war or by the pre-war authoritarian regimes, thereby undermining any potential opposition to the Communists. In particular, the political parties of the democratic centre and left had been weakened by the war, as many leaders had been imprisoned, killed or had fled abroad.

All non-communists had to account for their activities during the Nazi occupation, which put most of them under considerable pressure, not allowing them to stand up to the Communists, who were relentless pursuers of wartime collaborators.

The non-communists had false perceptions of what the West could and would do for them. They were generally unaware of the emerging Cold War and cooperated with the Communists in the belief that this was internationally desirable.

The West responded feebly to Soviet expansion after 1945, even when help was specifically requested, for example in 1947 by F. Nagy, Hungarian Premier and leader of the Smallholders' Party.

Specific errors on the part of individual non-communist politicians made it much easier for the takeover to be effected, such as the mass resignation of non-communist members of the Czechoslovak cabinet in February 1948.

Main instruments of external Soviet control

Soviet-type socialism implied:

* recognition of the Communist Party's 'leading role within society';

- a hierarchical and centralised structure of command within the Party, with decisions being made in a top-down fashion;
- an economy based on state ownership and central planning instead of a market economy;
- loyalty to the Soviet Union;
- dedication to the unity of the socialist bloc, that is, to international socialism.

However, the definition of 'socialism' was to be the prerogative of the Soviet leadership alone, which meant, *inter alia*, that the Soviet leaders had ultimate control over the selection of ECE Party and state leaders and insisted on being kept informed of any major changes of policy in ECE. In addition, there were various instruments of external control that the Soviets had at their disposal:

The Council for Mutual Economic Assistance (COMECON)

The CMEA, usually known by its acronym COMECON, was established in 1949, as the Soviets' answer to the USA's Marshall Plan for Western Europe. There was little for the CMEA to coordinate, however, since the Soviet Union had no intention of giving aid to ECE. (On the contrary, the USSR collected substantial reparations from those countries it considered former wartime enemies, i.e. East Germany, Hungary, Romania and Bulgaria.)

Khrushchev recreated COMECON as a regional planning agency, whereby there would be an enforced country-by-country division of labour, with each country specialising in the production of certain goods, according to production quotas that were all determined centrally in Moscow. For example, Czechoslovakia, Poland and the Soviet Union built cars; Hungary made buses; and Lithuania produced most of the silicon chips for the whole COMECON bloc. Each country would import what it needed from the others. (Although it continued as a COMECON member, Romania did not participate in Khrushchev's plan and Yugoslavia was never a member of COMECON, having been excluded from the Soviet bloc from 1948 onwards.)

In this economic sense COMECON now became a major instrument of Soviet power, especially when the Soviets were able to make ECE totally dependent on its oil deliveries.

Warsaw Pact

The ECE armies were carefully integrated with the Soviet army, first through a series of post-war bilateral treaties, then, after May 1955, through the Warsaw Pact (the Warsaw Treaty of Friendship, Cooperation and Mutual Assistance). This meant the armies could be standardised. Most top officers were trained in Moscow; their appointments were at least ratified by Moscow. Arms and equipment were made according to Soviet specifications, and most tanks and aircraft were purchased from the Soviet Union.

The Warsaw Pact also provided the framework for stationing Soviet forces throughout the region and for conducting joint manoeuvres. In theory, Soviet forces were based in ECE to guard against an invasion from the West. In reality, they constituted an army of occupation which would ensure that the ECE satellite states remained within the Soviet bloc. 'Joint manoeuvres', for example, were used to put down the Hungarian and Czechoslovak rebellions in 1956 and 1968, respectively.

The largest number of troops were stationed in East Germany – more than 500,000 soldiers. No Soviet troops were posted in Yugoslavia, Albania, Romania and Bulgaria. Yugoslavia never joined the Warsaw Pact because of Tito's split with Moscow in 1948; Albania left the alliance in 1961; Romania refused to allow Soviet forces inside its borders, although it remained a nominal Warsaw Pact member; Bulgaria was an obedient satellite which did not need the Soviets to maintain internal order.

The Brezhnev doctrine

This was otherwise known as the 'doctrine of limited sovereignty' and named after the Soviet Party leader Leonid Brezhnev. The doctrine was evolved to justify the 1968 invasion of Czecho-slovakia and affirmed that no action in any socialist country 'should do harm either to socialism' in the country concerned 'or to the fundamental interests of other socialist countries'. In effect, the Kremlin was claiming the right to intervene within any state in the socialist bloc to prevent any weakening of Communist Party control or any anti-Soviet activity. In essence, the sovereignty of all ECE states was limited by the fact that they still operated as a 'safety zone' against the West.

Russian language and culture

As the Communists incorporated ECE into the Soviet bloc, they tried to strengthen and deepen cultural ties. Russian language instruction became required in most ECE primary and secondary schools, even though it was very often resented.

Resistance to communism in ECE

Once established in power, the Communists never showed any intention of relinquishing their position of dominance. Even so, there were occasional revolts and resistance against Communist leadership.

Plzen, Czechoslovakia, 1953

A sizeable revolt broke out in Plzen in June 1953 (three months after Stalin's death), with workers protesting against the currency reform which meant, in practice, 500 per cent inflation of prices and destruction of all savings. Demonstrations spread to large factories in other cities, before the Communist government modified its policies slightly and attempted to alleviate the workers' situation by increasing the production of consumer goods, halting the collectivisation of agriculture and allowing some farmers to recommence private production. This was the first mass protest against a Communist regime in ECE.

Workers' strikes in East Berlin, 1953

In June 1953, the East German regime raised work quotas to increase output. East Berlin construction workers went out on strike in protest. They were soon joined by other workers and the strike spread quickly to other East German cities, developing into anti-communist riots. The Party leader, Walter Ulbricht, had to call on Soviet troops to suppress the revolt, which they did, killing over twenty demonstrators in the process. A further seven activists were executed later.

Poznan, Poland, 1956

In June 1956, approximately 50,000 workers rioted against higher prices and increased work quotas in the industrial city of Poznan, demanding 'bread and freedom'. Then university students joined the protests, which thereby intensified into a more general anti-regime revolt. The Communist Party leadership employed the Polish army to crush the protests: fifty-four protesters were killed and hundreds were wounded.

Wladyslaw Gomulka (formerly under house arrest) was appointed new Party leader. He brought in various liberal social measures: he released political prisoners, eased press censorship, gave greater autonomy to the Catholic Church and ended the attempted collectivisation of Polish agriculture. However, he did not change the centralisation of the economy and he allowed no political competition to the Communist Party.

Full-scale revolution in Hungary, 1956

Following Khrushchev's criticism of Stalin and the events in Poland, students and young people went on to the streets of Budapest demanding free elections, the withdrawal of Soviet troops, the dismissal of the hard-line Stalinists and the appointment of the 'Hungarian Gomulka', Imre Nagy. They even toppled Stalin's statue and broke into the headquarters of the secret police, killing some agents. Within a matter of hours a full-scale revolt was spreading throughout the nation.

Nagy was duly appointed and, under his brief leadership, non-communist political parties re-emerged and their leaders entered Nagy's coalition cabinet, which advocated a middle way between capitalism and communism. However, within a matter of days, massive Soviet military intervention crushed the rebellion. Nagy and the other leaders were arrested, tried and executed in 1958. The Soviet retaliation thus confirmed that Hungary in particular and ECE in general still lay within the Soviet sphere of influence. Nagy had appealed desperately for Western help, but his appeals remained unanswered. Altogether, some 32,000 died in the uprising and over 250,000 Hungarians fled to the West, especially to the USA (although some 100,000 later returned).

Janos Kadar was chosen new Party leader: he ended the police terror and after 1968 allowed Hungary to develop its own path to communism through a partial and gradual marketisation of the economy, which became known as 'Kadarism'.

The 'Prague Spring' reforms in Czechoslovakia, 1968

The events that became known as the 'Prague Spring' of 1968 really began at the beginning of the 1960s, when several reformist Communists proposed a 'third way': a combination of the free market system and state planning. It was almost inevitable, however, that the desire for economic change would eventually lead to the need for political change and the possible dismantling of one-party Communist rule.

In 1968 Alexander Dubcek became head of the Communist Party and initiated a series of progressive economic and political reforms in an attempt to create 'socialism with a human face'. During the 'Prague Spring' Czechoslovakia moved towards political pluralism, and freedom of the press, of assembly and of travel. This reformist movement was crushed by the military invasion of Soviet troops and those of five other Warsaw Pact countries on 21 August 1968. Under Russian direction Dubcek was dismissed in April 1969 and the country returned to harsh Stalinism under Gustav Husak – a period known euphemistically as the 'process of normalisation'.

Poland from 1970 and the Solidarity trade union movement

In 1970 demonstrations against increased food prices by workers in the Polish ports of Gdansk and Szczecin brought down the

Gomulka government. In 1976 similar strikes and demonstrations against the Gierek government (again for raising food prices) quickly developed an anti-regime character and, for the first time, brought workers and intellectuals into an alliance: the KOR Workers' Committee, the forerunner of the Solidarity movement.

In 1978 a small group of workers in the shipyards along the Polish coast illegally formed the 'Committee of Free Trade Unions for the Baltic Coast' (one of the founding members was Lech Walesa). In the summer of 1980 there were yet more strikes throughout Poland because of increased food prices. This time the government accepted the strikers' list of twenty-one demands, including free trade unions independent of the Party. This led to the founding of Solidarity.

In the following year, some 10 million people (out of a total workforce of 16 million) joined the Solidarity trade union or its rural equivalent. Of 3.5 million Polish Communist Party members, 800,000 resigned and many of them joined Solidarity. In September 1981, Solidarity held its first congress – condemned as 'anti-socialist and anti-Soviet' by Moscow.

On 21 December 1981, with Soviet approval, but without Soviet military support, General Jaruzelski declared martial law, arrested the Solidarity leadership and banned the independent union, which simply continued its activities underground, until its re-legalisation in 1989. This was a classic military coup to avoid system breakdown, but it was primarily to avert any possibility of Soviet invasion.

Totalitarianism, Stalinism and the Communist regimes

It has been said by several authors that the regimes of Nazi Germany, fascist Italy and Stalinist USSR demonstrated a particular type of twentieth-century personalised dictatorship, which they claimed represented a new sort of 'totalitarian' government.

The totalitarian state attempted to extend its influence over the whole of life, both the private and public spheres, and required submission of the individual to the demands of the state.

Totalitarian states were naturally dictatorial, but differed from imperialist or autocratic regimes and military dictatorships, such as in post-war Latin America or inter-war ECE, because of the idea of the 'totality of the state', whereby the role of the individual citizen was one of 'subject'. This was achieved only with a comprehensive monopoly of modern communications: hence 'totalitarianism' being a twentieth-century phenomenon. As C. J. Friedrich and Z. K. Brzezinski concluded: 'Broadly speaking, totalitarian dictatorship is a new development; there has never been anything quite like it before'.

It was Benito Mussolini who in the early 1920s used *totalitario* to describe his idea of the new fascist state: 'All within the state, none outside the state, none against the state'. In this concept, all aspects of any individual's life were subordinated to the authority of the state.

The term *totalitarianism* itself was given wider usage in 1951 when Hannah Arendt published her monumental *Origins of Totalitarianism*. Professor Arendt traced the origin of modern totalitarianism to nineteenth-century anti-Semitism and imperialism, and saw its growth as the outcome of the waning of the traditional nation state. She was concerned with totalitarianism of both the right (Hitler) and the left (Stalin).

Within the context of the Cold War, Friedrich and Brzezinski first published their definitive work on totalitarianism in 1954: *Totalitarian Dictatorship and Autocracy*, concentrating on the Communist regimes, especially the USSR under Stalin. Their conclusions have since been somewhat developed and enlarged upon by various authors, including, *inter alia*, L. Shapiro.

The term totalitarianism was adopted by ECE dissident academics and writers, who used it mostly in a very pejorative sense: but it certainly had meaning in the reality of the societies in which they found themselves. The first post-communist President of Bulgaria, Zyelu Zhelev, for example, wrote a famous critique of Marxism in which he compared 'real existing socialism' to totalitarianism.

What follows is a résumé of the characteristics of a totalitarian state according to both the originators of the term and everyday usage within ECE during the Communist era.

Stalinism – real totalitarianism

'Stalinism' refers to a particularly centralised, hierarchical and brutal type of dictatorship which characterised the Soviet Union from 1927 to 1953: a really totalitarian system, of which there were three main features.

(1) *The Stalinist leadership cult.* In the USSR, Stalin built up an amazing personality cult whereby he was seen as 'Father of the Nation' – a superhuman, with superior knowledge and wisdom, who could never be wrong and whose slightest whim could have the force of law. In post-war ECE an extreme personality cult was built around the Soviet leader, with statues, streets, parks, mountains and factories all bearing his name. The region's press reported everything he did and said. Leaders of the ECE satellite states often copied his political style (e.g. Gottwald in Czechoslovakia, Hoxha in Albania, Ceausescu in Romania, and Ulbricht in East Germany), and, in turn, built up their own personality cults.

(2) *Stalin's emphasis on absolute obedience to the Soviet line.* Stalin demanded that Communists all over the world duplicate Moscow's policy to the letter: from the purges to enforced collectivisation of agriculture. Such devotion to the leadership principle was particularly strong among the Party faithful of the 1930s and 1940s, which included many of the future leaders of ECE Communist parties then in exile in Moscow.

(3) *Show trials, purges and deportations.* Stalin, not Hitler, was responsible for the greatest genocide in history. Some 9–12 million people died during the enforced collectivisation and industrial modernisation of the First Five-Year Plan (1928–33); 3 million were executed during the Great Purge, during which another 5–9 million were arrested and deported. In addition, there were mass executions of thousands of people during 1937 and 1938, many of whom were Communist Party members from ECE – almost the entire leaderships of the Polish and Romanian Communist Parties were exterminated, for example.

In the immediate post-war period, with the exception of Poland and East Germany, every ECE country staged a major public trial of leading figures within the Communist Party at Moscow's instigation.

The characteristics of a totalitarian state

Clearly, there is no doubt about applying the term 'totalitarianism' to Stalin's rule over the post-war Soviet bloc. In ECE eyes, however, communism and totalitarianism have always been interchangeable and the latter often constituted a form of political abuse (see Adam Michnik's quote at the beginning of this chapter).

The following would be the main characteristics of a totalitarian state:

1   the predominance of the leader in all matters;
2   one ruling party;
3   one single ideology;
4   extensive police/army/secret police repression/terror, often directed randomly against the whole population and not just against 'enemies of the state';
5   all the economy under state control;
6   subservience of all intermediary state and non-government organisations to the Party;
7   direct and overt control of the mass media and practice of government censorship;
8   expansionist foreign policy, which usually included the ultimate goal of world domination or world revolution;
9   absolute control of the means of coercion;
10   consistent deception of the masses outside the Party;
11   frequent party purges to demonstrate the guiding principle, 'those who are not with us, are against us';
12   great emphasis placed on the role of rituals and symbols, such as the marches around Red Square in Moscow, stage-managed expressions of goodwill for Party leaders, mass participation at elections, and so on.

Application of characteristics to ECE Communist states

Almost all of the various characteristics identified above can easily be applied to the Stalinist period within ECE.

(1) The leader dominated any ECE Communist movement. Early leaders were ambitious Party members who, to a certain extent, still believed in the utopian ideology of the perfect and classless society. Within ECE a leadership cult could not develop to the same degree, because, clearly, Stalin was 'the leader' for the whole Soviet bloc. Only in Ceausescu's Romania, Hoxha's Albania and (partially) Tito's Yugoslavia did the same sorts of country-wide personality cults emerge (all three quite independent from Moscow).

(2) All ECE Communist states were ruled by a single party, even though there was superficial pluralism in many ECE parliaments. These satellite parties always upheld the leading role of the Communist Party, which, in its turn, upheld the leading role of the Communist Party of the Soviet Union. There were no opposition parties or organisations representing any view contrary to that laid down by the Party.

(3) All ECE regimes were based on the official ideology of Marxist-Leninism, although this meant different things at various times. In theory, this ideology was leading all the socialist republics to the utopian perfection of the classless society. In practice, for the overwhelming majority of East Central Europeans this was an ideology imposed from the outside, representing an alien political system and was resented as such, reviving traditional anti-Russian sentiments especially in Poland, Hungary, East Germany and Romania.

(4) All ECE Communist states were subject to intensive, random and ubiquitous terror campaigns by the secret police. The security forces – usually under the interior ministry – kept files on anyone who dissented, had contacts with foreigners, or who travelled abroad. Part-time informants for the secret police were everywhere, so people had to be very careful about what they said in public. It is reckoned that such terror campaigns in most ECE countries touched upon most families in some way or another.

All ECE states had security services modelled on and connected to the Soviet KGB. The security forces were effectively a type of paramilitary force which existed to carry out the orders of the Party. Usually, the top officers of the satellite countries had been trained in Moscow and most reported back to the KGB headquarters, so that the Soviets always knew what was happening. Even so, the system never achieved the total subservience of most individuals: it led rather to a type of social schizophrenia, whereby everyone had a public face and a private opinion (which was shared only with the closest friends and relatives).

(5) All ECE economies were almost entirely in the hands of the state, under a central planning agency, which promoted heavy industry at the expense of consumer goods. In most countries farming was collectivised and production and international trade were tied heavily to the military and technological needs of the Soviet Union and other socialist nations. In Czechoslovakia, for example, 98 per cent of gross domestic product was in the hands of the state. The consequence of this centralised approach was a concentration on heavy industry, with very large plants, each sizeable town having its own massive factory, combined with a reckless attitude towards the environment, especially in respect of energy resources.

(6) Everywhere intermediary organisations were mostly under the control of the Party. There was no need for autonomous trade unions, for example, since no worker could have any interests which would not reflect the will of the Party. The Party attempted totalitarian control over every aspect of life, in both the private and public spheres, aimed at values as well as organisations. Anything that could promote diversity or enhance a nascent civil society was destroyed. In short, societies were 'atomised' so that they could be more easily controlled: all individuals were expected to conform to Party dictates.

(7) The Communist regimes had to suppress any alternative source of information if they were to remain in power, so there was extreme press censorship and no private media were allowed. Each ECE country had a Communist Party daily newspaper that was a propaganda broadsheet. Although many of the satellite parties had their own newspapers, no viewpoints could be published that differed from the official Party line. Likewise, all television channels and radio stations were kept under tight state

control, and were used indiscriminately to publish the Party line on whatever issue. All other forms of communication – films, music, painting, literature, the theatre, and so on – were also censored with regard to ideological content.

The news black-out was never complete, however, as many citizens had access to alternative sources of information. The Catholic Church, in Poland and elsewhere, presented its own version of events from the pulpit or within Church publications. Most people had access to Western news reports, through foreign radio broadcasts by Radio Free Europe, Voice of America, Deutsche Welle, or the BBC. With several stations broadcasting from West Berlin in German, East Germany, for example, was inundated with Western radio. Moreover, 85 per cent of East Germans could receive West German television, Czechoslovaks could pick up Austrian television channels, and so on. Even though outside broadcasts were often jammed by the Communists, the news got through somehow.

(8) As an ideology communism was expansionist, but an expansionist foreign policy was not practised by the ECE Communist states. Firstly, they were too small, and secondly they were fully dependent on the Soviet Union militarily speaking. However, an integral part of Soviet foreign policy was the support of the armed insurgencies throughout the world, for example in Mozambique, Angola, or Vietnam. In these instances the ECE Communist states contributed to the policy by helping to finance it, especially Czechoslovakia, Hungary and East Germany.

(9) Absolute control of the means of coercion applies to all states and, in any case, the means of coercion were never used to their full capacity, except in isolated instances like 1956, 1968 or 1981. On the whole, during the 1970s and 1980s, force was not usually necessary to keep the system in place, except against actual dissidents and opponents of the regime.

Post-totalitarianism

Stalin's death in 1953 was followed by a visible process of de-totalitarianisation within the Soviet Union. For example, the vast police empire was reduced, many concentration camps were closed, full-scale purges and show trials against suspected 'enemies of the state' ceased.

According to Arendt, totalitarianism came to an end in the Soviet Union and ECE after Stalin's death and Khrushchev's repudiation of the Stalinist era. A period of 'post-totalitarianism' began, during which, according to G. Schöpflin, there was a 'totalising ideology' and a 'potential for totalitarian intervention', but little of the 'real totalitarianism' described above.

Jan Sokol, a leading Catholic dissident in Czechoslovakia, explains the difference between totalitarianism and post-totalitarianism very simply. 'Under totalitarianism you still had people who believed in the communist utopia, under post-totalitarianism no one believed in it any more … but you still had to obey.'

Features of these post-totalitarian regime were the following.

- Terror was more administrative, almost invisible, but just as pervasive, in that people universally believed that the state would levy sanctions against anyone for the slightest misdemeanour, that is, there was almost complete material dependence of the individual on the state and the 'politics of fear' were still present everywhere.

- Nascent forms of disobedience were allowed and there was even limited toleration of criticism, for example in Yugoslavia, where anyone could be criticised except for Tito himself.

- The post-totalitarian system could no longer base itself on the use of arbitrary power and brute force: it had to justify its actions to a more inter-dependent world, particularly after the USSR and ECE countries signed the Helsinki Accords in 1975–76.

- The atomisation of society and general apathy became more important than attempts at outright control and mobilisation.

- The system's main ally was the individual's conviction that nothing could be changed in the given circumstances and that cooperation with the authorities was the only way to have a trouble-free existence.

- There was a distinct change in the function and influence of the ruling ideology, which now became entirely ritualistic. Ideology in post-totalitarian societies, according to Vladimir Tismaneanu, was a 'residual construct' which never inspired the populace with any degree of loyalty. The Communist elite manipulated ideology for no other reason than holding on to power. Likewise, in the post-totalitarian society the dominant structures seemed to be exhausted. There was a general malaise in the functioning of all institutions, which even the Communists themselves began to take less seriously.

- There was a noticeable bureaucratisation of the entire system, which had become socially, economically and politically ossified – minor reforms enabled the system to prolong its existence but not to survive. This meant that corruption was endemic: if anyone wanted cement to build a weekend cottage, if a plumber was needed to repair the bath, or even a doctor to examine someone's eyes properly, then the bribe had to be paid up front. There was a popular joke that the greatest know-how was to know to whom to give the envelope first.

Difference between the various communist states of ECE

Within the context of the Cold War, Westerners developed a type of ideological anti-communism, which prevented us from distinguishing between the various Communist one-party dictatorships throughout the Soviet bloc. There was just as much variety among the communist states of ECE as among states within Western Europe. For example:

- in Poland collectivisation of land was reversed so that agriculture remained under largely private ownership;
- in both Hungary and East Germany some private entrepreneurship was permitted (but not encouraged) – in

Hungary economic private ownership was allowed under 'Kadarism' after 1968 in particular;

- in Poland, Hungary, Czechoslovakia, Yugoslavia and East Germany a certain degree of political party pluralism was tolerated, although this was mainly window-dressing for the West;

- culturally speaking some states remained Catholic, for example Poland, Slovakia and Croatia, and, although religious worship was not encouraged, only Albania was officially atheistic (in Poland the Catholic Church represented a focal point of Polish nationalist opposition to the externally imposed communist regime);

- levels of economic development between various communist countries were just as great as in the West – the difference between Czechoslovakia and Albania, for example, was just as great as the economic disparity between West Germany and Portugal.

Conclusion

By the 1980s the communist regimes had become clearly illegitimate: the Communists held on to power for power's sake and the ECE economies were deteriorating rapidly in comparison with their Western neighbours. The collapse of these regimes was inevitable – it was only a question of time.

Further reading

Hannah Arendt, *The Origins of Totalitarianism*, Harvest, 1975.

Zbigniew Brzezinski, *The Soviet Bloc: Unity and Conflict*, Harvard University Press, 1971.

R. V. Burks, *The Dynamics of Communism in Eastern Europe*, Princeton University Press, 1961.

Carl J. Friedrich and Zbigniew K. Brzezinski, *Totalitarian Dictatorship and Autocracy*, Praeger, 1967.

Carl J. Friedrich, Michael Curtis and Benjamin R. Barber, *Totalitarianism in Perspective: Three Views*, Pall Mall Press, 1969.

Joseph Rothschild, *Return to Diversity: A Political History of East Central Europe Since World War II*, Oxford University Press, 1989.

Jacques Rupnik, *The Other Europe*, Weidenfeld and Nicholson, 1989.

George Schöpflin, *Politics in Eastern Europe*, Blackwell, 1993.

Leonard Shapiro, *Totalitarianism*, Pall Mall Press, 1972.

Vladimir Tismaneanu, *Reinventing Politics: Eastern Europe from Stalin to Havel*, The Free Press, 1992.

Stephen White, John Gardner, George Schöpflin and Tony Saich, *Communist and Post-communist Political Systems*, Macmillan, 1990.

3
The revolutions of ECE

The real question, however, is whether a revolution that is negotiated or 'velvet' can rightly be called a revolution at all. (Jacques Rupnik)

We didn't win. They ran away and left us to take power. (Jan Urban)

The year 1989 will go down as one of the most important years in the twentieth century. Never before have so many countries undergone such dramatic changes in regime in such a short space of time.

Some were brought about by round-table negotiations, as in Hungary; some by 'people power', as in Romania, East Germany and Czechoslovakia; some by a combination of the two, as in Poland, Albania and Bulgaria; and one by internal disintegration, in the case of Yugoslavia.

In every case the speed of the changes was breathtaking and the ease with which the peoples of ECE removed the Communists from power was quite astonishing. Regimes that were considered well entrenched simply collapsed and the ruling elites gave up power almost at the first instance of concerted opposition. With the sole exception of Romania, all of these changes occurred peacefully.

Was it really a revolution?

'Revolutions' or 'refolutions'?

There is actually a considerable amount of debate as to whether the dramatic changes that took place during 1989 constituted real 'revolutions'. Jakub Karpinski, for example, claims that 'there was no anti-communist *revolution* in ECE, but rather a "velvet evolution"'. Timothy Garton Ash calls what happened a 'refolution', that is, 'a mixture of reform and revolution' from above, led by 'an enlightened minority in the still ruling Communist parties' and 'mediated by negotiations between ruling and opposition groups'. However, Garton Ash distinguishes between what occurred in 1989 in both Hungary and Poland (*refolution*) from what happened in Czechoslovakia, East Germany and Romania (*revolution*). Bulgaria and Albania have aspects of both.

Hannah Arendt asserted the following about the course and meaning of revolutions:

- revolutions necessarily have a degree of violence;
- revolutions bring about 'something altogether new', with a 'complete change of society' being the overriding goal;
- the ultimate aim of all revolutions is freedom;
- all revolutions entail 'irresistibility' (an overwhelming urgency), that is, the revolution has an unstoppable dynamic all of its own;
- in all revolutions 'novelty is connected with the idea of freedom'.

Rebellions, coups d'état, so-called 'palace revolutions' and civil wars are not revolutionary, as they usually result in the simple transferral of power among different elites. Revolutions, on the other hand, challenge the way society is organised.

To return to Arendt's criteria in respect of ECE:

- dramatic change took place everywhere, and the 'revolutions' of 1989 certainly brought about 'something altogether new' in comparison with the previous forty years or so;
- there was concerted action from below everywhere;
- the changes occurred very swiftly, with more than an element of 'irresistibility';
- the changes were far reaching and radical, and had 'freedom' from the Soviet colonial system as their ultimate goal;

- the 1989 revolutions certainly brought about the end of an old order and the birth of something new.

However, Jacques Rupnik still has problems with the appellation 'revolution' to the events of 1989, and asserts that the ECE revolutions are 'unique in history', since none of them claimed to have a 'new societal project', as the dissident leaders simply copied Western economic and political systems. In comparison with the 1789 French or the 1917 Russian revolutions, according to Rupnik, 'the negotiated transitions of 1989 were quick, easy and non-violent'. In a similar vein, François Furet prefers to label what happened a 'revolution-restoration'.

Moreover, the extent of the 'revolution' in terms of social structures is questionable. Even before the revolutions actually took place, several leading Communists were already planning change. They were well equipped to take advantage of the new economic freedoms after 1989 and so have become the new capitalists and the holders of extensive economic power throughout ECE today. Since the electoral victories of the ex-communists in Poland, Hungary and Bulgaria, they possess both economic and political power.

Common features of all 'revolutions' in ECE

Suddenness of the collapse

In January 1989, Solidarity was still a banned organisation and Vaclav Havel had just been imprisoned for nine months. Six months later Solidarity won the first partially free elections in the Soviet bloc and in December 1989 Havel was appointed Czechoslovak President. In all ECE countries, except Albania and Yugoslavia, the 'revolutions' took place within the course of seven months, from the beginning of June to the end of December 1989.

Ubiquity of the collapse

The course of events during 1989 was rather like a 'domino effect', whereby one Communist nation after the next followed the pattern set by Poland or East Germany. The televised crowds demonstrating in the GDR or camping in the grounds of the American Embassy in Prague influenced events in Czechoslovakia, Bulgaria and, eventually, even in isolated Albania.

Completeness of the collapse

By 1989 the Communist regimes were devoid of all legitimacy, so that when they were challenged by vast numbers of their citizens, they simply collapsed, abandoning all the main pillars of the former regime – press censorship, control over people's private lives, the leading role of the Communist Party, the Warsaw Pact, and so on. They just capitulated, as if they had never expected the 'people' to be against them. By early 1990 communism had become a dirty word and most ECE inhabitants wanted to dispense with anything that reminded them of the previous regime.

Unpredictableness of the actual collapse

Very few people expected such a sudden disintegration of the Soviet bloc, politicians and academics alike. Many experts on the area were writing as late as September 1989 that the future would probably entail the Communists gradually incorporating the opposition into the government, but retaining the important posts for themselves – as was actually happening in Poland at the time.

Long-term inevitability of the collapse

By the end of the 1980s communist Eastern Europe had fallen so far behind the West, especially with regard to computerisation and modern technology, that it was evident to rulers and ruled alike that the centrally planned economies could not be maintained.

Moreover, many leading reformists within the various Communist parties had already reached the opinion that the centrally planned economies needed a complete overhaul in the direction of the free market, rather than superficial tinkering with the planning system. It was also realised that no enduring solution to these problems would be feasible without more political freedom.

Existence of elite groups aware that change was near

In quite a few countries, but especially Poland and Hungary, there were groups within the Communist elite who understood the enormity of the social and economic crisis facing the region and who realised the need for compromise with the emerging opposition groups. It is very difficult to judge, however, whether such 'reform Communists' had a deep conviction of the need for reform or whether they were simply interested in maintaining themselves in positions of power.

Existence of opposition groups

In each country, with the exception of Romania, there were clearly identifiable opposition groups that could take advantage of the new situation as it materialised during 1988–89, such as Polish Solidarity, which had over 10 million members, or the elitist Czechoslovak Charter 77, signed at first by only 253 intellectuals and artists.

Opposition intensified after the signing of the Helsinki Accords in 1975, as groups focused on the abuse of human rights and began to propose real alternatives. Such groups were often quite varied. In Croatia and Slovenia, for example, opposition forces launched campaigns for greater rights of the various nationalities living within the Yugoslav Federation. In Hungary opposition of intellectuals began in earnest at the beginning of the 1980s, with the appearance of hundreds of *samizdat* publications. Their number increased dramatically in 1987–88 when embryonic opposition political parties emerged.

The importance of people power

There was concerted action 'from below' in all ECE countries during 1989. Sometimes it was limited to isolated events, as with the reburial of Imre Nagy in Hungary in June; sometimes it was regular and accumulative, like the Monday night processions in Leipzig, which grew 100-fold during the course of September and October; sometimes it was most dramatic, such as hundreds of thousands of people filling Wenceslas Square, or the crowds breaking down the Berlin Wall – both in November.

Its effect was always far reaching, as with the heckling of Ceausescu in Bucharest, which triggered his attempted flight from the country in December, or the large demonstrations in Sofia after Zhivkov's dismissal in November. The Communist leadership simply disintegrated when faced with such outright opposition of the masses, as they did not know how to respond to the challenges from below, other than to resort to brute force, which they could no longer use because of possible sanctions by the international community.

The emphasis on negotiated transition

By 1988, leading figures within both the Communist regimes and the opposition groups in Poland and Hungary realised that some sort of compromise between the two groups was necessary for the sake of their respective countries. In the cases of Czechoslovakia and Romania, this 'realisation' dawned on the Communist leaders much later in the day, after the revolutionary process had already begun.

The idea of compromise divided not only the regimes and their Communist parties, but also the opposition in each country. Within Solidarity, radical opponents formed their own break-away group in opposition to the conciliatory approach adopted by Lech Walesa and his team. In Hungary the issue of how far to collaborate with Communist Party reformists bitterly divided the Hungarian Democratic Forum (MDF) from the other, more radical opposition group, the Alliance of Free Democrats (SZDSZ).

Aspects of the revolutions in each country

Strikes and round-table negotiations in Poland

In Poland revolutionary events were brought to a head by two waves of strikes and demonstrations in April and August 1988, when the strikers called for the legalisation of the banned Solidarity trade union. The Communist government agreed to this last demand, in return for an end to the strikes.

After Solidarity's leaders had helped to negotiate an end to the strike, the Communists stalled on legalisation. It was not until General Jaruzelski threatened to resign in January 1989 that the Party then approved a variety of political reforms, including the legalisation of Solidarity. Consequently, round-table talks between the Communists, the Catholic Church and Solidarity began on 6 February 1989 and ended on 5 April 1989.

The agreement reached between the Communist government and the opposition amounted to the following:

- Solidarity, the farmers' Rural Solidarity and the Independent Students' Association were all legalised;
- these organisations received air time on radio and television as well as their own national and regional newspapers;
- new parliamentary elections for the Sejm, the lower legislative chamber, were to take place in which the Communist Party (PZPR) was pre-allocated 38 per cent of the seats (i.e. Communist candidates were unopposed in 175 seats), 22 per cent of the seats went to its satellite parties – the United Peasant Party (ZSL) and the Democratic Party (SD) – while a further 5 per cent were reserved for Catholic organisations, meaning that only 35 per cent of the seats were open to contest from Solidarity candidates;
- elections for the newly established upper legislative chamber, the Senate (100 seats), were to be totally free;
- in all constituencies there were to be two rounds of elections, unless a candidate received 50 per cent of the vote plus one vote in the first, in which case there was only one round;
- the Sejm and Senate in joint session were to elect the President of the Republic – a post with some considerable powers of patronage and appointment (it was implicitly accepted by all concerned that General Jaruzelski would become President).

In the early June elections Solidarity surprised everyone, including the Communists, with an overwhelming 'victory', winning all the contested seats for the Sejm and ninety-nine of the hundred seats for the Senate. Indeed, in the first round only seven of the Communist or satellite candidates won overall majorities in their reserved seats, despite being unopposed. The majority of the electorate simply deleted the Communists' names.

After the elections, Walesa persuaded the PZPR's former allies, the ZSL and SD, to switch sides and support a Solidarity-led coalition. General Jaruzelski then appointed Tadeusz Mazowiecki Premier of the first non-communist government in ECE since 1946. Within this government, most cabinet posts went to Solidarity, while the Communists were allocated the key Ministries of the Interior and Defence, as a gesture to the Soviets.

General Jaruzelski was then elected President by a one-vote margin on 19 July, as agreed, even though most Solidarity deputies opposed his candidacy. This allowed Adam Michnik to refer to the new situation as: 'Their President, our Government'.

The real importance of the Polish events, however, was Moscow's acquiescence in, if not Gorbachev's active encouragement of, the first profound changes within ECE. This sent a clear message to the rest of the region.

The opening of the Iron Curtain and more normal party politics in Hungary

The first steps to Hungary's revolution really occurred in 1956 with Imre Nagy's attempts to instigate political pluralism and economic liberalism. After 1968 the New Economic Mechanism (NEM) introduced gradual and limited market reforms without any political changes.

By the 1980s dissident groups were beginning to press for greater political pluralism. A burgeoning number of *samizdat* journals began to criticise the Communist regime openly for its moral bankruptcy, political and economic shortcomings.

Even communist reformists were criticising the regime. In 1987 Imre Poszgay claimed that the communist system 'cannot be reformed because it has clearly failed'. On 22 May 1988, General Secretary Kadar was replaced in a Communist Party back-room coup by the more reformist Karloly Grosz – again with the consent of the Moscow.

Various opposition groupings emerged after Kadar's departure. Some were resurrections of pre-war parties – such as the Christian Democrats (KDNP), the Independent Smallholders' Party (FKGP) – while others were brand new political forces – the MDF, the SZDSZ, the Federation of Young Democrats (FIDESZ), free trade unions, environmental groups, and so on.

As a result, there was no one single, identifiable 'revolutionary' event in Hungary. Two pronouncements in February 1989 were of crucial importance however: the Hungarian Communist Party (MSZMP) officially agreed to the establishment of independent non-communist political parties and declared that the 1956 Hungarian revolt had been a 'popular uprising', not a 'counter-revolution'.

There followed two very symbolic events: the ceremonial cutting of the barbed wire of the Iron Curtain on the newly opened Austro-Hungarian border in May. On 16 June the reburial in Budapest of Imre Nagy and four other heroes of the 1956 revolution was attended by 200,000 people – including Poszgay and other reformist communists.

On 13 June the Communist government and representatives of eight opposition groups began round-table talks, within which the reformists under Poszgay played a prominent role. The participants agreed on constitutional reform, the creation of a multi-party system, the holding of free elections under a new electoral law and a new name for the Republic (dropping the word 'People's'). But they disagreed on direct elections for the presidency. The more radical groupings (FIDESZ, SZDSZ and some trade union representatives) refused to sign the accord and forced a referendum on the timing and method of the presidential elections, winning the poll by a very narrow margin in late November. This represented a major setback for the MSZP, MDF and Imre Poszgay. Now the President was to be appointed by parliament after the general elections. (By now the MSZMP had changed its name to the Hungarian Socialist Party (MSZP), replaced Grosz with the more reformist Nyers and renounced Marxism-Leninism totally.)

In April 1990 Hungary held the most 'normal' elections in the former Soviet bloc. The elections were not a simple plebiscite on communism as elsewhere, as the opposition parties also competed against each other most vehemently. As a result, the two-round election in March–April 1990 produced a centre-right MDF/ FKGP/KDNP coalition opposed by a Western-type opposition of the more radical parties, SZDSZ and FIDESZ.

Demonstrations and emigration in East Germany

With the advent of political pluralism and a free market in East Germany, the whole *raison d'être* of the GDR as a separate entity from West Germany disappeared. The GDR state itself was threatened, not just the communist regime. Hence, the East German leadership continually criticised Gorbachev's reform process.

After the opening of the Austria-Hungarian border in May 1989, thousands of mostly young East Germans started 'voting with their feet'. During the summer thousands occupied the gardens of the West German embassies in Warsaw, Prague and Budapest, while hundreds of thousands camped elsewhere. In September/October they were allowed to leave for Austria or West Germany. Thereafter visas were required for travel to other ECE countries and requests for such visas were normally refused.

At the GDR's fortieth anniversary in East Berlin on 7 October, President Gorbachev tried to persuade the country's hard-line leadership to reform. He was welcomed enthusiastically by over 100,000 people and there were several demonstrations during his visit. After his departure, the protests spread to other cities, with people demanding free emigration, the resignation of Party leaders and the legalisation of the New Forum opposition. In addition, the odd poster demanded unification with West Germany.

In Leipzig, regular Monday evening protest marches across the city began in mid-September with 2,500 people, growing to about 500,000 participants by early November. There were frequent clashes with the police and, on occasions, the Politburo even contemplated using the army against the demonstrators.

In mid-October Egon Krenz replaced Erich Honecker as Party leader and on 7 November a new government was formed which ended all travel restrictions and opened crossing points in the Berlin Wall on 9 November. This event more than any other symbolised the collapse of the Soviet empire throughout ECE.

By now, 500,000 people were demonstrating in Leipzig and East Berlin, where several posters now demanded 'One German Nation'. People were leaving the country *en masse*, even though Krenz promised further reforms. The country was on the brink of revolt.

In mid-November the media exposed the extent of the opulent lifestyle of the former Communist Party leaders. Several people reacted violently by storming the headquarters of the secret police (*Stasi*) and destroying files. Krenz and the new Politburo resigned in early December. Krenz was replaced as Party Chairman by Gregor Gysi, a lawyer who had defended dissidents in the past.

The Communist Party (SED) now renamed itself the Party for Democratic Socialism (PDS) and voted to end the Communists' 'leading role', approving free elections for the spring of 1990.

By early December, the momentum had been lost to the process of unification of the two German states. Once West German *Bundeskanzler* Helmut Kohl began pressing for quick reunification, groups like New Forum (advocating a more gradual reunification process) lost their political appeal. There was a headlong rush to rejoin the West and gain access to its higher living standards.

On 18 March 1990, the East German Christian Democrats won the elections with 48.1 per cent of votes. But the real 'winners' were Kohl and the West German parties, not the indigenous East German politicians. In mid-April 1990 a care-taker government was formed under Premier Lothair de Maiziere, to oversee the process of reunification, which lasted until October 1990, when the GDR was incorporated into the Federal Republic.

The 'velvet revolution' in Czechoslovakia

The hard-line leadership in Czechoslovakia also rejected Gorbachev's reforms, as they resembled those of the 1968 Prague Spring. The subsequent twenty years of 'normalisation' (increased Stalinisation) had meant a total renunciation of such policies.

During the 1980s Charter 77 activists began to chronicle the regime's human rights abuses and protests started. Some 100,000 people marched through Prague on the twentieth anniversary of the Warsaw Pact invasion; 500,000 people signed a petition demanding religious freedom; in January 1989, thousands demonstrated for five days on the twentieth anniversary of Jan Palach's death (he had burnt himself to death as a protest against the 1968 invasion). The police used quite blatant force to suppress the protests, imprisoning Vaclav Havel and other members of Charter 77 in January 1989.

By late summer of 1989 the Czechs and Slovaks could see what was happening in Poland, Hungary and East Germany, since the emigrating East Germans were using Prague as a departure point to the West and many people could watch the events in Leipzig and Berlin on Austrian television. Even so, the dissidents – mainly the 2,000 intellectuals and artists who had signed Charter 77 – were hardly prepared for change. Even as late as 15 November they decided that pushing for round-table talks and opposing the Communists with official candidates in the next year's elections were 'too risky'.

On 17 November, nearly 100,000 unarmed students marched towards Wenceslas Square – to commemorate the fiftieth anniversary of the killing of sixteen students by the Nazis. They were brutally attacked by riot police and several were badly injured. This action sparked off further nationwide demonstrations and strikes.

The opposition formed itself into the Civic Forum (OF) in Prague and the Public Against Violence (VPN) in Bratislava. Their leaders – mainly from Charter 77 – pressed for total economic and political reform and demanded the resignations of the Party leader, Jakes, and President Husak.

On 25 November, 350,000 to 500,000 people gathered in Wenceslas Square to hear Alexander Dubcek and Vaclav Havel speak. That day the entire Party leadership resigned, to be replaced by younger reformists. On 27 November a general strike forced the government to agree to the formation of a Communist–OF coalition government, free elections and freer travel to the West.

On 29 November the Communist Federal Assembly abolished the Party's 'leading role' and the Communist-controlled mass media began to advocate political pluralism. Faced with mass action on the part of ordinary citizens, the Communists simply capitulated. Hence the term the 'velvet revolution'.

On 3 December, 'reformist' Ladislaw Adamec proposed a new twenty-one-member cabinet with only five non-communists. It was rejected by the OF leadership and Adamec resigned under the threat of a general strike. Seven days later, Marian Calfa formed a 'Government of National Understanding' with a majority of non-communist ministers. (Most of the eight Communist ministers – including the Premier himself – soon left the Party and joined OF or VPN.)

The Communists then aided the legal transfer of power by allowing themselves to be replaced within the Assembly by co-opted members from the opposition. President Husak resigned on 10 December after swearing in the new government. On 28 and 29 December this newly co-opted Federal Assembly then elected Dubcek Speaker of the Federal Assembly and Havel President.

In the June 1990 elections, OF won a clear majority in the Czech Republic and VPN took 34 per cent of the votes in Slovakia. Calfa, now a member of VPN, became Premier of an OF/VPN coalition government with the Slovak Christian Democratic Movement (KDH) and Havel was re-elected President.

Ecological protest and evolving revolution in Bulgaria

During the Communist era the Bulgarian Communist Party (BKP) always followed the Soviet lead. Between 1954 and 1989 there was only one leader, Todor Zhivkov, and no rebellion of any sort. Zhivkov was also the first ECE leader to copy Gorbachev's reforms, when he called for political democratisation, greater press freedom, multi-candidate elections and so on in his 1987 'July Concept'. Nothing materialised from the intended reforms, but Zhivkov had commenced a process he could not control. Independent trade unions, organisations promoting human rights, revived political parties and an organised ecological movement (later called Eco-glasnost) all entered the political arena.

Strikes and protests now spread among Bulgaria's ethnic Turks, who had been subject to assimilation campaigns in the 1980s. In June 1989 Zhivkov forced 315,000 ethnic Turks to return to Turkey, until the borders were closed by the Turkish government. The policy gave Bulgaria worldwide negative publicity and also back-fired economically, as the Turks were efficient farmers.

In early October 1989, 5,000 people marched on the parliament in Sofia to protest about environmental pollution, but the demonstration became anti-regime. There were further protests in subsequent weeks, several being organised by Eco-glasnost.

The mounting protests and Zhivkov's 'Turkish' policy convinced BKP's Politburo of the need for a 'palace coup'. (Gorbachev apparently gave his advance support to the change.) On 10 November, they achieved Zhivkov's 'resignation', as both Party leader and President. The Party was then purged of many of Zhivkov's closest supporters and other hard-liners. On the streets, however, the protests continued, with the demonstrators demanding nothing short of the end of Communist Party rule.

The new Communist leadership now organised a 'refolution' from above. They halted the persecution of the ethnic Turks, inviting those who had fled to return. On 10 December they permitted the legalisation of opposition parties. The Party then abolished its 'leading role'. Finally, in January 1990, Zhivkov was arrested for inciting ethnic hostilities and misusing government funds.

In December, Eco-glasnost and ten other opposition groups formed the Union of Democratic Forces (SDS). In mid-January

1990 the BKP and the SDS began round-table talks, where the opposition won some concessions, but had clearly lost the initiative to a reforming government. The SDS refused to join in a coalition with the ex-communists in February 1990.

The BKP, meanwhile, changed its name to the Bulgarian Socialist Party (BSP), adopted the market economy and pluralistic democracy, and voted in Petar Mladenov as interim President. The SDS opposition was badly prepared for the June elections, which the BSP won. The Bulgarian electorate had wanted change, but could not yet fully trust opposition parties. In any case, the ex-communists were carrying out real reforms.

However, the victorious BSP was soon faced with continuing economic collapse and increasing demonstrations by an independent trade union movement. Moreover, on 6 July 1990, Mladenov was forced to resign as President, after a videotape showed him ordering army tanks against peaceful demonstrators in December 1989. In August 1990 Zyelu Zhelev of the SDS became interim President.

After the elections, the SDS again refused all offers of a BSP/SDS coalition and waited until October 1991 before forcing new elections on the minority BSP government. The SDS gained a narrow election victory and formed Bulgaria's first post-war non-communist government, relying on the parliamentary support of the Turkish Party (DPS). Finally, Zhelev became President in direct elections in January 1992 and the revolution was complete.

Violent overthrow in Romania

The regime in Romania was more repressive and its leadership more personalised than elsewhere in ECE. Nicolae Ceausescu had a monopoly on power within a dynastic version of socialism, with both the Communist Party and the secret police (*Securitate*) being subordinate to himself and his wife (number two in the Party).

After coming to power in 1965, Ceausescu pursued an independent foreign policy (e.g. not permitting Warsaw Pact manoeuvres within Romania, not following the Soviet line on the

Middle East and China). This gained him respect in the West, despite his draconian domestic policies.

After 1985, Ceausescu refused to initiate any Gorbachev-type reforms, despite Romania's deteriorating economy. In fact, he criticised Gorbachev publicly on several occasions for abandoning the principles of Marxism-Leninism.

Under his regime, the mildest form of criticism was stamped out by the *Securitate,* so there was no organised dissident opposition. Similarly, there were virtually no reformists in the Party. When six prominent Communists (including two former General Secretaries) criticised Ceausescu for his monopoly of power in a letter to the BBC as late as March 1989, they were immediately placed under house arrest and their relatives and friends harassed.

In Ceausescu's Romania there were food shortages, bread and petrol rationing, unheated homes and appalling pollution. Yet the historical centre of Bucharest was bulldozed in order to build a new marble palace for the Stalinist dictator. He also initiated the proposed destruction of about 7,000 (mainly ethnic Hungarian) villages in a massive drive for modernisation and progress.

When *Securitate* forces attempted to arrest a Hungarian Protestant church minister, Father Laszlo Tokes, in Timisoara on 15 December 1989, hundreds of his parishioners blocked their path. Later some 10,000 people protested against the Ceausescu regime and *Securitate* forces opened fire on the unarmed demonstrators, reputedly killing hundreds. There was a riot in Timisoara, while demonstrations also broke out in Bucharest and elsewhere.

On 21 December, Ceausescu was heckled and booed during a televised speech. He declared martial law, but the army refused to enforce it and many army units mobilised against the *Securitate.* Ceausescu and his wife fled Bucharest by helicopter, but were captured and tried by a military court on Christmas Day. They were both condemned to death and executed by firing squad. The next day, their corpses were shown on national television.

A provisional government was formed by a group of leading ex-communists, calling itself the National Salvation Front (FSN).

Ion Iliescu was named interim President. The FSN promised democratisation and called free elections for 1990. There were rumours that the FSN had been secretly formed months before and had provoked the protests and violence in order to seize power.

The FSN included only a very few dissidents, and consisted mainly of former Communists who now blamed Ceausescu for the country's economic backwardness and political problems. Most Communist officials and *Securitate* members remained in their posts.

During and after the 1990 elections, students protested at the way former Communists had 'stolen' the revolution and demanded their resignation. They were denounced as 'fascists' by Iliescu, and many were beaten up by miners who were bussed to Bucharest by the government in mid-June to restore order through terror. Iliescu publicly thanked the miners for the role they had played.

Although the FSN would probably have won the elections of May 1990, it took the usual precaution of rigging the result. While claiming the communist regime was over, the FSN was in effect the vehicle whereby the old Communist elite held on to power.

Nationalist fragmentation in Yugoslavia

Since 1948, Yugoslavia had pursued its own path of socialism, independent of the Soviet Union. The country was more open than other ECE countries and, in some regions, had developed a thriving tourist industry geared to the West.

It was a federal and multinational state consisting of: Serbs, Montenegrins, Slovenes, Albanians, Bosnian Moslems, Macedonians, Croats and Hungarians. This diverse country had been held intact primarily by Josip Tito, ruler since 1945, the Communist Party (SKJ) and the army.

With Tito's death in 1980, both the Federation and the economy began to collapse. The federal Presidency was replaced by a collective leadership which rotated among five republics and three autonomous regions of Serbia (each representing a different nationality). This caused the federal government to be dominated by ethnic tensions and resulted in weak leadership.

Governmental immobilism ended with the rise to power of Slobodan Milosevic after May 1987, when he manipulated renewed tensions between Albanians and Serbs in Kosovo to become the leader of the Serbs. He fashioned the newly named Socialist Party of Serbia (SPS) into a vehicle of populist nationalism and became the instant champion of all Yugoslavian Serbs by advocating a 'Greater Serbia' (25 per cent of all Serbs lived outside Serbia's borders). He thus also pre-empted the challenge of any nationalist opposition to the SPS inside Serbia.

In the late 1980s, Croatia and Slovenia (later followed by Bosnia and Macedonia) reacted against Milosevic's blatant nationalism, by insisting on greater autonomy for all Yugoslav republics within a loose confederation. But the Serbs refused to accept any changes without the creation an enlarged Serbia.

The worldwide recession and growing economic crisis in Yugoslavia only exacerbated the differences between the richer Slovenia and Croatia and the other republics. In January 1989, federal Premier Ante Markovic spoke of the failure of socialist planning and announced major new free-market initiatives.

In January 1990, the SKJ relinquished its 'leading role' and adopted the market economy. But the process of disintegration was proceeding faster than the Party's capacity to change. In the 1990 multi-party elections in four republics, the Communists were defeated by nationalist oppositions.

In Slovenia a coalition of seven opposition parties (DEMOS) won the election with 55 per cent of votes. The former Communist leader, now nationalist, Milan Kucan was then elected President. In Croatia, the nationalist Democratic Community (HDZ) emerged as the winner and Franjo Tudjman, the former Titoist general, was appointed President by parliament. On 23 December 1990, Slovenia's electorate voted overwhelmingly for full independence in a referendum. It was the death knell for Tito's Yugoslavia.

In June 1991, after a pretence at negotiations, Slovenia and Croatia declared independence. The Yugoslav Federal Army engaged in a brief civil war with Slovenia to maintain the Federation, but was defeated. In any case, Slovenia had no major Serbian minority and so did not arouse Serbian national passions. When Croatia and Bosnia (with their large Serb minorities) declared independence, however, the Yugoslav army (predominantly Serb) and local Serb militias responded with much greater violence. The region then drifted into a major civil war of horrific proportions, first in Croatia and then Bosnia, involving widespread destruction of towns and villages, cold-blooded massacres of civilians, concentration camps and 'ethnic cleansing'.

The multi-racial Yugoslav state was unable to resist the resurgence of nationalism at the end of the 1980s. The 'revolution' when it came was the reassertion of national identity and the disintegration of the federal state (see Chapter 7), not necessarily a transition to democracy.

End of isolationism in Albania

Albania did not experience the revolutionary fervour of 1989, although it went through very dramatic changes in 1991–92. Albania had left COMECON in 1961 and had remained a most rigid and Stalinist regime, in self-imposed isolation under the very personalised leadership of Enver Hoxha. Economically it was the most underdeveloped country in Europe (even though it had significant reserves of exportable chromium, nickel and hydroelectric power).

Before he died in April 1985, Hoxha installed his protégé Ramiz Alia as President, under whom the Albanian Communists totally refuted Gorbachev's reforms throughout the late 1980s. In January 1990, Alia criticised the other 'revisionist' ECE regimes for compromising the socialist state. Yet, the government moved to restore diplomatic relations with many West European countries.

When Albanians realised that Hoxha's dictatorial state was vulnerable, then it was doomed. The first demonstrations took place in the north of the country in late 1989 and over the next six months spread to Tirana, where many young people sought refuge in foreign embassies. In June–July 1990 Alia allowed them to emigrate, hoping to dispose of the main troublemakers.

Like the Bulgarians, Alia now endeavoured to pre-empt the rise of the opposition by introducing reforms himself, although the opposition of Hoxha's powerful widow and other hard-line members of the Politburo constrained his freedom to manoeuvre.

During 1990, Alia began his 'refolution' from above in earnest, ending the ban on religion, introducing real land reform, encouraging private ownership, permitting citizens to travel abroad, and so on. This forestalled many demands made by the opposition and prevented the latter from making any real impact. However, the reforms 'from above' released greater demands 'from below'. There was an exodus of several thousand people in the summer – mainly to Greece – and increasing student unrest. Opposition groups now challenged the regime to introduce full-scale political pluralism. By the end of 1990 the Communists had agreed to the legalisation of political parties and the holding of free elections in 1991.

In February 1991, at a huge demonstration in Tirana, protesters symbolically toppled Hoxha's statue in the capital's central square. This act, however, caused reprisals by Communists and members of the opposition were threatened or beaten. The crisis led to another mass exodus – this time by sea to Italy – and the country appeared to be approaching civil war.

On 31 March 1991 the first multi-party elections in Albania since 1923 took place, with the Communists gaining a two-thirds majority, thanks mainly to their success in the countryside and small villages and towns. The opposition Democratic Party (PD) performed well in the larger towns and particularly in the capital: even Alia himself was defeated in his Tirana constituency.

The mass exodus to Italy continued, while a general strike and more demonstrations in May compelled the Communists to form a coalition with the PD. This coalition survived various crises and disagreements over proposed legislation – mostly over fundamental economic reforms and the regime's continued control of the media – until December 1991 when the PD pulled out and demanded new elections. (By this time, Alia had already said that he would resign as President because of bad health.)

The new parliamentary elections in March 1992 were won by the opposition PD, which this time campaigned strongly in the countryside, where it won a great deal of support. Alia resigned as President, the Democrats constituted a non-communist government and the PD's leader, Sali Berisha, was elected President: all within two months.

Why the revolutions occurred in 1989

There was not one single reason which brought about the revolutions in 1989, but rather numerous causes which all interacted to make change both immediate and unavoidable. As one communist system after the next simply collapsed, these causes became increasingly interconnected.

The Gorbachev effect

Events in Poland in 1989 might have triggered the revolutionary wave throughout the region, but far more important was Moscow's acquiescence in, if not active encouragement of, this cataclysmic change. As soon as the Soviet leadership under President Mikhail Gorbachev had demonstrated that the Soviet Union would not longer use brute force to protect socialism, then revolution everywhere in ECE was just a matter of time. His reforms – including a reassessment of the post-war spheres-of-influence policy – were a crucial catalyst to the events that led to the collapse of communism within the region.

Renunciation the Brezhnev doctrine. It would seem that Gorbachev had already decided to reject the Brezhnev doctrine when he came to power. He and his Foreign Minister Edward Shevardnadze certainly abandoned all intervention in the affairs of any ECE country from the spring of 1985. The nearest to a formal rejection of the Brezhnev doctrine came on 7 July 1989, when Gorbachev addressed the Parliamentary Assembly of the Council of Europe in Strasbourg, saying that 'any attempts to limit the sovereignty of states ... are not admissible'. At the Warsaw Pact summit meeting in Bucharest one day later, Gorbachev proposed transforming the alliance into a mainly political organisation. At the end of the summit Gyula Horn, then Hungary's Foreign Minister, said: 'the period of enforcing the so-called Brezhnev Doctrine is over once and for all'. In mid-October 1989, G. Gerasimov was to suggest that the Brezhnev doctrine had now been replaced by the 'Sinatra doctrine', by which each ECE nation could now follow its own path towards a multi-party system and a free-market economy.

Encouraging change elsewhere. Not only was a different approach now permitted within ECE, but it was actively encouraged. Consistently, Gorbachev pushed for greater changes and in the late 1980s went out of his way to aid the reform Communists against the Stalinist hard-liners. For example, Gorbachev told Jaruzelski that there was no Soviet objection to the legalisation of Solidarity; reformers in Hungary were backed and a multi-party system encouraged; the Soviet leader openly criticised Honecker's refusal to consider changes; hard-line leaders from Czechoslovakia and Bulgaria were not supported when they appealed for help from the Soviet Union, and so on.

Leadership by example. The new Soviet leadership after 1985 also provided the example to be followed in attempting wide-ranging reforms of both the economy and political system within the USSR itself. Gorbachev's reforms have usually been referred to by their Russian names: *perestroika* (i.e. restructuring the economy); *glasnost* (i.e. opening up of the political system – more open discussion, freedom of the press, etc.); *democratcie* (i.e. introduction of democratic procedures and practices throughout society, e.g. multi-candidate elections, legalisation of independent pressure groups, etc.). There was also a new thinking in terms of Soviet foreign policy (in particular, the abandonment of the arms race and a new approach to ECE).

It was natural that a loosening of control at the centre would lead to a desire for greater economic and political freedoms at the periphery. Indeed, leading dissidents like Adam Michnik saw the prospects of Polish freedom depending directly on the success of Gorbachev's reforms in the USSR. Within ECE these reforms were heartily endorsed in Poland, Hungary and parts of Yugoslavia, and were superficially acknowledged in Bulgaria. Otherwise the more hard-line regimes of Albania, Czechoslovakia, Romania and the GDR rejected them out of hand as being 'unnecessary' for their own regimes.

However, the effect of these reforms on ECE should not be overestimated, since they were almost identical to those advocated during the 1956 Hungarian revolution and the 1968 Prague Spring. Of greatest importance, perhaps, was the concept of *glastnost*, which led to more open reporting of worldwide events throughout the Soviet bloc.

Generational change

'It took a generation which did not know that it could not be done,' is how Ralf Dahrendorf described the revolutions of 1989. In other words, older generations had been discouraged by the failures of 1953, 1956 and 1968, and were reluctant to experiment once again. 'The young had a go because they did not realise that it was impossible to dislodge regimes, and so they dislodged them,' concludes Dahrendorf.

Political illegitimacy

By the end of the 1980s, it was clear that very few people still believed in the utopian socialist model. The illegitimacy of the regime was especially apparent to younger people who had benefited from greater access to travel and from various cultural exchanges with Western Europe during the 1980s.

In reality, communism never gained the acceptance of more than a very small minority who held power. Moreover, within ECE it was an 'alien' regime imposed and protected from outside and maintained by a bureaucratic Party elite, whose only legitimacy had become 'power for power's sake', and who were backed by the Soviet military.

Economic bankruptcy

The centrally planned systems simply could not compete in the world market. They had an in-built bias for heavy industry, ridiculously outdated industrial structures, a total lack of private initiative, no capacity to modernise and an overriding aim of just meeting planners' targets, not satisfying consumers.

By the 1980s COMECON was stagnating under the dead weight of the Soviet economy, as the attempt to 'keep up with the West' militarily was draining the resources of the whole Soviet bloc. The economies of ECE, in particular, were annually falling behind their Western counterparts, especially in computer technology, for example. The dependence on Western loans from the mid-1970s just exacerbated the deteriorating situation.

Once the twin evils of economic bankruptcy and political stagnation occurred simultaneously, leading intellectuals of both the Party and the opposition movements realised that partially reforming the system would not solve its major problems: full-scale economic and political change was needed.

Influence / pressure from the West

In the approach to the events of 1989, the West played a key role and operated as a catalyst in the revolutionary process, directly within the field of human rights and the Helsinki process, and indirectly via globalisation of political and economic relations.

The Helsinki Accords. Western pressure exerted on the communist regimes by both governmental and non-governmental agencies with regard to their fulfilling international treaties within the field of human rights was of crucial importance during the 1980s – although its real power lay in its linkage with Western assistance. In the process leading up to the signing of the Helsinki Final Treaty in 1975, the West had insisted on the maintenance of some standards of human rights within ECE. Thereafter, it was specifically the monitoring of the adherence of the communist regimes to these documents by both internal (e.g. Charter 77 in Czechoslovakia) and external groups that helped to undermine the legitimacy of those regimes.

Star Wars. President Ronald Reagan, by speeding up the space race, exposed the backwardness of the Soviet space programme. With the advent of 'Star Wars' (an expensive programme proposing to use satellite technology to destroy inter-continental ballistic missiles in flight), the USSR finally gave up competing with the West, because of spiralling military costs. (Note that the USA has not been able to afford the Star Wars programme either.)

Western assistance. The growing Soviet need for Western assistance also played a significant role in undermining the political legitimacy of the Communist regimes. The Soviet bloc could no longer exist in isolation beyond the bounds of the global market and became dependent on Western assistance, especially within the field of high technology. Once the West linked economic assistance with the Soviets fulfilling their Helsinki pledges on human rights (e.g. the Reagan embargo on technological equipment), change was in sight.

Global communications

One of the big differences with previous rebellions against Soviet rule during the 1950s and 1960s was the preponderance of global radio and television networks. In 1989 news of the revolution in each individual country could not be suppressed as in the past, and news of revolutionary events somewhere in ECE was an everyday occurrence throughout the region in the latter half of 1989. The various ECE governments had also ceased jamming Radio Free Europe and the BBC World Service. Consequently, people throughout ECE knew what was going on in their own and neighbouring countries.

This relatively free flow of information was crucial for the 'domino effect' whereby revolutionary fervour became 'irresistible'. When Poland was seen to create an anti-communist government with apparent Soviet acquiescence, it was only a matter of time before other countries would follow suit. When even East Germans could demonstrate freely every Monday night in Leipzig without being shot at, then it was inevitable that anti-communist demonstrations would take place elsewhere.

Conclusion

The impact of the West on the degree and speed of the changes in ECE was just as important, in the long term, as the more immediate process of liberalisation under Gorbachev after 1985.

Even though the 'revolutions' were generally unpredicted and occurred with unbelievable speed, there had been an overall inevitability about the collapse of the communist system throughout the Soviet bloc. By the end of the 1980s the twin evils of economic bankruptcy and political illegitimacy united to undermine the regimes. Both Communist and opposition intellectuals realised that the outdated economic and political system had to be scrapped.

The question then came of what other system to adopt. After forty years of centralised communism, it was always going to be most difficult to reintroduce political pluralism and economic free-market forces. In a sense the 'revolutions' were the easy part: democratisation and privatisation of market relations would be more difficult to achieve, or so it seemed in 1990.

Further reading

Hannah Arendt, *On Revolution*, Penguin Books, 1990.

Crane Brinton, *Anatomy of Revolution*, Prentice-Hall, 1952.

Ralf Dahrendorf, *Reflections on the Revolution in Europe*, Chatto and Windus, 1990.

Roger East, *Revolutions in Eastern Europe*, Printer Publishers, 1992.

François Furet, *L'énigme de la désagrégation commmuniste*, Fondation Saint-Simon, 1990.

Timothy Garton Ash, *The Magic Lantern: The Revolution of '89 Witnessed in Warsaw, Budapest and Prague*, Random House, 1990.

Timothy Garton Ash, *We The People*, Granta Books, 1990.

Misha Glenny, *The Rebirth of History: Eastern Europe in the Age of Democracy*, Penguin Books, 1990.

Jakub Karpinski, 'Velvet Evolution', *Transition*, 2 (6), 22 March 1996.

David S. Mason, *Revolution in East-Central Europe*, Westview Press, 1992.

John Simpson, *Despatches from the Barricades*, Hutchinson, 1990.

4
Transition to democracy in theory

Democracy is by far the worst form of government ... except for all the others. (Winston Churchill)

East Central Europe must construct in very short order what the West took a long time to build. This is an unprecedented experiment, and it is *not* being conducted in laboratory-like isolation (where there is leisure to observe, and to perfect theories about democracy). (Jacques Rupnik)

Definitional problems

In recent decades democracy has re-established itself in much of Central and South America, southern Europe, ECE, parts of what was the USSR, South Africa and various parts of Asia. Nowadays most states in the world would like to think of themselves as being 'democratic'.

Before examining the process of transition in theory and in practice, it is worth contemplating what ECE and other countries are making a transition towards. Generally speaking the term 'democracy' has become somewhat meaningless because of the wide range of systems to which it has been applied. Before 1989, all ECE Communist states, for example, also styled themselves 'People's Democracies', although they were far from being 'democratic' according to normal criteria.

The textbook definition of democracy stems from two Greek words, *demos* and *kratia*, and means 'government by the people', or, to use Abraham Lincoln's more intricate phrase, 'government *of* the people, *for* the people and *by* the people'. But this is extremely vague in its conceptualisation, since 'government by the people' is clearly impossible in a large industrial state.

Over time, therefore, 'democracy' came to imply 'government by the majority' via a representative assembly. But, there is still the danger of the 'tyranny of the majority', as Aristotle called it, where the rights and opinions of the minority are ignored or oppressed. Thus, protection of minority rights and opinions is the main test of any state claiming to be 'democratic'.

In modern, industrialised states democracy became related to a particular set of institutions and practices (e.g. constitutions, parliaments, executives with restricted powers, independent judiciaries). The distinctive aspects of a democratic system are its emphasis on competition, representation of different interests, recognition of rules and equal application of the law. This makes democracy a most intricate form of government, which assumes a different pattern in diverse states.

All this seems to imply that there is no absolute definition of democracy, that 'democracy' is rather a matter of degree whereby countries are 'more' or 'less' democratic. In this sense, all countries have some elements of democracy, be they capitalist or socialist, Christian or Arab, East or West.

If there is no absolute definition of democracy, at least an overriding *aim* of democracy can be identified: the ability of people to affect the decisions that shape their everyday lives. This is true of decisions made within the home, at the workplace, in the school or university, in the town council, at the national or federal levels of government, or, finally, within intergovernmental organisations like the EU. It is within this broader context that we will use the term 'democracy' throughout this volume.

Characteristics of a democratic state

An ideal democratic government would be one whose actions *always* reflected the attitudes and wishes of *all* of its citizens *all* of the time. Such complete responsiveness of government is clearly impossible, but it serves as an ideal which democratic nations should at least attempt to approximate. Therefore, we might say that a democratic regime is characterised by a *high degree* of responsiveness to the wishes of a *substantial number* of its citizens *most* of the time.

The following are the main characteristics of such a democratic regime (note that the mere existence of these features does not guarantee democracy, as it still depends on how they are practised by both citizens and governments):

1   free, fair, competitive elections at regular intervals;
2   various personal freedoms and basic human rights that are considered inviolable – the freedoms of speech, association and assembly; freedom of the press; freedoms of thought and religion;
3   the general adherence to the 'rule of law' – implying that the laws of the land apply equally to everyone, are understood and appreciated by everyone and are seen to be basically just;
4   some form of separation of powers in order to provide for certain checks on the behaviour of the executive in particular;
5   the independence of the judiciary;
6   some form of distribution of powers between the centre and the periphery, that is, between central and local or regional government, to guard against an over-centralised state;
7   equal access for all to most information and the absence of unjustifiable secrecy;
8   feedback – the idea that there is a relation between the rulers and the ruled which is a two-way process and benefits both sides simultaneously, allowing the 'people' to express their wishes and respond to the actions of governments outside of electoral periods.

Application of these characteristics to ECE

As far as these characteristics are concerned within ECE since 1989:

1   free, fair, competitive elections at regular intervals have taken place throughout the region, although some governments have manipulated elections on occasions, for example in Romania and Albania;

2   by now most countries have accepted or are working on a new, post-communist constitution, which contains most of the personal freedoms listed, and some countries have even passed a separate Bill of Rights, such as Hungary and Czechoslovakia in 1990;

3   adherence to the rule of law is impossible to measure, but it would seem that many parliamentarians and government ministers have problems in accepting legal judgements that go against their own views, therefore the rule of law exists on paper, not in practice, because the courts cannot enforce it;

4   separation of powers is another area which remains somewhat vague constitutionally speaking, since many of the governments have created constitutional laws that leave too much unchecked power within their own hands;

5   likewise, there are still some states which regard the judiciary as an extension of the executive;

6   most states remain extremely centralised and those efforts to introduce true federalism failed, for example in former Czechoslovakia, 1989–93, and the former Yugoslavia, 1990–92;

7   none of the democratising states has passed anything that vaguely resembles a Freedom of Information Act;

8   there is very little feedback between the rulers and the ruled – it is certainly not a two-way process, political parties do not yet act as mediators and pressure groups are not yet fully functional.

Procedural and substantive notions of democracy

There is a tendency in the Western industrialised world, where 'representative democracy' predominates, to perceive democracy simply in terms of free elections. So, as soon as free, competitive elections had taken place in the former ECE communist regimes, then 'democracy' was presumed to have been established. In this case all the emphasis is placed upon the procedures established and less attention is paid to the actual quality or substance of the 'democracy' introduced. It is crucial, then, to distinguish between the procedural and the substantive notions of democracy.

The German Weimar Republic (1918–33) represents a very good example of this point. The procedures established under the 1919 constitution – president with limited powers, bicameral parliament, federalism, constitutional government, rule of law, proportional representation, and so on – appeared to satisfy all the basic criteria of a democratic regime. In hindsight, however, the Weimar regime has been described as a republic without republicans and a democracy without democrats, in that many of the key political actors in German society – major landowners, judges, civil servants, military personnel or top business people – wanted to return to the semi-authoritarian rule of the Prussian monarchy and *Rechtsstaat*, rather than to experiment with democracy. Since there was so little support for the Republic in elite positions and since a general passivity prevailed among the German people, it is not surprising that the regime was ended with comparative ease by Hitler in 1933.

The crucial question for the inhabitants of the newly democratising post-communist states is whether the existing social structures are adequate and deeply enough entrenched to support democracy after the authoritarian, paternalistic and totalitarian regimes of the past.

Comparative transitions to democracy

The consolidation of democracy is an ongoing, evolutionary process throughout the world and is hardly ever static, even in well established pluralist democracies like the UK or USA, Switzerland or Holland. Over time most states are usually evolving towards a better or more perfect democracy, even if the process is interrupted for a long period.

Historically speaking, the establishment of democracy has occurred gradually within the rich, capitalist nation states of Western Europe and North America, where the industrial and agricultural revolutions were concomitant with the revival of democracy and the emergence of the nation state. This process led eventually to both full, adult suffrage (procedural democracy) and the emergence of a democratic, political culture (substantive democracy), characterised by tolerance and the ability to compromise. The UK can be seen as the classic example of this evolutionary process – beginning in 1215 with the Magna Carta, right up to 1993, when the ruling monarch became subject to taxation.

Conventional wisdom also postulates that the transition to democracy proves much more difficult within those countries where there are rapid changes in regime and the apparent lack of a democratic political culture. In such countries there is a real danger of backsliding in the transition to democracy, as occurred in France, Germany and Italy during the nineteenth and twentieth centuries. Owing to its history and political traditions, all of ECE would also be placed within this group.

Certain theories of long-term transition

Barrington Moore in his *Social Origins of Dictatorship and Democracy: Lord and Peasant in the Making of the Modern World* tries to demonstrate why some states became democracies and others not. His emphasis is on the historical transformation of agrarian societies into modern industrial societies – otherwise known as the process of 'modernisation'. Democracy emerges where a strong, independent bourgeoisie opposes the *ancien régime* and where the influence of the peasantry is almost non-existent because it has been transformed by the lords and others through the commercialisation of agriculture, as occurred in the UK. This model could not be further removed from the experience of ECE, where feudal-type relations continued right up to the twentieth century in some cases.

Goran Therborn also claims the transition to democracy is linked to the process of 'modernisation' brought about by the industrial revolution, that is, capitalism becomes well entrenched first and then democracy comes into existence. Therborn's theory is restricted to Western industrialised nations and is of little help for the peasant-based economies of ECE.

The process of transition within ECE does not fit well with the accepted theories of the historical transition to democracy. The rapidity of the changes, in months and years, hardly corresponds with theories of evolution to democracy over centuries.

Rustow's model of transition to democracy

In 1970 Dankwart Rustow produced a comprehensive model of the origins of democracy, which could be used in any country at any stage of economic development: in short, with any particular type of political regime.

Rustow saw democracy as evolving through four very important stages – each of which will then be applied to ECE post-1989.

(1) *National backdrop*. This means there must be a very well defined territorial community within which the transition takes place. It does not matter when national unity is achieved – it could be decades or days before the transition begins; nor is it important how such unity is achieved, for instance through war, defeat, natural geographical factors and so on.

In ECE, the transition to democracy cannot always occur against the backdrop of a clearly defined national territory and the resurgence of previously dormant nationalism has had to be resolved before the transition to democracy and the transformation of the economies could be attempted in earnest.

For example, the transition to democracy within the Czech and Slovak Federal Republic was seriously delayed while the new political elites attempted to resolve the (Slovak) nationalist question, leading to partial immobilism in the federal parliament on constitutional matters of state. Likewise, there could be little emphasis on a transition to democracy in former Yugoslavia until the nationalist question was resolved once and for all, by dissolution.

(2) *Preparatory stage: prolonged and inconclusive conflict.* Within this clearly identifiable community, a crucial division between well entrenched forces among the people needs to be resolved – a religious, regional, ethnic or ideological conflict that threatens the cohesiveness of the state.

All the post-communist societies were born from a struggle to dispose of the former regime. Within Albania, Czechoslovakia, Hungary, Poland, Romania and Bulgaria, the revolutions of 1989 were the ultimate protests against Soviet-type post-totalitarianism.

(3) *Decision-making stage.* To resolve this conflict a conscious decision is made to opt for democracy: in other words, people seek a peaceful resolution to the conflict and rely upon compromise between the opposing factions to solve the dispute in hand. This might be one major decision made by various protagonists at one particular moment, or it might be a whole series of decisions spread across years.

'Democracy' was obviously a driving force behind the ECE revolutions of 1989, as far as the emerging political elites were concerned. For the people, however, it was often just another slogan and was understood very much within economic terms (i.e. access to Western goods and Western standards of living).

In terms of the actual decision made, it could be disputed that a decision was rationally made to 'opt' for 'democracy' on the part of most East Central Europeans. At the time people knew what they did not want politically speaking – communism – but they had little idea of the procedures and institutions needed to replace the former regime.

(4) *Habituation stage.* Democracy cannot be said to exist, or rather to have been consolidated, until peaceful resolution of conflicts by compromise has become a way of life for the citizenry. This implies that in any sort of dispute there is automatic recourse to democratic procedures. Thereafter, even the most divisive conflicts will be addressed in a democratic fashion.

This applies to equality between the sexes, democracy at the workplace, decentralised or regional decision making, a lack of social racism, as well as the institutionalisation of democratic governmental and parliamentary institutions.

In terms of historical and contemporary examples, this theory can hope to explain why some established democracies do not succeed (e.g. the aforementioned Weimar Republic), as they never complete the 'habituation stage'. The question for the new ECE democracies, therefore, is whether democracy will become a habit among ministers, parliamentarians, bureaucrats, and others, or whether the decision-making process will continue to be characterised by the authoritarian attitudes and behaviour that are residues of previous, undemocratic regimes. At the moment any answer to this question is pure conjecture.

More general theories of transition related to ECE

Seven distinct periods of transition in the twentieth century

During the course of this century, there have been seven major, distinct transitions towards democracy:

1   in ECE after the First World War;
2   in post-war Western Europe in both the occupied countries (e.g. France and Belgium) and the defeated countries (i.e. West Germany and Italy – and similarly Japan, outside Western Europe);
3   throughout South and Central America, since 1945, but particularly since the 1970s;
4   in Greece, Spain and Portugal since the mid-1970s;
5   within the post-colonial regimes throughout the Asian and African continents since the late 1950s, with the addition of South Africa in 1990;
6   in ECE and the various republics of the former Soviet Union since 1989;
7   in Palestine and elsewhere in the Middle East, only just beginning in the mid-1990s.

Huntingdon's various waves of democracy

In his book *The Third Wave*, Samuel P. Huntingdon identifies three great waves of democratisation, two followed by reversals:

1   The first wave began in the 1820s in the Americas (1848 in ECE) and lasted up to the First World War in Europe – a process reversed in the inter-war period, when ECE, in particular, was characterised by non-democratic, authoritarian dictatorships.

2   The second (post-war) wave affected the defeated Axis powers first, then the Third World colonies as they gained independence. The reversals occurred from the 1960s onwards among the newly independent colonies – meanwhile, ECE had succumbed to Soviet post-totalitarianism.

3   The third wave began with the Portuguese revolution and the end of the Franco regime in the mid-1970s, continued in Latin America, spread to Asia and finally touched even ECE. The short time so far elapsed means it is too early to identify any reversals.

Huntingdon draws two conclusions about the countries involved in these various 'waves':

1   there is always disenchantment after the euphoria of the establishment of democracy and often a noticeable frustration at the slowness of change – this is when reversals can begin – and in ECE this has certainly been the case;

2   the consolidation of democracy becomes real only after the 'two-turnover test', that is, when a country experiences two changes of government peacefully, as a result of fair elections – by the end of 1995, only three ECE countries had managed the 'two-turnover test', Bulgaria, Hungary and Poland.

O'Donnell's three possible outcomes

In their mammoth comparative study of regimes undergoing more recent transitions from authoritarian rule to 'something else' in southern Europe and Latin America, G. O'Donnell, P. Schmitter and L. Whitehead propose three possible outcomes:

1   a consolidation of democracy;
2   a slip back into a (substantively) more authoritarian but (procedurally) still democratic regime;
3   recourse to yet another military or authoritarian dictatorship (in ECE's case a return to a one-party Communist regime).

In ECE the first outcome will occur only if the region's governments can substantially improve the living standards of the vast majority of their citizens, which is not at all certain in some countries like Romania or Bulgaria. The third outcome is quite unrealistic. The second outcome is the most likely and, in fact, some ECE countries are already moving in this direction, for example Slovakia under Premier Meciar and Albania under President Berisha.

Rothschild's three different patterns of transition

Looking particularly at ECE, Joseph Rothschild points to three distinct patterns of transition that occurred in 1989–90:

1   countries where the Communists were able to control the reform process and dictate the terms of the first elections, with no need for negotiations with the (perhaps weak or even non-existent) opposition, such as in Albania, Bulgaria and Romania;
2   countries where Communists experimented during the Soviet period with a gradual shift to more relaxed positions, such Communists invariably finding themselves obliged to bargain with the opposition, typically in 'round-table' talks (these cases usually featured 'reform communists' and relatively smooth and long processes of change, such as in Poland and Hungary);
3   countries in which a Communist dictatorship collapsed suddenly after the Soviet Union withdrew its support and

changes were beginning to happen elsewhere (in some of these cases, the opposition forces were able to dictate the terms of the transition and the former elite was simply forced to accept the new rules, such as in East Germany and Czechoslovakia).

The optimistic scenario

Giuseppe di Palma argues optimistically that democratic attitudes can develop quite quickly, even within a state with few democratic traditions. He points to the 'rapidity and eagerness' with which new political actors have learned the 'rules of the democratic game' within a relatively short time in more recent transitions. He predicts that a 'bandwagon effect' will emerge within ECE and the lack of viable alternatives will reinforce democratic consolidation, to the extent that 'the likelihood of anti-democratic backlashes has been exaggerated'. In his opinion, even extreme economic discontent will not suffice to turn people against the democratisation process.

The realistic scenario

Gordon Smith, however, warns against euphoria or complacency within the present transition by pointing to the experience of the Weimar Republic as 'the classic European case of a transition to liberal democracy which failed'. He emphasises that within the transition process 'no country will follow precisely the same course' and 'only one route of several may lead to the consolidation of a liberal-democratic regime'. In his opinion, 'there are several feasible outcomes', which include both total and partial reversal of the process of democratisation.

He further argues that, in terms of ECE, little can be gained by making comparisons with Latin America or southern Europe and elsewhere. According to Smith, it is extremely difficult to 'generalise about countries with vastly different historical experiences and problems' and ECE – along with the former Soviet Union – will always be a very particular case.

Jan Ake Dellenbrant also claims that the transition to be undergone in ECE is without precedent, so that 'models drawn from elsewhere are of little use'. He refers to Huntingdon and points out that the key question for ECE is 'whether this third wave [of democratisation] will be allowed to develop fully, or whether it will die out or be diverted into authoritarian channels as happened before'. Only time will tell.

The process of transition in ECE since 1989

It is important to place the transition being attempted within ECE since 1989 in its rightful context. It is a monumental event which will have far-reaching ramifications for the future development of the whole of Europe.

Just as ECE could not be seen as a monolithic bloc under communism, the post-communist transition is occurring at varying speeds and with different priorities in each of the ECE states.

Among the post-communist governing elites, there has been nothing short of a frantic pursuit of Western models – in order to achieve the most rapid transition possible and to catch up with the West.

As far as democracy was concerned, it was seen as the process by which the free market could be achieved, that is, the emphasis within the transition was on people getting rich and having access to the sorts of goods and services available in the West. There was little awareness of what 'democracy' meant in terms of individual responsibility, or accountability of elected governments.

A process of multiple transitions

In none of the seven periods of transitions mentioned before have the countries concerned faced such a multiplicity of transitions – economic, political, national, social and psychological – to be achieved at one and the same time. It is the simultaneity of multiple transitions that poses the greatest problems for ECE countries in their attempt to rejoin the liberal democratic and free-market organisations of Western Europe.

In reality, no one, from former Soviet President Mikhail Gorbachev to Harvard economist Jeffrey Sachs, knows how this process of multiple transitions can be completed successfully. Hence, the West is concentrating on the economic transformation – opening up the markets to Western firms and goods and allowing the countries concerned to join (eventually) Western global institutions like the EU and NATO.

The simultaneous 'double difficulty'

Ralf Dahrendorf originally identified the main impediment to democratisation within ECE since 1989 as 'the double conundrum of how to "marketize" collectivist economies and how to privatize communist parties', that is, as a double and simultaneous transition from post-totalitarianism to democracy and the transformation of the economy from central planning to the free market.

By way of comparison, the transition to democracy in southern Europe took place *after* economic growth had been secured by military regimes in the 1960s. In Latin America, the Far East and post-war Western Europe, the transition took place within well established market economies with strong traditions of private ownership and entrepreneurial attitudes.

The simultaneous triple transition

C. Offe extended Dahrendorf's idea to a simultaneous triple transition, as follows:

1   a transition to democracy, after a totalitarian, Communist dictatorship, which strove to control both the public and private spheres of everyone's life;

2   a transformation to a free market from an effectively bankrupt centrally planned economy, which had failed to keep up with economic development in the West;

3   the resolution of often deep-rooted nationalist problems – a
        reflection of the fact that the nation-building stage in this
        part of the world was never completed.

Some other countries did not even attempt to achieve the
multiple transition. For instance, among the Far Eastern 'tigers'
(Singapore, Malaysia, Taiwan, South Korea and Thailand) there
was a transition to democracy only at a very superficial level after
independence. Most of these countries developed into one-party,
authoritarian states, where democracy was initially put to one
side. Indeed, in some of these countries there was a specific
policy of reforming the economy first and looking to democracy
much later on (e.g. in Malaysia and Singapore).

The resurgence of an emotive and utopian brand of ethnic
nationalism (see Chapter 6) has obstructed the democratic transition and economic transformation of some ECE countries (e.g.
Slovak nationalism within Czechoslovakia during 1990–92 or
various nationalisms within the former Yugoslavia since 1990).

Again, by way of comparison, most of the countries involved
in the other transitions – in particular, in post-1945 Western
Europe, or southern Europe after the mid-1970s – possessed a
significant degree of national unity. Even the countries of South-
East Asia had clearly defined, imperial boundaries, while all Latin
American countries were well established nation states dating
from the beginning of the nineteenth century.

The psychological dimension

A psychological dimension to the problem has been suggested by
Peter Frank to account for the atomisation of society and the total
undermining of normal, horizontal social relations during the
communist era. He claims that none of the previous countries
undergoing a transition to democracy had to cope with such a
social deficit.

Dahrendorf, too, sees the monopoly of the Communist Party
over the state, the economy and society as one of the main
differences between the transition process in ECE and transitions

elsewhere. 'There was no such thing as society, or an economy, or indeed the state; there was only the Party pervading everything else.' This means, in his opinion, that a true democratic transition in ECE is going to be measured in terms of generations rather than years.

Of the other transitions, only West Germany, Italy and, to a limited extent, France had to overcome a 'totalitarian experience' after 1945 and in all three cases that experience was short lived and not so deeply ingrained socially speaking. Latin America and southern Europe made the transition from authoritarian (not totalitarian) military dictatorships, which did not attempt to take over people's private sphere of activity to the same degree.

The global dimension

If this quadruple transition were not difficult enough, it must take place within a global economy:

* without the countries concerned being given the chance to put their own house in order first before competing on the world market (compare West Germany, Japan and France in the 1950s);
* and without the necessary massive amounts of capital investment coming from the West (compare enormous USA aid to post-war construction in Western Europe via the Marshall Plan).

Previous transitions all took place when the individual nation state was the predominant economic and political actor, as in post-war Western Europe. In Latin American countries, consolidation to democracy has taken place within a more global economic environment because of their proximity to and dependence on the USA. Only in southern Europe was there a rapid adaptation to the constraints of the global market, with a rather swift entry into international organisations, especially the European Community and NATO. (Spain, Portugal and Greece gained enormously from the integration process as they became immediate recipients of substantial amounts of financial aid from the Community's structural funds.)

Economically speaking, the Far Eastern 'tigers' made a dramatic transformation from predominantly rural-based to successful export-oriented market economies within the confines of the world market. However, that spectacular process began with the basic capitalist infrastructure already installed by the previous imperial regimes. Similarly, all post-war states in Western Europe received substantial (Marshall) aid to kick-start war-ravaged economies and build up their own economic infrastructures before subjecting themselves to the rigours of the global market.

In terms of the post-1989 transitions, only the territory of the former GDR has received such massive outside aid: more than $500 billion in five years from the federal government of the reunited Germany. (In comparison, approximately $75 billion went to all ECE countries between 1989 and 1995 – including former East Germany – from international and European organisations in the form of loans, grants and gifts.)

Furthermore, there is a very interesting contrast between post-war Marshall aid and the post-revolutionary ECE aid programme (West German grants to the former GDR excepted): Marshall aid was 85 per cent outright grants and 15 per cent loans, whereas recent aid to ECE from international organisations has been 85 per cent loans and only 15 per cent outright grants.

The sextuple transition

Thus, the process of transition within ECE needs to be put into its proper context: the post-communist regimes are all undergoing a simultaneous sextuple transition:

1   *politically* from a one-party communist to a democratic pluralistic state;
2   *economically* from a centrally planned to a free-market economy;
3   *nationally* from a quasi-colonial state of occupation within the post-war Soviet empire to free nationhood;

4   *psychologically/socially* from a post-totalitarian or totalitarian, atomised society to a free society;

5   globally from a unit within COMECON isolated from world markets to part of the dynamic world economy;

6   *financially* from a state-owned system to capitalism – moreover, this transition is being imposed without capital, specifically without a Marshall-aid-type package to kick start the economies.

Conclusion

Each of these transitions would be difficult on its own. Accomplishing all six simultaneously must represent an almost impossible task. As a result, it can be argued that the transitions in ECE face greater difficulties than those that have taken place in Latin America, Western and southern Europe and the Far East.

This process of transition is also considerably more complicated than the transitions attempted in ECE (including Germany) after the First World War. Those transitions failed – with the exception of Czechoslovakia – and royal or military authoritarian dictatorships were the outcome.

Further reading

Jan Ake Dellenbrant, 'Parties and Party Systems in Eastern Europe', in *Developments in East European Politics* (Stephen White, Judy Batt and Paul Lewis, eds), Macmillan, 1993.

Ralf Dahrendorf, *Reflections on the Revolution in Europe*, Chatto and Windus, 1990.

Samuel Huntingdon, *The Third Wave: Democratisation in the Late 20th Century*, University of Oklahoma Press, 1991.

Samuel Huntingdon, 'Will More Countries Become Democratic?', *Political Science Quarterly*, 99, 1984.

Paul Lewis, 'Democratisation in Eastern Europe', *Coexistence*, 27, 1990.

Paul Lewis and Geoffrey Pridham (eds), *Stabilising Fragile Democracies*, Routledge, 1996 (compares ECE with southern Europe).

Barrington Moore, *Social Origins of Dictatorship and Democracy: Lord and Peasant in the Making of the Modern World*, Allen Lane, 1967.

Guillermo O'Donnell, Philippe C. Schmitter and L. Whitehead (eds), *Transitions from Authoritarian Rule: Tentative Conclusions About Uncertain Democracies*, Johns Hopkins University Press, 1986.

Claus Offe, 'Capitalism by Democratic Design? Democratic Theory Facing the Triple Transition in ECE', *Social Research*, 58, 1991.

Giuseppe di Palma, 'Why Democracy can Work in Eastern Europe', *Journal of Democracy*, 1 (1), winter 1991.

Geoffrey Pridham and Tatu Vanhanen (eds), *Democratisation in Eastern Europe*, London, Routledge, 1994.

Joseph Rothschild, *Return to Diversity*, Oxford University Press, 1993.

Dankwart Rustow, 'Transitions to Democracy: Towards a Dynamic Model', *Comparative Politics*, 2, 1970.

Philippe Schmitter, 'The Consolidation of Democracy and the Choice of Institutions', *East–South Systems Transformations Conference*, January 1992, Toledo, Spain.

Gordon Smith, 'Transitions to Liberal Democracy', in *The New Institutional Architecture of Eastern Europe* (Stephen Whitefield, ed.), St Martin's Press, 1993.

Goran Therborn, 'The Rule of Capital and the Rise of Democracy', *New Left Review*, 103, May–June 1978.

Stephen White, Judy Batt and Paul Lewis (eds), *Developments in East European Politics*, Macmillan, 1993.

5
Transition to democracy within ECE in practice

We have similarly overestimated the pace of post-communist transformation.... We tended to assume initially that a few rearrangements, largely of an economic nature initiating a free-market economy, would produce not only a stable free market but a functioning democracy. We now know that both are much more complex processes than we initially assumed. (Zbigniew Brzezinski)

The most dangerous time for a bad regime occurs when it tries to improve itself. (Alexis de Tocqueville)

There are several different types of problem facing the transition to democracy within ECE which would seem to point to a very slow 'habituation' of democratic practices and a possible revival of authoritarianism within the region. Foremost among these is a predominance of authoritarian attitudes and behaviour that is a residue from previous regimes, but which has all sorts of ramifications for minority rights, the role of women in society, the way parliaments operate, the relations between presidents and parliaments, and so on.

Furthermore, true to the 'messianic tradition' of the past, democracy was accepted as an 'easy solution' in 1989–90 and was understood primarily in economic terms – that is, it would automatically lead to Western levels of living standards. This is not a solid foundation on which to build a democratic transition, particularly when the future economic prospects for most of ECE are hardly encouraging so far.

Overcoming the legacies of the past

Throughout the region there is the continuation of certain attitudes and behaviour which are more reminiscent of the former totalitarian or post-totalitarian regime than of democracy. As with the failure of democracy in the pre-war German Weimar Republic and in many of the ECE inter-war regimes, such attitudes could undermine the whole process of democratisation.

Ken Jowitt claims that the 'old rule residue' or 'Leninist legacy' is an insurmountable problem facing ECE after 1989. Thus, non-democratic attitudes remain to bedevil the new regimes – for example the post-1990 campaigns of revenge against 'old structures' and collaborators with the secret police in some countries; the blatant disrespect for minorities, especially gypsies, throughout the region; particularly strong anti-Semitic statements made by many (even young) people; and outdated attitudes concerning the role of women in society.

Decommunisation or 'lustration'

The clearest case in the immediate post-revolutionary period has been the desire to settle scores with former Communist officials and secret police 'collaborators' through a process of screening or 'lustration'.

In the former East Germany and the Czech Republic, there has been nothing short of a full-scale purge of former officials and a 'witch-hunt' of previous collaborators. In Poland a similar purge failed for constitutional reasons and in Hungary the issue seriously divided the 1990–94 governments. The matter still divides the non-communist political elites in Bulgaria and Croatia. In Albania all former Communists have been forbidden to engage in politics until after 2005.

The issue never made it on to the agenda in Romania (although it caused some controversy when President Iliescu was incriminated as being a *Securitate* informer) and it was purposely taken off the political agenda in Slovakia after 1993. The governments formed by the communist successor parties in Poland, Hungary and Bulgaria have usually ignored or refused to implement anti-communist legislation passed by previous, non-communist governments, hoping that the issue will eventually disappear.

The arguments for 'lustration' were the following:

- Communist officials and ex-secret-police agents or collaborators could undermine the transition towards democracy;
- some previous collaborators could be exposed to blackmail;
- society needed to feel that a real break was being made with the past.

The counter-arguments ran thus:

- in many cases reform Communists had played a leading role in bringing about the revolution in the first place;
- many reform Communists were stalwart democrats, and many Communists had become some of the region's best capitalists, so they had no interest in undermining the system;
- it was almost immoral to rely on the doctored records of the former secret police – who had had time to shred the documents of the most important agents and top officials, leaving only the small-time collaborators to be punished;
- there were many different reasons for people collaborating or working within the Communist Party before 1989, and this type of blanket purge made no attempt at differentiation of motives;
- dissidents and members of the opposition were often not qualified enough to replace the former economic officials, high-level administrators and judges, and so lustration would lead to a great loss of expertise within the state apparatus;
- 'lustration' allowed a type of collective self-purification to take place – Vaclav Havel's insistence on collective guilt was soon forgotten as the vast majority of the population could point their fingers at former Party members, yet very often those who shouted the loudest against secret-police collaborators were themselves guilty of a different type of complicity with the former regime.

Generally speaking, the 'big fish' or former Party leaders, who were ultimately responsible for the policies of the previous Communist regimes, have not yet been prosecuted for crimes against humanity. In the countries where former leaders were prosecuted there were often strong political motives for such trials taking place. Bulgaria was the first country to prosecute its former Party leader, Zhivkov, but this was a device by the first ex-communist government to lay all the blame on one person, exonerating themselves in the process. Similarly, the former Communists in Romania's FSN prosecuted some of the members of the Ceausescu dynasty, but these were more or less token trials, since the sentences were either quashed or derisory. In Albania many leading Communists were imprisoned after due legal process, depriving the main socialist opposition of many of its leading figures – although several were later granted an amnesty by President Berisha.

Only in East Germany has due legal process been used to prosecute leading Communist Party officials systematically, including former leaders like Erich Honecker and Egon Krenz. Even so, most of the successful prosecutions so far have been of former GDR soldiers who killed people attempting to flee the communist regime. Otherwise former Communist leaders are still free to use their capital and connections – accumulated and established under the previous regime – to make the most of the new capitalist environment. It was only in November 1995 that Krenz and five other members of the former Politburo were brought to trial for the murder of some of the people who were killed while trying to escape into West Germany.

Old attitudes versus old structures

The real problem is one of 'old attitudes' (authoritarianism), not necessarily 'old structures' (i.e. former Communists). Many of the people replacing the Communists are just as much products of the old system, in that they are just as dogmatic, authoritarian and unskilled in compromise, whether within the ministries, the new parliaments, universities or schools.

This was very marked in many of the 'new' politicians who emerged throughout the region during the immediate post-revolutionary period. Such politicians tended to promote and accept ideas and policy for ideological rather than rational reasons. They took up positions of principle on most issues, which meant that debates were often an airing of entrenched ideas, and it was most difficult to reach any consensus.

Many former Communists, on the other hand, had criticised the socialist regime before 1989. Indeed, some were already laying the groundwork for fundamental political and economic changes and were ready to dispense with the whole socialist system. Such people were often becoming far less authoritarian in their attitudes and more open to new ideas from the West.

Respect of human rights and inherent racism

The respect of minority rights within ECE has been a problem throughout the history of the region. As in the past, there is very often a considerable discrepancy between practice and the consti-tutional guarantees of human rights in many ECE states. The 1992 Slovak constitution serves as a perfect example: it guaran-tees the (Hungarian) minority the right to use their own language in education, cultural events, business, and so on, yet Article 6 states that Slovak is the national language. It was Article 6 that was used as justification for removing bilingual road signs and for passing legislation enforcing the use of Slovak in all schools. In passing the new language law at the end of 1995, the Slovak government conveniently ignored the constitutional guarantees made in 1992, as well as some of the promises it made when joining the Council of Europe.

On the whole, the situation of the larger minorities – such as Hungarians in Slovakia (10.7 per cent of the population), Albanians in Macedonia (21 per cent), Turks in Bulgaria (9.7 per cent) and Hungarians in Transylvanian Romania (7.1 per cent) – is somewhat precarious, since they are usually seen as a threat to the integrity of the state by the majority ethnic group.

It is difficult to talk of respect of human rights when there is inherent, but usually passive, racism within most ECE societies. In a June 1995 survey conducted within the politically stable Czech Republic, 58.2 per cent of those questioned inclined to 'full racism and part intolerance', and 12.5 per cent towards extreme racism. In the same survey 25 per cent of Czechs saw racism as a serious problem.

Much of this racism is directed against gypsies – the smallest, but the most visible minority throughout ECE – for whom there is almost no tolerance at all, but Muslims who look like gypsies also suffer. In 1995 there were some quite horrific attacks made on gypsies: a father being beaten to death by young people with baseball bats in front of his family; a young gypsy being sprinkled with petrol and set on fire by a group of white youths. Gypsies have been subject to a curfew in Slovakia and gypsy areas have had to endure astronomical levels of unemployment (60–90 per cent in parts of Bulgaria and Romania).

Blatant sexism

Sexual attitudes in ECE did not undergo the social revolution of the 1960s and 1970s as in Western Europe. It was one of the greatest contradictions of the communist era that while far more women worked full time and there was much greater equality of the sexes at the workplace than in the West (e.g. earlier acceptance of women bus\train drivers, engineers, parliamentarians, for similar rates of pay) women continued to suffer sexual discrimination at the social level. Women were in the classic situation of always having to do 'two full-time jobs' while men were the traditional 'masters of their own castles'.

Very little has changed since. There is still tremendous social pressure from mothers (and especially grandmothers) for young married women to look after the man of the house, do everything to keep him happy and not make their own demands as women. Judith Acsady even claims that within Hungary in particular, there is a 'growing trend toward supporting the traditional view that a woman's true place is in the home.'

Since 1989, women have generally been the first to lose their jobs in the event of redundancies and have seen a reduction in social security payments. The woman's role in society has been compromised through burgeoning pornography and prostitution. The representation of women's issues is almost non-existent, firstly because women's organisations are extremely weak and ineffective, and secondly because the number of women parliamentarians has dropped significantly since 1990 (from 34 per cent to 4 per cent in Romania, from 21 per cent to 7 per cent in Hungary, and from 30 per cent to 9 per cent in the Czech Republic).

Things may change with the new generation, which is travelling more and experiencing other cultures. Furthermore, women are beginning to attain positions of influence within the new market economies, particularly in the Czech Republic, where overall unemployment is very low. But, anecdotally, over most of ECE it seems that many young women still prefer the traditional man–woman relationship because they understand it and feel safe within it.

Rampant corruption

Corruption is still endemic in ECE societies, as it was under communism, ranging from personal gifts to doctors in order to obtain better medical treatment to outright bribery of high-ranking public officials in order to secure the purchase of a profitable company within the privatisation process. Throughout ECE the housing, cigarette and other markets are almost totally in the control of Mafia groups, which, though usually foreign, are run locally by former black marketeers.

This also occurs in the West, but in the Mafia-ridden 'Wild East' it touches upon all aspects of life. If you want anything very quickly – ranging from a personal parking place near your office to a permit to allow you to establish your own business – then you have to be prepared to pay several bribes, which may quadruple the cost of a transaction. Given that the same bureaucrats are still in their posts and that there is a lot more money around, it is difficult to see why they would suddenly change from the way they behaved under the old regime.

Control of the media and avoidance of criticism

Most countries passed 'media laws' very soon after 1989 to allow for privatisation and to give the image of an independent media (Hungary being a notable exception). In some cases (e.g. the Czech Republic) this meant that the mass media were sold almost entirely to foreign companies. In some countries ownership and control of the media became highly politicised (e.g. in Albania, Bulgaria and Hungary).

There is still some overt censorship and direct control of the media in Romania, Slovakia, Serbia, Croatia and Bosnia, where television and radio in particular are still mainly mouthpieces for the government. Serbian President Milosevic's manipulation of television, radio and the press is probably the most blatant censorship in the region. This can be far less overt, such as the Czech Premier Klaus's weekly column and bimonthly interview in *Lidove Noviny*, and his weekly twenty-minute television slot on the private Nova television channel in which he quite openly presents government policy (the programme beginning nine months before parliamentary elections!).

Individual journalists can be physically intimidated in Serbia or arrested in Albania if they criticise the governing regime of Milosevic or Berisha, respectively. They can also be sacked by a television chief, who is usually a government supporter, as happened to the seven journalists sacked from Bulgarian state television in December 1995 by its pro-Socialist director.

Radio and television stations have been closed down (eighty private radio stations in Macedonia), anti-government television programmes have been cancelled in Slovakia, newspapers have been banned (*Borba* in Serbia and *Smena* in Slovakia), or their activities overseen by the government, as in Serbia. Similarly, programme schedules have been controlled and appearances of the opposition parties regulated, as in Croatia during the run-up to the 1995 elections and in Albania before the 1996 elections.

In terms of top appointments, there have been politically motivated purges within the radio and television stations, for example in Bulgaria every time the government changed. In Hungary, the MSZP government after May 1994 immediately appointed new (more sympathetic) heads of television and radio, who then dismissed or silenced a number of reporters who were biased in favour of the previous, conservative government.

Financial controls have also been applied, such as manipulating the price and supply of newsprint, printing facilities or the distribution networks, as in Romania and Serbia. Some governments have even levied special taxes in order to control specific publications; for example, the Croatian government crippled one anti-government weekly with a series of libel suits and levied an extortionate 'pornography tax' on another (non-pornographic) anti-government political weekly. Serbia has used similar techniques. In Albania tax concessions have been given to pro-government newspapers.

The government's prerogative of granting frequencies to private radio and television stations has clearly been abused in Serbia, Macedonia, Bulgaria and Romania. Legislative obstruction has also been used, with the constant delays in adopting a media law in Hungary and in regulating private television and radio in Albania.

Most ECE leaders eschew criticism at all costs and are very bad at learning from their own mistakes. This is a residue of the lack of competition in the past. Criticism is seen as undermining their status and prestige. Therefore, government leaders constantly criticise the media for its lack of objectivity and complain that the media fail to give the government enough opportunity to explain its views, for example Premiers Antall and Horn in Hungary, also the Czech Premier Klaus (who considers journalists 'the biggest enemies of mankind').

Rebuilding a civil society

The next group of problems probably constitutes the region's greatest challenge: the rebuilding of a civil society or civic culture – that is to say, a prevailing political culture in which many, if not most, citizens are active participants in their economic and political society.

The importance of the civil society

In this respect it is worth noting how Gabriel Almond and Sidney Verba – in their classic volume *The Civic Culture* – refer to the difficulty of nations attempting the transition from a 'subject' (totalitarian) to a 'participatory' (democratic) political culture. They claim that this process requires a great deal of time, if not intergenerational change. Their overall conclusion is that, in terms of democratic stability, the closer the approximation to the 'participatory' type of civic culture, the more stable the democracy is likely to be.

The legacy of the communist period was a non-participatory citizenry: the involvement of the individual in politics was dictated by the state. People accepted the duties and laws that were imposed from above and performed the many rituals demanded by the regime. The tradition of an active civic society was totally absent: past behaviour was based on passive obedience.

'New evolutionism', which was invented by Adam Michnik, was an idea whereby Solidarity would encourage a participatory political culture from below, so that eventually the Polish people would press for economic and political changes and unseat the Communists. 'Civil society' in this sense could almost be equated with the act of thinking for yourself and behaving in a way that was blatantly anti-regime.

In Ralf Dahrendorf's opinion, the procedural aspects of democracy can be implemented very quickly: constitutional reform can be accomplished in as little as six months and genuine economic reform in at least six years. But a viable civic society that will 'transform the constitution and the economy from fair-weather into all-weather institutions' will take over sixty years to be established.

Conflictual societies

Stephen Heintz, of the East–West Studies Institute in Prague/ New York, has studied the various factors that could delay or undermine the transition process in ECE. A section of his analysis appertains to the 'phenomenon of post-totalitarian [i.e. post-communist] confusion about the role of power in society', particularly as it affects the relationship between the individual and the state. The 'confusion' relates to the way that power is established, used, and distributed within the emerging democracies of ECE. He alludes to a more authoritarian, top-down decision-making process in which there are:

- a persistent addiction to conflict rather than a culture of compromise (many minor issues become massive problems which are then presented as almost unresolvable, for instance the relationships between Czechs and Slovaks, from the debate over the name of the state in April 1990 to the 'velvet divorce' of 1993);
- a very weak culture of competition, whereby ECE leaders are loathe to tolerate any type of opposition within the party, or the governing coalition, or from any expert or foreigner who might challenge his or her opinion (this applies to anyone from President Milosevic in Serbia to Premier Klaus in the Czech Republic);
- a very strong personalisation of power in various ECE parliaments or during electoral campaigns (e.g. the 1994 elections in Slovakia, when the four-week campaign was more or less dominated by heated exchanges between Premier Moravcik and the challenger Meciar, as well as by continuous criticism of President Kovac, who expressed serious concern about the 'confrontational developments' within the campaign);
- a lack of institutional apparatus by which to arrive at some overall consensus and the ineptitude of the main political actors in the art of compromise, leading to an outright refusal to contemplate new ideas (whether in respect of

new legislation or different teaching methods at universities)
or a serious lack of rational debate in most parliaments;

- a lack of the 'politics of trust', which have not yet replaced
the 'politics of fear', which was a key feature of the former
totalitarian state. There is still of fear of doing *anything* that
someone in a position of authority might get to know about
and possibly use against the person or institution involved.
This is particularly the case when a signature is required on
pieces of paper.

The atomisation of society

One of the most difficult legacies of the past to be overcome in
rebuilding a civic culture is the atomisation of society, that is, the
breaking of all horizontal relations between people, which meant
that people formed very small groups of close friends and
relatives and were not able to build up areas of communal activity.
It was too dangerous: everyone not known intimately could be an
informer for the secret police.

In this way, the Communists succeeded in destroying all the
intermediary institutions and associations that normally serve as
the foundations of a civil society. For over forty years, societies
were purposely atomised and controlled, suspicion was rampant
and the 'politics of fear' predominated. As Vaclav Havel described
it, each person was 'driven into a foxhole of privacy'.

Weak pluralism

In a functioning pluralistic society, non-governmental organisations play a mediating role between the individual and the state.
They provide a functional type of representation that both
supplements and complements the formal institutions of representative democracy, and act as a constraint on the power wielded
by the central government.

For a civil society to develop, there must be a real increase in
the number of active voluntary associations (the third sector). One
of the things that is most striking about ECE in general is the

total lack of collective action. The development of this third sector remains in an embryonic stage and, at the time of writing, was hardly encouraged by the various governments.

Bureaucratic way of thinking

A bureaucratic way of thinking and behaving is an important legacy of the past, stemming from the bureaucratic traditions of both the Austro-Hungarian and Ottoman empires. This persists today and can be specifically seen in the inability or reluctance to question bureaucratic regulations or accept any degree of personal responsibility in decision making.

There is bureaucracy in any polity, but Heintz calls what exists in ECE 'bureaucracy squared' because of the plethora of minor regulations that bedevil almost every transaction. Sometimes this can be very counterproductive because things that are important to the process of transition cannot be accomplished. The existence of this myriad of regulations will certainly cause problems in the region's attempts to enter Western organisations like the EU.

The tenuous economics–democracy linkage

The most pressing problem for the present, though, is the economic backwardness of the entire region, which has to be remedied if democracy is to become firmly established and if the countries are to be integrated into 'Europe'. But a rapid transition to a capitalist system with price liberalisation and private ownership will not bring about the desperately needed economic restructuring that will have to take place to overcome dilapidated infrastructure, outmoded productive capacity, environmental pollution, exposure to economic competition from abroad, and so on.

The problem is that economic restructuring and the transition to pluralism are intrinsically linked. If the new political leaders of the state fail to satisfy the material needs of the nation, then they will be penalised by the electorate, even though there might be no alternative economic policy among the other political parties.

This is the major reason for the rejection of the first post-communist elites almost everywhere and the return to power of former Communists in Poland, Hungary and Bulgaria: the ECE electorates feel the need to shield themselves from the ravages of unbridled capitalism.

Some of the most immediate socio-economic problems that have emerged within ECE as a result of a rather rapid trans-formation towards a free market are discussed below.

Excessive consumerism

This is a natural consequence of the pent-up demand of forty years of isolation from the marketplace and from the flood of Western products and Western advertising now sweeping the region. Such excessive consumerism (mainly in the big towns and cities) is still being financed by personal savings or a sudden influx of money via restitution (i.e. property being returned to the families of the original owners before its expropriation by the Communists), letting of property to foreigners, entrepreneurship and trade (all for a small minority of the population). Since the majority of savings are being spent on imported foreign goods, this has serious implications for future domestic output and the balance of trade.

Growing disparities of incomes and wealth

Enormous differences in income are emerging throughout ECE. Those able to start up businesses are quickly becoming million-aires. The vast majority, however, are still tied to their low-paid state jobs and will have very little access to luxury goods once all their savings have been spent. A true under-class is currently juxtaposed to a rich economic elite, with the majority stagnating somewhere in the middle.

According to World Bank figures, in 1990 some 4 per cent of the ECE population was adjudged to be living in poverty; by 1993 that figure had risen to 18 per cent. Often those verging on the edge of poverty are single parents in state jobs – which includes many people in vocational professions like university lecturers, teachers, doctors and nurses, all of whom are very badly paid compared with the normal secretary working for a Western company.

The other problem with the new economic elite is that they often benefited under the communist regime. When the process of small privatisations began, very few groups within society were able to take advantage of the new economic freedoms: former Communist Party members; former black marketeers; green-grocers, butchers and certain other retailers who, in the past, sold second- or third-class goods as first-class and pocketed the difference; prostitutes, waiters, and taxi drivers, who had contact with foreign tourists. Hence there exists a culture of envy throughout ECE, whereby the vast majority associate present-day wealth with corruption and links to the previous regime.

Crisis in housing

Housing is one of the major problems facing ECE in terms of its transition to a free-market economy, since it seriously restricts mobility of labour. Millions of people are still living in heavily subsidised state housing at rents far below market rates. Foreigners and members of the (very small) *nouveaux riches* are the only people able to afford to rent or buy on the private real-estate market. In a sense, the state has entered a vicious circle from which there seems to be little chance of escaping, barring a massive influx of capital:

- the state dare not raise rents dramatically to anywhere near market levels – it would lead to high levels of indebtedness and, eventually, homelessness;
- at the same time, hundreds of thousands of families are still waiting for apartments and are having to remain living with relatives;
- on the other hand, the state is building hardly any new

housing stock, because it cannot be rented to the indigenous population at a profitable rate, and no ECE state possesses adequate financial resources to finance a larger state housing sector;

• because of the minute supply of private rented accommodation, prices are so inflated that only foreigners can afford them;

• therefore, the vast majority of people cannot move from their subsidised state apartments;

• this results in an immobile labour force at a time of rising unemployment.

Unemployment

At the time of writing, unemployment is still under 5 per cent in the Czech Republic; in regions of Poland, Hungary, East Germany, Romania, Bulgaria and Albania, however, it is in excess of 15 per cent. In some individual cities, it is well over 25 per cent and rising – indeed, in some parts of former East Germany and Romania 40 per cent has not been uncommon. Among gypsies unemployment can reach 80–90 per cent.

Unemployment is an especially complex social problem in societies in which there was previously no unemployment at all. The major reason for the high rates of unemployment has been what is called the 'transitional recession' – so, in theory, unemployment should begin to drop as recovery occurs. Unfortunately, there is no indication that this is yet happening. Furthermore, a comparative study conducted by the Institute of East–West Studies shows that the long-term unemployed are the fastest growing section of the unemployed throughout ECE.

Deepening criminalisation of society

Perhaps as an expected offshoot of high unemployment, crime has increased rapidly since 1989, especially economic crimes, with some ECE countries now being cited in official comparative statistics as having the greatest incidence of burglary, car theft, rape and pickpocketing per capita in the world. This both relates to the darker, anarchic side of freedom, but also reflects the less human side of capitalism: unfettered greed.

Unachievable expectations

Dahrendorf was one of the first authors to point to the possible disenchantment on the part of the general public with the new democratic regimes, once the euphoria of unseating the Communists had been replaced by the realisation of economic hardship ahead. By 1991 many people were arguing that one political elite had simply replaced another, albeit democratically.

Opinion polls conducted in mid-1994 did indeed demonstrate that economic realisation had dawned on the vast majority. The proportion of people claiming their economic situation was worse than under communism was: 70 per cent in Slovakia, Hungary, Bulgaria and Romania, 55 per cent in Poland and just over 50 per cent in the Czech Republic.

On the whole many people believed that the end of communism would automatically mean improved living standards, with the introduction of a free market and democracy. This blind acceptance meant a growing gap between the rising expectations of the population and the limits of the existing system. By 1993–94, people's main concerns were with the stagnant living conditions and the increasing social costs of the reforms. Hence the victory of the communist successor parties in Poland, Hungary and Bulgaria.

Conclusion

Democracy involves more than free elections and elected parliaments; the free market means more than private ownership and price liberalisation. Both imply far-reaching changes in attitudes and values. As has been proven so often in the past, it is far easier to change institutions and structures than it is to change patterns of thought and behaviour, ingrained over previous decades.

The transition towards democracy and the free market has certainly proved much more problematic than had been generally supposed beforehand. The old communist order has collapsed, but a new order universally welcomed by the vast majority has not yet been created in its place.

Further reading

Judith Acsady, 'Shifting Attitudes and Expectations in Hungary', from the issue entitled 'Women Changing Roles?', *Transition*, 1 (6), 8 September 1995.

Gabriel Almond and Sidney Verba, *The Civic Culture*, Little Brown, 1964.

Ralf Dahrendorf, *Reflections on the Revolution in Europe*, Chatto and Windus, 1990.

Stephen Heintz, 'Where Does the Former East Bloc Go?', *Social Venture Network Conference*, Lucca, Italy, 6–9 April 1995.

Ken Jowitt, *New World Disorder: The Leninist Extinction*, University of California Press, 1992.

Juan Linz and A. Stepan, *Problems of Democratic Transition and Consolidation*, Johns Hopkins University Press, 1995.

George Schöpflin, 'Post-Communism: Constructing New Democracies in Central Europe', *International Affairs*, 67.

Gyorgy Szoboszlai (ed.), *Democracy and Political Transformation. Theories and East-Central Realities*, Hungarian Political Science Association, 1991.

Peter Volton (ed.), *Uncertain Futures: East European Democracy*, Institute of East–West Studies, 1990.

Peter Volton (ed.), *Bound to Change: Consolidating Democracy in ECE*, Institute of East–West Studies, 1992.

6
Nationalism

The Nation is essentially the source of all sovereignty; nor can any individual, or any body of men, be entitled to any authority which is not expressly derived from it. (*La Déclaration des Droits de l'Homme*, Clause III, 1789)

It is the State which makes nations, and not nations which make the State. (Josef Pilsudski)

Men make nations. (Ernest Gellner)

The nation state remains the most enduring political structure of the twentieth century, and nationalism is certainly one of the most frequently manipulated, most emotive and most powerful of all political doctrines.

Since the collapse of the Soviet empire, several new nation states have emerged in ECE, and this resurgence of nationalism represents one of the greatest obstacles to a successful transition to democracy that the region has to face.

Nationalism before 1900

In the Ancient World people expressed their loyalty to their city (e.g. Athens or Sparta), so loyalties were local or regional, rather than national. In the Middle Ages, Europe was formed of empires, kingdoms and principalities, and loyalty was given to the king or queen, emperor or empress.

It is only from the end of the 1700s that people in Europe really began to identify with the 'nation', after the advent of industrialisation and the exodus of people from rural areas to the cities. Previous 'face-to-face communities' (as Benedict Anderson calls them) began to disappear and the nation state now emerged as a new source of identity.

Thus the old sources of legitimation – monarchical rule, feudal loyalties, hereditary lineage, or religious affiliation – lost their importance through the steady increase in the power of parliament (Great Britain) or the violent overthrow of the *ancien regime* (France). As the people began to participate in politics, the 'nation' (Benedict Anderson's 'imagined community') grew as the centre of people's allegiance.

The USA is often depicted as the first of today's modern nations, when it established its independence from Britain in 1776. Within Europe, though, it was the French Revolution and the subsequent Napoleonic Wars which played the greatest role in expanding the doctrine of nationalism. The legacy of the French Revolution was the idea that people possess inalienable natural rights and that society should promote those rights, including the right to live and organise society within one's own nation. Napoleon continued this tradition and looked upon his conquests throughout ECE as freeing various 'nations' and different peoples from imperial occupation.

By the mid-nineteenth century nationalism had become a real political force, challenging imperial rule throughout ECE and justifying the colonising 'mission' of many European states on the African and Asian continents. By the end of the century, the nation had become the prime source of territorial loyalty and began to be the main cause of many inter-state wars and regional conflicts.

Major waves of nationalism

There have been five major waves of nationalism throughout history, which have usually followed the collapse of empires:

1   the foundation of the new states in Latin America in the early nineteenth century when they gained independence from imperial Spain and Portugal;

2   the gradual process of unification of both the Kingdom of Italy and the first German Empire during the period 1830–71;

3   the new countries of ECE that emerged as a result of the fall of the Habsburg and Ottoman empires and from the principle of self-determination built into the 1919 Paris Treaties (Czechoslovakia, Hungary, Yugoslavia and Poland);

4   the rapid growth in the number of states in the African and Asian continents, as a result of decolonisation and the decline of the British, French, Portuguese and Dutch empires after 1945;

5   the independent nations emerging from the collapse of the Soviet bloc towards the end of the 1980s, leading to the disintegration of the USSR itself in 1991.

The role of history in ECE nationalism

When examining nationalism within ECE, it is impossible to avoid the crucial role of history over preceding centuries.

In the 1800s, ECE was an assortment of races, ethnic groups, languages and religions under imperial rule, and there was a general separation of nation and state. The Habsburg Empire was a very powerful state – but it was not a nation; Prussia was the prototype state, but it was not a nation; the Polish constituted a 'nation', but were stateless, like several other ECE nations under various empires.

The region's history is a chronicle of war and conquest over centuries, with the same territory being dominated by different empires at varying times. Frequently a nation's very survival was at stake. For example, the once powerful Polish kingdom disappeared from the map in 1795, and the first Polish Republic was invaded by Hitler in 1939.

The region's collective memories, therefore, tend to be of defeat and suffering at the hands of foreigners. Some ECE nation states tend to see themselves as 'victims' of frequent injustices, as did the Serbs, for example, under the Ottoman Empire.

Traditionally, adjacent states were often seen as aiding and abetting the foreign invaders, which led to intense animosity between neighbouring peoples, such as the intense rivalry between Croats and Serbs.

During the nineteenth century, there were many abortive 'nationalist' revolts against the multinational Habsburg and Ottoman empires. In the end, independence was largely bestowed by the victors of the First World War, when President Woodrow Wilson's insistence on the doctrine of 'self-determination' allowed several nations of the Austro-Hungarian Empire to become sovereign states.

Therefore all ECE states can be considered 'late nations': Bulgaria, Serbia and Romania gained independence from the Ottoman Empire in the late 1870s; Czechoslovakia, Yugoslavia, Albania, Hungary and Poland were created or re-established in the post-war treaties of 1918–19.

However, precise ethnic borders were impossible to draw in ECE in 1918 and many areas remained with mixed populations, such as the Romanian and Hungarian-speaking populations in Transylvania; Czechs, Slovaks, Hungarians, Ukrainians and Sudeten Germans in Czechoslovakia; Slovenes, Croats, Bosnians, Macedonians, Serbs and Albanians in Yugoslavia; finally, the Jews, Germans and gypsies who were spread over the entire region.

The fact that the state and national boundaries have rarely coincided in ECE has been one of the region's greatest problems since the early 1800s. In the inter-war period Germans inhabited most ECE states, and Hitler's attempts to unite all Germans into one German Reich led to the Second World War. Likewise, Milosevic's campaign for a Greater Serbia and Tudjman's desire for a Greater Croatia led to violent civil war and ethnic cleansing in former Yugoslavia.

The fluidity of national and state borders in ECE also caused problems over political loyalty and national identity. Hungarians in southern Slovakia, for instance, have been Austro-Hungarian,

Czechoslovak, Hungarian or Slovak at different times since 1900.

As a result the history of ECE since 1900 can be read as a succession of nationalistic conflicts and atrocities:

- the First and Second World Wars, both of which began in the region;
- various inter-war skirmishes, such as between Bulgarians and Macedonians, Croats and Serbs, Hungarians and Romanians;
- attempts at genocide during the Second World War, especially of Jews in Poland and of Serbs and Croats in Yugoslavia;
- the immediate post-war 'ethnic cleansing', beginning in 1945 with the murder and expulsion of Germans and Hungarians, in particular;
- the nationalistic revolts in Kosovo (1968) and Croatia (1971);
- President Zhivkov's campaigns of assimilation and expatriation of ethnic Turks from Bulgaria in the 1980s;
- the split in the Czechoslovak Federal Republic after 1992;
- the Yugoslavian conflict since the late 1980s;
- in particular 'ethnic cleansing' of the populations in Bosnia-Hercegovina, Croatia and elsewhere in former Yugoslavia since 1991.

Pan-nationalism in ECE

The idea of pan-nationalism is that several nation states join a supranational governmental authority – for religious, historical, economic or defence reasons – but still retain their separate ethnic identities. The gradual process of post-war unification within Western Europe is the clearest recent example.

Pan-Slavism was probably the earliest of such European movements, attempting to unify the various Slav 'nations' of the Habsburg and Ottoman empires into one Slav state in the early

1800s. The idea behind this movement was that the Slavs were a potentially great people with a common history, shared destiny, and closeness of language and culture. Yet they were also weak and fragmented, precisely because they were divided among different empires. If they could obtain political unity, then they might realise their potential greatness.

The first Pan-Slav Congress was held in 1848 in Prague, but the movement was effectively stifled at birth through Austrian opposition and Russian manipulation. (Russia claimed to be the natural leader of all Slavs – but really wanted to extend its influence over the whole of ECE.)

King Alexander and the Serbs revived the idea of pan-Slavism during the First World War, by proposing a Kingdom of the Southern Slavs – the origin of Yugoslavia. Such ideas of pan-Slavism were also used by the Soviets in the post-war period to justify the USSR's occupation of ECE.

Definitional problems

Definition of nationalism

As a political ideology, nationalism is a belief in the primacy of nations, with national unity or independence being the main goal of all political activity. This implies that the borders of the administrative state (providing goods and services to its citizens) and the 'sentimental nation' (evoking a feeling of belonging and of community for its inhabitants) are more or less congruent.

The main tenets of nationalism are the following:

- the world is naturally divided into nations and only into nations;
- each nation is organised within its own clearly defined sovereign territory (i.e. the borders of the state and nation are the same);
- each individual belongs to only one nation;
- the only type of legitimate government is national self-government.

According to Ian Adams, however, nationalism is only a 'partial ideology' since it provides no indication as to how society is to be organised afterwards. Nationalist movements can thus be right wing, like F. Tudjman's HDZ in Croatia, or left wing, like the Slovak Nationalist Party.

Definition of 'nation'

Nationalism is one of the most influential ideologies of this century. Yet, it is quite vague as an ideology, because of the difficulty in understanding its core concept: the 'nation'.

A 'nation' has two major characteristics:

1   a body of people recognised as distinct by virtue of their historical, linguistic, cultural or ethnic characteristics (of which language is the most obvious outward sign) and usually the sense of a shared past (which could be an 'invented past');

2   an overwhelming desire by the vast majority of the population to assert that distinctiveness in the form of a separate and independent political organisation (this also includes the ruling elites leading the population into the formation of their own nation state on the basis of representing the majority of the 'people').

The main problem with this traditional definition is that it remains highly subjective and quite emotive. There are no absolute criteria by which a 'nation' can be categorically distinguished from a region, a province or any other unit of devolved power within a unitary state. If Slovakia calls itself a separate 'nation' – on the basis of language, history, culture and national economy – then Scotland, the Basque country, French-Canadian Quebec, or the Flemish-speaking part of Belgium could all claim national status on similar grounds. Since there are approximately 2,000 separate languages in the world, there is the potential for just as many nation states.

Similarly, the term 'nationalist' has been adopted by a variety of movements over time. For example, in the case of the territory covered by the former Yugoslavia, over the past 150 years 'nationalists' have at various times advocated:

- independent Serbian, Croatian, Bosnian, Macedonian and Slovenian states;
- the creation of a south Slav nation state during the nine-teenth and at the beginning of the twentieth century;
- an all-embracing pan-Slavic state, incorporating the whole of ECE and western parts of the Russian Empire.

Generally speaking, there are four different types of nation:

1   an ethnic majority ruling its own state, such as today's Poland (99 per cent Polish), Hungary (98 per cent), Albania (98 per cent) or the Czech Republic (97 per cent);

2   an isolated ethnic minority within a state run and controlled by a different ethnic majority, such as the Slovaks in Czechoslovakia (this ethnic minority often seeks a degree of administrative autonomy and equal treatment for its native language);

3   those minorities which belong to another nation, such as inter-war Sudeten Germans in Czechoslovakia (who wished to be part of Austria immediately after the First World War), the Hungarians living in today's Romanian Tran-sylvania and southern Slovakia, the Albanians in Macedonia and Kosovo and the Serbs in Bosnia (this type of 'nation' can wish to be united with the mother country);

4   transnational minorities, such as Jews and gypsies – very often these groups face the greatest discrimination, es-pecially in ECE; there has even been a rise in anti-Semitism in Poland since 1989, which is surprising as there are now fewer than 10,000 Jews in the country.

Two different conceptions of nationalism

From the beginning, it is necessary to distinguish between two very different conceptions of nationalism: ethnic and civic.

(1) 'Ethnic nationalism' occurs when simply belonging to a particular ethnic group is given primacy. The ethnic community regards itself as distinct because of its shared history, common ancestry, similar culture (traditions, myths and folklore), same religious background and/or identical language.

Ethnic groups do not need states in order to become nations. The Poles, Czechs, Hungarians, Serbs, Albanians, Macedonians and Bulgarians were all 'nations' during their centuries-long occupation under imperial rule. Similarly, between the wars a single Hungarian 'nation' was distributed among four states – Hungary, Romania, Yugoslavia and Czechoslovakia.

When nation states are formed around ethnically homogeneous populations they tend to be stable, cohesive political units, like Poland, Hungary and the Czech Republic since 1990. But a 'mixed' state founded on the basis of ethnicity often excludes foreigners or 'others' from the 'national' community, as with German nationalism from the early 1800s to 1945, or the exclusive nationalism in former Yugoslavia since 1987.

In such a 'mixed' state, ethnic nationalism can have profoundly destabilising effects, for example: the persecution of minorities by the dominant ethnic group (Serbs by Croats, Hungarians by both Slovaks and Romanians); the non-violent (Czechoslovakia) or violent (Bosnia) break-up of existing multi-ethnic states; and inter-state conflict (e.g. First and Second World Wars).

(2) 'Civic nationalism', on the other hand, permits identity and citizenship through membership of the state irrespective of ethnicity or common ancestry, which means that all members of the state are equal. The emphasis here is on shared participation within a political community, on civic and democratic values and identity through residence within the state, rather than membership of the ethnic group.

Both French nationalism, which stressed the 'Rights of Man and of the Citizen' for everyone, or US statehood, with its constitutional guarantees of equal treatment for all citizens, are of this type. This means that the criterion for belonging to the French or US nation is not one's mother tongue or ethnic background, but rather French or US citizenship.

Civic nationalism, based on political equality for all citizens, encourages social cohesion and is less inclined to lead to the persecution of minority populations within any ethnically mixed state. But civic nationalism is quite rare and usually implies well developed political and legal institutions within a relatively evolved political culture (e.g. the UK, Switzerland or the USA).

Ethnic and civic nationalism

Link between civic nationalism and democracy

Nationalism in most of Western Europe consists of both civic and ethnic elements, and has generally been, and will probably remain, a positive force *for* democracy and social harmony within the region. In fact, democracy and civic nationalism are intrinsically linked: both enjoyed a revival at the end of the eighteenth century, since both were reactions against the *ancien regime*.

This was illustrated by most of the 'nations' within the former Austrian Empire, whose goals in the 1848 revolutions were *both* their independence from the Habsburgs *and* their desire for greater democracy and decentralisation of imperial power. The Hungarian revolutionaries, in particular, endorsed the call of the 1789 French Revolution for greater 'freedom, equality and fraternity'.

Ethnic nationalism in ECE can also help a specific population develop a feeling of national unity and evolve its own sense of identity. Present-day nationalism in Poland can be said to be 'healthy' in that it fosters a sense of national unity during a difficult period of economic and political transition.

However, there are usually negative consequences when ethnic nationalism plays a dominant role within any society where the civic culture is weak. Indeed, one of the main reasons why democracy generally failed in ECE during the inter-war period is that ethnic nationalism predominated and ethnic and political boundaries were not congruent. This was particularly important in states where ethnic minorities constituted 25–30 per cent or more of the population (Poland, Yugoslavia, Czechoslovakia and Romania).

The dangers of ethnic nationalism

Ethnic nationalism can be extremely dangerous, as it plays on very powerful and irrational emotions, and has the potential to become exclusive, dogmatic and violent.

The dangers of ethnic nationalism are particularly evident in ECE countries, where:

- there is a strong propensity to 'ideological thinking', with most events being explained in terms of nationalist rhetoric (e.g. the country's economic and political difficulties will be solved if only the country gains independence);

- ethnic nationalism has been used by opportunistic politicians as an extremely efficient method of political mobilisation and has become little more than a basis of legitimacy for those seeking or retaining power (e.g. Milosevic manipulated Serbian nationalism to achieve power in Yugoslavia in 1987, and Meciar used nationalism to regain power in Slovakia after 1991);

- ethnic nationalism becomes the main division within society, since it is most difficult to compromise over one's ethnicity (a person is either Serb or Croat, Hungarian or Romanian, Bulgarian or Turk);

- the collective rights of the ethnic (majority) nation are given prominence over the individual rights of the citizen (e.g. the 1992 Slovak constitution equates citizenship with Slovak nationality, basically excluding the Hungarian minority from nationhood; and the 1991 Croatian constitution similarly barred the Krajinian Serbs from citizenship);

- the majority nationalist group sees itself as the 'embodiment of the nation', and regards members of 'other' or minority groups as 'enemies of the nation' and 'unpatriotic';

- the other group is usually discriminated against by the majority community (e.g. restrictions on the use of their minority language; filling key political and economic posts with members of the dominant ethnic group only; the closure of minority language schools or universities; and

criticism of the minority group within the national media –
this is the sort of treatment meted out to the Hungarian
minorities in both Romania and Slovakia, to the Albanians
in Kosovo, and to the Krajinian Serbs in Croatia).

The danger is that a nationalist 'vicious circle' can emerge.
With the various degrees of repression, many of the minority
groups loyal to the nation state will be alienated, to the extent that
they might even seek reunion with a neighbouring state or
independence. At this point the ethnic majority will criticise the
minority for destabilising the new state, will view them as an
internal 'enemy', and will blame them for all the current economic and political problems, which only alienates the minority
even further. A major internal conflict or civil war could be the
outcome of this vicious circle, as has occurred in former Yugoslavia.

Nationalism and communism

Nationalism under communism

According to Marxist theory, the whole idea of the nation state
was an illusion, used by the capitalist bourgeois to rationalise their
exploitation of the working classes. Nationalist or regionalist
movements were therefore a 'bourgeois deviation', manipulated
by the middle classes to divert the workers from their real
struggle: overturning class relationships within society.

Thus, nationhood was not a primary concern of early communists, and nations were seen as irrelevant. It was not until the
Stalinist era that nationalist movements figured among groups
considered as 'enemies of the communist revolution'. Only then
were they outlawed as ideological competition and their leaders
persecuted.

Similarly, some post-war ECE Communist leaders viewed ethnically based or minority movements in their own countries as a
threat to their power base. This meant they had to suppress any
opposing nationalist ideologies. Hence even 'national communists'

paid only lip service to nationalism and never used it openly as a means of mobilisation. Even when Communists reverted to nationalist rhetoric, as in Yugoslavia, they were not 'real nationalists', but were just using nationalism to defend their positions of power.

Under Stalin in the immediate post-war period, the following measures were taken to stamp out any growth of nationalism:

- purges of nationalist leaders;
- suppression by force of any truly regionalist or nationalist movements, such as the Hungarian-speakers in Romania, the Turks in Bulgaria;
- organisations of a specifically nationalist character (e.g. associations of Hungarian writers in Romanian Transylvania or various Slovak cultural organisations within Czechoslovakia) had to be officially permitted by the regime and their activities were usually stringently controlled;
- the assimilation of leading nationalist politicians into the communist system (e.g. many Czechoslovak leaders were Slovak);
- attempts to create a universal, socialist identity through an international 'brotherhood' cutting across national borders;
- domestic propaganda endeavouring to glorify workers first and playing down national affiliations (e.g. the GDR was to be a communist, peasant/worker state first before it was German);
- an all-pervasive campaign of Russification, which tended to be carried out spasmodically;
- national histories were rewritten, national symbols were removed or changed, so that even Martin Luther and Bismarck became proto-communists in East German history books.

In this way, Communists destroyed all overtly nationalist political organisations. So when leading Communists like Tito and Brezhnev claimed to have 'solved' the nationalist problem, they were reflecting the fact that totalitarian control had kept any sort of nationalist opposition muted for most of the post-war period. In fact, ECE nationalism did not disappear, but remained dormant, below the surface, waiting for the right moment to express itself openly.

Sub-surface nationalism under communism

Sub-surface nationalism had various forms under communism.

To begin with, Z. Brzezinski notes that each communist regime inadvertently promoted a political culture of nationalistic chauvinism, based on its own excellence and achievements. 'Nationalism was thereby nurtured, rather than disturbed, in the communist experience,' he concluded.

Somewhat ironically, communism actually strengthened ethnic differences, in that each minority looked back longingly to its own national heritage in order to escape the bland uniformity of communist society.

'National communism' emerged as early as 1948 when Yugoslavia left the Soviet bloc. Thereafter it survived in the sense that communism in each individual country would reflect the country's national character and political culture (e.g. Gomulka's rule in Poland 1956–70 and Romania from the mid-1960s under Ceausescu).

Nationalism also lay behind the post-war revolts against the Soviet hegemony. The 1956 Hungarian revolution, the Polish 1956 revolt, the 1968 Prague Spring and the creation of Solidarity were all attempts to escape from Soviet hegemony, as were the 1989 'revolutions'.

Whenever reform movements emerged in ECE, long-suppressed national feelings returned to the surface. During the Prague Spring in Czechoslovakia, for example, the issue of Slovak autonomy again came to the fore (as in 1918 and 1938) and the federal structure evolved during 1968 was almost the only institutional change to survive Dubcek's attempt to give socialism a 'human face'. Likewise, the limited amount of political freedom in Tito's Yugoslavia was bound to give rise to nationalist aspirations of the different republics, expressed for example in the 1971 Croatian revolt and the 1968 demonstrations in Kosovo over Serbian centralism. This was especially true after Tito's 1974 constitution was introduced, which gave much greater autonomy to the existing republics and created some new autonomous regions.

Moreover, hatred of foreigners, prevailing anti-Semitism, discrimination against gypsies, and the violation of minority rights were all practised under the Communists, for example the assimilation campaigns against the Turks in Bulgaria, the Romanisation campaigns against Hungarians in Transylvania, the attempted compulsory sterilisation of gypsy women in Czechoslovakia, or various anti-Jewish campaigns throughout the region.

Similarities between ethnic nationalism and communism

Ethnic nationalism is similar to communism in several important respects:

- as an ideology, it tries to give people a sense of belonging;
- under both communism and ethnic nationalism people think in ideological terms, being either for or against something, seeing everything in black and white;
- elites dominating the state specifically exclude other groups from power positions, that is, there is a type of 'ideological enemy';
- both communism and ethnic nationalism are collectivist ideologies, that is, the individual is of less importance than either 'class' or 'nation';
- both are part of the messianic tradition of easy solutions – everyone will be prosperous as soon as individual nations become independent or the working classes become free;
- both encourage conspiracy theories, in the sense that they look for 'bourgeois' or 'unpatriotic' internal enemies and view the rest of the world as hostile;
- both are ideologies claiming that one particular political form is inherently natural and therefore right – meaning

that people take up positions from which they will not move and are unable or unwilling to compromise.

Nationalism in post-communist ECE

J. F. Brown characterises the exclusive form of messianic, ethnic nationalism that has emerged in ECE since 1989 as 'hyper-identification with one's nation'. Both Czechoslovakia and Yugoslavia have disintegrated because of ethnic nationalism and nationalist issues are potentially destabilising elsewhere within the region.

Nationhood remains on the political agenda in ECE for the following reasons.

Nation building has resumed again, with some nations claiming sovereignty for the very first time in the 1990s, such as Slovakia, Croatia, Slovenia, or Macedonia (ignoring the Nazi wartime puppet regimes in the first two countries mentioned).

'National rehabilitation' is seen as the primary post-revolutionary task throughout the region, because in some cases borders are still in dispute, for example Macedonia (involving Bulgaria, Greece and Albania), and Kosovo (which opposes Albania against Serbia), not to mention the impossibly fluid borders of Bosnia-Hercegovina.

There are still large areas of mixed nationalities on the same territory, such as the Hungarians and Romanians in Transylvania, Hungarians and Slovaks in southern Slovakia, Turks and Bulgarians in Bulgaria, as well as former Yugoslavia's mixed populations.

Democratic traditions are generally weak, so it is difficult to counteract the rule of strongly nationalistic and authoritarian leaders, such as Milosevic in Serbia, Karadic in Bosnia, Tudjman in Croatia, Meciar in Slovakia and Iliescu in Romania.

There is a conflictual political culture, so countries have found it difficult to 'solve' their minority problems through compromise and consensus, as illustrated by the dissolution of federal arrangements in both former Yugoslavia and Czechoslovakia. (In Western

Europe such problems *are* usually resolved with democratic devices of federalism, regional autonomy, and so on.)

Nationalists are not particularly concerned about the transition to democracy, especially in those countries where nationalism has been used as a means of mobilisation, such as Slovakia, Serbia, Croatia and Romania.

Reasons for the resurgence of nationalism

Once communism collapsed, nationalism was the one easily comprehensible concept to restore a new sense of identity within the political vacuum. Indeed, it was the only concept by which the electorate could be mobilised immediately after 1989 – little else could serve as a clear source of identity or voter alignment.

There are several reasons for the resurgence of nationalism throughout ECE after 1989:

(1) *A reaction to the failure of Soviet-imposed universalism, internationalism and artificial cosmopolitanism.* Under Soviet communism national differences were considered secondary to the theory of international solidarity and the goal of a worldwide unified proletariat. But these remained purely theoretical abstractions, which failed to replace or erode national identification, as is proved by the various revolts against the Soviet-imposed regimes during the 1950s and 1960s (in East Germany, Poland, Hungary and Czechoslovakia), and the independent foreign policy pursued by Romania, Albania and Yugoslavia.

(2) *A reaction to global political and economic relations after 1990.* With the collapse of communism, the emerging democracies needed a new set of beliefs to give them stability within a rapidly changing world. The vast majority of ECE citizens feel lost within the process of globalisation and cannot always identify with Western models. Nationalism can compensate for that loss.

(3) *A reaction to the failure of the newly independent states to provide economic prosperity for the vast majority.* The first post-communist elites failed to provide the expected economic prosperity for the vast majority, so that the new states did not attract the loyalty of their citizens. Such elites could not compete

with nationalism when it was used by other politicians to galvanise electoral support, appealing to the emotions and promising an 'easy answer', for example Meciar's clever use of nationalism in Slovakia.

(4) *Nationalism being a major distraction from everyday reality.* Nationalism has been used by some members of the new political elites as a mechanism of mobilisation to distract attention from the day-to-day problems of the transition process by stressing the glories of the nationalist past.

(5) *Other sources of identification, in particular religion, being either too diverse or too compromised to counteract nationalism.* Nationalism might not be so attractive as an 'easy solution' in ECE if other ideologies were to act as countervailing forces. Religion, for example, is either too diverse or too compromised to compete with the attractions of nationalism, apart from in Poland, where the Catholic Church has been the repository for Polish national identity since the beginning of the nineteenth century. In other parts of the region the religious heterogeneity of the population and the impact of over forty years of state-organised atheism means that no one church can speak for the whole nation. With the notable exceptions of the Polish Catholic Church and certain leading members of the East German Lutheran Church, very few churches in ECE can claim to have been opposed to the communist regime. Indeed, many of the state churches were compromised by their cooperation with the Communists (e.g. the Romanian Orthodox Church under Ceausescu).

(6) *Strong identification of a people with the nation or minority group being a function of the post-communist search for community.* Ronald Linden has shown that ECE national minorities tend to distinguish between the central government representing the *political* nation and the regional authorities representing the *ethnic* nation. This explains both the Slovene and Croatian demands for independence from the Yugoslav Federation, and the Istrian, Dalmatian and Krajinian Serb regionalist demands against the unitary Croatian state.

(7) *The opening up of the political and media arenas* (Gorbachev's *glastnost*). With the arrival of democratic reforms, nationalist

opinions and the views of minorities could now be published and distributed freely throughout most of the region: nationalist demands were being expressed openly for the first time in decades.

(8) *The weakness of civic culture, which is a legacy of both the pre-war and communist regimes.* A country with a weak civic society is highly susceptible to nationalist idealogues. If the civic culture had been stronger in post-1987 Yugoslavia, for example, the intense violence committed in the name of ethnic nationalism might have been avoided. But, since such nationalism appeals strongly to the more basic emotions and prevailing prejudices, it is very difficult for democratically elected governments to counter the claims made by nationalists.

(9) *The existence of post-communist elites intent on using nationalism for their own ends.* The division of Czechoslovakia and the civil war in Yugoslavia would not have happened if leading politicians had not knowingly manipulated nationalism for their own political agenda, for example Premiers Klaus and Meciar in Czechoslovakia and Presidents Milosevic, Kucan and Tudjman in former Yugoslavia.

Differences with the past

The real question in terms of nationalism is whether there will be a reversal of the democratic consolidation in ECE, as there was after the First World War, in favour of more authoritarian, nationalist regimes. Superficially, several similarities exist with the inter-war period. In the inter-war period, nationalism had particular appeal to those states which lost either territory or pride as a result of the First World War. In Germany, Hungary and Bulgaria the appeal of nationalism lay in part in its promise to reverse the terms of the 1919–20 Paris Treaties and overturn the democratic governments that had negotiated and fulfilled those terms. There was the same sort of reaction to the communist-instigated federations since 1989.

On the surface, some post-communist states are still burdened with sizeable ethnic and religious minorities for whom the problems of assimilation are just as difficult as in the past. Such ethnic minorities continue to instil a fear of the possible disintegration of the state (e.g. Albanians in Macedonia and Serbian Kosovo, Hungarians in Slovakia and Romania, and Turks in Bulgaria).

Ethnic nationalism still seems to dominate various countries' political and economic lives to an even greater extent than in the inter-war period (e.g. Slovakia in 1990–93 and Yugoslavia since 1987).

On the other hand, there are also substantial differences with the periods before the First World War and between the wars which should militate against a repetition of the collapse of democracy and rise of authoritarian, nationalist governments in the region. Several ECE countries have 'regained' independence after the collapse of the Soviet empire: they are not being created for the first time. The Great Powers have withdrawn from ECE, and the region is no longer subject to external pressure from any expansionist nation, such as fascist Italy, Nazi Germany or Soviet Russia. Indeed, any interference from the West seems to be directed at calming nationalist excesses and avoiding any conflict that might spill over into the West (e.g. attempts at a peaceful resolution of the Bosnian and Croatian crises).

As before, many ECE states could advance territorial claims against their neighbours, and there are co-nationals on both sides of present borders. But for the moment ECE governments are firmly and officially renouncing demands for territorial changes, as evidenced by the series of bilateral treaties signed by Hungary, guaranteeing the integrity of its frontiers with its neighbours. Except for former Yugoslavia, this is a major difference from the inter-war period.

One of the greatest differences between the two periods is the existence of a network of well established international institutions operating in Europe (e.g. OSCE, NATO, EU, EBRD and the Council of Europe) which are both a point of reference and a source of moral and financial aid for the ECE countries in their present transition.

Furthermore, the new governments are the creation of their own populations and enjoy a greater amount of legitimacy than did the inter-war governments (although that support does not often hold for minority groups).

However, the ability of the new governments to retain the loyalty of their populations depends on their skill in offering the majority of citizens a better standard of living, approaching levels of West European prosperity. If they fail in this task, it might allow nationalist parties to exploit a deteriorating economic situation by looking for minority scapegoats (Slovakia) or adopting an aggressive stance against neighbours (former Yugoslavia).

Conclusion

Ethnic nationalism is 'an easy answer', which appeals to collective emotions, and presents new elites with a quick route to both legitimacy and popularity. Politicians like S. Milosevic, V. Meciar, V. Klaus and I. Iliescu have used ethnic nationalism for their own personal ambitions, manipulating politically inexperienced populations in a populist way.

When nationality becomes the sole source of identity for the community, the civic dimension and democratic rights of any social or ethnic minorities can be ignored. There is a correlation here: the more prominence is given to ethnicity within any state, the weaker are democratic and civic values. Hence civil society will take some time to develop in most ECE countries.

The problem for the future arises when nationalist problems assume a greater priority than the process of transition itself. Then another vicious circle sets in, as the longer the process of transition is delayed, the more nationalist issues will tend to dominate the politics of the region.

Further reading

Ian Adams, *Political Ideology Today* (chapter 4), Manchester University Press, 1993.
Benedict Anderson, *Imagined Communities*, Verso, 1992.

J. F. Brown, 'The Resurgence of Nationalism', *RFE/RL Research Report*, 24, 14 June 1991.

Ernest Gellner, *Nations and Nationalism*, Basil Blackwell, 1983.

John Hall, 'Nationalism: Classified and Explained', *Daedalus*, July 1993.

Eric Hobsbawm, *Nations and Nationalism since 1780*, Cambridge University Press, 1990.

Michael Ignatieff, *Blood and Belonging: Journey into the New Nationalism*, Farrer, Straus and Giroux, 1994.

Elie Kedourie, *Nationalism*, Hutchinson, 1966.

Charles Kupchan (ed.), *Nationalism and Nationalities in the New Europe*, Cornell University Press, 1995.

Ronald Linden, 'The Appeal of Nationalism', *RFE/RL Research Report*, 24, 14 June 1991.

George Schöpflin, 'National Identity in the Soviet Union and East Central Europe', *Ethnic and Racial Studies*, 14, January 1991.

George Schöpflin, *Nationalism and National Minorities*, Europa Publications Ltd, 1992.

Anthony Smith, *The Ethnic Origins of Nations*, Basil Blackwell, 1986.

7

The break-up of nations: Czechoslovakia and Yugoslavia

Jiri, what am I to do? He's forcing me to split the state. (Vladimir Meciar, Slovak Premier, to Czechoslovak Foreign Minister Jiri Dienstbier, referring to Vaclav Klaus, Czech Premier)

It's no use pretending that there are perfect innocents in this conflict and that there is one side which is pure white, the victims, and another side which is pure black, the aggressors. (Lord David Owen, EU peace envoy)

The Europeans couldn't handle it on their own and the US should not have withdrawn from the issue [i.e. Bosnia]. This was the great collective failure of the West. The greatest one, in my view, since the late 1930s. (Richard Holbrooke, US Assistant Secretary of State and US peace broker)

The case of Czechoslovakia

Czechoslovakia was created in 1918 out of five distinct regions of the Austro-Hungarian Empire: Bohemia, Moravia, most of Slovakia, and parts of Silesia and Ukrainian Ruthenia. Ruthenia and Slovakia had been under Hungarian dominion and were primarily agricultural, whereas the Czech lands of Bohemia and Moravia and (Polish) Silesia were much more industrialised.

When the joint state was first founded, despite the obvious differences in industrial structure, there was considerable homogeneity between the Czech lands and Slovakia: the Slovak language seems much more of a regional dialect of Czech than a separate and distinctive language (it was 'invented' as a language in the early nineteenth century and, in any case, was based on Old Czech); the Czechs and Slovaks had a common history to a certain extent, being under the same ruler for more than 400 years; their cultural traditions and folklore bore a marked similarity.

However, since the time of the First Republic (1918–38) the Slovaks have felt like a little brother in relation to the Czech part of the country. The unitary Czechoslovak Republic was very centralised, with most decisions being taken in Prague, with no autonomy to any of the large minorities living within the state: Sudeten Germans, Slovaks, Ukrainians or Poles.

Immediately after the end of the Second World War, non-communist ministers of the provisional government, led by President Benes and based in London during the war, repatriated up to 3 million Sudeten Germans – disposing of one minority problem through expulsion. Ruthenia was arbitrarily annexed to the Soviet Republic of Ukraine.

Under the Communists the Slovaks also had very little autonomy. The only concession given to the Slovaks was the establishment of the Czech and Slovak Federation after the 'Prague Spring' in 1968 – but, under communism, this gave the Slovaks autonomy only in theory, not in practice.

With the end of communism, nationalism in Slovakia enjoyed a resurgence, with all Slovak political parties advocating a strong stance towards the 'Pragocentrism' of the Czechs. Vladimir Meciar, Slovak Premier from January 1990 to April 1991, from June 1992 to March 1994 and again since October 1994, while being a champion of the Slovak national cause, also wanted to keep some sort of common state with the Czechs (for sound financial reasons). However, owing to what seems to be a lack of understanding of what is possible in politics and of how the political process functions with compromises and so on, the question of Slovak independence became a matter of honour and people took up extreme positions, from which both sides would not budge. The split in the country could be said to have been engineered by the elites for their own purposes, against the prevailing public opinion of the time. (It was very much a split by default, rather than by design, as far as the majority of the population of the common state were concerned.)

It is doubtful that the Slovak people actually wanted to be a separate nation, since in almost all opinion polls during 1990–93, 75–85 per cent of Slovaks expressed the wish to live in a common state with the Czechs. Well over one year after the 'velvet divorce', 57 per cent of Slovaks still regretted the division of the Czechoslovak nation and desired the re-establishment of a common state with the Czechs.

The discussion about the split of Czechoslovakia hampered most of the political debate in the country and considerably delayed discussion on most constitutional matters, seriously impeding the whole transition process. However, once the split was achieved it allowed the Czech Republic to proceed at a much greater speed than would have been possible with the Slovaks as equal partners. (It is worth emphasising that the so-called 'velvet divorce' itself was accomplished in a remarkably short time and with comparatively little acrimony.)

After initial adjustment difficulties during 1993 and early 1994, the Slovak economy is now also quite buoyant and has undergone some major restructuring of its industries. However, there is little foreign investment and the country has fallen behind in the race to enter the EU. Furthermore, there is also a strong tendency towards the assertion of Slovak nationalism and concomitant increasing hostility towards the Hungarian and gypsy minorities, particularly with regard to the use of the Hungarian language in public places and education.

The case of Yugoslavia

The Yugoslav 1991–95 conflict has seen the largest loss of life, the greatest destruction of property and the most massive movements of people in Europe since the Second World War. Wanton massacres of civilians, purposeful and total annihilations of whole villages, people subject to indescribable tortures, concentration camps where prisoners lived in the most horrific conditions, all seemed to reflect a total disregard for human life. The conflict resembled something out of the more barbaric Middle Ages and the whole international community demonstrated a complete inability to handle the crisis.

(A comprehensive chronology of the events in Yugoslavia can be found in the Appendix, beginning on page 326.)

The region in history

Superficially, the different inhabitants of former Yugoslavia – Serbs, Croats, Slovenes, Bosnians, Montenegrins, Macedonians and Albanians (in Kosovo and Macedonia) – have much in common. Most can speak some form of Serbo-Croat, they share a common history under foreign rule, they are all Slavs, and many people saw themselves as 'Yugoslavs' rather than Serbs, Croats, and so on. However, there are five key differences:

1   there is enormous dialect variation in the former Yugoslavia and the language used in Slovenia is not really Serbo-Croat; Macedonian is akin to Bulgarian and Albanian is a language of its own;
2   there is wide diversity of religion within the area – Slovenia and Croatia are predominantly Roman Catholic, Serbia and Montenegro are mainly Eastern Orthodox, Macedonia is a mix of Islam and Eastern Orthodox, the Kosovo region of Serbia is chiefly Muslim, and Bosnia is still a mixture of all three religions;
3   in terms of historical background, Slovenia, Croatia and Serbia were all once independent states with their own histories – the Serbs, for example, had their own strong empire in the Middle Ages before being conquered by the Ottoman Turks in 1389;
4   there have always been considerable cultural differences – for example, the south of the country was based on a clan system of different 'tribes', with the usual inter-tribal conflicts, and so violence and warfare have been a permanent feature of their political culture;

5   before the recent ethnic cleansing the republics comprising
the former Yugoslavia each had different large minorities –

- Croatia had a sizeable Serb minority (10–12 per cent)
  in the Krajina district – the centre of the civil war in
  1991 and 1995, after which the region was 'cleansed' of
  almost all Croatian Serbs; Serbs also inhabit eastern
  Slavonia near the Serbian border in northern Croatia;
- Serbia has a substantial Albanian minority in Kosovo;
- Macedonia has a large Albanian minority (22 per cent);
- Bosnia, at the start of the war, was 44 per cent Muslim,
  31 per cent Serb and 17 per cent Croatian – there was a
  large amount of overlapping of ethnic areas, which
  makes division of the country into homogeneously
  ethnic areas extremely difficult;
- Slovenia is almost homogeneous, with only a small,
  Italian minority – causing occasional problems with
  neighbouring Italy.

The extensive campaigns of ethnic cleansing since 1991,
however, have dramatically altered the ethnic mix of the area.
Almost all 250,000 Serbs living in the Krajina region of Croatia
left their homeland for Bosnia or Serbia after the Croatian army
retook the region in its summer 1995 offensive. Before the war in
northern Bosnia-Hercegovina there were an estimated 500,000
Muslims, yet within three years that number had fallen to 30,000.
At the time of writing, it seems that the vast majority of Bosnian
Serbs have left their part of Sarajevo, rather than live under a
Bosnian Muslim government.

Recurring features of the Yugoslavian conflict

It is impossible to understand what happened over 1990–95 in the
former Yugoslavia without looking back in history to the roots of
the conflict. Elements of the recent problems have been present
within the region for centuries: ethnic cleansing, massacres, mass
rapes and the drive to extend territory.

The area has often suffered from foreign occupation. For
example, Serbia was subjected to Turkish occupation for almost

500 years from 1389; likewise, during the Second World War the Serbs were treated cruelly by the German occupiers and the pro-Nazi Croats (the Ustasi).

There were frequent uprisings against the foreign rule and acts of retaliation by those in power. For example, after the first of fourteen national uprisings by Serbs against the Turks in 1805, the Ottoman authorities held a mass execution of thousands of Serbian soldiers; during the Second World War, Serbia was heavily bombed and occupied by the Germans in 1941, causing the Serbs to engage in a fierce civil war against the occupiers and their Croatian/Bosnian allies; after the war the (mostly Serbian) communist partisans exacted terrible revenge on their wartime opponents: 250,000 Croats and 2,000–3,000 Slovenes were massacred.

There have been several implantations of peoples by the occupying powers over the centuries. For example, in the mid-1700s the Habsburg Empire had non-Turkish areas colonised by German-speakers from Austria and Poland; after Bosnia was occupied by the Austrians in 1878, over a quarter of a million Catholics were 'imported' in the same way; during the Second World War, the Italians colonised Serbian Kosovo with 100,000 Albanian families, expelling Serbs from the region – a policy continued by Tito.

Mass movements of people have been part of Yugoslav history since the mid-1800s. For example, during 1876–78 about 2 million Bosnian Muslims were driven from their homes; after the 1878 Austrian occupation, at least 140,000 Muslims emigrated to Turkey and 90,000 Serbs were forced to leave Bosnia; between 1941 and 1945, 250,000 Serbs and 200,000 Croats emigrated from Bosnia to Serbia and Croatia, respectively.

Massacres have occurred quite often. During the German occupation, 1941–45, the Serbs underwent a veritable holocaust – it has been estimated that 400,000–600,000 of them were killed by pro-Nazi Croats (Ustasi) and their Muslim allies, many in Nazi-type concentration camps; altogether over 2.5 million Yugoslavs died during the Second World War, and it is said that more Yugoslavs were killed by compatriots than by the enemy.

Mass rapes of women are also traditional in this region. In 1840 the Muslims raped countless Bosnian Serb women after their military victory; Serbian women were also subject to multiple rapes in the concentration camps during the Second World War.

The religious and national cleavages overlap and nationality has a distinct religious interpretation. It was religion that sharply divided the Serb, Croat and Muslim communities of Bosnia, in particular, separating Christians from Muslims.

Serbia has wanted to create a Greater Serbia from 1860s onwards. The Serbs ruled the inter-war Kingdom of the Serbs, Croats and Slovenes (renamed Yugoslavia in 1929) as a centralised state. Both Croats and Slovenes were unhappy with Serbian dominance, hence the Croatian attempts to destabilise the regime, including the assassination of King Alexander in 1934. Likewise, Croatia has always wanted a Greater Croatia, seeing Bosnians as Islamic Croats.

The formation of Yugoslavia

In 1917, the Croats and Serbs concluded the Deal of Corfu, by which a southern Slav nation was formed, with its own Serbo-Croat language. The 1920 constitution established a unitary state for the Kingdom of the Serbs, Croats and Slovenes, which the Serbs dominated. The Croatians boycotted the constituent assembly and infighting began in the early 1920s, including several political assassinations (e.g. in 1928 Croatian political leaders were shot on the floor of the parliament).

In 1945 there was a brief civil war in Yugoslavia between Tito's communist partisans and the former German allies (Croatian Ustasi and Slovenian Medics) plus the Cetniks (supporters of the royal government-in-exile), with the partisans emerging victorious. Thereafter, Tito's partisans assumed control, abolished the (Serbian) monarchy, and promised equality of all nationalities as well as an end to all inter-ethnic fighting.

Thus, Yugoslavia became a centralised communist state with the facade of a federation of equal and separate republics. Tito claimed to have solved the nationalist issue – albeit through mild repression – and nationalist demands remained more or less muted.

Dissolution of Yugoslavia

Even so, there were minor revolts against this centralised control, such as the demonstrations by the Albanian majority in Serbian Kosovo in 1968 and 1981 and the Croatian uprising of 1971. In 1974 a new constitution was promulgated, which gave greater powers to new autonomous republics; for example Serbia was divided into three separate regions – Serbia, Vojvodina and Kosovo – which had the same status as republics. Bosnia became an autonomous Muslim state despite the ubiquity of the three religions. The 1974 constitution perhaps marks the beginning of the disintegration of the country.

When Tito died in 1980 leadership of the country rotated among the leaders of the different republics, while decisions were made by majority vote in the meetings of the eight heads of the various republics, which became the real powerhouses within the Yugoslav Federation and began to accentuate their nationalistic differences. This all took place within the context of severe economic decline and the loosening of Communist Party control. In effect, the transition to democracy stressed greater ethnic rights rather than improved individual liberties.

These new political elites used nationalism as a means of mobilisation in order to gain, or hold on to, power. Slobodan Milosevic united all Serbs against Albanians in Kosovo; Franjo Tudjman reawakened the traditional Croat hatred of the Serbs; in Slovenia Milan Kucan reacted against Yugoslav centralism.

The new leaders could not agree on the structure of the state. The Serbs wanted a strong central, federal government, while other republics wanted the weakest possible confederation with all powers remaining with the republics. At the same time, Milosevic continued to advocate a Greater Serbia. (Approximately 24 per cent of Serbs lived outside Serbia, mostly in Croatia and Bosnia.)

Nationalism in Yugoslavia has always been egocentric: nationalities want their own autonomy or unified lands, but are never willing to apply this to their own minorities; this is apparent in the Serbs' adamant refusal to allow the Albanian community in Kosovo any sort of autonomy. In fact, the prelude to the civil war was a massive rally in Kosovo in 1987 on the anniversary of the Serbs' defeat by the Turks at Kosovo Field. Milosevic promised to keep Kosovo within Serbia, by force if necessary. To the other republics it seemed the Serbs were planning to dominate Yugoslavia as they had before 1945.

In late 1989 the last federal Prime Minister, Ante Markovic, attempted to introduce a new union for the republics, along with other economic and political reforms. In January 1990, the plan was resoundingly defeated at a special Congress of the Yugoslav Communists, who then formed their own republican groups, ending all central authority. Disparities in economic development among the various republics also exacerbated nationalist differences; Slovenia complained that it was supporting the poorer regions.

Nationalist candidates and parties were elected in all of the republics in 1990 – for example Slobodan Milosevic in Serbia, Milan Kucan in Slovenia and Franjo Tudjman in Croatia (all former Communists) and Muslim fundamentalist Alija Izetbegovic in Bosnia. In Yugoslavia, therefore, communism was ousted by voting for nationalism, that is, for independence.

A brief civil war between Serbia and Slovenia

In October 1990 Slovenia and Croatia, encouraged by both Germany and Austria, proposed a loose confederation of quasi-independent republics, but Serbia dismissed the idea. In the Slovenian referendum held in late 1990, however, 88.5 per cent of Slovenes voted for independence, making its secession inevitable.

Slovenia had a negligible Serbian minority, and so did not figure in Milosevic's Greater Serbia. When Slovenia declared independence in June 1991, a few units of the Yugoslav army (2,000 strong) entered the country, in order to re-establish the federal customs posts and maintain the federation. The army withdrew, however, when Slovenes retaliated and killed forty members of its forces in small skirmishes. The federal army wanted to invade properly and take the country within 24 hours, but Milosevic did not give the go-ahead.

Not long afterwards – again with the strong encouragement of Germany – Croatia, Bosnia and Macedonia declared their independence from Yugoslavia.

Bloody civil war between Serbia and Croatia in Croatian Krajina

Croatia's secession was a different matter, as more than 600,000 Serbs lived in its Krajina region in 1991 (12.5 per cent of the Croatian population, occupying 30 per cent of its territory). The Krajina region was also an intrinsic part of Milosevic's Greater Serbia.

The minority Serb population in Croatia feared the reversion to an anti-Serb, nationalist dictatorship. In mid-1991, after the Croatian declaration of independence and the promulgation of a new constitution depriving Serbs of some of their rights, including the right to use their Cyrillic script, about 350,000 Serbs moved to Serbia, while those remaining declared the Krajina region an independent republic within Croatia. Serbs were dismissed from all government posts and anti-Serb propaganda appeared in the Croatian mass media. The Croats refused to accept the independent Serbian state and armed conflict ensued between the Croats and Krajinian Serbs.

The mostly Serbian Yugoslav army intervened in the conflict, engaging actively on behalf of the Krajinian Serbs. Atrocities were committed against civilians by both sides, with concentration camps, massacres of hundreds of people and the complete destruction of several towns and villages.

The first bout of fighting ended in December 1991 when the United Nations (UN) sent in its peace force, effectively protecting the Serb gains (by this time the Krajinian Serbs controlled about 25 per cent of Croatian territory). Both sides had engaged in massive 'ethnic cleansing' of the regions they controlled, and refugees now posed enormous financial problems for the strained Serbian and Croatian economies.

In January 1993 the Croats launched their second major offensive against the Krajinian Serbs, without success. However, in mid-1995, Croats retook the region in a matter of days – this time the Yugoslav army was not involved in the conflict. A mass migration of 150,000–200,000 Serbs occurred as people fled into Serbian Bosnia. Retaliatory moves were made by the Serbs, who began 'cleansing' towns in Serb-held northern Bosnia, in order to rehouse the Krajinian Serbs. They also emptied several Croatian Serb villages, sending their inhabitants back to Croatia.

(The predominantly Serb eastern Slavonia in north-east Croatia could still pose a problem for the peace process into the more distant future.)

Civil (religious?) war in Bosnia-Hercegovina

Until 1990–91 in Bosnia-Hercegovina the three peoples (Orthodox Serbs, Catholic Croats and Muslim Bosnians) had lived together relatively peacefully for centuries, with only rare instances of inter-group violence and very many mixed marriages. From early 1992 onwards, however, the small republic became the centre of an intense ethnic conflict in which former neighbours, close friends and even relatives became arch enemies.

The civil war in Bosnia can be seen as:

- a struggle against the threat of Islamic fundamentalists, seeking to create an Islamic republic in the heart of Europe;
- a response to Serbian imperialism and attempts to create a Greater Serbian state;
- in the very early stages an attempt by the Yugoslav federal army to preserve the integrity of Yugoslavia;
- a traditional conflict over the possession of land and power;
- the resurgence of centuries-old enmities;
- an outcome of religious differences, in that the leading protagonists in the conflict have played upon those differences;

- a result of Serbian and Croatian collusion to divide up Bosnia between them.

Independence was supported by the vast majority of Muslims and Croats in a referendum, held over 29 February to 1 March 1992, but boycotted by the Serbs. (Constitutionally, agreement of all three religious groups was required for secession.) Bosnia declared independence in March 1992 and received international recognition one month later.

The Bosnian Muslims began the war on 1 March 1992, by attacking a Serbian wedding in Sarajevo and then killing Serbian women and children in Siekovas. The Serbs responded with roadblocks throughout Sarajevo (one-third of the population of which was Serb before 1995). Small massacres were committed by all sides. After the first mass murder of Muslims (in Bijeljina) in April 1992, all-out war began, including the siege of Sarajevo by the Serbs. Intense fighting also broke out between Croats and Bosnians in western Bosnia, around the ancient town of Mostar, which was declared capital of the Bosnian Croatian state of Herceg-Bosna.

In mid-March 1992 the European Union had proposed a partition of Bosnia along ethnic lines acceptable to all three parties. In the end, however, the Bosnian Muslims refused to sign, as they were now sure of international recognition and were hoping for international aid (which never arrived). By the end of the summer of 1992, the Bosnian Serbs (supported by the Yugoslav army) had captured two-thirds of Bosnia-Hercegovina and had implemented large-scale 'ethnic cleansing' of both Croats and Muslims.

Although the Bosnians and Croats made several pacts with each other from April 1992 onwards, the Croatian and Serbian presidents met on at least two occasions to discuss dividing up Bosnia between Serbia and Croatia. The Bosnian Serb and Bosnian Croat leaderships also met to discuss the same proposition. In early 1994, however, at the urging of the USA, the Croats and Muslims joined in a federation. The war against the Serbs continued, with atrocities on all sides, constant ethnic cleansing of various regions, occasional cease-fires (thirty-six in

all between 1991 and 1995) and even peaceful 'population exchanges' between Croat and Bosnian allies.

In mid-1995 NATO aeroplanes and the French/British Rapid
Action Force began strategic bombing of Bosnian Serb positions
around Sarajevo, in retaliation for the second bombing of a
Sarajevo market (killing thirty-seven and injuring eighty-five
civilians). Even as late as July 1995, it still seemed that the fate of
Bosnia was going to be decided on the battlefield, rather than at
the negotiating table.

Western response to the conflict

For four years international policy in the region rested on
continuous diplomatic activity to achieve a lasting cease-fire,
while maintaining a small contingent of UN peace-keepers on the
ground and making continual threats of air strikes against
Bosnian Serb aggression.

It is argued by some commentators that right from the
beginning, during late 1991, the West – especially Germany and
Austria – were too swift in pressing for international recognition
of both Slovenia and Croatia, in particular as this ignored
Croatian authoritarianism, war crimes and abuse of (Serb) minority rights. The European Union's almost immediate recognition
of Bosnian independence in April 1992 is also seen as seriously
exacerbating the situation, if not triggering the actual conflict.

From 1991 onwards the overall tendency of European and US
policy led to the dissolution first of Yugoslavia, then of Bosnia,
since Westerners generally believed that dividing the countries
into ethnically homogeneous districts would end the conflict (a
vindication of ethnic cleansing). The 1992 Vance–Owen plan,
the 1994 Contact Group's plan (Russia, Germany, France, the
UK and the USA) and the 1995 American Dayton peace plan all
partitioned the republic along ethnic lines, even though the
population is still thoroughly mixed. The last two plans divided
the republic into two areas (51 per cent Muslim/Croat and 49
per cent Serb), which the Bosnian Serbs had always rejected up
until 1995, since they already held 70 per cent of Bosnian

territory. But with the 1995 Muslim–Croat joint offensive they began to lose much of that territory in western and northern Bosnia, and were more willing to accept peace terms.

From the outset, Western policy was anti-Serb, even though atrocities were committed by all sides in this war. It also failed to recognise that the Serbs and Bosnian Serbs were two distinct groups of people. The Serbs were viewed as the original aggressors and that image remained. As a result, only Serbia was subject to the UN economic embargo imposed in 1992. Even when Milosevic withdrew the Yugoslav army from Bosnia, and blocked all but humanitarian aid to the Bosnian Serbs, leaving them to fight on alone, there was only a partial lifting of sanctions in terms of travel and cultural/sports exchanges. Economic sanctions against Serbia remained in place until the signing of the Dayton accord in late 1995 and went on to cripple an already declining economy. They also hurt the economies of other states in the region for which Serbia was a key export market, such as Macedonia and Bulgaria.

In May 1993 the UN Security Council established an international war crimes tribunal to investigate war crimes committed during the civil war. In July 1993 NATO planes carried out limited air strikes against Serbs for the first time. The threat of air strikes had led to the implementation of a heavy-weapons exclusion zone around Sarajevo, although this did not completely halt the shelling of the city.

On the whole, the UN peace-keeping forces in former Yugoslavia were simply onlookers to a continuing conflict. They could not actually keep the peace, as there was no peace to keep between the main combatants, although their presence helped to keep the Croats out of the Krajina region for some time. For three years the international community in general and the EU in particular seemed incapable of solving the war. It was not until the UN peace-keepers were partially withdrawn, a French/British Rapid Action Force was assembled around Sarajevo and an intensive air-bombing campaign began (August 1995) that the Bosnian Serbs were forced to sue for peace on the basis of the 1995 American Dayton peace plan.

Meanwhile, back in Macedonia

During the 1990s Macedonia has been the only republic of the former Yugoslavia to have avoided war. There were some skirmishes on its border with Serbia, but these ended in June 1993, with the deployment of UN troops. In 1992 the country's leaders formally declared that Macedonia would not attempt territorial expansion or interfere in the internal affairs of another country.

Internally the country's greatest problem is tension between the Macedonian Slavs and the ethnic Albanians (22 per cent of the population). Issues involving use of the Albanian language (e.g. in education) have caused the greatest tensions. The dispute has been exacerbated by the occasional intervention of the Albanian government on behalf of the Macedonian Albanians, some of whom have advocated total secession from the republic.

Externally, Macedonia was unable to achieve full status as a member of the international community because of opposition by Greece to the use of the name Macedonia and of the five-starred Greek/Macedonian emblem on its flag. The Greek government also claimed Macedonians were making irredentist claims on parts of northern Greece. The Greeks therefore applied economic sanctions against the new republic which, coupled with the loss of Serbia as its chief export market, crippled an already ailing economy.

As part of the 1995 US peace mission in former Yugoslavia, however, the Macedonians and Greeks were persuaded to settle their differences, which they did through a treaty signed in October 1995, by which the Macedonians agreed to alter their flag and the Greeks to end the economic boycott. The only issue remaining to be resolved was the name of the republic.

Apportioning the blame

Between 1991 and 1995 within former Yugoslavia, over 250,000 died and over 4 million were subject to ethnic cleansing. The Serbs have always borne the blame for this conflict, because:

- they are by far the most numerous nationality and therefore are seen to commit more crimes;
- Milosevic triggered the conflict originally with his speeches about creating a Greater Serbia;
- Serbs initiated the armed conflict by sending troops into Slovenia in 1991;
- Serbs and Bosnian Serbs originally stalled all plans to find a constitutional settlement in the early years of the conflict.

But the Muslims and Croats have obstructed the peace process and broken the cease-fires just as often as the Serbs. Croats and Muslims have also committed atrocities against Bosnian Serbs. In fact, there is proof of atrocities committed by Bosnian Muslims against their own people in Sarajevo in order to lay blame on the Serbs and secure Western assistance. For example, it is reputed that the infamous 'bread-line massacre' on 27 May 1992 (when sixteen people were killed in Sarajevo while queuing for bread) was attributable to Muslim forces, as was the aforementioned Sarajevo market bombing in June 1995. After Operation Storm, by which Croatia retook the Krajina region in 1995, older Serb inhabitants who had been unable to flee were systematically murdered by Croatian soldiers. So, atrocities were committed by all sides, as has been the case in this region for over a century.

In hindsight, there is also no doubt that the Western powers made several mistakes that exacerbated the conflict: recognising the break-away states too early in 1991–92; for much of the war merely threatening to use NATO air strikes; constantly disagreeing among themselves; expecting too much from the various protagonists with regard to their capacity to compromise and make binding agreements; sending in a peace-keeping force with little more than observer status.

Concluding remarks

The latest peace treaty has come about through exhaustion, a general realisation that conflict and genocide were leading nowhere, and Milosevic's desperate need to end UN sanctions. At the time of writing, it does seem that peace has emerged – or perhaps it would be safer to use the words of Martin Bell, the BBC's correspondent in Bosnia since 1992: 'the indefinite closing-down of the war'. With the amount of aid that is now being promised to Bosnia from the International Monetary Fund (IMF) and World Bank, it is very unlikely that war will break out again in the more immediate future. But peace has been achieved only by the splitting up of Bosnia.

Post-Dayton Bosnia will remain an ethnically mixed country, although much less mixed than before. There will certainly be minor skirmishes and several 'isolated incidences'. Four flash points for the future could be:

1   the refusal of Bosnian Serbs to remain in a Sarajevo governed by Bosnian Muslims;
2   potential conflict in eastern Slavonia as it falls under Croat control again in late 1997;
3   continuing localised conflict between Croats and Muslims in Mostar and other regions 'shared' by the Croat–Bosnian Federation;
4   the possible desire for the Bosnian Serbs to attempt to incorporate their 49 per cent of Bosnia into Serbia.

Finally, one aspect of the Dayton Treaty will never be fulfilled, not in the more immediate future in any rate: most people will not return to their former homes and property, as many of them are no longer standing – they have been destroyed during the war or blown up subsequently – or have been occupied by members of the other ethnic groups. In fact, it is very doubtful that free movement of peoples within Bosnia (one of the main provisions of Dayton) will ever be achieved.

Two attempts at forming a south Slav state have now failed and ended in the same types of atrocities and ethnic cleansing. There could never be a third 'Yugoslavia' after such gruesome occurrences.

Further reading

Magas Branka, *The Destruction of Yugoslavia*, Verso, 1993.

Milovan Djilas, *Tito, the Inside Story*, Weidenfeld and Nicholson, 1980.

Misha Glenny, *The Fall of Yugoslavia: The Third Balkan War*, Penguin Books, 1992.

Florence Hamlish Levinsohn, *Belgrade – Among the Serbs*, Ivan R. Dee, 1994.

George Schöpflin, 'Yugoslavia', in *Regulation of Ethnic Conflict* (B. O'Leary and J. McGarry, eds), Routledge, 1994.

Laura Silber and Allan Little, *The Death of Yugoslavia*, Penguin Books/BBC Books, 1995.

In OMRI's *Transition* and the Radio Free Europe/Radio Liberty weekly journal, there are several articles on nationalism, the problems of minorities in ECE in general and the split of Czechoslovakia in particular (e.g. *Transition*, 2 (1), 12 January 1996). The *Nationalist Papers* journal also contains several articles on the ECE region since 1989 (vols 18–23).

8
Social cleavages

all social problems are overruled by the concept of nationhood. (Gyorgy Markus)

The monopoly on all aspects of society by the Communists specifically prevented the organisation of any independent group interests. Accordingly, when the communist regimes began to collapse in 1989, intermediary groups were almost non-existent – they were certainly not numerous or strong enough to act as the foundations of new party political systems. Social cleavages will certainly re-establish themselves in the future, but it will necessarily be a very long and slow process. At the moment, though, it is like starting with a completely clean slate.

Definition of social cleavage

A social cleavage is a division within society whereby a certain number of people or organisations oppose each other within the context of some political or economic conflict. But, it is a *social*, rather than a purely *political*, division.

Cleavages occur in any political system as a result of conflicts or issues that need to be tackled within the decision-making process. They divide society into various groups, around which voters align themselves and political parties organise. People's voting behaviour can usually be explained by looking at the cleavage structure within any society.

According to Gallagher, Laver and Mair, any social cleavage possesses the following features:

- it reflects a major *division within society*, that is, it is not simply an ideological division about different ideas, and it juxtaposes clearly identifiable groups within society, for example farmers against town dwellers, employees against employers, Catholics against Protestants, Slovaks against Czechs;

- people clearly *identify themselves with the group*, so that they are very conscious of belonging to the group – for example Hungarian-speaking Romanians in Transylvania feel different from the majority of Romanians, Muslim Albanians in Serbian Kosovo feel a world apart from the Christian Orthodox Serbs;

- a cleavage has to find *organisational expression*, primarily through a political party, but also through a pressure group or church; the group then uses the organisation in order to express their demands within a conflictual situation.

These are more than differences in ideas. In post-communist society there were many identities associated with different ideas, for example rapid versus gradual economic reform, West versus East: such divisions exist as ideological differences between the new political elites, not as cleavages within society.

Traditional cleavage structure

In their classic work *Cleavage Structures, Party Systems and Voter Alignments*, S. M. Lipset and S. Rokkan identified four types of cleavages within Western European societies: the centre–periphery, church–state, employee–employer, and rural–urban cleavages. They demonstrated how cleavage structure and voting behaviour were related. They also concluded that social cleavage structure had altered very little in Western Europe since the extension of the franchise in the 1920s. The political party systems of the late 1960s were, therefore, still the result of the great cleavage lines at the end of the nineteenth century.

These cleavage lines became linked with the establishment of certain *categories* of political parties: liberal, agrarian, conservative, socialist, social democratic, or Christian parties. The relations between cleavage lines and the respective political parties varied in intensity, and the structure of any country's party system emerged from the interaction of the various cleavages. For example, England's primarily two-party system was a result of the predominance, if not exclusivity, of the class cleavage, while Holland's multi-party system derived from the interaction of the prevailing religious and class cleavages.

In terms of socio-economic cleavages, socialist, social democratic or labour parties organised workers against owners in order to reform capitalism. Agrarian parties defended the interests and values of traditional farming communities against the commercial and industrial classes of the cities.

In the nation-building process, liberal parties, focusing on democracy, individual rights and the free market, opposed the conservative, nationalist forces represented, for example, within the Catholic Church. Regional parties arose against the centralist system of the nation state and defended the interests and values of certain ethnic or regionalist sub-cultures.

It should be emphasised that:

- the conclusions reached by Lipset and Rokkan were based on data and opinion poll research up to the mid-1960s;
- political behaviour and voter alignment have altered considerably in the succeeding thirty years – leading to sometimes dramatic changes within existing party systems.

However, the overall framework of their analysis is still as relevant today as it was in the late 1960s, and serves as a basis on which to examine emerging social cleavages in ECE.

Social cleavages in inter-war ECE

In the inter-war period, the social cleavage structure of ECE societies was at an embryonic stage, being much less structured and less organised than in Western Europe. There were several reasons for this – some country specific, others more general.

In 1918 most of the countries of ECE were brand new (e.g. Czechoslovakia) or re-established nations (e.g. Poland). Their political culture was, therefore, rather underdeveloped, and prone to paternalistic and authoritarian tendencies. It was not really surprising, then, that normal democratic politics lasted a very short time (seven years in Poland, ten in Yugoslavia) before the advent of dictatorial and authoritarian regimes, which usually suspended parliamentary politics and abolished political parties. In addition, the region's economies were still largely peasant based (except for the Czech lands), so their societies were highly conservative and traditional by nature, with little involvement of the peasant majority in politics.

There was very little industry in most of these countries – with the exception of northern Bohemia and northern Moravia in Czechoslovakia and odd regional pockets in Poland, Romania, Bulgaria, Yugoslavia and Hungary. This meant that the *class cleavage* was hardly apparent and social democratic parties were generally weak and under-represented in parliament (being minute parties in Yugoslavia and Romania, and never gaining more than 13 per cent of votes in Bulgaria or never more than 10 per cent of seats in Hungary).

In terms of the *religious cleavage*, Christian democratic parties did exist and achieved moderate representation in some countries, such as Czechoslovakia before 1938 and Poland before 1926. On the whole, though, strong religious affiliation and voting behaviour were regionalised, for example Hlinka's People's Party in Slovakia and the Christian Democrats in Slovenia. Generally, religion – whether Roman Catholic, Eastern Orthodox or Muslim – tended to play a deeply conservative role in politics, reinforcing the authoritarian tendencies mentioned above (e.g. in Hungary, Poland and Czechoslovakia).

As a rule, the peasant party emerged as the largest party in most parliamentary assemblies, for example in Hungary and Bulgaria (before the Bulgarian Peasant Union split into several factions), reflecting the fact that *the rural–urban split* was the major cleavage within society between the wars. Given the distinct agricultural and rural character of these societies at the time, this was hardly surprising. This cleavage was particularly strong in Hungary, where there was a very clear division in society between the liberal, modern, Western, intellectual and partially Jewish urban forces centred in Budapest and the conservative, traditional, nationalist, peasant-oriented and anti-Semitic populist groups in the outlying provinces. It also dominated Bulgarian and Romanian politics, although electoral support for the various peasant parties could not always be translated into parliamentary seats because of party splits (Bulgaria after 1927) or rigged elections (Romania).

Throughout the inter-war period, as during earlier and later periods, *nationalism* was by far the strongest social cleavage, and was used as a mechanism of mass mobilisation by many politicians. As a result, there was much political intolerance towards the ethnic minorities – particularly Jews and gypsies – within all of these states, which acted as a precursor to the emerging fascist movements. Furthermore, the ethnic split existing in Yugoslavia led to violent clashes between the different nationalist groupings just as intense as anything in the 1990s.

The ECE societies were quite fragmented along ethnic or regionalist lines, with each country possessing its own minority within its borders (except for Hungary which became a much more homogeneous nation after the loss of most of its minority populations in the 1920 Trianon Peace Treaty).

Politically speaking, Czechoslovakia was the only country within the region that possessed a normal 'European' party system and even then the Agrarian Party played a crucial role within the famous '*petka*' (an almost permanent coalition of five parties – or rather five party leaders – which formed the basis of all inter-war governments in the country).

Social cleavages under communism

It is impossible to talk of social cleavages during the communist era because of the total dominance by the various Communist parties of the whole political system and the complete subordination of all intermediate bodies to the Party. The normal Western cleavage structure was basically non-existent: social classes hardly existed because of the enforced egalitarianism; divisions between town and country were turned upside down, as explained below; nationalist or ethnic differences were not allowed to express themselves; religious affiliation was suppressed, even in Roman Catholic Poland. The main division in society was therefore a strictly political one: them versus us, the Communists versus the people.

This division in society expressed itself in different ways: in the revolts against the state during the 1950–70s; in the emergence of politically motivated opposition groups like Charter 77 in Czechoslovakia or Solidarity in Poland; in the general apathy, disinterest or resentment of the vast majority in the countless rituals they were expected to perform; and, finally, in the 'revolutions' of 1989 onwards.

The class divide

In theory there was no class cleavage during forty years of enforced egalitarianism – with no private owners, there could be no worker–owner conflict. In any case, communism stood the normal Western class differences on their heads, since blue-collar, manual workers had both higher status and greater pay than many white-collar workers, professionals and intellectuals.

Religion

Religious observation was either curtailed (Albania), persecuted (Romania and Bulgaria) or only just tolerated in situations where the Catholic Church agreed some sort of *modus vivendi* with the communist state (Poland and Czechoslovakia). In any case, within a strictly one-party state, religious affiliation was not allowed to offer any ideological alternative to the ruling Marxist-Leninist doctrine.

In many places a residue of religious affiliation remained, whatever the authorities attempted – even in Albania. In Poland, for example, the vast majority of the population remained avowedly Roman Catholic, and the Church became a centre of nationalist opposition to the Soviet-imposed communist regime. (Many leading Polish Communists themselves were Catholics.) Slovenia and Croatia also remained predominantly Catholic, Hungary and Slovakia mainly Catholic, and there were significant Catholic minorities in the Czech Republic and Bosnia. In some places a Christian democratic party was allowed to survive as a satellite party within the communist regime, for example the People's Party in Czechoslovakia, and the Christian Democratic Union in the GDR.

Rural–urban split

The same applied to any potential peasants' movements or parties, with the added disadvantage that it was particularly the peasant/agrarian parties and their leaders that were subject to the most severe persecution by Communists in the immediate post-war period. Only in Poland was a United Peasants' Party (ZSL) allowed to exist after 1948 – again as a Communist satellite party, not an independent organisation. (Its aim was to ensure the compliance of the many Polish peasant farmers to communism.)

In any case, the collectivisation of the agricultural sector which started in the 1950s in all ECE countries changed the social structure rapidly – except in Poland where the process was ended in the mid-1950s. The interests and values of the rural population emanating from the collectivised agrarian sector differed widely from those of the pre-1950s rural population. In fact, the cooperative farmers were quite rich in some countries (e.g. Czechoslovakia, Hungary, Bulgaria and the GDR) and far better off than the normal city dwellers, especially when the peasantry were modernised and given the right to grow their own produce on the side. Such countries under communism were characterised by poor cities and towns surrounded by rich villages: it was as if the rural–urban split had been stood on its head.

Ethnic/regionalist cleavage

The one social cleavage that was kept under tight control during the communist era was the ethnic/regional divide. Ethnic divisions within Yugoslavia, for example, were still present under the surface but hardly ever expressed themselves openly – the revolts in Albanian Kosovo (1968) and Croatia (1971) being notable exceptions. The activities of most ECE ethnic minorities were constrained by force – such as the Hungarian-speakers in Romanian Transylvania, Croats in Yugoslavia, and Turkish-speaking Bulgarians. Campaigns of assimilation were often carried out against such groups in the name of the Marxist revolution – the most comprehensive being Todor Zhivkov's campaigns against the Bulgarian Turks between 1984 and 1989.

Cleavages in ECE since 1989

The present social cleavage structure in ECE has similarities with that in Western Europe, but it is in an embryonic state. On the whole, parties are supported by a variety of groups, and it is impossible to make a clear and definite correlation between social groups and the emerging party structure. The new parties that appeared after 1989 tended to receive support right across the social spectrum, and it will take a considerable time before social cleavages are a major factor in people's electoral behaviour.

This is because beliefs, ideas or issues are much more important than social standing or group association. The ordinary 'worker' in the Czech Republic, for example, feels that capitalism and the continuation of free-market economic reforms are more important than identification with his or her peer group, trade unions or social democrats.

The latent class cleavage

The traditional class cleavage – between workers and owners – was basically destroyed by the communist regimes, along with all interest organisations, independent trade unions and other intermediary bodies which could have expressed workers' interests outside of the parameters of the Communist Party. In most ECE elections after 1990, there were no clearly cohesive working-class groups and very little self-perception according to social class. One of the reasons why the revived social democratic parties – many re-established by émigrés returning from the West – failed to make any impact on the first elections was that there was no distinct worker-oriented class constituency on which to build. As a result no party could claim to speak for the workers, who therefore tended to vote for all parties across the whole political spectrum. In the Polish 1991 elections, for example, the manual workers voted for parties of the left and right, Catholic and secular: in fact, the strongly nationalist Confederation for an Independent Poland (KPN) gained the largest segment of worker support (12 per cent).

Similarly, the managerial/capitalist class is not represented by a well defined social group, although there are several parties that appeal to the new entrepreneurs. At present this group represents only a very small minority in society – about 10 per cent.

For this reason, therefore, a latent class cleavage – or an 'under-developed labour-capital cleavage' as Gyorgy Markus calls it – is emerging in a rather nineteenth-century form, between a small number of very rich/millionaire entrepreneurs and the vast majority of very poor state employees, or the employees in small, privatised industrial plants (e.g. textiles or simple machinery), whose wages have improved only minimally, if at all. In addition, a type of underclass is developing already, since sizeable numbers of people, especially pensioners, are being forced to rely on the quite inadequate state benefits that are leaving most of them close to or below the poverty line. Middle-aged people in areas of high unemployment also tend to belong to this underclass.

The blurred class cleavage

Immediately after the revolutions, the left–right ideological division became blurred throughout ECE, because almost all political parties, including the successor communist parties, were overwhelmingly committed to dismantling state ownership, introducing a Western-type market economy and encouraging private ownership as soon as possible. As a result, the economic programmes of all parties were almost identical, with most parties remaining very vague about the specifics of the economic transformation. Very often parties normally considered 'left' were keener on a swift transition than the more nationalist/conservative parties of the 'right'.

Disagreement came later over the speed of economic transformation, when it became clear that the transition process would benefit only a small minority of people. Then the communist successor parties, in particular, began to defend the interests of the disillusioned majority – leading to their electoral successes after October 1993 in Poland, Hungary and Bulgaria. No doubt class voting will grow in the future when these differences become more clearly defined.

The hidden rural–urban split

Throughout ECE there has been the resurrection of the previously important agrarian parties. Apart from 15 per cent of votes attained by the communist successor Polish Peasants' Party (PSL) and 11.4 per cent for the Hungarian FKGP in the 1993 and 1990 elections, post-1989 agrarian parties have all achieved less than 10 per cent of the vote – or have disappeared completely, as in the Czech Republic – and have had little impact on the emerging party systems. (The FKGP was part of the first conservative–centre-right Hungarian coalition government for a time, until that government partially reneged on its promises concerning restitution of land to peasant farmers; the PSL has been part of the centre-left, ex-communist Polish government since 1993, providing the Premier until early 1995.)

The agrarian parties that attempted to reorganise after 1989 – like the Hungarian FKGP and the Romanian Peasants' Party – found that their constituencies had changed dramatically. The conservative and traditional rural electorate tended to remain loyal to the ex-communist parties in many instances. In Poland the ex-communist PSL and the Solidarity Peasant Alliance garnered 52 per cent of the peasant electorate between them in the 1991 elections, but the main reason for that was the continuity of support for the PSL.

The distorted rural–urban split

The rural–urban split emerged in the first post-revolutionary elections in a different guise. It was reflected in a difference of attitudes between the more conservative and traditional communist voters in the countryside and the more progressive and reformist non-communist voters, found mostly in sizeable urban centres. Several polls revealed continuing support for the former Communists in the rural areas because of the inability to break entrenched habits. In some countries this was particularly marked (e.g. Albania, Bulgaria and Romania). In fact, this trend was noticeable as early as 1990 in the first Hungarian municipal elections, in which the two reformist liberal parties won in the cities, while villages voted for former Communist functionaries running as independents. A similar phenomenon was also observable in the 1990 Czechoslovak parliamentary elections.

Peasants farmers are still a distinctive social group in ECE, especially in Poland, Hungary, Bulgaria, Romania and former Yugoslavia, and peasant parties can still play an important role (in Poland and Hungary, for example). But the peasant farmers now do not vote primarily for the peasant parties as they did before the war, except in Poland.

A weakened religious cleavage

There is little evidence of a religious cleavage because of the attempted or enforced atheism of the post-war Communist dictatorship – except in Poland, where 95 per cent of today's 38 million Poles consider themselves (at least nominally) Roman Catholic.

Generally speaking, though, religion seems to have had only a minor effect on voting behaviour; for example, in the 1992 federal elections in Czechoslovakia, there was only a slightly lower vote for the Christian democratic parties in the Czech Republic than Slovakia (8.6 per cent compared with 8.9 per cent), where there are substantially more Catholics. Moreover, Catholic parties obtained only 10.8 per cent of total votes in the 1993 Polish elections (down from 21 per cent in 1991). Elsewhere their voting totals are very low: 5.5 per cent in Hungary, almost non-existent in Albania, Bulgaria and Romania. Only in Slovenia (14.5 per cent) and East Germany (41 per cent) did they perform particularly well. (It is difficult to consider the East German result along with the rest, since the electoral campaign was dominated by West German politicians and political parties and the result was distorted by the Christian Democratic Union (CDU) being the clear champion of the rapid unification of the two Germanies.)

The sporadic religious cleavage

Throughout most of ECE, religious disputes still emerge in the odd policy difference with the state, for example over the restitution of former Church property confiscated by the Communists. In Poland, however, the Catholic Church has meddled in the affairs of state, particularly moral and constitutional issues.

The new Polish media law states that journalists must maintain 'Christian values'. The Catholic Church was instrumental in pushing a very controversial anti-abortion act through parliament, which seriously damaged the standing of the ex-Solidarity Suchocka government in 1993. Likewise, the Church's insistence on being given a constitutional role within the state prevented a full constitution from being drafted and seriously divided previous centre-right, Solidarity governments between 1989 and 1993.

The coalition between the Democratic Left Alliance (SLD) and PSL (ex-communist parties) delayed a bill regulating the Church's role in Polish society from late 1993 onwards, blocking it for the last time in September 1995. Hence, the Church entered the 1995 presidential campaign, giving its full support from the pulpit to (Catholic) Lech Walesa, and being wholeheartedly against (atheist) Alexander Kwasniewski, the SLD candidate, claiming the choice was between 'Christian' and 'pagan' values. This did not have the desired effect. A survey taken in September/October 1995 indicated that two-thirds of regular churchgoers in Poland thought the priesthood should not instruct them on how to vote. Moreover, in the presidential elections Kwasniewski performed just as well in the rural areas (where the Church's influence is stronger) as in the urban centres.

Otherwise, the only place where religion seems to have played a real role of cleavage is in former Yugoslavia, within the context of the various civil wars between Catholics, Orthodox Christians and Muslims, where religion intensified the ethnic divide and was used as a symbol to justify nationalistic differences. In other places, such as Slovakia, tension between the different churches – Greek Catholic and Roman Catholic – remains strong, but does not manifest itself in actual conflict.

Predominance of the ethnic/nationalist cleavage

The lack of the cleavages mentioned above means that the only existing cleavage with which the electors in ECE can really be mobilised is the ethnic/nationalist cleavage. This is clearly the case where ethnic or nationalist differences are apparent: Czechs versus Slovaks, Serbs versus Croats, Bulgarians versus Turks, Romanians versus the Hungarian minority, Slovaks versus the Hungarian minority, and so on.

Nationalist problems even affected the seemingly homogeneous Hungarian state, in the sense that the post-1989 political leaders felt obliged to pay attention to the abuse of human rights of Hungarians abroad, for example in Slovakia, in Romanian Transylvania and in the Vojvodina area of Serbia. Former Premier Josef Antall claimed to speak 'emotionally and spiritually' on behalf of all 15 million Hungarians in Europe – that is, including those living in neighbouring countries.

An economic form of nationalism also arose in homogeneous Poland, where people were mobilised by certain political forces to oppose the influence of foreign businesses within the privatisation process (selling the 'family silver'). Laws on large-scale privatisation were defeated in parliament and the whole process of economic transition was severely retarded in the spring of 1993. Economic nationalism was also used as a major argument in the split of Czechoslovakia by Czech Premier Vaclav Klaus – that is, the Czechs would be better off without the Slovaks.

Elsewhere, the ethnic/nationalist cleavage plays a crucial role in the body politic, and nationalism is a major means of electoral mobilisation, for example Milosevic using the SPS as a vehicle to re-advocate a Greater Serbia and thereby achieve personal power. In similar fashion, President Tudjman promoted the idea of a Greater Croatia.

Often the presence of ethnic minorities is used as a rallying point for parties speaking on behalf of the majority nationalist group; for example, in Romania the Party of Romanian National Unity (PUNR) takes a very strong anti-Hungarian stance. In Slovakia, the HZDS, led by Meciar, has also used the Hungarian minority (11 per cent of the population) as scapegoats and has endeavoured to deprive the Hungarian community of some of their constitutional rights. The ethnic Bulgarians have attempted to minimise the impact of the Turkish DPS politicians by banning all parties which had a specifically ethnic character. Similarly, Greek ethnic parties have been banned in Albania.

The principal problem with the predominance of the ethnic or nationalist cleavage throughout ECE countries is that cultural-ideological issues are far less open to compromise than, say, socio-economic issues, as has been demonstrated for decades in Northern Ireland, Corsica or the Spanish Basque country. The Yugoslav situation since 1987 is the classic example in ECE.

Issues rather than cleavages

It is rather a question of different issues or political divisions that emerged as the basis for party competition in ECE during the first five to six years after the revolutions, rather than the parties expressing basic social cleavages.

Quick versus slow economic reform. The dominant political division is related to the speed and extent of economic reform – between those parties favouring rapid economic changes in a Polish-type 'shock therapy' and those parties promoting a more gradual approach, giving more importance to social welfare. Initially, the new, mainly ex-dissident post-communist parties advocating rapid economic change were supported at the polls – with the implicit proviso that they would improve the material living standards of the majority. When immediate improvements did not materialise, voters turned to those parties taking a more gradualistic approach, that is, to the communist successor parties.

In Hungary the pace of economic reform was one of the principal issues that divided the main democratic forces in the 1990 elections, with the neo-liberal SZDSZ favouring a Polish-type 'big bang' approach and the MDF proposing a less painful transition. In Bulgaria, the non-communist SDS represented the former approach, the ex-communist BSP the latter. Even in the Czech Republic, where the necessity of the economic reforms is widely accepted, the Social Democrats dramatically increased their vote in the June 1996 elections (from 6.5 per cent to 26.4 per cent), by advocating a slower, more humane process of transition.

This difference in economic approach was also one of the principal reasons behind the split in the Czechoslovak Federation. The Czechs, under the then leadership of Finance Minister Vaclav Klaus, pursued a rapid process of both small-scale and large-scale privatisation, with a very definite neo-liberal orientation in rhetoric. In Slovakia, however, the government under Vladimir Meciar advocated a slower process of privatisation, paying more attention to the social costs of the transition.

It should be stressed that this is not a 'reform versus anti-reform' cleavage, as some observers have suggested, since no one doubts the validity of total economic reform – it is rather the way in which the reforms are to be achieved. Even in those countries where the reform process has sometimes stalled (Bulgaria or Slovakia) or was very slow to start (Romania), there is no party that would campaign to end the reform process and the prevalence of market forces – although the Association of Slovak

Workers (ZRS) and the Czech hard-line Communist Party (SCK) are not far from an anti-market stance.

In Poland, Hungary, Bulgaria and Slovakia market reforms have been considerably slowed down – principally by the communist successor parties – but this has been in response to the majority of the electorate, which wants a slow-down.

The Polish SLD/PSL and Slovak HZDS/SNS/ZRS governments have come closest to a reversal of the reform process by claiming the government should control all future top positions within newly privatised companies and by allowing former communists to regain positions of economic power: a feature now known as 'cronyism'.

Eastern versus Western international outlook. Parallel to the 'pace of reform' issue, there is a certain West versus East division in terms of foreign policy issues, which is again much more a question of speed rather than substance. All ECE countries look westwards and seek to participate in Western European institutions – NATO, the EU, the European Free Trade Area, and the Council of Europe. No ECE nation contemplates rejoining a string of alliances dominated by Russia and all would criticise President Yeltsin for warning against a NATO expansion eastwards. But there are some countries that are being careful not to annoy Russia and want to remain on good terms if possible (e.g. Bulgaria and Slovakia).

This issue really reflects itself in the difference between a pro-European and a more nationalist/populist approach. Poland, the Czech Republic, Slovenia and Hungary seek as swift as possible integration into the economic, cultural and political communities of Western Europe under both centre-right and centre-left governments. Such governments also welcome foreign investment and foreign companies in the economic restructuring of the country.

Other governments advocate a nationalist and populist approach, looking to keep the 'family silver' for the nation itself and deciding not to sell the country to foreigners. Such governments remain somewhat suspicious of foreign economic investment and integration into Europe. The Bulgarian, Romanian and Slovak governments fit into this category. (In the spring of 1996 the Bulgarian BSP government went as far as to reject the country's potential future membership of NATO.)

De-communisation. The issue of de-communisation, and the whole question of how to deal with former organisations and supporters of the communist regime, particularly collaborators of the secret police, has also caused deep and sometimes antagonistic rifts between various parties, particularly in Poland, Hungary and the Czech Republic. In Poland, the communist successor parties and the more liberal members of several ex-Solidarity parties have argued against recrimination, as have President Havel and other Czech liberals. The main concern of such liberals is the need to look into the future and to achieve a successful economic and political transition, rather than dwell on the past. Conservative and Christian parties, however, often became preoccupied with the presence of former Communist officials in the state administration and in key positions within the economy. Most of these parties argued vehemently for some rectification of the past, aimed at removing all supporters of the former regime from the top political, economic and administrative positions in society.

In Poland the six-month-old, Catholic-led Olszewski government fell in June 1992 over the issue of de-communisation, in that it accused some prominent politicians from the Solidarity opposition of collaboration with the secret police during the communist years, including President Walesa himself.

In Hungary, the process of de-communisation was one of the main issues which divided the main right-wing parties within the 1990–94 Christian democratic coalition: the MDF, FKGP, and KDNP wanted a 'screening law' while the neo-liberal SZDSZ was against such a process.

The first and most comprehensive 'screening law' was passed in 1991 in the former Czechoslovakia. Not only did it split the various parties along the lines mentioned above, it also represented another major difference between the Czechs and the Slovaks, since the latter's governments took no steps to implement the law within Slovakia.

The one thing that has become abundantly clear in recent years is that the process of de-communisation is not a vote winner. Indeed, one of the main reasons why the MDF lost so abysmally in the 1994 elections was their concentration on the need to carry through a comprehensive process of de-communisation throughout society. In the 1995 Polish presidential elections, Lech Walesa's anti-communist campaign also did not find favour among the electorate. Voters are far more concerned about their declining living standards than they are about a 'velvet restoration' of Communist officials.

Personal differences among elites. Personal differences, not social cleavages, have often been the basis of party differentiation in all ECE countries. The first new political parties after 1989 were created at the 'top' and then superimposed on society at large. The ensuing break-away groups and splits from the original formations – for example Solidarity fragmented into fifteen different groups within eighteen months of its June 1989 election victory, and the Czech Civic Forum split into six different groupings within nine months of their 1990 electoral success – occurred mainly at the level of the political elites.

This meant that during the first parliaments political differences were more frequently articulated within the various parliamentary assemblies rather than within society in general. This has usually led to a very complex set of political alliances within most ECE parliaments, with very few parliaments reflecting dominant social cleavages. This is why Attila Agh described the political parties as 'floating' over the weak cleavages of the society.

Conclusion: lack of identification

The political parties in ECE did not emerge along existing cleavage lines, as was the case in Western Europe at the end of the nineteenth century. Party formation is not rooted in conflicts within the society or a representation of interests. Rather, the parties have been constructed at the level of a polarised and highly ideological political elite.

It is difficult to identify the social bases of support for different parties. Post-communist societies are characterised by a high level of change and flux. The interests of individuals and elite groups are changing rapidly as a result of the economic transition – hence, the very high level of volatility in electoral support for the parties.

Further reading

Attila Agh, 'The Emerging Party System in ECE', *Budapest Papers on Democratic Transition*, No. 13, Budapest University of Economics, 1991.

Stefano Bartolini and Peter Mair, *Identity, Competition and Electoral Availability: The Stabilisation of European Electorates, 1885–1985*, Cambridge University Press, 1990.

Geoffrey Evans and Stephen Whitefield, 'Identifying the Bases of Party Competition in Eastern Europe', *British Journal of Political Science*, 23, October 1993.

Michael Gallagher, Michael Laver and Peter Mair, *Representative Government in Western Europe* (chapter 4), McGraw-Hill, 1992.

Herbert Kitschelt, 'The Formation of Party Systems in ECE', *Politics and Society*, 20 (1), March 1992.

Samuel M. Lipset and Stein Rokkan, 'Cleavage Structures, Party Systems and Voter Alignments: An Introduction', in *Party Systems and Voter Alignments* (S. M. Lipset and Stein Rokkan, eds), The Free Press, 1967.

Gyorgy Markus, 'Parties, Camps and Cleavages in Postcommunist Hungary', *Probleme der Internationalen Zusammenarbeit*, 129, September 1992.

9
Elections

The most efficient way to retain democracy is to have constant voting. It defeats the principle of democracy, not to have regular elections. (J. Madison)

Free and competitive elections are the cornerstone on which liberal democracies are built (compare violent force, co-option or inheritance, which are the means of authoritarian regimes). Universal adult suffrage is thus the only legitimate basis of power within a democracy.

Role of elections

Elections play four important roles:

1   representative government (i.e. the parliament) is formed as an outcome of elections;
2   they are a mechanism of control, as governments are created, maintained or changed as a result of elections at regular intervals;
3   they provide the citizenry with their main mechanism of participation in the political system;
4   they give the political system its legitimacy.

Elections in inter-war ECE states

Between the two world wars, only Czechoslovakia and East Germany had any significant historical tradition of free, competitive elections. Before 1939 in Poland, for example, the only perfectly free elections took place between 1918 and 1926. In Hungary, Romania and Bulgaria almost all inter-war elections were rigged in favour of the government. (The most blatant distortion of results probably took place in Romania and Bulgaria.) Once the royal or military dictatorships assumed power everywhere – except in Czechoslovakia – elections were a charade.

Elections under communism

In terms of communist ideology, elections were considered inferior to direct democracy in the evolution towards full socialism and the classless society. Ideologically speaking, the voters did not need to be given a choice between the Communist Party and any opposition group, since, supposedly, there were no conflicts in socialist societies. Even so, unlike certain fascist regimes, elections in communist states were seen as an important vehicle of participation and system legitimation.

As far as the individual ECE voter was concerned, other than Party members, voting had very little meaning. It was simply a ritual – another of those small compromises to be made with the communist regime in order to ensure a peaceful co-existence. Voting in communist states was only one type of controlled participation among many.

In Western eyes, however, elections in ECE communist states were traditionally seen only as facades to camouflage totalitarian dictatorships, so their only real purpose was merely to maintain a ruling minority in its position of power: they had only a formalistic meaning, therefore.

Electoral choice before 1989

Alex Pravda distinguished between 'plebiscitary' and 'limited-choice' elections within the former Soviet bloc. 'Plebiscitary elections' were non-competitive, with only one election programme and only one candidate (of the Communist Party or a sister party) standing in single-member constituencies. In this type of election the Communist Party had an absolute monopoly (e.g. post-war Albania, Bulgaria and Czechoslovakia). 'Limited-choice' elections were characterised by a somewhat greater degree of political pluralism – even though this might have been entirely cosmetic – along with some scope for the interpretation of the Party line by individual candidates (e.g. Hungary and Yugoslavia).

In both types of election, it was claimed that a substantial element of voter choice existed at the candidate nomination and selection stages, where electors within the constituencies would choose from several candidates in a number of quasi-primary elections. At such meetings criticism was sometimes voiced of local governmental organisations, local issues were occasionally discussed and demands were made on the prospective deputies.

In practice, however, the Communist Party played the predominant role in the selection procedure. Moreover, no type of independent party-political activity was ever permitted. Only in Yugoslavia did outside organisations really influence the nomination process – and then it was mostly at the local level.

In any case, all candidates advocated the same (Communist Party) electoral programme. In fact, there were no electoral campaigns as such, just blanket mobilisation, within which Communist Party policies were never discussed openly or challenged. So, the choice presented was one between personalities, not policies. Some independent candidates were successful in Yugoslavia – but mainly because of their promises to promote specifically local interests.

Role of elections in the one-party communist states

Elections had an important function in post-war ECE communist systems, in contrast to many authoritarian regimes, since they were interpreted by the communist authorities as a true expression of the popular will and therefore played similar roles as in any Western democracy in terms of legitimising the state, despite their non-competitiveness.

Mobilisation. Communist governments spent much time and effort publicising both the elections themselves and their results. Strenuous attempts were made to attain the maximum participation of the voters in the pre-electoral process and the election itself. This usually included mass mobilisation of Party activists to ensure personal contact with a large percentage of the electorate. Pravda estimates that most families were visited at least once during any campaign and that a third to a half of the electorate participated in election meetings, if only passively.

Political socialisation. Election campaigns were viewed as mass socialisation. Political information dominated the mass media and there was direct contact with the electorate through meetings, the distribution of electoral literature and massive canvassing. Elections provided the citizenry with an important mechanism of participation in the political system. Voting for the Communist Party was the most symbolic civic ritual the individual made, but, in reality, it represented little more than an enforced personal compromise with the regime. And the overwhelming majority did vote (not the 100 per cent or 99 per cent that was sometimes claimed, but usually well over 90 per cent).

Integration. Elections also performed an important integrating function, as they were seen as uniting the people and their rulers. In fact, voting was more a duty than a right – a public expression of identification with the system, rather than a personal choice. Furthermore, in terms of the deputies elected, there was often a concerted attempt to achieve a proportionate balance according to gender, occupation, ethnicity and minority groups. It was hoped such positive discrimination would lead to the groups concerned accepting the political system as a whole.

Legitimation. Legitimation (both internal and external) was by far the most important function performed by non-competitive, one-party elections in communist systems. Whether or not voting in ECE communist states was a free, natural choice, the Party still used high levels of electoral support to legitimise the regimes externally at international conferences and meetings with foreign dignitaries. Communist participation levels compared especially well with the USA or Switzerland, where often only 50 per cent of the electorate voted. Non-participation was usually regarded as opposition to the regime and subject to possible sanctions. This was very different from many other authoritarian regimes, where political apathy tends to be viewed as passive support for the regime.

Representative link. No clear representative link between the various Communist parties and the electorate existed anywhere in ECE. There was little responsiveness by the ruling party to the electorate and almost no feedback from the voters. Representative government therefore could never have been the outcome of the elections.

Mechanisms of control. During the election campaigns voters could sometimes express their opinions on matters of local concern, and such viewpoints were occasionally acted upon in some way by the authorities. This limited feedback was restricted mainly to matters of local interest and administrative detail, but was significant in Yugoslavia, for example, where the different nationalities could vent their grievances. Overall, though, elections were clearly not a mechanism of control to hold the government to account.

The best electoral system for ECE after 1989

Under the communist regimes, people simply cast a vote for one candidate or a single list of candidates. In some countries like Serbia or Macedonia, this straightforward system has been retained. Elsewhere in ECE after 1989 the systems adopted have contained some measure of proportional representation.

Some countries adopted pure party list systems, like Poland with one national list or the Czech and Slovak Republics with regional lists. Other countries adopted a mixed majority–proportional system, including East Germany, Bulgaria, Hungary and Albania. In Bulgaria half of the 240 parliamentary seats are filled by party lists and half are contested in single-member districts by simple plurality, with a second round of voting in those constituencies where no individual candidate attained 50 per cent of the vote in the first round. Hungary has single-member and multi-member constituencies, as well as national and regional party lists, and uses the second round at the constituency level. In Albania the 100 members of parliament elected in single-member constituencies are 'topped up' by another forty deputies elected by a proportional list system, in order to give a more or less proportional final result. Croatia and Slovenia have also adopted mixed systems.

There were certain clear arguments for adopting proportional representation:

- proportional representation had been used extensively throughout ECE during the inter-war period, so it was 'traditional';
- there was the natural inclination to reject the plurality electoral system used under communism;
- there were a large number and variety of political opinions present after 1989 which militated against simple plurality, in particular in Poland (although a simple plurality system was used for the Senate elections and this produced a fragmented chamber);
- a pure majority system would have produced highly distorted results throughout the region – parties gaining 33 per cent of the vote would have won over 90 per cent of the seats, for example the Hungarian MDF (1990), the Czech Civic Democratic Party (ODS) (1992) and the Slovak HZDS (1992 and 1994);
- in this respect, there was a fear of the possible resumption of a one-party state.

The problem with returning to proportional representation was that it allowed greater differentiation of ideas and excessive fragmentation of the political party spectrum in a way that was reminiscent of the inter-war period, when parliamentary immobilism led eventually to regime collapse. In this respect, the Polish Sejm after the 1991 elections was a perfect example: twenty-nine parties were represented in parliament, with no one party gaining more than 13 per cent of the vote and with the two leading parties – both receiving 12.5 per cent of the vote – unable to work together in a coalition.

Therefore, in most countries there was an electoral threshold to guard against too many small political parties (e.g. 5 per cent in the Czech Republic for the 1992 and 1996 elections, Poland (1993), Hungary (1994) and Slovakia (1994), 4 per cent in Bulgaria, Albania and Hungary, and 3 per cent in Romania and Slovakia (1990 and 1992)). After the introduction of a 5 per cent threshold for the 1993 elections in Poland, only six parties entered the Sejm.

The first electoral campaigns

Lack of understanding of the democratic process

The electorate did not comprehend the mechanisms of electing someone – which was quite natural after such a long absence of democratic practice. The link between a politician, the political party and the electors was quite simply not understood.

The attitude of many voters was just to elect 'new faces' untainted by the past and then just let them govern. There was little thought of holding elected individuals to account in any way. The new political parties, too, had little concept of how to play a mediating role between the government and the electors, primarily because of the heritage of the past.

Starting from scratch

The electorate was potentially very volatile and had no particular loyalty to any specific political grouping (except for the 10 per cent of the population who were former Communist Party members). The political parties had little idea who was a potential voter. Some parties – like the Communist, peasants' or people's parties – had a traditional electorate and existing membership on which to build, but the new parties often had no links with the electorate and were starting from scratch. This was the case even within Solidarity (the only anti-communist movement with mass support among the population before 1989).

State support

All potential political parties were supported by the state to some extent, that is, they received money to establish themselves in

Czechoslovakia, Romania and Hungary, and were given free airtime on state television everywhere. In Czechoslovakia the parties also received financial support after the elections, when parties gaining more than 2 per cent of total votes obtained 15 crowns per vote (38 pence or 52 cents), with votes to both chambers of parliament and the republican parliaments counting separately. In the 1996 Czech elections this amount was effectively doubled to 90 crowns per vote for a single chamber.

Ignoring polls

The electorate was confused about whom to vote for and there was a general lack of trust in official data, so electors tended both to disbelieve and to ignore all opinion polls. The reference point for what was going to happen was still one's small circle of close friends and relatives, as before 1989 in relation to other events.

Voter turnout

Voter turnout was extremely high, ranging from the peaks of 96 per cent, 92 per cent and 92 per cent in the Czech Republic, East Germany and Albania, respectively, to the lows of 63 per cent, 62 per cent and 43 per cent in Hungary, Serbia and Poland (1991), respectively – turnout in other countries was around 80 per cent. However, voting percentages were particularly low in some local elections (e.g. in 1990 42 per cent in Poland and 30 per cent in Hungary). The lowest figures were recorded for mid-term parliamentary by-elections in Hungary in 1991, when only 7 per cent and 17 per cent of electors voted.

Negative campaigns

The first elections were primarily negative plebiscites on communism, aimed at not allowing the Communists to remain in power: it was not a question of vote *for* us, but more a question of vote *against* them. (Under the circumstances it is very difficult to imagine how this could have been otherwise.)

No specific policies

During the first election campaigns, the political parties dealt most often in symbols – such as 'democracy' and 'free-market economy' – saying little about how these could be achieved in reality and being very imprecise about their own political programme. As a result, most of the programmes were extremely general and very similar, since not even the reformed Communist parties disagreed with the basic principles of political and economic reform.

Large number of parties

A very large number of parties registered for the first elections: in Hungary over fifty parties registered and twenty-eight contested the elections, but only twelve presented national lists of candidates; in Czechoslovakia over 120 registered and forty-two presented republican or national lists; in Poland 140 parties registered and ninety parties contested the 1991 elections. This often meant that votes were spread very thinly across all parties.

There were basically three reasons for this:

1 people were 'drunk on democracy', and had a somewhat anarchic reaction to the new political freedom;
2 the inability for groupings with similar ideologies to compromise on their (sometimes insignificant) political differences;
3 financial incentive – several parties founded by business people never fielded candidates (e.g. in the 1992 elections in Czechoslovakia), and money raised presumably went into small-scale privatisation; the unemployed members of various gypsy communities in Romania also used the elections as a way of raising money, with whole communities sponsoring each other as political parties so they could each claim the founding fee.

Anti-communist alliances, not political parties

When fighting the elections, many of the small parties formed very loose anti-communist alliances to ensure the defeat of the

Communists. Civic Forum (OF) in Czechoslovakia, for example, was an anti-communist alliance of fourteen different political groupings, the Bulgarian SDS was composed of seventeen different groups, while in Slovenia DEMOS combined seven major parties (from Christian and Liberal Democrats to Greens) into one umbrella movement.

These anti-communist alliances tended to be more like social movements, for example the Polish Solidarity, and often attempted to be non-political. In its 164-page electoral programme, the MDF described itself as a 'democratic, centrist party, committed to Hungarian traditions ... not an ideological or class party. It rejects socialism ... collectivism ... nationalism and chauvinism'.

There was also a concerted effort to avoid the appellation 'party' because of the links with 'the Party' of the past. Rather the name forum, union, movement, community or alliance was used.

Pressure groups not parties

Several single-issue pressure groups stood as political parties – business and entrepreneurial parties, groups of old-age pensioners and retired people, women's movements, students' federations, committees of war veterans or the police, and so on. It was a way of making themselves rich, in those countries where parties received state financing, but also a way of establishing a profile for themselves, given the difficulties of non-governmental groups within an apathetic political culture.

Fun parties

There was an array of non-serious parties, like the Winnie the Pooh Party in Hungary, the Rock and Roll Party in Serbia, the Party of Car Drivers in Romania, the Sexual Erotic Initiative in Czechoslovakia, the Anti-Prohibitionist Freedom-Loving Party in Croatia, and the Party of the Friends of Beer in Poland and Czechoslovakia. The vast majority of these parties did not often contest the elections, although the beer drinkers' party won 2–3 per cent and had sixteen deputies in the Polish Sejm after the 1991 elections.

Voting for insignificant parties

Usually 20–30 per cent of ECE electorates voted for parties that either did not manage to clear the electoral hurdle or had only one or two representatives. There was no basis of rationality in these first ECE elections: electors simply did not realise that in giving their votes to parties that failed to cross the electoral hurdle they were effectively giving their votes/seats to other parties. Moreover, some parties received minute proportions of the vote: in 1992 in Romania only seven out of seventy-nine parties cleared the 3 per cent threshold and fifty-five received less than 0.3 per cent of total votes. In 1994 in Hungary, 100 of the 120 registered parties were of very minor and dubious status. In the first East German elections, twenty-two parties contested the elections, but eleven of them together obtained 0.13 per cent of the total votes – one party receiving no votes at all.

The Communist parties

Most Communist parties disposed of their hard-liners, and advocated a pluralistic society and free-market economy like everyone else. They therefore expected to do quite well in the first post-revolutionary elections and many Western observers also predicted that the elections would result in some power-sharing arrangements between the Communists and the new opposition.

In fact, many anti-communist parties also expected a Communist victory in the first elections, since the Communist parties were better organised, could rely on their large memberships and had greater financial resources.

In the end, the Communists remained in power – usually after a name change – in Albania, Bulgaria, Romania and Serbia, winning 67 per cent, 47 per cent and 66 per cent of the vote and

78 per cent of seats, respectively. Former Communists, as individual candidates, also won presidential elections in the nations of former Yugoslavia (Slovenia, Croatia, Serbia and Montenegro and Macedonia). Elsewhere, however, the Communists were shunned by the voters, as they had been in Poland in June 1989. They scored 16 per cent, 15 per cent, 14 per cent and 12 per cent in East Germany, Hungary, the Czech Republic and Poland (1991) respectively.

Basically, the Communists received votes from former Party members, older members of the electorate unable to break with past habits and the more conservative voters in the countryside.

Ethnic minority parties

Each ECE country had its own ethnic minority parties, with the exception of East Germany (in 1990). Such parties were usually small – for example, the German Minority Party or the Silesian Autonomy Movement in Poland, the Turkish Minority Party in Macedonia and the Democratic Union of the Greek Minority (OMONIA) in Albania all received only 1–2 per cent of total votes. Sometimes small regionalist parties combined in an electoral alliance; for example, the Dalmatian Action, Istrian Democratic Association and Rijecka Democratic Alliance won six seats together in the 1992 Croatian elections. The very small Italian and Hungarian minorities are allocated one seat each in the Slovenian parliament, with national minorities also guaranteed thirteen seats in Romania. Otherwise the Serbian National Party in Croatia and the Reform Forces of Vojvodina in Serbia won two seats each in their respective parliaments. Finally, gypsy or Romany parties fielded candidates throughout ECE, and usually attained 0.5–2 per cent of votes cast, gaining one seat in the Macedonian assembly.

But some ethnic minority parties were much larger and even played crucial roles in the region's first governments, such as the Turkish DPS in Bulgaria and the Albanian Party for Democratic Prosperity (PDP) in Macedonia, which were both periodically involved in government coalitions. Support for such parties usually ranged between 5 and 8 per cent (e.g. the Hungarian Alliance in Slovakia, the Moravian and Silesian Party in the Czech Republic, and the Hungarian minority party in Romania). In Bosnia the vote was split along ethnic lines, with 27 per cent going to the minority Serbian Democratic Party of Bosnia-Hercegovina (SDS BiH) and 15 per cent to the Croatian Democratic Community of Bosnia-Hercegovina (HDZ BiH).

Complete failure of social democrats

One of the surprises of the first elections was the poor perform-ance of the independent social democratic parties (i.e. not communist successor parties) – with the exception of East Germany in March 1990 when they scored 22 per cent of all votes. Otherwise they failed to achieve 5 per cent across the whole region, falling below 1 per cent in Romania, Slovenia, Macedonia and Bulgaria. Basically, this was because there was no workers' constituency to which appeal could be made along class lines. Workers throughout the ECE countries tended to vote right across the political spectrum for a variety of parties.

Similar failure of peasants' parties

The same could be said of the peasants' parties, which were often founded by returning émigrés or pre-war/immediate post-war veterans of agrarian parties. The rural constituency had changed dramatically under the Communists, so that there was a greater tendency for farmers and their families to remain loyal to the former Communists than return to the political behaviour of their forbears. With the notable exceptions of Poland (1991) and Hungary (1990) where the combined totals of two peasants' parties was 14–15 per cent in both cases, peasant parties usually scored below 10 per cent, and often below 5 per cent – for example, the East German Democratic Peasant Party with 2.2 per cent, the Serbian Peasant Alliance with 2.7 per cent, the two minute peasant parties in Slovakia, or the Albanian Agrarian Party with 0.1 per cent of votes cast.

The results of the first free elections assessed

Two patterns of elections

J. Rothschild points to two different patterns of elections between Central Europe (i.e. Poland, East Germany, Czechoslovakia and Hungary) and the 'Balkan' countries (i.e. Bulgaria, Romania, Albania and parts of Yugoslavia). In the former group the communist regimes collapsed at the first sign of resistance and their communist successor parties lost badly in subsequent elections. Having witnessed that collapse in the north, the Communist parties in the Balkan countries attempted to retain power in competitive elections by exploiting the divided and fragmented opposition parties and playing on the weak civil society. Accordingly, they started the reform process themselves and then called quick elections, giving the opposition parties little chance to organise. Hence they were able to retain the initiative and win the first elections.

Three stages of elections

There were basically three stages within those two patterns.

(1) In the first stage, either the Communists continued in power (Albania, Bulgaria, Romania and Serbia), or former dissidents won – especially Poland (Solidarity), Czechoslovakia (OF and VPN), and Hungary (MDF). (Only in East Germany did the former dissidents – the New Forum – fail to make any impact in the first election, because of the way in which the campaign was taken over by professional politicians and parties from West Germany.) In Bulgaria, Albania and Romania the opposition was not yet united or professional enough to win power. Indeed, in Romania opposition to the ex-communists of the FSN was virtually non-existent.

(2) In the second stage, there was a marked dissatisfaction and rejection of the first post-1989 elites, who had failed to solve the economic and other pressing problems (e.g. nationalism in Czechoslovakia), including the ex-communist elites in Albania, Bulgaria and (partially) Romania. The only countries in which

this trend was not so prominent were the newly independent nations of the former Yugoslavia, where nationalism dominated the political debate.

(3) In the third stage, there was a return to power for the communist successor parties in Poland, Hungary and Bulgaria (see below), while the communist successors in former Yugoslavia, Romania and (partially) Slovakia held on to power.

Voters for the ex-communist parties

The victorious ex-communist parties usually combined a more left-oriented approach in economic policy with a tinge of nationalism and blatant populism. They addressed their campaigns to the majority of the voters who were faced with declining living standards and increasing social problems, and were therefore disillusioned with the economic reform process.

Across all Poland, Bulgaria and Hungary, the victorious communist successor parties tended to be supported by older people (aged forty-one and above, but especially old-age pensioners), people on lower or average incomes or welfare payments, often employed in the state sector and often with only lower levels of education. In particular, 56 per cent of the votes received by the Bulgarian Socialist Party in December 1994 came from people aged fifty-one and above – indeed, half of all old-age pensioners voted for the BSP. This should be compared with the 13 per cent of votes received by the BSP from electors between eighteen and thirty, and the meagre 7 per cent of its voters who were university graduates.

In contrast, the ex-dissident parties, like the Democratic Union (UD) in Poland or SDS in Bulgaria, tended to be supported by a younger electorate (particularly those aged twenty-five to thirty-five years) with higher incomes and higher education, especially those benefiting from the new economic freedoms within the private sector.

Viewed objectively, this should mean that the communist successor parties are faced with a declining electorate over the next two decades (although Alexander Kwasniewski received the backing of young voters in the Polish presidential elections). Everything, though, depends on the success of the economic reforms, since the communist successor parties are clearly being supported by the disadvantaged.

The reasons for the return to power of former Communists

It has often been said that 'revolutions devour their children', and those in ECE were no exception. By the end of 1994, Solidarity in Poland, the vast majority of the post-revolutionary dissidents in the Czech Republic, most of the post-1989 dissident elite in Slovakia, the SDS in Bulgaria, the Hungarian MDF and the East German New Forum had all been rejected by their respective electorates. Klaus in the Czech Republic was an exception: as former Finance Minister, he took the message to the people and convinced them of the need and benefits of economic reforms. Others used nationalism to mobilise the population into continued support, for example in Romania, Croatia, Serbia, Slovenia, and Macedonia, as well as the post-1992 Slovakian leadership.

As a result, the former Communists have returned to power in Poland, Hungary, Bulgaria and (partially) Slovakia, or have remained in power (in different guises) in Romania, Croatia and Macedonia. There are several reasons for this.

In ECE countries the reforms have not been very pleasant for the vast majority, and have led to declining living standards, sometimes hyperinflation, often very high unemployment and abject poverty – the last three almost unknown under communism. In Poland, for example, during the period 1989–92, unemployment stood at 14–15 per cent, with some regions experiencing 30 per cent, while real wages declined by 26.6 per cent. The universal social security net available under the former communist regimes has also disappeared. In Hungary, by the time of the May 1994 elections, countless surveys of public opinion demonstrated how people believed themselves to be worse off than under communism, and they specifically blamed the 1990–94 Christian-conservative government for their economic problems. Polish Solidarity and the Bulgarian SDS were similarly blamed for their respective countries' economic predicament. Therefore, voters wanted to slow down the pace of economic reform and return to the social security of the communist era.

There has always been deep resentment on the part of the majority at the emerging disparities of income. The very small number of *nouveaux riches* are often considered to have earned their money through corruption or links to the old regime. In Poland, in particular, economic reform was depicted as '*nomenklatura* privatisation', that is, the idea that former Communist officials were still in charge through their ownership of leading firms that they had once managed. Many ordinary people are especially irritated the most blatant display of wealth by the *nouveaux riches* (otherwise known as the culture of envy).

In Poland, Hungary and Bulgaria, therefore, the communist successor parties have tried to project the image of caring parties which want to help those who have not benefited from the economic transition. They advocate something resembling capitalism with a human face. At the same time, their electoral programmes stress the need for pressing ahead with a degree of economic reform and seeking integration with Europe. (There is no desire to revert back to a communist-type dictatorship with central planning.)

The former Communists were also seen as more professional than the dissident leaders, who, because of their exclusion from public office, had had no experience whatsoever of government and had spent much of their time bickering openly about minor, trivial or side-tracking issues – in particular, the 'war at the top' among the Solidarity leadership in 1990–91.

Other problems which the new elite could not solve – particularly the problems related to nationalism, independence or treatment of minorities – also led to their demise. This very much refers to the rejection of the Czech dissident elite who were in charge of the negotiations with the Slovaks during the first (1990–92) government. Eventually the Czech electorate tired of the old brand of dissidents who wanted to keep the negotiations going and looked for firm leadership from someone who would 'stand up to the Slovaks'.

The post-revolutionary dissident movements rested their appeal on simply being against the Communists, and did not really have anything positive to propose, other than somewhat intangible concepts. No dissident group was really an organiser and very few of them understood the need to create a solid party-political base within the electorate, with the exception of Klaus in the Czech Republic.

Part of the rejection of the post-revolutionary dissident elite in Hungary lies in the fact that in their election campaigns the MDF and FIDESZ focused on the need to call former Communists to account (FIDESZ even wanted to apply the policy to offspring of former Communists within both the economic and political fields). Both parties fared particularly badly in May 1994, with FIDESZ only just scraping over the 5 per cent electoral hurdle (having at one time been the most popular party in Hungary, with 18 per cent support in opinion polls). Ordinary people do not care too much about the past – they are far more concerned about rising costs than they are with historical grievances.

Dangers of a return to power by former Communists

Adam Michnik often refers to the 'velvet restoration', that is, the return of former Communist officials to their positions of power and influence, involving the following:

- the sacking of state officials appointed under the previous, non-communist regime;
- the reinstatement of former Communist officials dismissed under the first post-revolutionary governments;
- the appointment of officials with much experience under the pre-1989 communist regimes and seen to be naturally

more loyal to the communist successor parties, in both the
state bureaucracy and the state-run media.

The 'velvet restoration' figures strongly in the return to power
of former Communists in Poland, Hungary and Bulgaria. The
post-1994 Hungarian government, for example, was supposed to
be a 'government of experts' but consisted mainly of professional
politicians and party loyalists who had made their careers during
the former communist regime.

Since former Communist Party officials are present at all levels
of leadership within the governing socialist/social democratic
parties, this means a return to the cosy types of close, personal
clientele–government relations, which could be more prone to
both corruption and lethargy, and which could re-establish the
old network of connections with everything functioning for the
benefit of the self-perpetuating political, economic and administrative elite, as in the previous regime. This has been called
'cronyism' or 'crony democracy'.

During the first year of the SLD–PSL government in Poland,
Premier Waldemar Pawlak gradually increased his power by
placing 'his' people in positions of influence in the public
administration and in the economy, which had a knock-on
effect, with other appointments made in the lower ranks. Slovak
Premier Meciar also staffed leading positions in society with
HZDS supporters, for example within the mass media and
throughout the economy.

Certainly, this will have the following consequences:

- the economic reform process will be slowed down and
  attempts will be made to widen the welfare safety net;
- there will be non-implementation or administrative obstruction of any laws discriminating against the employment of
  former Communists in top administrative and educational
  posts;
- there will be an end to any other forms of 'de-communisation';
- 'friendly' journalists and administrators will be appointed

to the state-run television and radio stations, to ensure the 'right' message gets across to the people.

Conclusion

Getting elected was the easy part; now the ex-communist socialists and social democrats have to prove that, with their professionalism, they are capable of solving the major economic problems faced by the majority of the people, where others have failed.

The communist successor parties throughout the region will remain committed to the economic reform process, which will still depend on attracting foreign investment, and will continue to seek their country's integration into the EU and other Western alliances.

In the process, however, the new socialist/social democratic governments are going to have to slow down the privatisation and liberalisation reforms in response to the needs of the majority of the population. But there is no guarantee that such a policy will improve the economic lot of the vast majority. Slowing down the reform process could quite easily prolong the misery of the majority, retard the country's entry into Western European institutions like the EU and delay the possibility of vaguely catching up with the West well into the twenty-first century.

Consequently, such governments are just as likely to disappoint the voters and to be ousted at subsequent elections. In this respect, what occurred in 1995 in local elections in Lithuania and parliamentary elections in Latvia was most illuminating. Having rejected the Communists for the dissident nationalists in 1991, then the dissident nationalist elite for the reformed Communists in 1993, the Lithuanian and Latvian electorates are now turning to the far right conservative/neo-liberal and right-wing populist parties as their saviours. The electoral merry-go-round seems set to continue.

Further reading

Vernon Bogdanor, *What is Proportional Representation?*, Martin Robertson, 1984.

Michael Gallagher, Michael Laver and Peter Mair, *Representative Government in Western Europe* (chapter 6), McGraw-Hill, 1992.

Enid Lakeman, *How Democracies Vote* (4th edn), Faber and Faber, 1974.

Alex Pravda, 'Elections in Communist Party States', in *Elections Without Choice* (Guy Hermet, Richard Rose and Alain Rouquie, eds), Macmillan Press, 1978.

Joseph Rothschild, *Return to Diversity*, Oxford University Press, 1993.

Stephen Whitefield (ed.), *The New Institutional Architecture of Eastern Europe*, St Martin's Press, 1993.

10

Election results and events since 1989

Albania

Political parties first formed in December 1990 and the Communists won an absolute majority in the first free elections (which had a 92 per cent turnout) on 31 March 1991. A Communist veteran, Ramiz Alia, continued in power as President. After a short period of majority communist government, the opposition Democratic Party (PD), Social Democratic Party (PSD) and Republican Party (PR) were brought into a broad coalition. However, the parties were unable work together and the coalition ended mid-December 1991, after only six months.

On 23 March 1992, the PD won the second elections (90 per cent turnout) with 62 per cent of the vote (Table 1), just missing the two-thirds majority required for constitutional changes. All overtly ethnic parties were banned from fighting the election, so the Greeks formed the Party for the Defence of Human Rights (PBDNJ). The PD formed a coalition with the very small PSD and PR, which began the reform process towards a Western-style liberal democracy and free-market economy.

On 9 April 1992, Sali Berisha, leader of the PD, became the first democratically elected President, after a campaign in which he stressed the need for protection of human rights, economic privatisation and a liberal democratic constitution. Just before the elections some quick changes were made to the country's constitution in order to enhance the President's power.

Berisha's government brought about positive signs of economic growth for the first time since 1990. Politically speaking,

Table 1   *The Albanian general elections, March 1992*[a]

Party	Votes (%)	Seats (no.)	1991 (%)
PD	62.0	92	38.7
PS	25.7	38	–
PSD	4.4	7	–
PPSH	3.1	–	56.2
PBDNJ (ex-OMONIA)[b]	2.9	2	–
OMONIA[b]	–	–	0.7
PR	0.7	1	1.8
PASH	–	–	0.1
Others	3.2	–	2.5
Total no. of seats		140	

[a] Results for the elections of May–June 1996 are not given here because they were rigged.
[b] Ethnic parties were banned in the 1992 elections, so OMONIA reorganised into the PBDNJ.
PD, Democratic Party of Albania.
PS, Socialist Party of Albania.
PSD, Social Democratic Party of Albania.
PPSH, Party of Labour of Albania.
PBDNJ, Party for the Defence of Human Rights (ex-OMONIA).
OMONIA, Democratic Union of the Greek Minority.
PR, Republican Party.
PASH, Albanian Agrarian Party.

however, there was considerable criticism – primarily from the newly constituted Socialist Party (PS) – of corruption and the use of the state media in favour of the PD.

There followed a concerted campaign against the Socialists: the 1991 Premier, Fatos Nano, was charged with corruption and all members of the former Politburo were arrested, including ex-President Ramiz Alia. This was seen as a means of dispensing with the main opposition to the PD. The Socialist Party engaged in an unsuccessful campaign for the government's resignation.

In September 1992 the coalition lost its two-thirds majority when a faction within the PD split and formed a separate opposition party, the Democratic Alliance (AD).

Rising political tension led to a delay in drafting a new constitution in the parliament. In October 1994, President Berisha therefore initiated a referendum on a new constitution giving increased powers to the President. The electorate rejected these proposals by 53.9 per cent and the PS demanded new elections. Instead, in early December, Berisha made radical changes within the cabinet.

Such activities were seen as a move towards an authoritarian type of personalised dictatorship, especially after a new screening law in 1995, which, *inter alia*, banned many leading members of the opposition Socialist and Social Democratic Parties from participating in all elections before 2005.

In June 1996 the PD won an overwhelming 'victory' in rigged elections, which were boycotted by the opposition on the last day and severely criticised by international observers for multiple voting, stuffing of ballot boxes, disqualification of opposition candidates, the banning of opposition rallies, media bias in favour of the governing PD, and so on.

Bulgaria

In the June 1990 elections the BSP, successor of the Communist Party, won a bare parliamentary majority. In August 1990 Zhelyu Zhelev – the leader of the opposition SDS – was elected President by the parliament.

During 1991 the opposition SDS cooperated with the BSP in adopting a new constitution and a new electoral law. Afterwards the SDS withdrew their cooperation and forced a general election, which they just won. They then formed a minority government relying on the informal support of the party of the ethnic Turks – the DPS.

In January 1992, Zhelev won direct presidential elections. During 1992 the minority government began the process of economic reform, to which there was considerable opposition from the trade union movement. There were also disputes over the role of the Church and the status of Church property.

Table 2   *The Bulgarian general elections, December 1994*

Party	Votes (%)	Seats (no.)	1991 (%)
BSP[a]	43.5	125	33.1
SDS[a]	24.2	69	34.4
NS[a]	6.5	18	–
DPS	5.4	15	7.6
BBB	4.7	13	1.3
DAR	3.8	–	–
BZNS[a]	–	–	3.9
BZNS–NP[a]	–	–	3.4
SDS-Centre (Social Democrats)	–	–	3.2
SDS-Liberals (Greens)	–	–	2.8
Others	11.9	–	10.3
Total no. of seats		240	

[a] In 1994 BZNS was divided into 3 groups: BZNS 'A. Stamboliski' was in alliance with the BSP, BZNS was in the NS coalition with the Democratic Party and most of BZNS-NP were affiliated with SDS.
BSP, Bulgarian Socialist Party.
SDS, Union of Democratic Forces.
NS, National Union.
DPS, Movement for Rights and Freedoms.
BBB, Bulgarian Business Bloc.
DAR, Democratic Alternative for the Republic.
BZNS, Bulgarian Agrarian National Union.
BZNS–NP, Bulgarian Agrarian National Union–Nikola Petkov.

In the autumn of 1992 the informal DPS–SDS collaboration ceased and the minority government had to resign. Instead of further elections, President Zhelev appointed Lyuben Berov to head a government of mainly non-party technocrats, which gained the parliamentary support of the BSP, DPS and a few former SDS deputies. On his appointment Berov claimed his cabinet would be the 'government of privatisation'.

During 1993 Bulgaria's main political problem was the return of the Muslim Turks exiled in 1989, who had to resort to hunger strikes in order to have their former property returned to them. Economically speaking, very little progress was made towards full-scale privatisation within either the agricultural or the industrial sector. (By May 1994 there was still no reform of the tax system and no law on bankruptcies.)

As a result, political support for the non-party government collapsed in May 1994, after a series of nationwide strikes by the trade unions. Although the Berov government survived a vote of no confidence in mid-1994, it resigned in early September and elections were called for December.

The BSP made a come-back in the December 1994 elections with 43.5 per cent of the vote and an absolute majority of seats (125 out of 240) (Table 2). The BSP's young leader, Zhan Videnov, pledged to slow down the economic reform process and improve the living standards of the poor in society. The minority Turkish ethnic vote was split three ways, so the DPS lost support.

In early 1995 a controversial amendment to the 1992 Land Law (requiring farmers to offer land they wish to sell to the government first) seemed to back-track on the reform process and caused a real conflict with President Zhelev.

In March 1995 the government published the 'White Book', which laid all the blame for the post-revolutionary economic problems on the SDS government of 1991–92. In June the BSP-dominated parliament appointed new ('more objective') directors of national television and radio, thereby confirming government control over the media. At the end of August, the government arbitrarily moved the Bulgarian Constitutional Court to smaller offices. This was seen as a political move to penalise the Court for its support of President Zhelev over the Land Law.

In December 1995, seven ('less objective') journalists were sacked by the new television chief. President Zhelev was most critical of the dismissals, emphasising that freedom of the mass media was a key feature of a functioning democracy and a standard condition for entry into the EU.

In the first half of 1996, the Bulgarian lev collapsed to one-third of its value against the dollar, prices rose dramatically (12.5 per cent in May, 20.3 per cent in June, for example), interest rates escalated to over 100 per cent, real wages plummeted, and there was a severe grain shortage.

On 1 June 1996 President Zhelev was defeated by Petar Stoyanov, deputy leader of the SDS (66 per cent of votes to 34 per cent) in a primary election to choose an opposition candidate for the autumn presidential elections.

Czechoslovakia

The Czech Republic

In the June 1990 elections, OF won a majority of votes in the Czech Republic and its sister party, VPN, won a third of the votes in Slovakia, where the KDH also performed well. An OF/VPN/KDH coalition was formed for the whole Republic.

Within nine months of the election, OF split and three months later the Slovak VPN also fragmented. The two-year constituent assembly was beset by problems of Slovak nationalism, which led to a total lack of agreement in parliament on almost all constitutional matters: a federal-wide constitution was never passed by the Federal Assembly.

In the June 1992 elections (Table 3), the former right-wing faction of OF, the ODS, won a third of all votes in the Czech Republic and the more left-wing, nationalist Slovak HZDS won a third of all votes in the Slovak Republic. The subsequent inability of both party leaderships to find a working relationship between the two republics led to the splitting of the state in the so-called 'velvet divorce' on 1 January 1993.

Since that date, the Czech Republic has proven to be one of the most stable polities in ECE. Former dissident Vaclav Havel was elected President in January 1993. The economist Premier, Vaclav Klaus, leader of the ODS since April 1991, successfully convinced the public of the need for economic reform, and then closely identified his party with those reforms, gaining respect abroad for his tough macro-economic line.

Substantial transfer of ownership via both small-scale privatisation and the voucher scheme (copied in other ECE countries) have proven popular with large sections of the population. Tight monetary and fiscal policy has kept unemployment below 4 per cent and inflation at approximately 10 per cent.

Table 3   *The Czech general elections, May–June 1996*[a]

Party	Votes (%)	Seats (no.)	1992[a] (%)
ODS[b] and KDS[b]	29.7	68	29.7
CSSD	28.4	61	6.5
KSCM[c]	10.3	22	14.1
KDU/CSL	8.1	18	6.3
SPR-RSC	8.0	18	6.0
ODA	6.4	13	5.9
SD/LSNS[d]	2.1	–	4.6
HSD-SMS	0.7	–	5.9
LSU	–	–	6.5
Total no. of seats		200	

[a] The 1992 election results are the elections for the Czech National Council, which became the Czech parliament after 1 January 1993.

[b] The KDS finally merged with the ODS on 31 March 1996.

[c] The KSCM fought the 1992 elections with the Left Bloc coalition.

[d] The SD/LSNS was a coalition of a few small liberal parties; the 1992 figures are for the Civic Movement (OH).

ODS, Civic Democratic Party.

KDS, Christian Democratic Party.

CSSD, Czech Social Democratic Party.

KSCM, Communist Party of Bohemia and Moravia.

KDU/CSL, Christian Democratic Union/People's Party.

SPR-RSC, Republican Party.

ODA, Civic Democratic Alliance.

SD/LSNS, Free Democrats/National Socialist Liberal Party.

HSD-SMS, Movement for a Self-Governing Moravia and Silesia.

LSU, Liberal Social Union.

The four-party coalition – ODS, Civic Democratic Alliance (ODA), Christian Democratic Party (KDS) and the Christian Democratic Union/People's Party (KDU/CSL) – was dominated by the ODS. Strict party discipline within the ODS and the weaker positions of the smaller coalition parties meant that very few issues divided the government in public: the delay in establishing the second chamber of parliament (Senate) and restitution of both Church and Jewish property, for example, caused only slight tensions within the coalition. On overall economic approach, however, there was almost complete agreement. (KDS merged with ODS on 31 March 1996.)

The only things that disrupts the Czech Republic's political life are the recurring scandals involving individual ministers, parliamentary deputies or public officials, such as the Minister of the Interior using the secret services to spy on leading politicians, corruption of officials overseeing the privatisation process, and large donations from state funds into the coffers of the ODS.

In local elections in November 1994 (64 per cent turnout) the coalition parties easily outshone the opposition and attained similar totals to the 1992 parliamentary elections.

The coalition partners finally agreed on the formation of the Senate and the majority system of voting in two rounds within eighty-one single-member constituencies for elections in the autumn of 1996. The government also introduced a restructuring of the social security system to benefit the less well off five weeks before the June 1996 parliamentary elections.

In those elections the right-wing coalition just lost its overall majority, following the dramatic rise in the vote for the CSSD, who gained 26.4 per cent of the vote. Having secured the leadership of the National Council and five key parliamentary committees, the CSSD agreed to support in principle the ODS/ODA/KDU/CSL programme, to enable the coalition to continue in power in a minority capacity.

The Slovak Republic

The Slovakian government under Vladimir Meciar, on the other hand, during the first three years of its existence was beset by serious economic problems and subject to major upheavals in the parliament and the cabinet. The HZDS nominee for President (Roman Kovac) was not elected by the parliament in January 1993, but in February Michal Kovac was elected – no relation, but still a member of HZDS.

In March 1993, Meciar dismissed the Foreign Minister, Milan Knazko, who subsequently left HZDS along with seven other deputies to form a new political party – the Alliance of Democrats

Table 4   *The Slovak general elections, September 1994*

Party	Votes (%)	Seats (no.)	1992 (%)
HZDS[a]	35.0	61	37.3
Common Choice coalition[b]	10.4	18	–
SDL	–	–	14.7
SDSS	–	–	4.1
Hungarian Alliance[c]	10.2	17	7.4
KDH	10.1	17	8.9
DU[d]	8.6	15	–
ZRS	7.3	13	–
SNS	5.4	9	7.9
ODU	–	–	4.0
DP	–	–	3.3
Others	13.1	0	12.4
Total no. of seats		150	

[a] The small Peasants' Party (RSS) formed an electoral alliance with HZDS.

[b] Common Choice was a coalition of SDL and SDSS plus the Green Party and the Peasant Movement.

[c] The Hungarian Alliance was a coalition of all three Hungarian parties: Co-existence, the Hungarian Christian Democratic Movement and the Hungarian Civic Party.

[d] In 1994 the DU became a coalition of the Democratic Union and the Alliance of Democrats, both formed by HZDS dissidents.

HZDS, Movement for a Democratic Slovakia.

SDL, Party of the Democratic Left.

SDSS, Social Democratic Party of Slovakia.

KDH, Christian Democratic Movement.

DUS, Democratic Union of Slovakia.

ZRS, Association of Slovak Workers.

SNS, Slovak National Party.

ODU, Civic Democratic Union.

DP, Democratic Party.

(AD). In the same month, the Economics Minister and leader of the SNS, Ludovit Cernak, resigned his post and drew his party out of the informal coalition with HZDS. In June 1993, the Privatisation Minister, Lubomir Dolgos, was also removed from his post after a disagreement with Meciar and subsequently left the HZDS.

All these resignations eventually led to the formation of a new HZDS/SNS government with a very slim majority in parliament in November 1993. The next month, however, the SNS split into two, and a group of SNS deputies founded the National Democratic Party (NDS).

In March 1994, President Kovac addressed the parliament and encouraged the opposition parties to unite to oust Meciar. This they accomplished in a no-confidence motion on 11 March. The parliament then voted to hold new elections in September, hoping thereby to end government instability.

A broad, left–right coalition government of five political parties, plus a number of independents, formed a caretaker government under Premier Jozef Moravcik for the six months leading up to the 30 September elections.

In those elections (Table 4), Meciar's HZDS won more or less the same total of votes as in 1992, emerging, once again, as the largest party by far. The government formed after those elections, however, brought together very odd bedfellows: Meciar's HZDS, the SNS and the ZRS (a left-wing SDL splinter group).

On assuming power, the new three-party government abandoned the coupon/voucher privatisation plans of the previous government, and initiated a scheme of direct sales of firms to political allies. They further replaced many of the top political, economic and media officials with their own appointments. The power struggle with the President intensified – including a bizarre kidnapping of the President's son in the summer of 1995, apparently at the hands of the Slovak secret service, run by Ivan Lexa, a Meciar ally.

On 19 March 1995 Slovakia signed a bilateral treaty with Hungary, establishing the inviolability of existing borders and the renunciation of any territorial claims, plus the guaranteeing of minority rights to the Hungarian and Slovak minority populations in both countries. This treaty had been made a prerequisite for either country's entry into NATO – but it still took the Slovak parliament a whole year to ratify it. Slovakia was also one of the first countries to sign the Council of Europe's Framework Convention on the protection of minority rights in early 1995. Even so, the Meciar government's relations with the minority Hungarian community have hardly improved.

In November 1995, all parties except the Hungarians voted for the new Language Law that promotes Slovak as the national language and restricts the use of Hungarian in the state and educational sectors. A Law Protecting the State was also passed – in March 1996 – making it more difficult to criticise the government openly.

East Germany

The East German revolution against communism evolved into a popular movement for the reunification of the two Germanies. With the collapse of communism, there was no reason for the 'two German states of one nation' to remain divided. In February 1990 a framework for unification was agreed at the 'Two–plus–Four' talks (the two Germanies and the four occupying powers) at Ottawa.

The first totally free ECE elections took place in East Germany on 4 March 1990. The election campaign itself was basically taken over by the main West German political parties, which provided technology and advice, and campaigned for their sister parties in the East.

The Christian Democrats won 41 per cent of the vote, the Social Democrats 22 per cent and the ex-communist PDS 16 per cent (Table 5). A 'Grand Coalition' – the Alliance for Germany, SPD and the Free Democrats (BFD) – was formed under the Eastern CDU leader Lothar De Maiziere. This was merely a caretaker government to preside over rapid unification – for which both Eastern and Western CDU parties had strongly campaigned. The real loser in the election was New Forum, which tried to stem the incredible dynamic that was driving the two Germanies together, emphasising instead reconstruction 'along democratic socialist lines' within a 'gradual process to-wards unification'.

On 1 July 1990 effective monetary and economic union occurred, with the Bonn government offering East Germans a

Table 5   *The East German general elections, March 1990*

Party	Votes (%)	Seats (no.)	1994(%)[a]
CDU[b]	40.8	163	38.5
DSU[b,c]	6.3	25	–
Democratic Awakening[b]	0.9	4	–
SPD-DDR	21.9	88	31.9
PDS	16.4	66	17.7
BFD	5.3	21	–
Alliance 90[d]	2.9	12	5.7
FDP	–	–	4.0
DBD	2.2	9	–
Greens[d]	2.0	8	–
Others	1.4	4	2.2
Total no. of seats		400	

[a] Results from the 1994 elections within the area of the former GDR.

[b] The first three parties campaigned together as the Alliance for Germany.

[c] In 1990 the DSU was a coalition of twelve different Christian, liberal and conservative groups.

[d] In 1994 Alliance 90 (which included New Forum) and the Greens fought the campaign in coalition.

CDU, Christian Democratic Union.

DSU, German Social Union.

SPD-DDR, Social Democratic Party.

PDS, Party for Democratic Socialism.

BFD, League of Free Democrats.

FDP, Free Democratic Party.

DBD, Democratic Peasants' Party.

one-to-one exchange of the Western and Eastern Deutschmark. In mid-July the Soviet Union stated it would allow NATO membership for the united Germany (even though Soviet troops would remain on East German soil for another four years). On 12 September 1990, the Treaty on the Final Settlement with Respect to Germany was signed by the four occupying powers, ending their occupation duties. On 3 October, Germany was formally united – less than a year after the fall of the Berlin Wall – simply by applying Article 23 of the West German Basic Law, which allowed the six *Länder* of the former East Germany to accede to the Federal Republic.

The final stage in process of political unification was the all-German legislative elections on 2 December 1990. The CDU with its Bavarian sister party the Christian Socialist Union (CSU) won 43.8 per cent of the vote, giving the CDU–CSU/FDP a working parliamentary majority with almost 400 of the 662 seats of the enlarged all-German Bundestag.

In the 'Eastern regions of Germany', as the former GDR is now called, there was just as close a linkage between political stability and economic recovery as elsewhere in the ECE. The Germans too, both 'Ossies' and 'Wessies', totally underestimated the economic difficulties and costs of the transition process.

From the start, there was massive investment and assistance from West Germany (about DM150 billion a year). Privatisation took place much more quickly than elsewhere (e.g. 15,000 small commercial and service companies and 900 large industrial complexes were sold off during the first three months of 1991). Moreover, the buyers were generally West German firms, which could incorporate the new companies into already well established markets within the EU.

The social costs of German economic integration, however, were enormous. During 1990, East German industrial production decreased dramatically, workers left for West Germany and hundreds of firms went bankrupt. By the end of 1991, over 16 per cent of East Germans were unemployed. It was estimated that it would take the eastern part of Germany twelve to fifteen years to attain Western standards of living at a total cost of one to two trillion marks (ten times the original estimate in 1989).

Such economic problems quickly caused disenchantment in both parts of the country. Many West Germans resented the money they were pouring into the East – especially after Chancellor Helmut Kohl's tax increase in 1991 (the so-called 'solidarity surcharge' of 7.5 per cent). The East Germans complained of being second-class citizens and resented the government's economic policies which had caused so much unemployment and had not yet produced the expected economic miracle.

Since the population of the former GDR constitutes a mere 20 per cent of the united Germany's total population, there is a tendency for the (West) German parties not to address the particular needs of East Germans other than verbally during election campaigns. Hence, there have been both increasing frustration with the economic climate in eastern Germany and a decline in popularity of the governing coalition in many of the regional (*Länder*) elections.

The October 1994 parliamentary elections, however, maintained the status quo, as there was little alternative to the programme of reconstruction in eastern Germany. The former communists (PDS) improved considerably on their December 1990 result within the eastern regions of Germany (up from 9.9 per cent to 17.7 per cent) – a pattern reflected throughout ECE as the disenchantment with the post-revolutionary situation set in. This pattern was reinforced in the October 1995 regional elections in Berlin: although the PDS won 14.5 per cent of the vote over the whole city, it scored 36 per cent in the districts of former East Berlin.

Hungary

The MDF emerged as the largest party in the first Hungarian elections, in March 1990. These were probably the most normal elections in ECE, with a hard-fought contest between non-communist groups – the SZDSZ, the FIDESZ, the KDNP, the FKGP and the MDF – as well as against the former Communists, the MSZP.

The centre-right government (MDF, KDNP and FKGP) was beset with problems from the outset: the FKGP leaving the coalition when land was not returned to the peasantry as promised; divisions over a 'screening law' to punish former Communists for their activities under the previous regime; a dispute with Slovakia over the Gabcikova dam; problems over government control of the media in the so-called 'media war' in which President Goncz also became involved, and so on.

Table 6   *The Hungarian general elections, May 1994*

Party	Votes (%)[a]	Seats (no.)	1990 (%)
MSZP	33.0	209	10.9
SZDSZ	19.4	70	21.4
MDF	11.7	37	24.7
FKGP	8.9	26	11.7
KDNP	7.1	22	6.5
FIDESZ	7.0	20	8.9
ASZ[b]	2.3	1	3.1
KP[c]	2.3	1	–
MSZMP	3.3	–	3.7
MIEP	1.4	–	–
MSZDP	0.8	–	–
Others	2.8	–	5.5
Total no. of seats		386	

[a] The voting percentages are taken from the county lists, which do not take into account the number of constituency seats won by the different parties: hence the discrepancy between number of seats won and overall national percentages. In 1990 MDF won 115 of the 176 single-member constituencies; in 1994 the MSZP won 149 of the 174 individual seats.
[b] The one ASZ deputy has since joined the SZDSZ.
[c] The KP's one seat was won in alliance with the MDF.
MSZP, Hungarian Socialist Party.
SZDSZ, Alliance of Free Democrats.
MDF, Hungarian Democratic Forum.
FKGP, Independent Smallholders' Party.
KDNP, Christian Democratic People's Party.
FIDESZ, Alliance of Young Democrats.
ASZ, Agrarian Federation.
KP, Party of the Republic.
MSZMP, Hungarian Socialist Workers' Party.
MIEP, Hungarian Justice and Life Party.
MSZDP, Hungarian Social Democratic Party.

There was almost a constant state of disagreement between the democratic parties. As a result, opinion poll support for both major anti-communist parties, the MDF and SZDSZ, declined steadily, while FIDESZ gained support, until it split in 1993. But the MSZP started doing well in local and by-elections.

In the May 1994 elections the MSZP won a convincing victory, gaining an absolute majority in parliament, with 209 out of the 386 seats (Table 6). The MDF was humiliated, obtaining less than one-quarter of its previous seats. The other two non-communist parties also lost votes, with the FIDESZ only just clearing the 5 per cent electoral threshold.

Despite its absolute majority, the MSZP established a coalition with the SZDSZ under its leader Gyula Horn, who became Premier, with the majority of the cabinet posts going to MSZP members. The coalition has the necessary two-thirds majority to pass constitutional laws.

During its first year of government, however, the MSZP/SZDSZ coalition did not fulfil its electoral promises. Initially the Horn cabinet was unwilling to support the tough austerity economic programme of its Finance Minister, Laszlo Bekesi, who eventually resigned in March 1995. In the end the government found the political will to implement a tough stabilisation programme, which attempted both to balance the budget and to introduce welfare reform. This restored economic confidence abroad, but brought protests from those groups that will suffer from the reform package, such as pensioners and students.

There were some foreign policy successes during the first year, like the signing of a bilateral treaty with Slovakia (including commitments on minority rights for Hungarians in Slovakia) and talks about a similar treaty with Romania. Domestically, however, there were constant disputes between the two coalition partners, as well as between various factions within the MSZP. As a result, opinion poll support for both government parties declined dramatically in the latter half of 1995, with the MSZP falling from 33 per cent to 23 per cent and the SZDSZ from 19 per cent to 15 per cent, while the opposition FKGP rose from 9 per cent to 24 per cent.

Poland

In June 1989, in the first partially free elections within the Soviet bloc, Solidarity won 99 of the 100 seats in the Polish Senate and all of the 35 per cent freely contested seats in the Sejm. T.

Table 7   *The Polish general elections, September 1993*

Party	Votes (%)	Seats (no.)	1991 (%)
SLD	20.4	171	12.0
PSL	15.4	132	8.7
UD[a,b]	10.6	74	12.3
UP[a]	7.3	41	–
'Homeland' (Catholic coalition)	6.4	–	–
WAK	–	–	8.7
KPN	5.8	22	7.5
BBWR[a]	5.4	16	–
NZSS[a]	4.9	–	5.1
PC[a]	4.4	–	8.7
KLD[a,b]	4.0	–	7.5
Party 'X' (Tyminski)	2.7	–	0.5
PSL–PA[a]	2.3	–	5.5
German Ethnic Minority	0.7	4	1.2
PPPP[c]	–	–	3.3
CHD	–	–	2.4
Labour Solidarity[a]	–	–	2.1
Others	9.7	–	14.5
Total no. of seats		460	

[a] Former Solidarity.
[b] UD and KLD merged into the Freedom Union (UW) in late April 1994.
[c] The PPPP split before the 1993 elections with the majority of the party's parliamentary deputies joining with the KLD.
SLD, Democratic Left Alliance.
PSL, Polish Peasants' Party.
UD, Democratic Union.
UP, Labour Union.
WAK, Catholic Electoral Committee.
KPN, Confederation for an Independent Poland.
BBWR, Non-Party Block in Support of Reform.
NZSS, Solidarity Trade Unions.
PC, Centre Alliance .
KLD, Liberal Democratic Congress.
PSL–PA, Polish Peasants' Party–Peasant Alliance.
PPPP, Polish Party of the Friends of Beer.
CHD, Christian Democrats.

Mazowiecki of Solidarity was appointed Premier by President Jaruzelski. During the following eighteen months, however, the Solidarity movement split into fifteen factions, mainly because of personality clashes among its leading members – the so-called 'war at the top', which intensified in the run-up to the first presidential elections (won by Lech Walesa in December 1990).

In the October 1991 elections twenty-nine parties won seats in the Sejm and a seven-party coalition government was formed, headed by Jan Olszewski (Christian Democrat). He immediately had problems with President Walesa and a struggle between parliament and President began. The Catholic-led government was strongly anti-communist and chastised previous governments for allowing former Communists to retain positions of influence.

There was more confrontation with the President on the issue of de-communisation when the Interior Minister, Macierewicz, prepared a list of sixty-four people who were actual 'agents' or potential 'candidates' for recruitment of the former secret police – including many of Solidarity's leaders and Walesa himself. The whole 'screening' process was then suspended by the Constitutional Court.

Walesa now dismissed Olszewski and nominated Pawlak (ex-communist leader of the Peasants' Party) as Premier, but the latter was unable to form a majority government. Then Solidarity parties managed to unite behind Hanna Suchocka, whose short reign was dominated by ideological conflicts involving the separation of the Church from the state, de-communisation and abortion.

The Suchocka government fell in June 1993, and in the October elections the SLD and the PSL, both communist successor parties, won 66 per cent of the seats in the Sejm (Table 7). Solidarity parties received little support, because of their constant bickering and their inability to solve most people's economic problems.

There were also personality divisions within the SLD/PSL coalition, but they were not as damaging. Under Pawlak as Premier the economic reform process was considerably slowed, former Communist officials regained their positions of influence and small peasant farmers received substantial state aid.

In autumn 1994, a new power struggle between the President and the government broke out over the position of Defence

Minister, after which Walesa was criticised by all parliamentary parties for manipulating the constitution. At the same time the Foreign Minister, Andrzej Olechowski, also resigned, criticising the SLD/PSL government's lack of coordination in foreign policy.

Walesa now attacked the government for slowing down the economic reform process and failing to produce a viable budget, and threatened to dissolve parliament (the Sejm threatened to impeach him if he did). The coalition backed down from confrontation, however, dismissed Premier Pawlak and nominated another ex-communist, J. Oleksy of the SLD in his stead. In the new cabinet, Walesa saw his own candidates appointed to the three posts over which he claimed jurisdiction: the Defence, Interior and Foreign Ministries.

In the first round of the November 1995 presidential elections, in which there were thirteen candidates, Walesa came second, with 33 per cent of the vote, behind the ex-communist leader of the SLD Alexander Kwasniewski (who received 35 per cent). In the second round between the leading two candidates, Walesa was again just narrowly beaten, 51.5 per cent to 48.5 per cent, reflecting the failure of his 'return to socialism' campaign, a dislike of his unstatesmanlike behaviour and a negative reaction to the chaos he had created in the past.

In early 1996 Oleksy was forced to resign after it was revealed (but not proven) that he spied for the Russians even after 1989. In fact, all charges were dropped against Oleksy in April 1996, on grounds of insufficient evidence.

Romania

The FSN – composed of former Communists – had won the first elections in 1990 with 66.3 per cent of the vote, but in late 1991 and throughout 1992 groupings within the FSN left to set up their own organisations, which proliferated.

The FSN's popularity dropped sharply in the February/ March 1992 local elections, when the party won only 33.6 per

Table 8 *The Romanian general elections, September 1992*

Party	Votes (%)	Seats (no.)	1990 (%)
FDSN[a]	27.7	117	–
CDR[b]	20.0	82	–
FSN	10.2	43	66.3
PUNR	7.7	30	–
UDMR	7.5	27	7.2
PRM	3.9	16	–
PSM	3.0	13	–
PDAR	2.99	–	1.8
PNL	2.4	–	6.4
MER	2.3	–	2.6
PNTCD[c]	–	(42)	2.6
PAC[c]	–	(13)	–
PER[c]	–	(4)	1.4
RP[a]	1.6	–	–
PDSR	0.9	–	1.1
PDSR[c]	–	(10)	0.5
National minorities	0.9	13	–
Others	8.9	–	10.1
Total no. of seats		341	

[a] The FDSN changed its name to the Social Democratic Party of Romania (PSDR) in July 1993 with the merger of FDSN, the Republican Party and most of the Romanian Social Democratic Party.

[b] The Democratic Convention of Romania (CDR) was an alliance of opposition parties and civic organisations founded in 1991, which included the Social Democrats, Liberals, National Peasants, Christian Democrats and the UDMR. Hungarian nationalists excluded the UDMR in February 1995 and the CDR broke up in March–April 1995.

[c] These parties were part of the CDR coalition in September 1992.

FDSN, Democratic National Salvation Front.

CDR, Democratic Convention.

FSN, National Salvation Front.

PUNR, Party of Romanian National Unity.

UDMR, Hungarian Democratic Union of Romania.

PRM, Greater Romanian Party.

PSM, Socialist Party of Labour.

PDAR, Agrarian Democratic Party.

PNL, National Liberal Party.

MER, Romanian Ecologist Movement.

PNTCD, National Peasants–Christian Democratic Party.

PAC, Civic Alliance Party.

PER, Romanian Ecologist Party.

RP, Republican Party.

PDSR, Party of Social Democracy of Romania.

PDSR, Romanian Social Democratic Party.

cent of the vote. The Democratic Convention of Romania (CDR) emerged as the major opposition group, with 24.3 per cent.

The FSN split in March 1992 after Premier Petr Roman and President Ion Iliescu had been in dispute for six months. The Premier accused the President of holding up the reform process and of being a neo-communist, for example in defending former *Securitate* officers. So the Democratic National Salvation Front (FDSN) formed to support Iliescu.

In the September 1992 elections (Table 8), the FDSN emerged as the largest party in parliament, with the CDR as the main opposition party, followed by the rump FSN. There were more members of the extreme nationalist parties, in particular the anti-Hungarian PUNR. Smaller parties advocating a return to national communism also gained representation. The National Liberal Party (PNL) under Radu Campeanu played the nationalist card (i.e. anti-Hungarian) and advocated a return of the monarchy. This tactic split the PNL and it fell below 5 per cent of the vote.

After the elections, Nicolae Vacaroiu formed an FDSN-dominated government, which included a number of technocrats. This government had to rely on the support of the national communists in parliament. In July 1993 the FDSN changed its name to the Party of Social Democracy of Romania (PDSR).

A formal agreement was made between the ruling PDSR and the PUNR, led by Gheorghe Funar, in early 1994. Even so, PUNR almost brought down the government in a no-confidence motion and almost supported a move to impeach the President, changing its mind at the last minute on both occasions. The formal agreement was extended to cover the Socialist Party of Labour (PSM) and the chauvinistic Greater Romanian Party (PRM) in a four-party coalition in January 1995. (The PSM's participation in the government split the party in two.) In February to March 1995 the opposition CDR split, and in October 1995 the coalition of PDSR and nationalist forces began to break up, with the departure of the PRM, because of the nationalists' persistent attacks on President Iliescu.

In mid-September 1995 President Iliescu said he would take the lead in bringing about a bilateral treaty between Romania and

Hungary in order to heal the rift in terms of the 1.6 million Hungarians in Transylvania. Such a treaty is a precondition of both countries' entry into NATO and other European organisations.

Former Yugoslavia

After Tito's death in 1980, the process of change and reform in Yugoslavia was marked by the rise of nationalism, with the rise to power of national communists (beginning with Slobodan Milosevic in 1987). (The dissolution of Yugoslavia and the resurgence of nationalism is described in greater detail in Chapter 7.)

In January 1990 both Slovenia and Croatia called for a multi-party system and a loose confederation. In April free parliamentary elections in both countries brought about nationalist-oriented leaderships. Elections in Bosnia (Table 9) and Macedonia also brought about nationalist victories at the end of 1990.

In December 1990 Slovenia voted by an 88.5 per cent majority to separate from Yugoslavia, as did Croatia in May 1991 when 94 per cent voted for independence (with an 86 per cent turnout) (Table 10), after which Croatia unilaterally declared its sovereignty. The Krajinian Serbs immediately called for the union of their territory with Serbia, leading to a proclamation of the Serbian Autonomous Region of Krajina (comprising 27 per cent of Croatian territory) in August 1990.

The ensuing civil war was really a product of the break-up of the Yugoslav Federation. After the effective defeat of the invading Yugoslav federal army by the Slovenes in June–July 1991, Slovenia was allowed to secede from the Yugoslav Federation. Secession by Croatia was another matter, and fighting began between the federal army and Croatian forces in July 1991. On 9 September Macedonia voted in favour of autonomy by 95 per cent, and six days later the country declared its independence. On 15 October Bosnia declared its sovereignty, and on 21 December the Bosnian Serbs declared their own republic within Bosnia.

Table 9   *The Bosnian general elections, November 1990*

Party	Votes (%)	Seats (no.)[a]
SDA	37.8	86
SDS BiH	26.5	72
HDZ BiH	14.7	44
SK BiH-SDP	6.0	19
SRSJ BiH	5.6	12
Others	8.4	7
Total no. of seats		240

[a] The number of seats is a composite total of the two Bosnian parliamentary chambers (Chamber of Muncipalities and Chamber of Citizens).
SDA, (Muslim) Party for Democratic Action.
SDS BiH, Serbian Democratic Party of Bosnia-Hercegovina.
HDZ BiH, Croatian Democratic Community of Bosnia-Hercegovina.
SK BiH-SDP, League of Communists–Party of Democratic Changes.
SRSJ BiH, Alliance of Reform Forces of Bosnia-Hercegovina.

In the November 1990 elections in Macedonia (Table 11), Kiro Gligorov, a former Communist, won the presidential contest, but victory in parliamentary elections went to the VMRO-DPMNE, an extreme nationalist party advocating a 'Greater Macedonia' (including parts of Bulgaria and Greece). It was not surprising that this assembly approved a declaration of independence on 25 January 1991.

At the end of February 1992 there was a two-day referendum in which the Muslims and Croats in Bosnia voted overwhelmingly in favour of independence, while the Bosnian Serbs boycotted the vote. On 27 March, Bosnian Serbs proclaimed their own constitution under their leader Rado Karadic. In April there was a Serbian offensive into Bosnia, marking the beginning of the siege of Sarajevo. On 27 April Serbia and Montenegro proclaimed the Federal Republic of Yugoslavia (FRY), of which, in June, Dobrica Cosic became President and Milan Panic was appointed Premier.

In May 1992 a new coalition government was formed in Slovenia, under President Milan Kucan. On 3 July the Croats

Table 10   *The Slovenian general elections, December 1992*

Party	Votes (%)	Seats (no.)	1990 (%)
LDS[a,b]	23.5	22	–
ZSMZ-LS	–	–	14.5
SKD[a]	14.5	15	13.0
ZLSD	13.6	14	–
SNS	10.0	12	–
SLS[a]	8.7	10	12.6
DS[a,b]	5.0	6	–
ZS[a,b]	3.7	5	8.8
SDSS	3.3	4	0.4
ZKS-SDP	–	–	17.3
SDZ	–	–	9.5
SSS[b]	2.8	–	5.4
Regional minorities[c]	0.5	2	0.0
Others	19.2	–	18.5
Total no. of seats		90	

[a] LDS, SKD, SLS, DS and ZS or their equivalent parties were part of the broad opposition DEMOS coalition in 1990 (receiving 55 per cent of the vote).
[b] In March 1994 the LDS, part of DS, ZS and SSS merged to form the Liberal Democracy of Slovenia (keeping the initials LDS).
[c] Italian and Hungarian.
LDS, Liberal Democratic Party.
ZSMZ-LS, Liberal Democratic Party.
SKD, Slovenian Christian Democrats.
ZLSD, Associated List of Social Democrats .
SNS, Slovenian Nationalist Party.
SLS, Slovenian People's Party.
DS, Democratic Party.
ZS, Greens of Slovenia.
SDSS, Social Democratic Party of Slovenia.
ZKS-SDP, Party of Democratic Reforms (reformed Communists).
SDZ, Slovene Democratic Party.
SSS, Socialist Party.

declared their own self-governing community within Bosnia. In August, in both presidential and legislative elections in Croatia, President Tudjman and his HDZ party won impressive victories. On 4 September a new Macedonian coalition government (including Albanians) took office, under Premier Branko Crvenkovski.

Table 11   *The Macedonian general elections, November 1994*

Party	Seats (no.)	1990 (no.)
SDSM[a]	58	–
SKM-PDP	–	31
LPM[a]	29	–
SRSM	–	17
SPM[a]	8	5
PDP	10	22
NDP	4	1
VMRO-DPMNE[b]	–	38
DPM[b]	1	–
SDPM	1	–
PCERM	1	1
DPT	1	–
DPJM	–	2
Independents	7	3
Total no. of seats	120	120

[a] These three parties supported President Gligorov and formed the presidential Alliance for Macedonia (SM), which won ninety-five seats altogether.
[b] VMRO–DPMNE and DPM as the main opposition parties before the elections boycotted the second round of the elections because of voting irregularities.
SDSM, Social Democratic Union of Macedonia.
SKM–PDP, Macedonian League of Communists–Party for Democratic Changes.
LPM, Liberal Party of Macedonia.
SRSM, Alliance for Reform Forces of Macededonia.
SPM, Socialist Party of Macedonia.
PDP, Party for Democratic Prosperity (Albanian).
NDP, Democratic People's Party (Albanian).
VMRO–DPMNE, Internal Macedonian Revolutionary Organisation–Democratic Party for Macedonian National Unity.
DPM, Democratic Party of Macedonia.
SDPM, Social Democratic Party of Macedonia.
PCERM, Party of Full Emancipation for Roma in Macedonia.
DPT, Democratic Party of Turks.
DPJM, Democratic Party of Yugoslavs of Macedonia.

In mid–September 1992 there were the first talks between warring Bosnian factions: an on-going process that was to continue for over three more years, along with continued fighting and ethnic cleansing. By late 1992 the Serbian forces controlled over two-thirds of Bosnia. In legislative elections in both of FRY's

Table 12   *The Montenegrin general elections, December 1992*

Party	Votes (%)	Seats(no.)	1990 (seats)
DPSCG	42.6	46	–
SKCG	–	–	83
NS	12.7	14	12
LS[a]	12.0	13	–
SRS	7.6	8	–
SDPR[a]	4.4	4	–
SRSCG	–	–	17
Coalition of Muslims and Albanians	–	–	13
Others	20.7	–	–
Total no. of seats		85	125

[a] In 1992 the LS and SDPR participated in the Opposition Bloc (OB) also including the Socialist Party and the Democratic Coalition. This alliance was opposed to the DPSCG's strong links with the Milosevic regime in Serbia.

DPSCG, Democratic Party of Socialists of Montenegro.

SKCG, League of Communists of Montenegro.

NS, National Party.

LS, Liberal Alliance.

SRS, Serbian Radical Party.

SDPR, Social Democratic Party of Reforms.

SRSCG, Alliance of Reform Forces of Montenegro.

republics (Serbia and Montenegro) the reformed Communists won parliamentary majorities (Tables 12 and 13). In presidential elections in Serbia in December 1992, Milesovic was re-elected, but the turnout was only 34 per cent.

During the spring of 1993 in Bosnia there was the collapse of the Croatian–Muslim alliance and the outbreak of armed conflict between Bosnian Croats and Muslims, particularly in and around Mostar. In December 1993 new parliamentary elections in Serbia were again won by Milosevic's Socialist Party (Table 13) and Nikola Sainovic became Premier.

In the spring of 1994, encouraged by the USA, Bosnia and Croatia formed a federation. In November 1994 elections in Macedonia (Table 11) the pro-presidential Alliance for Macedonia (SM) won an overwhelming parliamentary majority

Table 13   *The Serbian general elections, December 1993*

Party	Votes (%)	Seats (no.)	1992 (%)
SPS	36.7	123	29.0
DEPOS[a]	16.6	45	17.3
SRS	13.8	39	22.8
DS	11.6	29	4.2
DSS	5.1	7	–
DZVM	2.6	5	3.0
PDD and DPA	0.7	2	–
SSS	–	–	2.7
Others	–	–	20.6
Total no. of seats		250	

[a] In 1993 DEPOS was formed from the Serbian Renewal Movement (SPO), a splinter group of DS, and the DSS (Democratic Party of Serbia), New Democracy (ND), and a faction of the SLS *inter alia*. After the 1993 elections ND defected from the alliance to support the Milosevic government and non-SPO deputies constituted a new DEPOS without the SPO in June 1994.

SPS, Socialist Party of Serbia.
DEPOS, Serbian Democratic Movement.
SRS, Serbian Radical Party.
DS, Democratic Party.
DSS, Democratic Party of Serbia.
DZVM, Democratic Community of Vojvodina Hungarians.
PDD, Coalition of the Democratic Action Party (Albanian).
DPA, Albanian Democratic Party.
SSS, Peasant Party of Serbia.

(95 seats out of 120) after the previously largest party, the VMRO-DPMNE, pulled out of the elections because of asserted irregularities in the first round of voting. International observers indeed corroborated that some irregularities had taken place.

In July 1995 the Croats launched a sudden attack on Serbian Krajina and retook the region within a few days. The following month, NATO aeroplanes bombed Bosnian Serb strategic targets in order to lift the siege of Sarajevo. The Bosnian and Croat armies joined forces and advanced into northern and western Bosnia, relieving the siege of Bihac and retaking towns that had been under Serb control since 1992.

Table 14   *The Croatian general elections, October 1995*

Party	Votes (%)	Seats (no.)	1992 (%)
HDZ	44.2	75	43.7
HSS[a]	18.6	14	4.2
HNS[a]	–	2	6.6
HKDU[a]	–	1	–
IDS[a,b]	–	4	3.1
SBHS[a]	–	1	–
HSLS	12.0	13	17.3
SDPH	9.4	10	–
SPH–SDP	–	–	5.4
HSP[c]	4.8	–	6.9
HSP-1861	1.3	–	–
HND	3.1	1	–
ASH	1.7	1	–
HKDS	0.8	–	2.6
SNS[d]	–	2	1.1
Independents	–	4	–
Others	4.1	–	9.1
Total no. of seats		128	

[a] HSS and HNS formed an electoral alliance with three other small parties.

[b] This was an alliance of three regionalist parties in 1992.

[c] HSP had two lists in 1995: HSP and HSP–1861.

[d] In 1992 most Serbs boycotted the elections, but they were allocated thirteen seats; in 1995 most Serbs had emigrated to Serbia or northern Bosnia and the SNS won only two direct mandates.

HDZ, Croatian Democratic Community.

HSS, Croatian Peasants' Party.

HNS, Croatian National Party.

HKDU, Croatian Christian Democratic Union.

IDS, Istrian Democratic Alliance

SBHS, Slavonia-Baranja Croatian Party.

HSLS, Croatian Social-Liberal Party.

SDPH, Social Democratic Party of Croatia.

SPH–SDP, Social Democratic Party of Croatia–Party of Democratic Changes.

HSP, Croatian Party of Rights.

HSP-1861, Croatian Party of Rights 1861.

HND, Croatian Independent Democrats.

ASH, Action of Social Democrats of Croatia.

HKDS, Croatian Christian Democratic Party.

SNS, Serbian National Party.

A cease-fire began in October 1995 and peace talks were held between Presidents Milosevic, Tudjman and Izetbegovic at the Dayton airforce base in Ohio, USA, at the very beginning of November.

Riding on a wave of popularity because of his recent military victories in Krajina and northern Bosnia, President Tudjman and his HDZ party won an overwhelming victory in early elections on 22 October 1995 (Table 14), but failed to secure his wished-for two-thirds majority in Parliament.

A provisional peace treaty was signed by the three Presidents at the Dayton air base on 21 November 1995, followed by a formal signing of the final document in Paris in December. Although not all territorial problems were solved, this was the first peace deal to be agreed by all sides simultaneously. Certain specific problems were resolved, such as the status of eastern Slavonia in Croatia, which is to return to Croat control by 1997. But, in mid-1996, other aspects of the Dayton accords looked far from fulfilment, in particular the free movement of people throughout Bosnia, peaceful resolution of the division of Mostar between Muslims and Croats, the return of people to their former dwellings, and the prosecution of former President Karadic and the previous Yugoslav army chief Mladic as war criminals at the International War Tribunal at the Hague.

Further reading

For the most up-to-date information and analysis of recent events in ECE, OMRI's bi-weekly publication *Transitions* and its *Daily Digest* (also on e-mail) are probably the best sources, particularly for post-Dayton events in the former Yugoslavia.

11
Parties and party systems

As long as the party systems are not consolidated, consolidation of the new democracies as a whole is very unlikely. (Geoffrey Pridham)

The current of anti-politics, the tendency of the new social movements to mirror the inclusive political fronts set up by the Communist Party, their antagonism to state authority, and inclinations to strive in political action broadly conceived symbolic expression rather than group representation, all seem in some ways to point as much back to the practices and structures of traditional Soviet-style communism as forward to the processes of modern democracy and the structures of Western pluralism. (Paul Lewis)

In Europe in the nineteenth century, the role of political parties was to express the emerging social cleavages in a political form. They were therefore closely linked to interest organisations. In ECE after 1989 there was a distinct lack of interests to be articulated or aggregated, primarily because of the atomisation of society under the communists. The new political parties were the only political actors of any importance within the post-communist regimes, but they were imposed by elite groups from above, rather than emerging to represent groups from below.

Definition and role of political parties

Definition

Giovanni Sartori defined political parties as follows: 'A party is any political group identified by an official label that presents at elections, and is capable of placing through elections (free or non-free) candidates for public office.' Perhaps it might be added that these groups have distinct ideological preferences in terms of their party programmes and that they all pursue the overall goal of political power.

Role of political parties

Political parties have become one of the key components of any functioning democracy, in that:

- they *mediate* between society and government – and this is a distinctly two-way process, with parties keeping the government informed of new policy needs and the impact those policies have on society at large;
- they *integrate* and organise various groups within society that have similar interests, values and goals;
- they *articulate* the needs of these different interests or social groups as political demands;
- they *aggregate* the many demands made by different groups on a variety of subjects into a series of policy proposals which become the party programme and, if elected, government policy;
- they *mobilise* potential support by competing with the other political parties during election periods, thereby making the electors aware of the dominating political issues;
- they are vehicles of *recruitment* since the political leadership of most democracies comes from the party or parties winning the elections;
- their goal is *power*.

Political parties in former communist regimes

Although the ECE communist regimes called themselves people's democracies and retained many of the procedural elements of democracy – regular elections, constitutions, elected parliaments, and so on – there was a total absence of pluralistic political parties and independent associations. In some countries, there was only a single Communist Party with its guaranteed 'leading role' in society. In other ECE countries, satellite parties were allowed to stand for parliament, but were always considered subordinate to the Communist Party, and were never allowed to adopt an independent policy line.

In terms of Sartori's broad definition, however, the Communist parties under the Stalinist and post-totalitarian regimes were proper parties. But because all power was kept in the hands of either the leader (Tito, Ceausescu, Zhivkov, *inter alia*) or the single hegemonic party, the roles played by these Communist parties were very different from those suggested above. They were certainly used as agents of mobilisation, information and recruitment, and their overall goal was definitely power, but, otherwise, the first four roles listed above hardly applied.

Parties in ECE since 1989

Political parties or social movements?

The initial transition from communism to democracy was performed by quite broad and unstructured social movements which appealed initially to the non-communist majority. Their supporters included people from all walks of life with a multitude of different political viewpoints. This meant that they did not speak on behalf of a specific group within society, but rather on behalf of 'everyone'.

These 'social movements' were coalitions of a large number of small groups, whether potential political parties or small interest groups. The Czech OF, for example, contained fourteen different entities, among them Social Democrats, Christian Democrats, neo-liberals, reformist communists, former dissidents and ecologists. The Bulgarian SDS was composed of seventeen separate groupings, again both parties and interest groups, including the revived Social Democratic Party, the environmental group Eco-glasnost and the Green Party. The Slovenian DEMOS combined seven different parties, including Christian Democrats, Liberals, Agrarians and Greens. Solidarity was a composite of workers' and peasants' groups, trade unionists and intellectuals, Christian and Social Democrats, and others.

With the possible exception of Polish Solidarity, these new movements did not focus their activities on the acquisition and retention of 'power', but rather on simply gaining adequate representation to defeat the Communists. In fact, they could be understood more as organised collective action directed against the previous regime: uniting the people *against* the former communist regime, rather than *for* any particular model of society.

In comparison with political parties, a social movement has the following characteristics:

- a very vague, non-specific ideology and/or programme – in 1989 this meant expressing little more than support for the market economy and pluralistic democracy;
- broad electoral support and a wide spectrum of viewpoints;
- a very general (and moralistic) electoral programme;
- 'catch-all' appeal that cuts right across the left–right spectrum as well as the religious divide;
- loose organisational structure;
- more characteristics of a pressure group than a political party;
- a tendency to mobilise on a single issue (in the case of the first 'founding' elections this was to defeat the Communists);
- an aim that is simply representation, not power;
- its parliamentarians lack interest in the organisational aspects of the party and have very little party discipline in parliament.

Such political groupings specifically refrained from using the word 'party' to escape from the connotations of the past, calling themselves front, forum, union, movement or community. They often referred to themselves specifically as 'social movements'. This applied to most anti-communist formations throughout the region in the immediate post-revolutionary phase, for example Solidarity in Poland, the Hungarian MDF, OF and VPN in Czechoslovakia, the FSN in Romania and the SDS in Bulgaria.

Typology of political parties in ECE

At present, the proto-parties of ECE find themselves at an embryonic stage of development, a type of pre-party-political phase, resembling Western Europe in the 1820–30s. It is difficult, therefore, to formulate a typology of political parties according to Western classifications, but certain points of similarity and contrast with Western Europe can be made.

(1) *The lack of mass parties.* Generally speaking in the West, mass parties represent large, well defined groups within society, such as social democratic or labour parties representing workers, Christian democratic parties standing for Roman Catholics, and agrarian parties acting on behalf of small farmers. These parties then build up a large membership and strong local, regional and national organisations based primarily on their core electorate.

In ECE countries, however, membership of political parties is extremely low, except for the communist successor parties, most of which inherited large memberships. Very few parties have established regional or local organisations, so there is little regular communication between leaders and members. Indeed, very few post-communist leaders appreciated the need for a well organised political party base. There were some exceptions though: Lech Walesa realised he required a loyal party behind him in order to win the Polish presidency in 1990; and the Czech Premier Vaclav Klaus understood the need for a strong party base in order to 'sell' the economic reform package to the population.

In fact, it is unlikely that mass parties could have developed out of the revolutionary dissident movements, as they were so exclusively tied to a very small intellectual elite – with the possible exception of Solidarity, which could have built upon its millions of former members to develop into a true workers' movement. Otherwise the only potential mass parties are the communist successor parties.

In any case, the ECE political parties still do not know whom they represent, so there is no targeting of core electorates. Mass parties are therefore at an embryonic stage and it is impossible to estimate how long this will last. It has been said, therefore, that the post-revolutionary situation resembles 'democracy without parties'.

(2) *The predominance of cadre parties.* 'Cadre' parties, on the other hand, are very small parties, usually focused on a narrow and particular ideology or intellectual group within society, which makes them more like the small cliques that were prevalent in Western Europe before the extension of the suffrage. They are in abundance in ECE.

Gyorgy Markus calls these parties 'intellectual milieu parties', in the sense that all the party activists have the same sort of life experience, similar familial and educational backgrounds, 'speak the same language', and so on, but have difficulties in communicating with the wider electorate.

(3) *The personalisation of politics.* Parties in ECE have therefore tended to centre around one or a few leading personalities, who often have quite similar ideologies, but are unable to work together. Very frequently there is a nuance of differentiation that separates the parties, which is often used to justify the personal enmity between the two party leaders.

The fragmentation of several parties, big and small, is more or less a product of the personalisation of politics. The Czech OF, Polish Solidarity, the Romanian FSN, the Bulgarian SDS, even the (very small) Bulgarian Agrarians: all of these groupings split mainly because of personality differences between political leaders. Only the communist successor parties – in particular SLD and PSL in Poland, and MSZP in Hungary – have managed to remain intact despite in-fighting among their members and leaders.

(4) *'Catch-all' parties in reverse.* Usually, the West European mass parties have broadened their appeal and targeted the centre of the political spectrum, as well as their core electorate, in order to become 'catch-all' parties, appealing thereby to a larger segment of the population.

In a sense, party politics in ECE is starting backwards: the 'catch-all' social movements appeal to all groups within society in order to rid themselves of the 'common enemy', then these movements break down into introspective 'cadre' parties, focused very much on one ideology or one group of intellectuals.

(5) *The non-applicability of 'left' and 'right'*. It is quite difficult to apply the terms 'right wing' and 'left wing' to political parties in ECE: they are very different entities from similar parties found on the right or left in Western Europe, even when they use the same names or have joined pan-European party political alliances.

Polish Solidarity and the Hungarian MDF were both seen as centre-right groupings, yet they were both statist in attitude, as well as being pro-Christian and nationalistic. In the 1991–93 Solidarity-led governments, the 'left-wing' SLD consistently supported privatisation measures, while the statist and nationalistic factions of Solidarity often tried to block some aspects of economic legislation.

In Slovakia throughout 1993 the Slovak Party of the Democratic Left (SDL, the successor party to the former Communists) criticised the nationalist and statist HZDS government for being far too left wing.

Post-electoral coalition behaviour also militates against there being any real concept of 'left' and 'right' in ECE. For example, the more welfare-oriented Hungarian MSZP and the neo-liberal, market-oriented SZDSZ formed a two-party coalition after the May 1994 elections.

(6) *Anti-system parties*. These usually took the shape of nationalist or regionalist parties pressing for independence along nationalist lines; for example, the main political parties emerging in Slovenia, Croatia and Macedonia in 1990–91 all advocated greater autonomy and the right to secede from the Yugoslav state. The same could be said of Vladimir Meciar's HZDS and the SNS in Slovakia, in terms of wanting an end to the Czechoslovak Federation after the 1992 elections.

(7) *Anti-party parties*. Overall, the emerging social movements were a special type of 'anti-party' – a barely organised social

movement, which rejected the title 'party', declined to represent specific interests, did not establish the usual national–regional–local party network that exists in most Western democracies, and did not require the party loyalty that is normal in most West European parliaments. These were sometimes conscious decisions taken on behalf of party leaders in order to escape any similarities with the past. More often, though, it was a lack of realisation of what is required for the proper organisation of political parties.

Political party families

When looking at different party families, it is crucial to examine where the party came from and what core interests the party intends to represent. The problem with this approach is that in most ECE countries political parties have had the same sort of beginning (within an intellectual clique) and are not firmly attached to any particular social group within society. Even so, in name at least, the same sorts of party political families that exist in Western Europe have established, or re-established, themselves in most ECE countries since 1989.

The communist family

The communist parties are very different from the pre-1989 'Party'. To begin with, they have usually shed their more conservative, hard-line wings, which have either disappeared or have become quite irrelevant electorally, like the Hungarian Socialist Workers' Party, the extreme left-wing Czech Communist Party (SCK) or the Bulgarian Communist Party. Such parties continue with the political orientation of the previous regime and have no real future in ECE.

Otherwise, most ECE 'communist' parties have rejected their communist ideology and turned into social democratic parties, undergoing a change of name and leadership, and a radical transformation of policy. The Hungarian MSZP, the Polish SLD, the Czech KSCM, the East German PDS and the Slovak SDL, are all such communist successor parties. In some cases the transformation of policy has been much less radical, for example with the Bulgarian BSP, the Romanian PDSR (formerly FSN) and the Serbian SPS. Moreover, most also managed to retain their local and regional party organisations, as well as a sizeable proportion of their former membership and finances to become by far the best organised political parties in the post-1989 period.

The ex-communist parties enjoy the greatest popular support in Romania, Bulgaria, Hungary, Poland, Serbia and Macedonia. In Romania the PDSR and the PD–FSN between them occupy about half the seats in parliament. The BSP, MSZP and Macedonian SDSM/SPM received 52 per cent, 54 per cent and 55 per cent of parliamentary seats respectively after the 1994 elections. In Poland the two communist successor parties – the SLD and PSL – obtained 66 per cent of the seats in the Sejm in 1993.

Most are fully committed to a West-European-style social democracy and market economy, so such parties are not a threat to the economic and political transition. Only the Romanian PDSR seems to have been 'hijacked' by members of the old Communist elite, who stuck to former behavioural patterns. The newly founded ZRS, under its leader Jan Luptak, also adopts a much more traditional left-wing stance, opposing both the concept of privatisation and any form of cooperation with the IMF. The Bulgarian BSP has also engaged in some back-sliding, for example in its attempt to make a partial return to collectivisation of agriculture. Otherwise, most leaders and members of the ex-communist parties have a vested interest in the success of the reform process.

The communist successor parties have gained support by criticising the adverse social effects of the economic transition. Hence their voters are mainly rural peasant farmers, urban industrial workers in large state-run companies, low-paid state employees and pensioners. Some former Communist parties have turned to nationalism as a means of retaining popular appeal, for example the SPS since 1987 under Slobodan Milosevic with his advocacy of a Greater Serbia.

The social democratic family

Social democratic parties had existed throughout the region in the inter-war period, but were eventually suppressed or abolished by various wartime fascist regimes. In the immediate post-war period they were forced into a merger with the Communists, and their leaders were often persecuted in the Stalinist purges of the early 1950s. This applies to the Polish Socialist Party, the Czechoslovak and Hungarian Social Democrats.

After 1989, social democratic parties (i.e. those which are *not* successor parties to the Communists) founded themselves all over ECE, but generally did not do well in the polls. They also had internal problems: the 'generation gap' was a source of conflict, with the older generation of social democrats often clinging to the ideas of 'socialism with a human face' or the 'third way' and rejecting the pragmatic and more realistic pro-market orientation of the younger generation.

The green parties

Green parties exist throughout ECE, but have made little headway in most elections, because the former centrally planned economies need to be transformed before environmental issues move to the forefront of political debate. As far as most governments in ECE are concerned, ecological considerations will always come second, since no ECE government has the enormous amounts of money that would be necessary for the massive injection of capital into environmental improvement. Whether or not this is a mistake as far as the region is concerned is immaterial – it is a necessary fact of life for the present. In late 1995 Bulgaria even re-opened its sixth reactor at the Kozloduy nuclear power plant on the Danube (adjudged 'unsafe' by international experts) because it could not find other affordable supplies of energy. Thus economic needs predominate for the moment.

The Christian democratic parties

Owing to the importance of the Catholic Church in many countries, it was almost inevitable that Christian democracy would be a major force in politics in ECE. But wherever pre-war Christian democratic parties were refounded as continuations of those parties which existed in the pre-communist period, they often returned to more conservative, if not authoritarian, traditions that are quite different from the West European Christian democratic parties; this is so, for example, with the Slovak KDH, the Hungarian KDNP, and the small Polish Christian National Union (ZCHN).

This means that Christian democratic parties are much less easily identifiable than in Western Europe. In Hungary, for example, there is a party calling itself the Christian Democrats (KDNP), but it is the MDF which is recognised by the West European Christian democrats as their Hungarian sister party, since the MDF is much more 'centrist'.

Similarly, in Poland, the Centre Alliance (PC) is the major Christian democratic party, and it is a member of the Christian Democratic International. But several other small Christian democratic parties exist – the Christian Peasant Alliance (SLCH), the Christian Democratic Party (PCHD) and the Christian Democracy (CHD), all of which formed themselves into the Republican Coalition. This coalition entered the Hanna Suchocka 1992–93 government and kept its ideological distance from the Centre Alliance.

The main party of this family within the Czech Republic is the KDU/CSL, which existed as a satellite party under the appellation 'People's Party' during the communist regime. A change of name and leadership, combined with internal reforms – but still retaining the grassroots network – has meant the party performed credibly in post-1989 elections (receiving 6–8 per cent of the vote) and is currently part of the Czech neo-liberal/centrist coalition government. The very small Christian Democratic Party (KDS) was also a member of the same government coalition, until the majority of the party merged with the ODS on 31 March 1996.

The secular neo-liberal parties

The Czech ODS, which emerged from a split in the OF, is probably the best example of this type. In rhetoric, it has adopted a typically Western neo-liberal stance in terms of ideology and economic policy, reflecting the personal conviction of its leader, the economist Vaclav Klaus. Under his leadership the ODS assumed an uncompromising position against the Slovaks concerning the future of the Federation. The party is avowedly secular, but fought the 1992 elections in alliance with the Christian KDS, and has also drawn the KDU/CSL into the governing coalition. The party also bases much of its appeal on anti-communist rhetoric.

The Hungarian SZDSZ is similar in ideology and also advocates radical and rapid economic reform. This party spurns nationalism, and is very wary of any signs of anti-Semitism in the public or private sphere. Since August 1994 the SZDSZ has been in a strange coalition with the MSZP: the non-party Economics Minister, J. Bielecki, refused to serve in the post-1994 MSZP-led government, unless the SZDSZ was part of the coalition. Otherwise, such parties tend to be quite small and have relatively little influence, like the Liberal Democratic Congress (KLD) in Poland, which has received 4–7.5 per cent of votes.

The secular conservatives

In ECE such parties tend to be linked with business groups, and remain quite small and on the periphery of politics. In ideological terms, such parties are very close to the neo-liberal parties (e.g. the Czech ODA, Poland's Party X, Bulgaria's BBB).

The classic liberals

The ideological position of these parties is centrist rather than right wing, which means greater emphasis on social welfare, while remaining pro-market. Neo-liberal economic policy is seen as too ideological and uncaring, so classic liberals prefer an approach which is more pragmatic and more humane, closer to social democracy.

Such classic liberal parties are few and far between in ECE, with the Czech Civic Movement (OH) – named the Free Democrats (SD) from 1993 onwards – representing the best example (it achieved only 4 and 2 per cent of the vote in the 1992 and 1996 parliamentary elections, respectively, and therefore failed to be represented in parliament). The Romanian PNL (which has received 4–6.5 per cent of votes) is also of this type. Such parties tend to be dominated by intellectuals, often former dissidents, and appeal to the urban professional middle classes.

The Freedom Union (UW) – the former Democratic Union (UD) – in Poland is also best described as a classic liberal party in the sense that it is closer to social democracy in terms of ideology and policy than neo-liberalism. However, the UW/UD has consistently supported radical economic reforms (known as the 'big bang' or 'shock therapy'). The UW leadership still contains many of the leading figures of the former dissident movement.

Some factions within the UD took their secularism to the extreme of being openly antagonistic towards Roman Catholicism in Polish politics and society. This anti-Catholic stance played a part in the fall of the UD government in June 1993 – partly over the issue of abortion, in which the Church and the UD were at odds. However, the UD's secularism did not prevent it from accepting the more traditional, and somewhat authoritarian, Christian parties into its 1992–93 government coalition. The UW/ UD is also firmly opposed to nationalism and anti-Semitism.

The agrarians

Throughout ECE this family was one of the strongest in terms of parliamentary representation between the wars – particularly in Czechoslovakia, Bulgaria, Poland and Hungary. Agrarian parties and their leaders were also among the most persecuted by the Communists – precisely because of their pre-war strength. Since 1989, only the Polish PSL and the Hungarian FKGP have played significant roles in their respective countries' politics.

In Poland agriculture was not collectivised during the communist period, so small peasant farmers continued to be the norm right up to 1989. The satellite United Peasants' Party (ZSL) was allowed to exist in alliance with the Communists. In the first totally free elections in Poland, in 1991, three peasant parties scored relatively well: the PSL (a successor to the ZSL) and the two-party Peasant Alliance (which had grown out of Rural Solidarity) received the support of the majority of rural peasant farmers. Differences in background and growing animosity between the party leaders meant there was little scope for cooperation, despite the obvious similarity of the party programmes.

The Hungarian FKGP was part of the first post-revolutionary coalition with the MDF and KDNP. It left that coalition when the government seemed to back down on its promise to restore land to peasants.

Fragmentation of the different peasant parties in Bulgaria meant that there was no coherent small-farmers' voice in parliament. In the Czech Republic, the Agrarian Party was left-oriented and fought the 1992 general elections in coalition with the former Socialist Party and the Greens: this coalition, the Liberal Social Union (LSU), attained 8 per cent of the total vote. The two Slovak peasants' parties are minute and field candidates in coalitions with other leading parties.

The far right

This group, with nationalistic, anti-foreigner, anti-immigrant and anti-Semitic overtones, is generally a small but disruptive fringe. For example, the Republican Party (SPR-RSC) in the Czech Republic is a far-right, neo-fascist party not dissimilar to those found in Western Europe – indeed, it is very similar to its namesake in Germany. Although numerically very small, the party has had a big impact on the Czech political scene: through the controversiality of its outspoken leader, Miroslav Sladek, its frequent public demonstrations, which often turn to violence, and its unrelenting opposition to Czech President Vaclav Havel.

Regionalist/nationalist parties

Nationalist parties seeking independence or greater autonomy. Because of the importance of the concept of nationhood since 1989, most parties have appealed to national sentiments at election time. For example, the largest Slovak party in the 1992 and 1994 elections, the HZDS, had a clear nationalist platform, advocating a quasi-independent status for Slovakia within the former Czechoslovak Federation in 1992 and playing upon the fears of the Hungarian minority in 1994. But there is also the Slovak National Party (SNS), which usually obtains 8–10 per cent of the vote, and which has now become crucial for post-1992 coalition politics.

Even though Poland is ethnically the most homogeneous country in ECE (being 98 per cent Polish), nationalism still plays a significant role in politics – as it has in previous centuries. The largest overtly nationalist party is the KPN, which receives 6–8 per cent support. Nationalists within all political parties – especially some Solidarity parties – played a role in delaying the large-scale privatisation partly because of the fear of selling the 'family silver' to foreigners.

Romania has two major nationalist parties: the PUNR, under Gheorghe Funar, is vehemently against the Hungarian minority in Transylvania, whereas the PRM seeks to incorporate the ex-Soviet republic of Moldova into Romania. Although these two parties had only 'nuisance value' for most of the post-1989 period, they began informally to back the ruling PDSR in parliament from 1994, entering into a formal coalition in early 1995 – only for that arrangement to end in October 1995, when the PRM persisted in criticising President I. Iliescu.

Parties representing ethnic minorities. There are also several nationalist/regionalist parties which represent a specific national or ethnic minority. Such parties seek to protect the human rights, language and/or culture of the minority group in the face of possible assimilation by the majority. Some advocate various degrees of regional autonomy, if not independence, and most are supported overwhelmingly by the minority they claim to represent. The Hungarian Democratic Union of Romania (UDMR) receives the votes of most of the Hungarian-speakers in Transylvania. In Slovakia, the four Hungarian parties unite at elections and obtain almost 100 per cent support from the Hungarian community. In Bulgaria the DPS speaks somewhat indirectly on behalf of the Turkish minority. The regionalist Movement for a Self-Governing Democracy of Moravia and Silesia (HSD-SMS) also advocates greater autonomy for its region within the Czech Republic. (This Movement split after 1992 and its electoral support collapsed to less than 0.5 per cent in the 1996 elections.)

Finally, it is worth mentioning that gypsy parties also exist throughout the region, but are usually too small to gain parliamentary representation, although they are usually assured of at least one parliamentary deputy in Macedonia.

Definition of a party system

A country's party system refers to the particular interaction of political parties that emerge from regular and competitive elections, that is, the number of party families that gain representation, their pattern of competition and their coalition behaviour. It is worth emphasising that the structure and stabilisation of the party system is crucial for the stabilisation of any emerging democratic regime.

However, given the novelty and unpredictability of ECE party politics, it is too early as yet to fit each of their new democracies precisely into Western models of party political behaviour. In fact, Barbara Misztal has specifically warned against describing the emerging party systems 'in terms of normal Western criteria', while Attila Agh has argued that it is too early to analyse party systems in ECE since they are still suffering from 'all kinds of "infantile disorders"'. Bohdan Szklarski even talks about 'non-party systems' within the region. But some initial comparative observations can be made which will serve as a possible guide for future developments.

Factors affecting the formation of party systems

These factors are:

- the specific history of each country;
- existing political cleavages – that is, to what extent diverse groups (social class, religious, ethnic, regional, farmers etc.) are represented within society;
- the degree of polarisation or consensus between the different party-political groups;
- constitutional constraints, such as whether there is a federal or unitary system, since the former will allow the emergence of a varied constellation of parties in the different federal units;
- electoral system – for example, proportional representation encourages a multiplicity of political parties, while a majority system can stifle representation of a sizeable group of the electorate;
- prevailing political culture – for example, can the various parties coalesce easily, as in the more consensual democracies of Scandinavia, the Benelux countries or Switzerland, or do too many parties or a conflictual political culture lead to parliamentary immobilism, as in the German Weimar Republic in 1918–33 or Czechoslovakia in 1990–92.

Sartori's theory of party systems

Giovanni Sartori developed a comprehensive theory of party systems that combined two variables: the number of parties in parliament and the style/behaviour of those parties. He elaborated six major types of party systems.

1   *single-party system*, when only one party is permitted (which can be left or right, communist or fascist), such as the Communist Party states of Eastern Europe, 1948–89;

2   *hegemonic party system*, where other parties are allowed and contest the elections, but one party is absolutely predominant, as in Mexico for the past sixty-five years;

3   *predominant party system*, where there are other competing
     parties but one party obtains the majority of votes or seats
     and governs alone over a long period of time (at least four
     consecutive elections), but can be and is defeated by the
     other opposition parties combining, as has happened in
     India, Japan, Ireland, Sweden and Norway;

4   *two-party system*, which is a very competitive system (e.g. in
     Great Britain, USA, Australia and New Zealand), where
     there is alternation of single-party government between two
     parties, either of which has the chance of winning an absolute
     majority of seats in parliament – one party then governs
     alone and the other goes into opposition, with the electorate
     seeing party competition in terms of only two parties;

5   *moderate pluralism*, in which three to five relevant or
     important parties with coalescent behaviour tend to form
     bipolar, centre-right versus centre-left, governmental co-
     alitions of two or more parties, with almost all parties being
     potential coalition partners. Voters' preferences are centrist
     and party competition is centripetal (moving to the centre).
     There is a relatively small ideological distance between the
     most relevant parties and most policies are moderate, so
     conflicts centre on day-to-day legislation and individual
     governmental policies. The fundamental 'rules of the game'
     are already firmly established

6   *polarised pluralism*, in which there are usually more than five
     parties, with considerable 'ideological distance' between
     them, often including significant anti-system parties which
     reject democratic politics. There is an 'ideological approach'
     to politics, with strongly polarised and centrifugal com-
     petition (moving to the extremes), leading to exclusively
     bilateral (i.e. incompatible) oppositions, the 'centre position-
     ing' of one party or a group of parties, 'irresponsible
     oppositions' and the 'politics of outbidding'. There is a
     polarised 'ideological patterning' to party competition,
     which becomes populist and antagonistic, based on prin-
     ciples, emotions and passions, rather than rational, reasoned
     debate and the ability to compromise.

Inter-war party systems in ECE

The inter-war ECE party systems were mostly very short lived. What happened in Poland was quite typical for the region: thirty-two political parties gained representation in the Sejm after the 1918 elections, all of which had great difficulty in working together. Parliamentary government became increasingly chaotic until it was eventually suspended by a military coup, led by Marshal Pilsudski, who then inaugurated a personal, authoritarian dictatorship. In Romania, Bulgaria and Yugoslavia it was monarchical dictatorship; in Hungary the military ruled. Everywhere assassinations of leading politicians and the rise of fascist parties played a role in undermining the new democracies.

For their short lifespan, the inter-war party systems were characterised by polarised pluralism:

- there were several extremist and fascist 'anti-system' parties that wanted to put an end to the liberal democratic systems (e.g. in Hungary, Poland, Austria, Germany);
- there were several parties in the various parliaments (e.g. the thirty-two in Poland) with great 'ideological distance' between them, and even when there were only two major parties, intense ideological differences made cooperation quite impossible (e.g. the political civil war and the ghetto-like attitudes in both Austria and Bulgaria);
- there was a centrist coalition in almost all of these countries (e.g. Hungary, Germany, Poland);
- political party competition was strongly polarised and centrifugal, with support for both left and right extremes gaining significantly during the 1930s, as in Germany.

The only possible exception to this scenario was a type of strongly coalescent party behaviour that emerged in Czechoslovakia under the strong moral leadership of their first President, Tomas Masaryk. The Czechoslovak government for almost twenty years was a semi-permanent coalition of the five leading parties (nicknamed the '*petka*') in which the party leaders governed consensually under the watchful eye of their paternalistic but democratic President. However, even here there were extremist, fascist parties, such as the Sudeten German Nationalists, who wanted union with Germany and who emerged as the largest party (15 per cent of votes) in the last elections to be held during the First Czechoslovak Republic in 1935.

Post-war Communist single-party systems

Usually only the Communist Party was permitted. When other parties were allowed (e.g. the Peasants' Party in Poland, and the People's Party in Czechoslovakia) they were subservient to the Communists. These were effectively single-party systems behind a facade of competition provided by satellite parties.

Party systems in ECE since 1990

In a repetition of the inter-war scenario, for the first six years the post-revolutionary party systems have been characterised by a multiplicity of political parties and a lack of consensus between most of those parties. It is not possible, however, simply to classify these party systems as 'polarised', since they are more 'in-between', with elements of both polarised and moderate pluralism.

The application of moderate pluralism

After the first or second elections, there were often three to five relevant or important parties with a degree of coalescent behaviour and lasting coalitions, for example in Hungary, 1990–94, the Czech Republic from 1993, and the 1990–92 DEMOS coalition in Slovenia.

The coalitions in ECE have been bipolar, centre-left versus centre-right, for example in Bulgaria, 1990–94, when the BSP reformed communists constituted one pole, the SDS democratic forces the other, with the party of the Turkish minority (DPS) playing the role of possible coalition partner for either pole.

On the whole, the coalitions before the return of the ex-communists were centre-right, like the Catholic–conservative MDF/FKGP/KDNP 1990–94 coalition in Hungary, the Catholic–neo-liberal ODS/ODA/KDS/KDU/CSL coalition in the Czech Republic, and the centre-right ex-Solidarity coalitions in Poland in 1989–93. Coalitions after the return of the ex-communists were strongly centre-left, like the ex-communist/neo-liberal MSZP/SZDSZ coalition in Hungary since mid-1994 and the SLD/PSL coalition in Poland since autumn 1993.

In the former Czechoslovakia, 1990–93, the right–left bi-polarity was expressed not by a two-party system but two *party systems*, each of them concentrated in one of the two republics. The party systems were clearly built around the national/ethnic cleavage represented by the two republics within the federation.

There is predominantly centripetal party competition and a 'centrist' tendency, with generally moderate policies accepted by (almost) all, as the vast majority of the electorate is not yet attracted by extremes – that is, hard-line Communist parties or extremist groupings from the right. But this in no way resembles the classic consensual polities where coalition government is of a very stable nature. Government stability has characterised the Czech Republic since 1993, but this has been mainly due to the domination of the four-party coalition by ODS and Premier Klaus (seriously undermined only since June 1996). Otherwise, all ECE party systems since 1989 have had a strong tendency towards 'polarised pluralism', making the consolidation of democracy more difficult.

The application of polarised pluralism

There are still some extremist and fascist parties, but these have been very small in size and electoral support, like Sladek's Republican Party in the Czech Republic; similarly, no really relevant hard-line Communist or extreme left-wing parties remain significant, with the possible exception of the Slovak ZRS.

Bulgaria had some extreme monarchist and ultranational parties, with the extreme 'left' being represented by several Marxist and neo-Marxist parties in the early 1990 and 1991 elections, but they all failed to cross the 4 per cent electoral threshold.

There was a very large grouping which dominated the centre in all ECE countries, such as the Hungarian MDF, Solidarity in Poland, SDS in Bulgaria and OF/VPN in Czechoslovakia: all these broad social movements attempted to become classic 'catch-all' parties through a primarily negative appeal to all sections of the population, demonstrating a perfect example of Sartori's 'centre positioning'.

The Slovak SNS and HZDS were both anti-system parties between 1990 and 1993 according to Sartori's definition, in that they both wanted to end the federal regime within which they were operating.

Political party competition was strongly polarised and centrifugal, but mostly directed 'against' the Communists in the first elections; thereafter polarisations emerged in respect of the speed of the economic reform process, the role of the Church in society and de-communisation.

There were several parties in the various parliaments, with great ideological distance between them and a lack of coalescent behaviour, even when those parties had similar backgrounds and/or policies, as did the different factions of the former Solidarity movement (which were very strongly divided on moral/ideological issues, like abortion, de-communisation and the role of the Church in the state).

In Bulgaria, ideological polarisation was very marked. The SDS, and especially its leader Filip Dimitrov, were driven by a strong anti-communism which made any cooperation with the BSP almost impossible. In Hungary, party competition was also highly ideological between the MSZP and MDF, mainly over the issue of de-communisation. The ideological distance between the other important parties was not as large in Bulgaria, hence the post-1994 neo-liberal/ex-communist coalition in Hungary.

In the former Czechoslovakia considerable ideological distance was expressed by the nationalistic differences between the two republics, to the extent that even pro-federal parties were organised at the republican level for the 1992 elections. In effect there were two separate sets of multipolar party systems within the joint federal republic.

During the various electoral campaigns in the region, there were several examples of nationalistic 'outbidding' (Slovakia and former Yugoslavia) and economic/social 'outbidding' (most communist successor parties, especially in Hungary, Bulgaria and Poland).

As a result of novelty and inexperience, the new parliaments in Czechoslovakia, Hungary, Bulgaria and Poland in particular had several parliamentary crises. In Czechoslovakia and Hungary this led to different degrees of parliamentary immobilism, in Poland and Bulgaria to frequent changes of government.

Fragmentation and instability in post-communist party systems

The political movements that emerged from the first elections tended to cover the entire left–right spectrum. For example, OF included among its leading members Petr Uhl, a self-confessed Trotskyite, and Vaclav Klaus, a well known neo-liberal monetarist economist. It was almost inevitable that such groups would begin to split into different factions once there was a normalisation of politics after the defeat of the former Communist parties.

Solidarity split into about fifteen different parliamentary groupings within eighteen months of its electoral victory in June 1989. The Czech OF, too, divided into three new factions and saw many former members join other existing parties. The Romanian FSN separated into two and the Bulgarian SDS split in various directions in the run-up to the 1994 elections.

There has been a proliferation of political parties in ECE, which is clearly affecting political stability. For example, there was incredible fragmentation at the 1991 parliamentary elections in Poland: twenty-nine parties attained representation, out of sixty fielded candidates (in all 111 parties were registered). In the subsequent parliament eleven parties were represented by only one deputy, and only two political parties scored over 9 per cent of the vote.

In the 1992 Czechoslovak elections, 126 groupings/movements/parties were registered, and forty-two presented lists of candidates, but only nine and five parties gained representation in the Federal Assembly from the Czech and Slovak Republics respectively – because of the 5 per cent electoral threshold. Similarly, in Bulgaria, eighty parties were registered, thirty-eight contested the October 1991 elections and eight gained representation. Many of these parties were extremely small and more like lobby groups on particular issues.

There was also a high degree of volatility among parliamentary factions, with some parties changing their leaders and their alliances with quite bewildering speed. In the Hungarian parliament – probably the most stable ECE parliament of the 1990–94 period – 10 per cent of deputies left their previous party to establish ten new parties, another 10 per cent changed their party allegiance to existing parties, and a further 5 per cent simply resigned.

A related problem was that of electoral volatility, whereby the first batch of post-revolutionary politicians have been rejected at the second or third round of elections. For example, almost the entire government elite changed in June 1992 in the Czech Republic, in May 1994 in Hungary, in October 1993 in Poland and finally in Bulgaria in December 1994.

Reasons for party fragmentation

No social basis on which to build. To begin with, as has been indicated, there are very weak cleavages within post-communist societies – a legacy of the communist period – so a party has no firm foundations on which to build.

No strong party identification. Understandably, party identification at the moment is almost non-existent, since:

• it is too early for such identification – which comes from personal approximation to a party's programme over a number of elections;

- all parties' programmes were more or less identical in the first elections;
- formal party links with emerging social groups have not yet been firmly established.

Natural fragmentation. The parties themselves are quite naturally fragmented as:

- they are new and non-institutionalised;
- it is unclear what the party stands for;
- no political party was able to gauge where its support lay;
- the whole electorate was open to political persuasion – anyone could have won the first elections;
- several parties were thus competing for the same social constituency, so they tended to strive for ideological purity in order to stress their differentiation.

Dominance of political issues. Political issues (over which it is much easier to disagree) were more prominent than political cleavages.

Parties as 'top-down' elite organisations. Instead of being anchored in group representation, political parties were created by 'top-down' elite initiatives – for reasons of both ideological distinctiveness and personal ambition, with the role of leading personalities being paramount.

Overwhelming lack of linkages. There is a lack of linkages between political parties and the electorate. There was a consequential 'representative abyss' which was exacerbated by the parties' search for ideological purity, which distanced the parties even further from the electorate.

Institutional factors. Institutional factors also added to the problem of fragmentation.

First, proportional representation exacerbated the social fragmentation by favouring smaller political parties – especially in Poland, where there was no electoral threshold before 1993. However, even with an electoral threshold in 1991, the fragmentation of the party system would still have occurred. Furthermore, no alteration in the electoral system could have dealt with the centrifugal forces which split the Czech and Slovak Federal Republic after the June 1992 elections.

Secondly, there is very clear sovereignty of parliament in most post-communist political systems, yet at the same time very loose party discipline, which automatically leads to a type of legislative anarchy and parliamentary immobilism.

It is noticeable that where there is tight party discipline of the leading political party (e.g. the Czech Republic since 1993, the communist successor parties in Poland, Bulgaria and Hungary since 1994) and some degree of accompanying executive dominance, there is greater party unity.

Personality clashes. The personal ambitions of many of the leading politicians also exacerbated the fragmentation of parties. The party was usually seen as a means of achieving something rather for oneself rather than an organisation with an intrinsic value in itself.

In all ECE countries, splits within the parties or party coalitions often occurred because of personal animosities between leading political leaders, not as ideological or political differences at the level of political programmes.

Conclusion

Instability within the party systems has waned somewhat since the return to power of the communist successor parties. Given that the behaviour of the political elites themselves is the crucial variable in this stabilisation process, then the professionalism and unity of the ex-communist elites was bound to be a stabilising factor.

The characteristics enumerated above are most typical of undeveloped party systems. To some extent, given the newness of the political situation, party fragmentation was inevitable. In a way, a transition to democracy needs several parties at the beginning, to cater to the divergent interests of the society emerging from authoritarian/post-totalitarian rule.

However they are viewed, most ECE parties still have a very long way to go before they achieve the level of organisation found in established democracies in Western Europe. So far it seems that the political parties in ECE have made only the first tentative steps as mediators between the voters and the central governments. From this embryonic stage, it will take time before political parties throughout the region emerge as fully fledged parties as we know them in the West.

Further reading

Attila Agh, 'The Emerging Party System in ECE', *Budapest Papers on Democratic Transition*, No. 13, Budapest University of Economics, 1992.

Sten Berglund and Jan Ake Dellenbrant (eds), *The New Democracies in Eastern Europe. Party Systems and Party Cleavages*, Edward Elgar, 1991.

Jan Ake Dellenbrant, 'Parties and Party Systems in Eastern Europe', in *Developments in East European Politics* (Stephen White, Judy Batt and Paul Lewis, eds), Macmillan, 1993.

Michael Gallagher, Michael Laver and Peter Mair, *Representative Government in Western Europe* (chapter 3), McGraw-Hill, 1992.

Herbert Kitschelt, 'The Formation of Party Systems in ECE', *Politics and Society*, 20 (1), March 1992.

Barbara A. Misztal, 'Must Eastern Europe Follow the Latin American Way?', *European Journal of Sociology*, 33, 1992.

Giovanni Sartori, *Parties and Party Systems: A Framework for Analysis*, Cambridge University Press, 1976.

Bohdan Szklarski, 'A Party "Non-system" – Relationship between Political Parties and Electorate in the Conditions of Systemic Change', discussion paper, Institute of Political Studies of the Polish Academy of Sciences, Warsaw, 1992.

Gordon Wightman (ed.), *Party Formation in ECE*, Edward Elgar, 1995.

12
The new legislatures

ECE countries themselves are huge Hyde-Park-Corners where everybody argues and nobody listens. (Attila Agh)

In every community there is a percentage of persons who are dishonest, stupid and incompetent. We are rather astounded by their over-representation in our Parliament. (E. Skalski)

The people who make revolutions know only how to destroy things, not to build things ... which is why they make very bad politicians. (Jan Urban)

In terms of the institutionalisation of democracy in newly democratising regimes, it is important to stress that without a strong parliament, central to the process of transition, there is little hope of meaningful democratisation taking place, even at the 'procedural' level.

David Olson, *inter alia*, emphasises the centrality of parliament during a period of transition, when the legislature is 'the key institution within which all of the other uncertainties in the political system find expression'. Parliament, therefore, 'is both a product of, and a contributor to, the broader political transformation process', according to Olson.

The role of parliament

Within any liberal democracy, parliament is the *one key* representative organ, and has a range of important functions:

- a *representative* function, in the sense that parliament is a forum of the nation, in which various public opinions can be expressed and balanced against each other through parliamentary representatives;
- *legislative* functions, that is, any major piece of legislation must pass through parliament in order to become law in any country calling itself a 'democracy';
- a *control* function, whereby parliament exercises a wide range of direct or indirect controls over the political executive;
- a *recruitment* function, whereby parliament usually serves as a sort of training school for the majority of government ministers in most European countries;
- a *communicative* function, that is, parliament can be seen as an important link between the electorate and the government;
- a *legitimating* function, with parliament serving as a bridge between the political elite and the population at large, legitimising the whole political system through its position of 'centrality';
- an *educational* function – parliament plays an important socialising role in that it sets an example to the nation, which is particularly important in a society undergoing a political transition from a previous totalitarian/authoritarian society.

Parliaments under communism

Parliaments under communism were not properly functioning legislatures. They were passive instruments of the ruling Communist Party and were little more than legislative facades. They were mere rubber stamps for the Communist Party leaderships in terms of law making, were full of compliant and obedient parliamentarians and did not engender any interest or trust from the general population. They played hardly any of the roles enumerated above, other than to perform a crucial legitimating function as far as the communist government and system were concerned.

M. Simon and D. Olson have argued, though, that during the 1980s the Polish Sejm and the Hungarian Assembly operated more as a 'minimal parliament' with 'a limited degree of influence over policy formation and implementation' – something that accompanied the decay of communism during that decade in both those countries.

The centrality of parliament in ECE after 1989

Under communism, the ECE parliaments had a range of constitutional powers that were to all intents and purposes non-operational. As soon as the Communist Party's 'leading role' was abolished, the post-1989 assemblies inherited a substantial degree of power within the new political system.

In addition, because of the enormity of the task of changing the old system so radically, ECE parliaments have tended to set the policy agenda and initiate new bills to a greater extent than would be normal in legislatures in established democracies. They really have become the central site of the transition, while the political parties developed into the chief actors of society's total transformation.

In fact, in many ECE countries, Romania and Poland excepted, it was a case of unbridled sovereignty of parliament. In some instances this was expressly stated in the new post-1989 constitutions. For example, the amended Article 19 of the Hungarian constitution reads: 'The supreme organ of state power and popular representation of the Republic of Hungary shall be the National Assembly'.

In occupying this central position in the transition process since 1989, ECE parliaments represent:

- the main organisational representative link between society and government, in that there is a distinct shortage or total absence of other political actors, such as well organised interest groups, and/or the lack of any external constraints, such as powerful executives;

- the principal decision-making body in respect of new legislation, especially all the new constitutional laws that form the very foundations of the new state (i.e. the 'rules of the game' themselves had to be changed and created anew);
- the 'central site' within which ECE political parties are constantly regrouping and reforming;
- the body which must initiate far-reaching socio-economic reforms in particular (not just keep the economy ticking over);
- a body playing a key legitimating role by helping the population accept the terms of the transition process as a whole;
- the only visible public forum which provides any level of political education in the practice of democracy (according to Liebert and Cotta, this is a distinct contrast with the transitions in southern Europe, where parliaments were 'relatively inert bodies' during the periods of transitions).

The inexperience of the new parliaments

As David Olson has explained, these new parliaments were also 'the least equipped of any parliaments' to make the vast array of choices that have to be made at the onset of any transitionary period. In particular, Olson claimed, the new parliaments lacked:

- an experienced membership;
- an internal structure of parties and committees;
- the support facilities of space, equipment and staff;
- established procedures for both raising and resolving policy disagreements.

Basic structure of the legislative chamber

The countries of ECE have adopted the following legislative structures:

Albania	unicameral People's Assembly, 140 seats, four-year parliament;
Bosnia-Hercegovina	bicameral Chamber of Communes, 110 seats, and Chamber of Citizens, 130 seats, (normally) four-year parliament;
Bulgaria	unicameral Grand National Assembly, 240 seats, four-year parliament;
Croatia	bicameral, lower house, the Chamber of Deputies, 128 seats, upper house, the Chamber of Counties, 68 seats, four-year parliament;
Czech Republic	bicameral from November 1996, four-year lower house, Chamber of Deputies, 200 seats, and five-year upper house, Senate, 81 seats;
Hungary	unicameral, 386 seats, four-year parliament;
Macedonia	unicameral, 120 seats, four-year parliament;
Montenegro	federal – the Assembly of the Republic of Montenegro, 85 seats, and then the Chamber of Citizens of the Federal Assembly of the Federal Republic of Yugoslavia, 30 seats, both four-year parliaments;
Poland	bicameral, lower house, the Sejm, 460 seats, upper house, the Senate, 100 seats, four-year parliament;
Romania	bicameral, lower house, the Chamber of Deputies, 328 seats, plus 13 seats for minorities, upper house, the Senate, 143 seats, four-year parliament;
Serbia	federal – the National Assembly of the Republic of Serbia, 250 seats, and then the Chamber of Citizens of the Federal Assembly of the Federal Republic of Yugoslavia, 138 seats, both four-year parliaments;
Slovakia	unicameral, 150 seats, four-year parliament;
Slovenia	bicameral, four-year National Assembly, 90 seats, and five-year National Council, 40 seats.

As can be seen, a notable proportion of parliaments in ECE are unicameral, with Serbia and Montenegro having a federal structure.

In actual fact, unlike West European legislatures, there is little differentiation made between first and second, lower and upper chambers, which are filled with the same sort of deputies and have the same structures and committees (e.g. in Romania), and can often meet in joint session for the purpose of debate, as happened with the short-lived Czechoslovak Federal Assembly (1990–92), which was unicameral in terms of its plenary sessions, nominally bicameral in that it was composed of two chambers (the House of the People and the House of Nations), but actually tricameral as far as voting was concerned, since all laws had to pass in both the Czech and the Slovak halves of the House of Nations.

Basically, unicameralism has been accepted because the ECE countries are so small and do not need two chambers in most people's opinion. The majority of those polled in the Czech Republic in 1994 and 1995 did not see the need for a second chamber, as stipulated in the constitution. (It took three years for the Czech parliament to decide to elect the senators by simple plurality over two rounds in eighty-one single-member constituencies, with the first Senate elections in November 1996.)

Three types of post-communist parliaments

Strongly authoritarian

This type is more or less a continuation of the communist era: a parliament that remains under the influence of a strong, authoritarian leader and a dominant party. Such a parliament behaves as if it is a rubber-stamp for a strong leader and rarely questions the leader's judgement; this is so in Serbia, Croatia and Macedonia from ex-Yugoslavia, Slovakia under a strong Premier, V. Meciar, and Romania under a strong President, Ion Iliescu.

Romania. As head of the Executive Body of the FSN Ion Iliescu was able to assume complete control of the FSN and the country right from the revolution. The FSN deputies behaved as a most compliant legislature in the early period, allowing the passage of a new constitution which gave considerable powers to the President. Those who supported Ion Iliescu were exactly the same people who had supported Ceausescu, and Romania's 'new' leaders were mostly former Communist officials.

Slovakia. The interesting point about Slovakia (under HZDS leader and Premier, Meciar) being included in this category is that constitutionally the Slovak National Council is in apparent control, as will be demonstrated below. But, like any constitution, its implementation depends on the political actors, that is, the individual parliamentarians and party members.

When Meciar and his party have been in power, government proposals have passed smoothly, usually without amendment, and the HZDS deputies have hardly ever commented on the actual laws passed. Only a small minority, less than 10 per cent of deputies, and usually from the opposition parties, have been active in making points of order, proposing motions, and so on, with the members of the SDL (reformed communists) constituting the nearest to a constructive opposition.

By various tactics Meciar slowly controlled every aspect of HZDS, side-lining his competitors, making himself the final arbiter in all decisions, placing all parliamentary committees under the chair of members of the HZDS and its two coalition partners, bringing Slovak radio and television under HZDS control, placing control of the state intelligence service in the hands of Ivan Lexa, his former secretary and, above all, ensuring a compliant parliament.

Even by the summer of 1993, former Foreign Minister Milos Knazko was already warning that Slovakia could return to a dictatorship with so much power concentrated in one person. Moreover, many of these (quite undemocratic) measures Meciar steered through a parliament in which he controlled only a very slender majority.

Macedonia. The presence of a strong person in control can be viewed positively as well as negatively – Macedonia has been seen as a haven of stability in the Balkans, and it was kept out of any conflict with its neighbours thanks mainly to the influence of its President, K. Gligorov, who was also responsible for the country being officially recognised in 1991 and for solving the on-going problems with the Greeks over the country's name, flag and emblem.

Basically the ruling four-party coalition government is held together by President Gligorov and simply supports his policies. (The country survived a potentially destabilising assassination attempt on President Gligorov in 1995.) As a result, there has been concern expressed in the press and mass media about his one-man rule.

Mildly authoritarian

This is where an inherently strong party discipline leads to a placid parliament which normally backs the leader, who maintains strong control of the government, the leading party and thereby parliament. Debates can still be quite acrimonious, but the opposition is usually weakened or divided, for example in parliaments with ex-communist majorities like Poland since late 1993, Hungary since mid-1994 and Bulgaria since late 1994, or parliaments where a right-wing party is very much in control, like the Czech Republic over 1993–96.

Democratically pluralist, but chaotic parliaments

This is where there is no one dominant party, a distinct lack of party discipline and generally conflictual patterns of behaviour among deputies, which leads either to chronic governmental instability, for example in Poland during mid-1989 to late 1993, the 'blocked parliament' in Bulgaria, 1991–92, or partial parliamentary immobilism, in Czechoslovakia in early 1990 to the beginning of 1993, Albania in mid-1992 to 1995 and, to a lesser extent, Hungary in spring 1990 to summer 1994.

Of this group, Hungary's legislature was seen as the most stable in ECE, since there was parliamentary and governmental continuity for the full four-year term. (Compare Bulgaria and Poland, with five and six governments respectively during the same period.)

Chaos into stability

Part of the 'chaos into stability' thesis is particularly evidenced in the behaviour of the parliamentarians, since there has been a shift in many ECE countries – Poland, Hungary, Bulgaria and the Czech Republic, in particular – from the third type into the second type, usually with the electoral victories of the more professional, more party-minded and power-oriented ex-communist politicians and parties.

General background to ECE parliaments after 1989

Working parliaments

The ECE parliaments quickly turned from rubber-stamping to working legislatures, with former secrecy being replaced by wide publicity and televising of parliamentary sessions.

To begin with, though, some of these parliaments:

- were more or less 'appointed' as a result of round-table agreements between former Communists and the dissident opposition (e.g. the 1989–91 Polish parliament);
- were intended primarily as constituent assemblies (e.g. the Czechoslovak Federal Assembly, 1990–92, and Bulgarian parliament, 1990–91);
- had to operate according to the constitutional rules of the previous communist regime, until a comprehensive constitution was drawn up – only Bulgaria and Romania passed a new constitution early on, in 1991.

Powers of parliaments

All parliaments have quite extensive powers, stipulated by a constitution or constitutional amendments.

Slovakia's 1992 constitution may be taken as an example. Article 84 lists some important powers of the National Council which require the consent of three-fifths of the members (i.e. 90 out of 150), for instance:

- electing and recalling the President;
- adopting constitutional laws;
- amending the constitution;
- declaring war (which balances the fact that the President is the Commander-in-Chief of the armed forces).

Article 86 lists other powers of the National Council, including: proposing referendums; ratifying treaties; electing the Constitutional Court; establishing government departments; debating all internal, international, economic and social policies; approving the budget; giving consent to the sending of any troops outside Slovakia; calling for the resignation of individual ministers; endorsing (or refusing) ministers proposed by the Premier.

Furthermore, the chamber is in continuous session and can be adjourned only by its own decision; it sets its own parliamentary agenda; and individual deputies control the government, through their oral or written requests for information (by law such interpellations *must* be answered). Finally, in the last resort, only thirty members of parliament (MPs) are needed to move a motion of no confidence against the government.

Bills may be proposed by the deputies, the committees and the cabinet, but not the President of the Republic. Most bills are proposed by the cabinet and most of them are passed, though sometimes with substantial amendments. The proportion of bills initiated by deputies from June 1992 to July 1994 in Slovakia was 27 per cent, which is considerably higher than in many democracies.

The Bulgarian Grand National Assembly and the Czech parliament have also been given such constitutional supremacy. But the Hungarian Assembly is counterbalanced by greater powers to the government, and especially the Premier, with the 'constructive vote of no confidence' (whereby a parliamentary assembly can vote out a premier and the government in a vote of no confidence only if it elects a successor immediately afterwards). This actually makes dismissal of the government extremely difficult. Likewise, the Polish 'Little Constitution' of 1992 still gives considerable powers to the President (see Chapter 13).

High expectations of MPs

After 1989, there were great expectations of the new parliaments, now staffed by 'our people'. During this generally euphoric period, parliaments achieved high approval ratings in most ECE countries and compared very favourably with other political institutions, like the government or president. (Confidence in the parliament reached 90 per cent in Czechoslovakia in June 1990, 64 per cent in Hungary in March 1989, and 89 per cent in Poland in October 1989 – the same level as the Catholic Church.)

Pre-eminence of political parties within parliaments

Political parties seemed to dominate everything in ECE in the immediate post-revolutionary period – not only the parliament, but also the media and public life as a whole. They stood out as the main political actors of the transition. But this was mainly due to the almost total lack of other intermediary organisations, like interest groups.

Legislative hyperactivity

The first post-revolutionary parliaments passed an enormous amount of legislation: the Czechoslovak Federal Assembly, for example, approved 168 pieces of major legislation during its two-year lifespan; the Hungarian National Assembly had accepted 289 major laws and substantial amendments by the end of 1992; in Bulgaria between October 1991 and November 1993, 283 bills were introduced into parliament; from June 1992 to July 1994 the Slovak parliament adopted 204 laws. (Compare a normal parliament in Western Europe, which might at the most pass fifteen major bills within one parliamentary year.)

Legislative initiative

Generally speaking, members of ECE parliaments have the right to initiate bills and have been very active in this respect. Between 2 May 1990 and 1 November 1992 in Hungary, for example, they, presented 132 new bills as opposed to 272 by the government. However, members' bills seldom become acts – of these 132 bills, only thirteen ran their full legislative course. In particular, a private member's bill moved by a member of the opposition has virtually no chance of being passed.

Likewise, of the 204 Slovak laws mentioned above, fifty-five were proposed by MPs. This 27 per cent of bills coming from private members is considerably larger than in many West European legislatures. In Bulgaria, too, of the 283 bills introduced into parliament between October 1991 and November 1993, only 129 were proposed by the government, indicating an active and participatory legislature.

However, because of poor preparation, new laws often had to be modified. For example, of the ninety-two laws passed in 1992 in Hungary, eleven were amendments of laws adopted earlier in the year.

Background to the post-revolutionary MPs

More elitist parliament

Communist parliaments had attempted to reflect precisely the stratification of society, with specific quotas among the deputies for workers, peasant farmers, women, young people, and so on.

Post-communist representatives tended to be middle-aged, highly educated men. In Hungary and Czechoslovakia, for example, 90 per cent and 85 per cent, respectively, of the new MPs were university graduates: poets, historians and intellectuals were common in Hungary; playwrights, actors and sportsmen stood out in Czechoslovakia; and in all ECE parliaments there were significant numbers of lawyers, teachers, journalists, doctors, economists, and priests. Their common feature would usually be non-complicity with the previous regime. (The drop in the percentages of women MPs was particularly noticeable, for example from 34 to 4 per cent in Romania, from 30 to 9 per cent in the Czech Republic, from 21 to 7 per cent in Hungary.)

The culture of dissidence

There was no one else other than the dissident groups to assume positions of power in 1989, since relying on reformed Communists was politically unacceptable at the time. So the dissidents represented the only group from which the new political elite could emerge, even in Poland, where Solidarity had been a broad-based opposition movement in the late 1970s and early 1980s.

The overwhelming characteristic of this new political leadership was that it had been more or less isolated from public life before 1989, and had had little exposure to public speaking or rational decision making, let alone public office. Under communism, these new politicians and parliamentarians had all been part of what has been called the 'culture of dissidence' (i.e. very small, closely knit groups of semi-intellectuals talking ad infinitum in smoked-filled rooms without ever reaching a decision, and with no power whatsoever to implement any decision if one were reached). J. Karpinski makes similar points about the Polish Solidarity 'dissident subculture', which was characterised by 'strong norms, rules of conduct, initiation rights, and an internal hierarchy', favouring 'personal authority over democratic procedures'. These people were now elevated into positions of governmental power literally overnight, without any sort of preparation.

Amateurs, not professionals

These dissident leaders were hardly prepared for professional politics: their pre-eminence was based on their expertise in the operating theatre, on the stage, in the lecture hall or on the sports field. The parties allowed them to feature on the party lists of candidates as they hoped their names would attract votes.

From the very beginning they could only be amateurs. In the April 1990 Hungarian elections, 90 per cent of the 386 people elected were not only MPs for the first time, but also complete novices in politics in general. Likewise, in Poland, Bulgaria, Romania and Slovakia, the first parliaments elected after 1990 included a large number of legislative beginners.

Some of the effects of this amateurism were:

- poorly prepared bills, which often emerged as purely ideological documents, which were then 'killed' in the committees, as they were quite unimplementable, in particular in Bulgaria and Hungary;
- non-consultation with organised interest groups, whose views and expertise could have been channelled into the legislation at either the preparation or implementation phases, everywhere;
- the wasting of valuable time in committee and plenary sessions;
- politicians engaging in hours of over-inflated, high-minded, ideological rhetoric, which had little bearing on the fate of the ordinary citizens, especially in Hungary and Czechoslovakia;
- a large proportion of bills had to be amended (fifty per cent in Hungary), because of their non-compliance with other existing laws or the impossibility of their actual implementation;
- the 'arena feature' of the parliament;
- confrontational and personalised politics, where very personal animosities were allowed to build up between various leaders, for example in Bulgaria, Romania, Czechoslovakia and Hungary;
- a strongly polarised party system which led to a blocked parliament in Bulgaria, partial immobilism in Czechoslovakia and fragmentation almost everywhere, but particularly in Poland.

The representative 'abyss'

In Poland, 90 per cent of respondents in an autumn 1989 poll thought that deputies were acting in the public interest; in late 1991, only 36 per cent of respondents still held such an opinion; and by May 1992 only 5 per cent thought that politicians were acting in the country's interest. Such a decline in public estimation was common throughout ECE: by 1993 the new political elites were perceived as basically corrupt career mongers, who were using a variety of economic and political privileges for their own benefit.

Clearly, there is a similar representative gap among politicians and other public representatives in the West, but this is more like a representative abyss for the whole ECE region. Some Hungarian citizens even went so far as to collect signatures for a people's referendum calling for new elections, since those representatives who constituted the then parliament were not able to represent the public and fulfil their duties.

Negative aspects of members' behaviour

Inability to pass a constitution

One of the earliest signs of impasse within the emerging democracies was the inability to pass a full constitution: Yugoslavia and Czechoslovakia because the enactment of a federal constitution became embroiled in nationalism; Poland because of the interference of both President Walesa and the Catholic Church; Albania because of disagreement on the balance of presidential powers; Hungary because of the new parliament's inability to resolve issues of the past and de-communisation. (Obviously, all these countries passed piecemeal constitutional amendments.)

Probably the clearest example was the inability of the Czechoslovak Federal Assembly over 1990–92 to come up with a constitution, when it was supposed to be acting specifically as a two-year constituent assembly. But the parliamentary authorities were afraid of the Slovak representatives voting down the constitution in the Slovak half of the House of Nations, so never presented the constitution to parliament.

In Albania, too, the delay in drafting the constitution caused an on-going political crisis from the summer of 1992 onwards. The matter was not even resolved when President Berisha took the matter to the people in a referendum in November 1994: his constitution was rejected by 54 per cent of voters.

The fragility of coalitions

It was a general feature of ECE politics during the first six years of chaos that coalitions came and went with great ease. Examples include the PD's decision to withdraw from the six-month-old Albanian coalition government under ex-communist Ylli Bufi in 1991; the FKGP withdrawing from the conservative–Catholic–agrarian coalition in Hungary in February 1992; the end of the Romanian coalition between the PSDR and certain extremist (nationalist) parties – the PUNR, PRM and the Socialist PSM – in September 1995; and the DPS allying itself with the BSP and bringing down the SDS government that it had previously supported.

Very often these coalitions ended because of personal disputes between the party leaders, or because of some minor aspect of policy difference between the party caucuses: it was disagreement mainly at the elite level.

The collapse of Hanna Suchocka's seven-party coalition in Poland in May 1993 is a classic case. The basically pro-government Solidarity Trade Unions Party (NZSS) put forward a vote of no confidence, just to give a warning to the government on public employee pay – they had no real intention of actually bringing down the government. But they miscalculated: the government lost the vote and had to resign.

The practice of walking out of the chamber

In some countries, instead of making strenuous efforts to compromise on important issues, parties simply abandoned the chamber temporarily or boycotted parliament altogether. In Albania, a long-term boycott was practised by the PD's coalition partner, the PSD, and the ex-communist PS, as a protest over the inability of the ruling party to draft a constitution by the summer of 1992.

In Bulgaria, opposition parties would often boycott parliament with the aim of provoking the government's downfall and initiating early elections; for example, the SDS, in the summer of

1991, in 1993 and 1994, boycotted all plenary sessions. These boycotts never worked, but they did lead to a slowdown of legislative activity and, in Bulgaria's case, the delay in debates and votes on crucial privatisation bills.

Frequent votes of no confidence

Another tactic used by opposition parties was the frequent use of no-confidence motions, even when parliamentary arithmetic pointed to clear failure in advance. This was a frequent practice in Bulgaria, both during the non-communist Dimitrov government between autumn 1991 and autumn 1992 (on 22 October 1992 the Dimitrov government failed to survive a confidence vote) and between January and July 1993, when the SDS moved six votes of no confidence against the technocratic Berov government.

During fifteen months of 1992–93, in Macedonia, the chief opposition party, the Internal Macedonian Revolutionary Organisation–Democratic Party for Macedonian National Unity (VMRO–DPMNE), moved a vote of no confidence on three occasions – and each time the government survived by only a small margin.

The frequent use of the vote of no confidence like this is merely a parliamentary device which when over-used simply undermines the legitimacy of the parliament and of the democratic institutions as a whole.

Lack of party discipline in parliament

On the whole, MPs see themselves as free agents, not at all bound by instructions from their party. This means that most votes were perceived as free votes and deputies stood by their right to leave their parliamentary group, join another party group or become independent: but there was no thought of referring back to their local or national electorates before taking such a step. Therefore, MPs tended to form ad hoc coalitions on individual bills, not necessarily voting with their party and hardly ever expecting any sort of retribution. The most obvious exception to this model was the traditional discipline of Communist Party members or the ex-communist social democrats. In the Czech Republic, V. Klaus also understood the importance of party loyalty and enforced it quite rigorously (to the extent that ODS members were to asked sign a pledge whereby they agreed to lose their parliamentary seat if they left the party faction). So, party discipline not only changed over time, but also varied among parties.

Splitting the party

Political parties throughout ECE exist primarily as parliamentary parties, working mainly in and through parliament, with their activities reported on the front pages of most newspapers as parliament plays the central political role. As a result, con-siderable distance has developed between the party leaders and party rank and file members. Moreover, given this central positioning of the elitist parliamentary party and the small propensity for compromise, frequent splits in the party – at the parliamentary level – were almost inevitable.

For example, the Czech OF split in six different directions in March 1991, so that by the Czechoslovak 1992 elections, eighteen parliamentary clubs had formed, while an additional set of MPs were 'unorganised'. In Bulgaria the number of party groups doubled from three to six, with groups splitting mainly from the dissident SDS. In Hungary, the number of parties in parliament grew from six after the 1990 elections to seventeen by October 1993. Besides that, MPs were continually switching allegiances between the different existing groupings. By 1992 in Poland at least fifteen different parliamentary groupings had emerged from the former Solidarity movement alone, ranging from the right-wing, Catholic Centre Alliance (PC) to the social-democratic Labour Union (UP).

So, by mid-1992, throughout ECE, a substantial number of MPs represented parties for which the electorate had never voted. In all ECE countries, these frequent desertions led to attempts to bind the MPs to the decisions of party conferences and/or the party leaders: such attempts usually failed.

Coming to terms with the past

Intense, personal animosities surfaced when linked with the 'past', for example during the course of many of the debates on the Czechoslovak *lustrace* (screening or vetting) law, or the various tense debates between the SZDSZ and FIDESZ over de-communisation, or the debacle caused by the release of the list of supposed secret police informers in Poland.

The point is that such acrimonious debates both seriously delayed key laws on privatisation and economic reform, and poisoned the general atmosphere in which the new parliamentary institutions were attempting to lay down new ground rules for the post-communist society. It is also no surprise, therefore, that the collapse in public support for the Czechoslovak Federal Assembly began with the televising of the *lustrace* debate in March–April 1991.

Ideological/philosophical debates

Debates often tended to concentrate on ideological, even philosophical, abstract goals and concepts, rather than the more constructive discussion of details, so that disputes became matters of fundamental principles rather than more reconcilable disagreements over policy.

The above was particularly true of any discussion that touched upon the relationship between different nationalities in Czechoslovakia. As early as March 1990, for example, the Czechoslovak Federal Assembly spent days debating the name of their joint republic and whether or not the word 'Czechoslovak' should be written with a hyphen, and whether a capital letter should be given to the word 'Slovak'.

In Hungary, many questions had an ideological dimension, even when it was a question of something like a new media law. Political/ideological debates were long and furious and absorbed a great deal of parliamentary time. As a result, more than half of the laws proposed for 1992 had to be left for the 1993 spring session, owing to lack of time.

More emotional opposition

Proceedings in most of the region's first parliaments were marked by the emergence of a more emotional (i.e. less rational) and more personalised, semi-responsible opposition. Debates usually degenerated into mud slinging and character assassination, rather than concentrate on reasoned discussion of the issues in hand. Again, although this can constitute a normal part of adversary politics in, say, Great Britain, there are rules and limits, and the degrees of viciousness that lay behind the point scoring in the Czechoslovak, Polish and Hungarian assemblies, for example, would have been quite out of place in most Western democracies.

This is how Attila Agh described the first six months of the Hungarian parliament:

> the parties behaved in plenary sessions as though they were still campaigning, echoing their old speeches regardless of the issue on the agenda. This was ... the only political role they had learned so far.... It seemed not to matter who was part of the coalition and who was in the opposition – during the first 6 months virtually all MPs had opposition attitudes. It was not clear who was fighting whom or what; it was only safe to say that every MP was fighting against – somebody.

It was rather like adversary politics twenty-four hours a day, and it mattered little whether privatisation, *lustrace* or pig farms were on the day's agenda – the MPs' behaviour was always the same.

The futile political conflicts discredited various parties and politicians in the eyes of the general public, which manifested its displeasure in the form of growing political apathy and worked to the benefit of the ex-communists, like MSZP in Hungary and SLD or PSL in Poland.

Engaging in non-rule-abiding behaviour

Given the inexperience of the newly elected MPs and the ineffectiveness of the political parties as representative organs, it was clear that the types of parliamentary rules and procedures which are usually adhered to within long-established democracies were more open to abuse and misuse in most of the newly democratising countries of ECE.

Unlimited debate. Whereas the time to speak in any one debate was often limited, the number of people wishing to participate in that debate was usually unrestricted. Everyone had a selfishly guarded right to be heard, even if they were reiterating ad nauseum points that had been made in previous speeches. Usually debate would not end until everyone had been heard – which meant that discussion sometimes lasted for days instead of hours.

The pre-meeting 'speech'. The pre-meeting speech was instigated in Hungary, to allow all MPs to introduce their own motions before the main debate. The overwhelming majority of these speeches covered topical political issues or remarks directed at an individual deputy, rather than a worthwhile piece of legislation.

The procedural remark. Throughout ECE the procedural remark or point of order was often quite blatantly abused to attack people personally rather than discuss the issue in hand. Any MP could make a point of order at any time within any debate and had the right to be heard immediately. Very often there would be recurrent re-use of the point of order between two parliamentarians hurling abuse at each other: a process which could sometimes last for twenty-five minutes and which was difficult to stop.

Legislative blackmail. In the bicameral Czechoslovak Federal Assembly, some parties (ODA and HZDS in particular) would vote for a bill in one chamber, only to reject it in the other, in order to have the bill brought before the twelve-member Conciliation Committee, where the party had equal representation with other parties and could perhaps achieve the sorts of legislative changes that had proven impossible in the plenary session.

Fluidity of amendments. Very often, *any* type of amendment that touched upon either the principles or the details of any bill could be made at *any time* within that bill's passage (this applied also to amendments on constitutional bills). This meant that MPs sometimes had to vote on 100 or more amendments and thereby consume a whole morning or afternoon session, taking up to twenty decisions per hour. Furthermore, amendments proposed on the floor were very often amendments to a committee's amendments, which usually led to almost endless debate. (In addition, in Czechoslovakia, there were often very long and technical debates as to what actually constituted an amendment!)

Abortive work in committee. Although the committees in most ECE countries were more or less filled with experts from various parties (e.g. most party representatives on the constitutional or law committees were lawyers), ordinary party members often distrusted their work. As a result, many of the amendments that had already been rejected in committee came up again in the full plenary session. In the end, debate in the committees was almost a waste of time, or at best reserved for highly technical matters like foreign affairs. (Compare this with most democracies in Western Europe, where many important decisions can be made at the committee stage in order to streamline debate.)

The consequences of chaos in parliament

All-change for the new elites

In most ECE parliaments, it was the same story: a dramatic turnover of 80–90 per cent of the parliamentary elites (although this was only 64 per cent in Hungary). The dissidents who had borne all the responsibilities of government, staffed most of the ministries and instigated most of the necessary radical changes – the OH and ODA in the Czech Republic, the ODU in Slovakia, Solidarity in Poland, the MDF in Hungary, the SDS in Bulgaria – were decisively rejected by the electorate at the polls, mainly because they were simply out of touch with the needs of the majority of the population.

Party fragmentation

As mentioned previously, former members of OF went in six different directions, whether to establish new parties or to join other existing parties; Solidarity split into about fifteen different groupings; and the MDF was constantly splitting and regrouping while in government, as was the Bulgarian SDS.

Government instability or partial parliamentary immobilism

In Poland there was inherent government instability (five governments in 1989–93).

In Czechoslovakia, there was partial parliamentary immobilism, in that nothing of a constitutional nature could be passed by parliament after late 1990. In Bulgaria there was a blocked parliament because of the intense confrontational behaviour between the equally sized SDS and BSP.

Collapse in support for parliament

Not surprisingly, there was a collapse in confidence in their parliaments expressed by voters in opinion polls throughout the region:

- from 90 per cent (June 1990) to 26 per cent (May 1992) in Czechoslovakia;
- from 89 per cent (October 1989) to 41 per cent (January 1993) in Poland;
- from 64 per cent (March 1989) to 29 per cent (May 1992) in Hungary.

It should be stressed that this is not a reflection of dissatisfaction with democracy itself, but a distinct dislike of the first parliaments and their MPs, that is, not of the difficulties of the transition, but rather of the disillusionment at the workings of parliament and the actual behaviour of the MPs, 'our people'.

Such a confidence gap, however, indicates a potential for anti-democratic behaviour and increased demands for strong leadership, whether from a president (Poland or Albania), or a returned monarch (Romania or Bulgaria).

Growing apathy

In 1990 in Hungary, only 30 per cent of the electorate voted in local elections and parliamentary by-elections had to be repeated five or six times before the necessary quorum of voters was reached. Even in the all-important general elections, 35 per cent of the electorate abstained.

In Poland, too, voting participation for the 1990 presidential, 1991 parliamentary elections and all local elections was below 50 per cent.

In Bulgaria apathy was high (40 per cent) in several major local elections in June and July 1994. Again, this is certainly due in part to a disenchantment with the workings of parliament and behaviour of their MPs.

Return to power of the ex-communists

In Poland, Hungary and Bulgaria ex-communists were returned to power, partially because they were perceived as being more professional and therefore better politicians. To a great extent, the first wave of new non-communist elites have only themselves to blame.

Changes under the ex-communists

In Poland and Hungary, in particular, there has been a marked change in attitude with the return to power of the ex-communists, including:

- the acceptance of the rights of smaller opposition parties in the legislative process;
- greater party discipline, even in cases where there are strong disagreements, for example within the majority SLD and PSL coalition in Poland;
- a greater capacity to accept the rights of coalition partners, such as the SZDSZ/MSZP coalition in Hungary;
- a distinctly less confrontational pattern of behaviour in the parliamentary chambers, especially in Bulgaria, for example.

Conclusion

Given the MPs' backgrounds, the lack of any civil society and the prevailing 'subject' political culture, the behaviour during the first six years of chaos, described above, is perhaps not surprising. It must be stressed, though, that the institutionalisation of parliamentary democracy within ECE is a *process* and is probably going to be a very long process that will have to take place within the context of ECE being absorbed into the more well established parliamentary practices of various European institutions.

Further reading

Gabriella Ilonszki, *Parliament and Parliamentarianism in Hungary in a Comparative Perspective*, Budapest Papers on Democratic Transition, No. 29, Budapest University of Economics, 1992.

Jakub Karpinski, 'Opposition, Dissidents, Democracy', *Uncaptive Minds*, 5 (2), summer 1992.

Ulrike Liebert, 'Parliament as a Central Site in Democratic Consolidation: A Preliminary Exploration', in *Parliament and Democratic Consolidation in Southern Europe: Greece, Italy, Portugal, Spain and Turkey* (Ulrike Liebert and Maurizio Cotta, eds), Pinter Publishers, 1990.

Lawrence Longley, *Working Papers on Comparative Legislative Studies*, Research Committee of Legislative Specialists (IPSA), Lawrence University, 1993.

Jill Lovecy, 'Parliamentary Politics', in *West European Politics Today* (Geoffrey Roberts and Jill Lovecy), Manchester University Press, 1984.

David Olson and Maurice Simon, 'The Institutional Development of a Minimal Parliament: The Case of the Polish Sejm', in *Communist Politics: A Reader* (Stephen White and Daniel Nelson, eds), 1986.

David Olson and Philip Norton, eds, *The New Parliaments of Central and Eastern Europe: Institutionalisation of the Democratic Transition*, Frank Cass, 1996.

Irena Pankow, *Sejm Deputies and Political Leaders: The Search for Political Identity*, Budapest Papers on Democratic Transition, No. 61, Budapest University of Economics, 1992.

13
The new executives

A careful comparison of parliamentarianism as such with presidentialism as such leads to the conclusion that, on balance, the former is more conducive to stable democracy than the latter. This conclusion applies especially to nations with deep political cleavages and numerous political parties; for such countries, parliamentarianism generally offers a better hope of preserving democracy. (J. Linz)

To attempt to propose today what the office of the president is to be in the future is like choosing a hat and adjusting the head to fit that hat. (Lech Walesa)

As the nations of ECE engage in their transition to democracy, the type of political regime chosen becomes of paramount importance. In this respect, the relationship between the executive and legislature is probably the most important institutional problem facing any political system. Achieving a balance between strong leadership and representative institutions has been one of the eternal problems of democratic political systems. Giving too many powers to the leader of the nation – either monarch or president – can easily lead to authoritarian government at best, dictatorship at worst, yet leaving all powers to the elected assembly can lead to parliamentary immobilism and system dysfunction.

Functions of the executive

The executive is the central and most visible institution of any government, usually giving direction to the whole of society. The functions of the executive are basically twofold:

1   *ceremonial functions*, whereby the head of state provides a
     sense of unity to the nation, represents it abroad, entertains
     visiting representatives of foreign countries, performs vari-
     ous formal functions of appointment and patronage, or has
     a symbolic role within the legislative system (e.g. the British
     Queen or the German President);
2   *governmental functions*, whereby somebody must actually
     head the executive branch of government within each
     country, proposing legislation, coordinating and overseeing
     government policy, and assuming responsibility for all
     government actions (e.g. the British Prime Minister or
     German *Bundeskanzler*, along with their cabinet ministers).

There are three principal governmental functions:

1   the *proposal*, *elaboration* and official *preparation* of policies;
2   the successful *implementation* of those policies by ap-
     pointing, coordinating and overseeing the administrative
     bureaucracy which puts those policies into operation;
3   the *coordination* of the individual policies into a consistent
     governmental programme.

In a parliamentary system there is a 'dual executive', in that
the monarch or president carries out all ceremonial functions,
while the premier discharges the governmental functions. In a
presidential system, however, the head of government and the
head of the state are one and the same person, and fulfil both
types of function.

Presidentialism, semi-presidentialism or parliamentarianism?

The debate concerning the executive hinges on whether there
should be the dominant influence of one person over the
governmental system, that is, a president, or whether the executive should be a collective body, that is, a cabinet chaired by a

premier. The options range mainly between three types of executives.

(1) Pure presidentialism

The USA is a prototype of this option. The American President:

- is both head of state and head of the government;
- is the sole executive, that is, the US cabinet is little more than a board of advisers to the President;
- is directly elected by the people, that is, the President has a personal mandate;
- is elected for a fixed term of office;
- cannot be forced out of office easily by Congress except by impeachment for serious crimes or misdemeanours;
- appoints the ministers who are responsible to the President alone (although these appointments are subject to ratification by the Senate);
- has a power of veto (which can be overturned by a two-thirds majority of both Houses of Congress);
- is responsible to the constitution and the electorate, that is, is not responsible to Congress in any way (although the President must work with the Congress);
- initiates and proposes legislation to Congress.

In addition, any member of the President's advisory staff cannot simultaneously be a member of the legislature.

Under this system, however, there is a rigid separation of powers between the executive and legislative branches of government, which is clearly elaborated in the American constitution and safeguarded by a constitutional court, so there is no concentration of power, rather a division of powers according to strict constitutional guidelines.

However, although there are checks and balances, the assembly is effectively supreme, as: it controls the allocation of money to all government projects; it can impeach the President; it can amend the constitution without regard to the President.

In much of Central and South America, which copied the US model, the presidential system has been distorted by dictatorship and these countries have generally been unable to enforce the strict separation of powers between president and parliament.

Advantages of presidentialism

First, there is executive stability, based on the president's fixed term of office and the inability of the legislature to force the president to resign except in cases of serious misconduct.

Secondly, the election of the president as chief of the executive is seen as more democratic than the informal, indirect, sometimes secret choice of premier by the legislature.

Disadvantages of presidentialism

First, there may be executive–legislature deadlock, when the one-person executive (with a powerful veto) is opposed by a different majority party within the legislature and both have democratic legitimacy.

Secondly, there is too much power for one person, so that dictatorial tendencies could emerge rather quickly, as they have in South and Central America.

Thirdly, the system is rigid and lacks flexibility – something that could be balanced by allowing the president to dissolve the legislature or have the parliament dismiss the president for political reasons.

(2) Pure parliamentarianism

This is where the head of state is either a constitutional monarch or republican president, as in Great Britain or Germany. Under this system:

- there is a dual executive, with the premier as head of the government, and the monarch or president as head of the state, performing the purely ceremonial functions;

- the government is a collective body, with the premier usually being little more than chair of the cabinet;
- the premier is indirectly elected to the post of chief executive by being leader of the majority party, or is sometimes formally elected by the legislature, as in Austria, Germany, and Switzerland;
- the head of state formally appoints the head of government, who then chooses his or her own ministerial team (the cabinet), which is again formally appointed by the head of state; sometimes the formality of the choice of premier is not so clear cut (e.g. in republican Italy or monarchical Belgium);
- the life of the government is not fixed, as the premier can usually choose a propitious date on which to hold an election, or the government can be censured prematurely;
- the government is responsible to the legislature, and its survival depends on its ability to maintain the confidence of the assembly, since the government can be forced to resign by votes of censure or refusal to support government bills;
- the premier and most of the ministers are usually members of the legislature (although sometimes civil servants or technocrats become ministers, as in Italy and France) so there is a 'fused' separation of powers.

The central institution within this type of system is the parliamentary assembly. If the parliament functions well, that is, debates and votes on most of its legislative programme without long delays or obstruction, then all other institutions will function normally and the government will pass most of its programme – presumably with parliamentary amendments. If, on the other hand, the parliament functions poorly, then none of the other institutions will perform efficiently and the entire political system could become dysfunctional.

Disadvantages of parliamentarianism

First, there can be instability of the party system, through too frequent use of the vote of no confidence, or simply through the loss of majority support within the legislature (e.g. the Weimar Republic, the French Third and Fourth Republics, and inter-war ECE). This can be corrected with a constructive vote of no confidence, as happened in Germany, Spain, and Hungary, when the premier can be removed only if a new premier is elected at the same time. However, parliamentary instability is a problem only when it is semi-permanent and extreme (e.g. the French Fourth Republic had twenty-five governments and seventeen prime ministers in twelve years).

Secondly, the indirect election of the chief executive, whether formally or informally, by the legislature is less democratic, especially when changes in the composition of a coalition government take place between elections, without any popular involvement of the electorate, as happens in Germany and Holland.

Thirdly, while the parliamentary system formally assumes legislative supremacy, in fact it often assures the dominance of the executive over the legislature, as in two-party Great Britain or multi-party Holland.

(3) Semi-presidentialism

France is the best example of this option – a sort of 'third way' between parliamentary and presidential forms of government. Under this arrangement, the president:

- both is the head of state and fulfils some of the functions of head of the government;
- is directly elected, so has his or her own mandate from the people;
- is elected for a fixed term, which is at a different electoral cycle from the legislative elections;
- cannot be removed from office during her or his term except for criminal misdemeanour;
- nominates the premier (usually subject to ratification by parliament) and then selects the cabinet ministers in conjunction with the premier (although formally the president

makes all appointments) (the president also has other quite extensive powers of patronage);

- can dismiss the premier or the entire cabinet under certain circumstances, usually possesses powers of legislative veto or can call referendums, and can dissolve the legislature and call new elections;
- often chairs the cabinet meetings (when the president and the cabinet are of the same party it is clearly the president's government);
- is usually given jurisdiction over foreign policy and defence;
- has emergency powers (when he or she can rule by decree) in a state of emergency.

The main characteristic of a semi-presidential regime is the dual executive (premier and president) and intricate sharing of powers and responsibilities between the premier, the cabinet and the president. Specifically, there is a dual responsibility of the premier to both the president and to parliament.

Under this hybrid type of semi-presidentialism, the president is strong only when backed by a large parliamentary majority (e.g. President de Gaulle, 1958–69, or President Mitterrand, 1981–86). As soon as there is a situation of 'cohabitation' however, that is, when the president and the parliamentary majority are of different parties, then the position of the premier strengthens enormously, whereas that of the president weakens considerably (e.g. France on occasions since the mid-1970s).

In such semi-presidential systems, the directly elected president can also often stand for the unity of the whole people against (for example) a fragmented parliament or unstable governmental coalition.

To a certain extent, the president is used as a safety net in such regimes, as a way of avoiding the basic problem of instability: the less the political parties are capable of cooperating, the more extensive the powers of the president become, and vice versa. Given a situation of parliamentary immobilism, the president can become the centre of the decision-making process – without any democratic control by parliament (something that would be almost impossible under pure presidentialism), for example the end of the German Weimar Republic from 1929 onwards.

Advantages of semi-presidentialism

First, alternation between presidential and parliamentary phases solves the problem of executive–legislature deadlock, in that presidentialism works well when the president has majority backing in the legislature, but when the president lacks a supportive majority in the legislature, there is a shift towards parliamentarianism, which avoids potential deadlock.

Secondly, the head of the executive is directly and democratically elected and has stable tenure, yet the system still has the flexibility of a parliamentary system.

Thirdly, there are effectively three sources of potential power – president, premier, and the cabinet, so there are better opportunities for building power-sharing coalitions than under pure presidentialism.

Fourthly, it provides 'dual leadership'.

Finally, the president can act as an above-the-parties arbiter, as long as he or she delegates the more controversial tasks to the premier.

Disadvantages of semi-presidentialism

First, if the president is backed by a very large parliamentary majority, dictatorial tendencies could emerge once again, especially if members of the majority party subordinate themselves to the president, for example by looking to his or her stature among the people to win the election for the party. This is what happened in many Latin American states and especially in France under President de Gaulle (1958–69).

Second, there could again be a different type of executive–legislature deadlock where both prime minister and president are very strong personalities and from different parties, so that each refuses to give up his or her powers. This is exactly what occurred for a brief period during Valery Giscard d'Estang's presidency when Jacques Chirac was prime minister.

Presidentialism in ECE in the inter-war period

In the democracies of ECE that were established after the First World War, there was the emergence throughout the region of an authoritarian personality heading a regime with different degrees of constitutionality and parliamentary democracy. This was not surprising given the past political traditions, mentioned before, coupled with the general failure of parliamentary institutions throughout the region.

Every ECE state started out after 1918 with a democratic constitution, but by the late 1930s only Czechoslovakia continued to function as a democracy. All the others ended up being led by nationalist generals, monarchical dictators, or, eventually, fascist movements, supported by authoritarian governments and arch-conservative parties – often as a consequence of rigged elections. The legacy of the 'unjust' Paris Treaties, the presence of dissatisfied minorities everywhere, the economic collapse following the 1929 Wall Street Crash, government instability and parliamentary immobilism: all of these interacted to bring about strongly authoritarian regimes.

In such a situation, the populations looked for a strong leader to solve the problems of political instability and parliamentary immobilism. In Poland Marshal Pilsudski introduced a quasi-military dictatorship and authoritarian rule in which political parties and the Sejm were gradually rendered powerless. Hungary was controlled by conservative and reactionary forces, led by the regent Admiral Horthy, whose power base was the populist and conservative Smallholders' Party: a classic semi-presidential system within a monarchical framework. As a reaction against nationalistic turmoil and political instability, King Alexander of Serbia proclaimed a royal dictatorship in 1929 throughout Yugoslavia. Romania, too, had an authoritarian and conservative, royal dictatorship under King Carol. After some period of bitter conflict between various political groupings, several coups and bloody assassinations, King Boris of Bulgaria, supported by the army, established a royal dictatorship. Similarly King Zog I had installed himself as royal dictator in Albania by the mid-1920s.

Pilsudski, Horthy, Kings Alexander, Carol, Boris and Zog – to a more limited extent, even President Masaryk of Czechoslovakia – can all be seen as early versions of France's General de Gaulle. All of them believed that a strong leader was the only thing that could save the unity of the nation. These were personal, authoritarian, mostly royal dictatorships: faith was put in the man, not the ideology or the state.

Presidential tendencies under communism

Under the various communist systems, power rested in the hands of a very small, elite group at the head of a massive political party. Decision making was hierarchical and, in effect, there were no democratic checks on the activities of this elite. Within this oligarchic system the president was often head of state and head of the Communist Party at the same time. This led to pure dictatorship by the Ceausescu family dynasty in Romania, and to strong personal leadership by Ulbricht and Honecker in East Germany and Tito in Yugoslavia. Whenever the president and the general secretary of the Communist Party were different people, the president usually played a less prominent role. This was true in the more collective, party-centred leadership group in Czechoslovakia and post-Tito Yugoslavia.

Presidentialism versus parliamentarianism in regimes undergoing the transition to democracy

Among Western experts, there is no consensus as to which is the best system. Furthermore, there are certainly no guidelines as to which regime might better suit a political system undergoing a transition to democracy.

In the past, in some West European political systems, pure parliamentary government has led to problems of legislative delay, parliamentary immobilism or system dysfunction, as in France during 1946–58, and Italy on several occasions since 1945. When a purely parliamentary system is superimposed upon a political culture which is not yet used to democratic procedures of compromise, tolerance, consensus and pragmatism, then political instability will be almost inevitable for some time. In such a situation, the appeal of the strong leader who gives the country a clear direction can be irresistible. But it could also indicate a return to authoritarianism.

Juan Linz posed the same sorts of questions in respect of the various transitions to democracy within Latin America. He concluded that the presidential type of government is more likely to undermine democracy and lead to the return to power of military regimes. In this case, therefore, parliamentary regimes are a much better safeguard of democratic practices and institutions.

Linz preferred parliamentary systems because they possess the greater flexibility required by developing democracies in the early stages; for example, if necessary, it is easier to dismiss a premier than a president without destabilising the entire regime. In his opinion, then, a parliamentary system was seen as better at aiding the transition to a democratic regime than a presidential or semi-presidential system, since the latter are not particularly conducive to the emergence of a multi-party system and are vulnerable to authoritarian and populist temptations.

F. W. Riggs made a study of seventy-six democratic countries within the Third World between 1945 and 1985: of the thirty-three presidential regimes, not one survived without serious inter-ruption; yet thirty out of the forty-three parliamentary regimes established managed to survive without any major reversal or backsliding.

Partial semi-presidentialism in ECE since 1989

In the beginning, most ECE countries adopted pure parliamentary systems, with the legislatures controlling both the government and the president, although Albania, Serbia, Croatia, Macedonia and Romania have a strong presidency, and presidents in Bulgaria, Poland and, at times, Hungary and Czechoslovakia have wielded considerable power. Only in Yugoslavia, where nationalist parties dominated the legislature, was there a marked preference for a nationalist strong leader (natural in a situation of war).

There was also a distinct change in Poland with the passing of the 'Little Constitution' in 1992, in which the Sejm was no longer designated as the highest organ of state power and the Senate lost power to the President. (A situation that is likely to be reversed with the enactment of a new, full constitution.)

It is not surprising that ECE countries have opted for a parliamentary regime, since they endeavoured to distance themselves from anything vaguely resembling the concentration of power under the communist regimes. Generally speaking, parliaments were made supreme, presidents were given very few powers and the executives – premiers and their cabinets – were made responsible to parliament. Those presidents who obtained power in the immediate post-communist period, and coming from the old regime, such as R. Alia in Albania, P. Mladenov in Bulgaria and General Jaruzelski in Poland, realised very quickly that they were somewhat of an anachronism and eventually resigned their posts.

In respect of the three typologies described above, the situation in ECE can be summarised as follows.

(1) There are no purely presidential regimes.

(2) There are purely parliamentary regimes only in Hungary, the Czech Republic and Slovakia. In these cases, the President is elected by and is clearly responsible to parliament, but is still not exactly powerless. Slovakia is probably the most extreme case of the three, as the President is very clearly under the control of the Slovak National Council, as he or she is both elected and can be removed from office by the Council under certain circumstances (this needs a three-fifths majority of all parliamentary deputies).

In all three, there is keen competition among the political parties, governments depend on simple votes of no confidence, they all have presidents elected by the parliaments and equipped with only weak powers – of which the most important is the legislative veto – and, currently, they have unicameral legislatures (except for the Czech Republic which became bicameral in 1996). As a consequence, their institutional frameworks are dependent upon the good performance of their parliaments.

In Hungary, the government has been strengthened vis-à-vis the parliament by the introduction of a 'constructive vote of no confidence'. Hence, during the whole period of the Antall government, the opposition did not once attempt to oust the Premier. (Compare Bulgaria, where the opposition was constantly raising no-confidence motions against the government.)

(3) There are semi-presidential regimes in Romania and most of the countries of former Yugoslavia, and there was one in Poland under Lech Walesa. Bulgaria and Albania have the potential to develop into semi-presidential systems. Parliament is very much in control in Bulgaria, but President Sali Berisha gained greater power and influence in Albania after parliament became deadlocked and especially after the rigged elections of 1996 when his PD party 'won' an overwhelming parliamentary majority.

Perhaps the countries of ECE represent something in-between pure parliamentarianism and semi-presidentialism: a situation where the government and parliament are very much in control, but where all the presidents have some powers which make them much more than a ceremonial head of state. 'Partial semi-presidentialism' might better describe the current state of affairs – resembling the situation of the French Third Republic, 1871–1940, when effective power resided in parliament and the majority party, but where the President still had some important powers: so it is not quite pure parliamentarianism. Some commentators have called these regimes 'presidential-parliamentary systems'.

Characteristics of 'partial semi-presidentialism' in ECE

Presidential elections

Nine nations elected their president directly: Poland (Walesa in 1990 and Kwasniewski in 1995), Bulgaria (Zhelev in 1992), Romania (Iliescu in 1990 and 1992), Slovenia (Kucan in 1992), Serbia (Milosevic in 1992), Montenegro (Bulatovic in 1992), Macedonia (Gligorov in 1992), Croatia (Tudjman in 1992) and Bosnia (Izetbegovic in 1990).

In other nations the presidents were elected by parliaments: Hungary (Goncz in 1990), Albania (Berisha in 1992), Czechoslovakia (Havel in December 1989 and June 1990), the Czech Republic (Havel again in January 1993 and June 1996) and Slovakia (Kovac in 1993). In the Czech Republic only an absolute majority of members is required, whereas in Hungary the president is elected by a two-thirds majority.

The only country in which the mode of the election of the president became controversial was Hungary, where the issue split the democratic opposition parties at the end of their round-table discussions with the Communists in autumn 1989. The FIDESZ and SZDSZ won a subsequent referendum by the narrowest of margins (50.1 per cent to 49.9 per cent) for the postponement of indirect presidential elections until after the parliamentary ballot. Goncz was subsequently voted into office by parliament in August 1990. In a further referendum on the method of electing the President in July 1991, called by the MSZP, who still wanted the President directly elected, turnout was only 13.8 per cent, indicating a lack of concern by the general public about the issue. This was also well below the required 50 per cent quorum (but 85 per cent of those who voted favoured direct elections). In consequence Goncz was reconfirmed in office by parliament on 3 August 1991. Actually, the choice of Goncz as President was effectively made by Premier J. Antall in 1990, as a sort of deal between the MDF and SZDSZ, represented by Antall and Goncz respectively. Goncz was to become President if the SZDSZ would agree to dropping the 'two-thirds' rule for passing important and constitutional changes into law, thus strengthening the powers of the government vis-à-vis the parliament. Both leaders did not inform their own party members about the agreement until it was a fait accompli.

Presidents and political parties

Generally speaking, the presidents are supported by a party, or other political groupings; for example, Hungarian President Goncz came from the SZDSZ, Czechoslovak President Vaclav

Havel from OF, Sali Berisha from the Albanian PD, and Croatian Tudjman from his HDZ. The one president in a weak position in this respect was President Walesa in Poland after the 1990 Solidarity 'war at the top': hence his creation at the 1993 legislative elections of the Non-Party Bloc to Support Reform (BBWR – the same initials as used in the acronym for Pilsudski's inter-war party).

Presidential terms of office

Most presidents serve a five-year term (Bulgaria, Poland, Slovenia, the Czech and Slovak Republics), but some have only four-year terms (Albania, Serbia, Hungary and Romania). The first two terms of Vaclav Havel were much shorter – six months and two years – as his tenure initially followed the parliamentary cycle.

Presidential ceremonial role

All presidents in ECE countries:

- represent their respective countries internationally, sign and ratify international treaties and receive foreign ambassadors;
- can grant amnesties and pardons and commute prison sentences;
- have extensive powers of patronage, over top officials of the state administration, top judges, university chancellors, army generals, and so on.

Symbolic role of presidents

Many presidents within the region play a key moral role of leadership within societies that are undergoing far-reaching and fundamental changes. In this situation, the head of state may provide a strong sense of national unity, continuity with the past, a feeling of stability – especially when compared with the parliamentary and political party confusion.

There is also a very strong tradition of paternalism in ECE. For example, President T. Masaryk, in the First Czechoslovakian Republic, 1918–37, had little more than ceremonial powers, but played a central role in Czechoslovak politics as the 'father of the nation'. Likewise, V. Havel was able to put his own moral stamp on the initial stages of the transition process as moral leader of the country – his initial choice of ministers was crucial for the formation of the first non-communist government in 1990.

With his tremendous revolutionary prestige, Walesa also saw himself as the 'father of the new nation' in Poland. After his popular election in October 1991, he had greater legitimacy than the Sejm and attempted to stand above the political chaos of the Solidarity era. (And yet much of that chaos was of his own making.) As a result, the potential for presidential rule was ever present. (Adam Michnik wrote a famous article entitled 'Why I'm not voting for Lech Walesa', which was first published just before the 1990 presidential elections; in the article, Michnik quoted Walesa extensively to demonstrate that the Solidarity leader wanted absolute, dictatorial power.)

The presidents' impartiality

The presidents are expected to play an impartial role, above the interests of the political parties. This often involves arbitrating behind the scenes between different party-political groups that find agreement and compromise very difficult at best, impossible at worst. The presidents can do this on the basis of their moral authority and reputation among the people. The role of impartiality was applied most strictly by President Havel in Czechoslovakia, 1990–92, who occasionally intervened in parliamentary debates so that consensus could be reached between the various party groups. In Bulgaria, President Z. Zhelev was a key player in behind-the-scenes negotiations to ensure that the ex-communist BSP did not become a party of government after the collapse of the centre-right coalition in October 1991. After January 1995 he often found himself in a constitutional impasse with the new BSP government.

Presidential powers

All the presidents in ECE are commanders-in-chief of their respective armies. However, the Hungarian President can give only guidelines, rather than orders, to the military; Walesa, as Polish President, on the other hand, claimed the constitutional right to oversee all defence and national security matters, including the choice of the Minister of Defence; finally, it is the National Assembly which declares war in Romania.

The presidents make many of the formal appointments, including the government ministers, top judges, and chancellors of universities. In some cases, the choice of premier can be left to the president's discretion, as in Poland on different occasions since 1990, in Bulgaria in 1991 and in Czechoslovakia in 1990. On other occasions, certain presidents have insisted on 'their' choice of certain government ministers – especially in Poland, where Walesa clashed with different Premiers over the choice of Foreign, Interior and Defence Ministers.

In the Czech Republic, the President has lost the powers of appointment possessed under the previous Czechoslovak Federal Republic, including choice of Premier. If the government is defeated on an important bill twice in a row, the Speaker of the Parliament nominates the candidate for the Premier and the President then appoints him or her as a matter of course.

In Hungary the President has a much freer and independent choice of the Premier, from a selection of candidates, and, according to the constitution, does not need to discuss the matter with the parties, and does not even have to ask them for advice. The Hungarian President can thus have a far-reaching function in forming the government.

The most evident case of powerlessness of the president vis-à-vis the premier can be seen in Slovakia, where Premier Meciar forced President Kovac to dismiss the Foreign Secretary Knazko simply because the latter had voted against Meciar's original candidate for the presidential post. (The Premier makes the appointments in Slovakia.)

In Poland, there were five Prime Ministers between 1989 and 1992 – the most of any European country – mainly because of

Walesa's personal interference in the Polish political scene. After the passing of the 1992 'Little Constitution', the President's powers of forming a government were enhanced. He therefore meddled in appointments to a much greater extent than might have been considered normal.

Presidents occasionally have the right to initiate legislation in parliament, for example in Hungary and Poland, plus Czechoslovakia in 1990–92, when President Havel presented bills to the Federal Assembly on several occasions.

Where presidents receive a direct mandate from the people (e.g. Poland, Bulgaria, Romania), they have a strong democratic legitimation, stronger, indeed, than many of the government coalitions.

One aspect which adds to presidential power is the fact that they have a fixed term of office, in contrast to the government, which must rely on the continual confidence of parliament. This applied particularly to Bulgaria, where motions of no confidence in the government (requiring only a simple majority of a minimum of one-fifth of MPs) were a quite frequent feature of political life between 1990 and 1994. President Zhelev's initial support for the Berov government (1991–94) was crucial, just as his lack of support for the same government during most of 1994 was critical.

All the presidents have some power of veto, although this might be limited to returning the disputed law to parliament for further discussion (e.g. Hungary, Slovakia and Bulgaria) rather than actual veto powers (e.g. Poland and the Czech Republic). In the Czech Republic this power of veto is very limited, and when President Havel has used the veto on a major bill, such as the continuation of the lustration law in 1995, the veto has been overridden by a simple majority vote in parliament – although he can be successful on a non-controversial issue, for example the bill proposing no smoking in public places. A veto cannot usually be applied for a second time, except in Poland.

In Hungary the President can initiate laws and reject legislation passed by parliament, as long as reasons for doing so are given. In Slovakia, the President possesses no veto over legislation but can ask the parliament to reconsider bills, as President Kovac did with the first two versions of the 1995 Language Law. In Poland, the President can veto legislation, but this veto can be overridden with a two-thirds minority in the Sejm. Furthermore, in Poland, the government can rule by decree and the President can veto that decree – in which case the matter goes to the Sejm for resolution.

Under certain circumstances, the presidents can dissolve parliament; for example, in Czechoslovakia the President could dissolve the Federal Assembly if parliament was unable to agree on the annual budget, but under the constitution of the Czech Republic the Czech President cannot dissolve the Assembly. The Polish President, on the other hand, can dissolve the legislature if it fails to pass a budget within three months.

Usually the various parliaments of the region can express a vote of no confidence in individual ministers or in the whole government, in which case the president is forced to dismiss them. However, there are clear instances in which governments have been dismissed by presidents, especially in Poland, or in which the presidents have played a key role in their dismissal (e.g. Slovakia, Albania, and Bulgaria in 1994).

Some presidents can participate in and often chair the cabinet sessions (e.g. in Romania, Bulgaria, Slovenia and Croatia). The Czech President can participate in parliamentary sessions and parliamentary committees and can speak on the floor of the Chamber at any time. Likewise, the President can participate in cabinet sessions, and can request reports from the government or any individual minister, but the President does not actually chair the cabinet.

Presidential interventions

Almost all presidents have flexed their muscles within ECE countries, in most cases going beyond the powers granted to them in the countries' constitutions.

In making key appointments. In the Czechoslovak Federal Republic, President Havel nominated the Premier and other government ministers, including assigning specific posts to the ministers concerned (i.e. he had a real element of choice) but his nominations were all subject to a vote of confidence in the Federal Assembly. Even so, the first six-month 'Government of National Understanding' and the 1990 OF government were very much 'his people', that is, his own choices had been crucial for the formation of those first two non-communist governments.

In terms of bringing down governments. In March 1994, President Kovac of Slovakia made a keynote speech within the parliament which was highly critical of the government of Meciar. He also participated in discussions with other political parties in preparing a multi-party coalition to replace Meciar. A little over forty-eight hours after Kovac's speech, Meciar was removed as Premier. It seems clear that Czechoslovak President Havel played a similar role when Meciar was unseated from government for the first time in April 1991.

In bringing about consensus. On many occasions ECE presidents have been responsible for consensus behind the scenes, for example in Bulgaria in terms of government formation in autumn 1991, in Czechoslovakia over the disagreements between political parties about the name of the state during the so-called 'hyphen war' and the division of government competences between federation and republics in 1990.

In Poland, during much of Lech Walesa's presidency, however, there was a persistent lack of consensus on major issues, with each of the different parts of the executive refusing to recognise each other's rights and with each claiming that they had responsibility for major policies and decisions.

In provoking conflicts. Walesa was by far the most interventionist President in the region and provoked constitutional crises on a number of occasions in order to have his way – for example, in his dismissal of individual ministers or premiers with whom he was displeased – the last one being W. Pawlak in early 1995. In fact, the situation was one of more or less permanent conflict between the President and various post-communist governments of whatever political persuasion. From his first day in office, Walesa demanded more powers in domestic affairs, even though he already had substantial jurisdiction over defence and foreign affairs. He clashed several times over this issue with parliament and government, and insisted on using his powers to dissolve the Sejm on his own initiative on two occasions, because of the perceived shortcomings of the government coalition – the last occasion in early 1995 when he claimed the Pawlak SLD/PSL coalition was not moving fast enough on privatisation. Such interventions only increased his unpopularity, leading to his eventual defeat in the autumn 1995 presidential elections.

Havel also made a bid for greater powers in late 1991, when he presented a list of six presidential initiatives to the Assembly (including calling for a referendum on the future of the federal state, proposing a new electoral system, and suggesting increases in presidential power to allow the President to dissolve the Assembly and rule by decree during periods of parliamentary immobilism). In the end, the Federal Assembly rejected four of his proposals and he withdrew the other two, demonstrating clearly that, in the final analysis, parliament controls the President.

In Hungary during the first post-communist government, a sort of power struggle emerged between President Goncz and Premier Antall, in which the latter reduced the presidential functions even before Goncz took office. President Goncz resisted such pressures, claiming that he represented the interests of the nation over and above party politics. Thereafter, they clashed frequently over the issue of calling former Communist officials to account and in the so-called 'media war', when the President joined the opposition in protesting against what was seen as the government's move to prevent journalistic criticism within the state-run media.

In former Yugoslavia, strong presidencies were created in the former republics of Croatia, Slovenia and Bosnia, with a mandate to resist Serb encroachment. In Serbia, too, the ex-communist, pro-nationalist Slobodan Milosevic has developed a very presidential style of government, as has President Berisha in Albania.

There has been conflict between President and parliament in Bulgaria, too. In October 1992 President Zhelev refused the nomination of the leader of the BSP as Premier, after a vote of censure had unseated the SDS government. Constitutionally speaking, the BSP leader should have been given the right to form a government, but President Zhelev (formerly of the SDS) wanted to prevent a former Communist from becoming Premier. President Zhelev also referred the ex-communists' plans to reintroduce collective farming to the Constitutional Court, which ruled against the government, saying its policy was against the whole notion of the ownership of private property.

In Slovakia, the attitude of President Kovac was also extremely important, even though he is in a much weaker position in terms of presidential power. On 9 March 1994, President Kovac gave his first State of Slovakia speech before the parliament and surprised everyone by ending with critical comments about Meciar, saying: 'Mr. Meciar doesn't need counsellors, collaborators, opponents, but just maids in order to realise his aims.' A little over forty-eight hours later, Meciar was removed as Premier for the second time in his political career. After returning to power in October 1994, however, Meciar spent much time and energy in attempting to remove President Kovac from office.

Conclusion

Under 'partial semi-presidentialism', all the presidents within the region possess some powers vis-à-vis both the government and the parliament. Nowhere is there a completely powerless president, as in Germany, for example, but nowhere is there a truly presidential system either. The actual powers of presidents vary from country to country, but, as indicated above, they are limited in favour of the parliaments.

Given the past political traditions mentioned above and in the first chapter, the emergence of an authoritarian personality as a leader, heading a constitutional, parliamentary democracy, was almost to be expected in ECE after the collapse of communism. The danger is that such a person might attempt to move into a more presidential-type system, particularly at a time of economic or political crisis. As far as can be judged, this is exactly what both Lech Walesa in Poland and Salia Berisha in Albania have attempted to do: the first through his moral authority, the second through manipulation of the constitution. It is also similar to the 'creeping authoritarianism' of Premiers Vaclav Klaus, Vladimir Meciar and Jozef Antall in the Czech, Slovak and Hungarian republics, respectively.

Further reading

Maurice Duverger, 'A New Political System Model: Semi-Presidential Government', *European Journal of Political Research*, 8 (2), 1980.

Donald L. Horowitz, 'Comparing Democratic Systems', *Journal of Democracy*, 1 (4), 1990.

Arend Lijphart (ed.), *Parliamentary versus Presidential Governments*, Oxford University Press, 1992.

Juan Linz, 'The Perils of Presidentialism', *Journal of Democracy*, 1 (1), 1990.

Juan Linz and Alfred Stepan, *Problems of Democratic Transition and Consolidation*, Johns Hopkins University Press, 1995.

Fred W. Riggs, 'Presidentialism: A Problematic Regime Type', in *Parliamentary versus Presidential Governments* (Arend Lijphart, ed.), Oxford University Press, 1992.

Matthew Shugart, 'On Presidents and Parliaments', *East European Constitutional Review*, 2 (1), 1993.

14
Conclusion

It is easy to turn an aquarium into fish soup, but not so easy to turn fish soup back into an aquarium. (Lech Walesa)

We are now still in the 'really existing' Absurdistan after the decades of the 'really existing' state socialism. (Attila Agh)

You can't build capitalism without capital. (CNN)

Enlargement is both a political necessity and a historic opportunity. (EU summit, Madrid, December 1995)

A Velvet Curtain of the Cold Peace is replacing the Iron Curtain of the Cold War. (Jaroslav Jaks)

The transition in perspective

As mentioned before, the simultaneous transition from communism to democracy and the transformation of the formerly centrally planned economies to the free market within ECE is a task without historical precedent: there is no blueprint. In addition, the global, especially European, economy is forcing these countries to adapt at a very fast pace, for which the existing ECE economic infrastructures are simply not prepared. ECE is being asked to construct in a very short time what it took the West decades, if not a century, to build.

It was always going to be much easier to dispose of politically illegitimate and economically bankrupt regimes than to re-establish democratic and entrepreneurial behaviour after such a long period of political and economic centralisation. Many previously hidden problems were bound to resurface once communism ended, including nationalist animosities.

The changes also affect the post-Cold-War development in the whole of Europe, not just the ECE states themselves. The collapse of communism throughout the Soviet bloc is causing just as many problems for Western Europe, which is going through its own identity crisis with the end of the Cold War. 'Europe' has to be redefined now that the bipolar East versus West military blocs have disappeared in a new post-Cold-War order.

Positive signs

All governments in ECE since 1990 have changed as a result of mostly free and competitive elections. Procedural aspects of democracy seem well established: political parties and parliaments are definitely pluralistic and the press is generally free.

There is no chance of a return to the Soviet-imposed totalitarian regimes of the past. (The ex-communists returned to power in Poland, Hungary and Bulgaria are clearly social democrats who can come to power only through elections.) Adam Michnik describes the 'velvet restoration' of the ex-communists in Poland as the process by which 'supporters of the old regime adapt themselves to the conditions of parliamentary democracy and market economy'. Their return to power, therefore, does not represent the re-communisation of Poland, 'but the continuation of the transformation process initiated in 1989'. Indeed, the return to power of the ex-communists seems to be ushering in a period of relative stability after the chaotic years of the 'dissident era' (compare Poland in 1989–93 with Poland in 1994–95).

Whatever type of post-communist societies emerge from the ruins of the previous regimes, as George Schöpflin has pointed out, 'they are going to be an immense improvement on communism'.

Negative aspects of the transition process

Both Westerners and Easterners totally underestimated the extent and magnitude of the economic transformation, even in East Germany. Expectations were extremely high everywhere. The ECE populations believed the transition would bring about almost immediate material wealth and the new political elites thought that the return to democracy and the free market could be resolved quickly. The EU and USA also built up ECE's expectations with regard to joining the EU and NATO – something which could never have been fulfilled in the short run.

All ECE regimes went from rampant euphoria to deep dis-illusionment within twelve months. After two to three years there was mass dissatisfaction due to the economic hardships to which the vast majority were subject and a subsequent rejection of the new political elites at the polls.

The transition to any substantial degree of democracy has hardly begun. The Leninist legacy still lives on and old attitudes still persist socially and politically, even among the younger generations. In particular, the absence of compromise and toler-ance has led to the emergence of several problems: unresolvable nationalism, oppression of ethnic minorities, excessive protection of the state, and ideological political parties in parliament.

Many of the former *nomenklatura* remain in positions of economic power and influence, intensifying the 'culture of envy' among the majority who have not benefited from the new economic freedoms.

To effect a successful transformation of the economy, much of the communist economic legacy must be destroyed or at least totally restructured. This can be achieved either by a massive injection of (presumably foreign) capital, as has occurred in former East Germany, or with the introduction of piecemeal changes over a very long period of time, as is occurring elsewhere. In 1991, the World Bank estimated it would take decades for ECE countries to reach the same levels of per capita income as the industrial countries of Western Europe.

Despite being ECE's largest market, the EU has proven a massive disappointment since 1989, erecting barriers against both ECE products and immigrant workers. It would seem there is a 'prosperity wall' or economic 'velvet curtain' which is going to exclude ECE from 'Europe' for some time to come.

The ECE electorates have tended to reject their governments outright if they fail to improve the material situation of the majority. Yet very unpopular decisions still remain to be taken throughout the region.

Post-communism

Post-communism is a phenomenon which has emerged in ECE since 1989: effectively, it is the transitional phase between communism and democracy, during which everything is still compared with what went before, namely communism.

Even though reformed communists are now in charge of the transition to parliamentary democracy and free-market capitalism, it is important to emphasise, as Jakub Karpinski does, that 'post-communism is not communism'.

Generally speaking, this post-communist phase will:

- be more difficult in some ECE countries than others;
- take a very long time to overcome the legacies of the past;
- see a considerable period of disillusionment and frustration;
- see great differences between the expectations of the people and the political/economic realities of the day.

Different degrees of post-communist development

Given the variety of the former communist and ECE inter-war regimes, it is not surprising to discover that each ECE country has followed its own particular path of post-communist development since 1989.

East Germany's political and economic transformation has been guided and generously financed by West Germany. The transition to democracy amounted to the imposition of well established political parties and well tested institutions through the unification of the two Germanies in October 1990. The East German economy was simply absorbed into the vibrant West German economy and thereby straight into the EU.

Poland introduced 'shock therapy' – overnight price liberalisation coupled with the beginnings of small-scale privatisation, resulting in high inflation (250 per cent in 1990) and spiralling unemployment (18.2 per cent in 1992, increasing from 0.6 per cent in 1990) – during a rather chaotic period of government by ex-dissident elites. The majority of the population felt excluded from the changes, so returned communist successor parties to power in October 1993.

Hungary had introduced a partial market economy under communism, so it has managed to attracted half of all foreign investment between the beginning of 1990 and the end of 1995. However, the country kept on borrowing from abroad, until the post-1994 MSZP/SZDSZ coalition had to instigate an austerity programme in order to contain the country's foreign debt and reduce the deficit. During the first post-revolutionary MDF-led government, 1990–94, political changes were made by an inexperienced ex-dissident government, which the electorate penalised by returning ex-communists to power in May 1994.

Romania saw former leading Communists retain power by 'hijacking' the revolution and continue previous behavioural patterns and policies for some time, so that a real process of reform, both political and economic, hardly began before 1995.

In Serbia, Croatia and Bosnia the reform process was sidelined with a reversion to nationalism: S. Milosevic manipulated Serb nationalism to remain in full control of a centralised communist-type state; F. Tudjman ensured reforms took second place to Croatian military campaigns; A. Izetbegovic also appealed primarily to nationalism, but, in any case, Bosnia's economic infrastructure was decimated in the 1992–95 civil war.

Bulgaria and Slovakia have both partially reversed the economic and democratic reform process, set in motion by a reformist government which ruled for only a very short period, before

subsequent ex-communist, or partially ex-communist, governments slowed down the reforms to the point that they are still
very much under the control of a centralised state.

The Czech Republic has experienced the most far-reaching
economic reforms, which have remained unchallenged. The
country benefited from very low foreign debt, a strong spirit of
entrepreneurship among the population, an important tourist
industry and the proximity of rich Western neighbours. As the
most productive republic of the former Yugoslavia, Slovenia also
began its reform process with similar inbuilt advantages.

Albania saw the Communists hold on to power for eighteen
months, before being defeated by the Democrats, who began a
limited marketisation programme, which enabled Albania to
experience the highest growth rate within Europe in 1994 and
1995 (8 and 15 per cent, respectively).

Characteristics of post-communism

Reflecting a certain degree of disappointment and disillusionment
in events within Czechoslovakia during the first two years after the
revolution, President Vaclav Havel defined post-communism in the
following way in 1991:

> Rancour and suspicion between ethnic groups;
> racism or even signs of fascism;
> brazen demagoguery;
> deliberate scheming and lying;
> political chicanery;
> wild and shameless squabbling over purely particular interests;
> naked ambition and lust for power;
> every kind of fanaticism;
> new and surprising forms of swindling;
> Mafia-style machinations;
> and a general absence of tolerance, mutual understanding, good taste, and a
> sense of moderation and reflection.

George Schöpflin lists a rather different set of criteria:

- a weak connection between elites and societies;

- no strong sense of involvement of the population in political institutions;
- the inability of public opinion to express itself coherently;
- people lacking a clear understanding of their own identity and role in the public sphere;
- the problem of identity being filled by nationalism;
- no sense of compromise or toleration, with people still unable to deal with diversity and to see both sides of any problem;
- a conflictual political culture;
- the legacy of atomisation in terms of lack of trust;
- the excessive personalisation of politics;
- societies which are still searching for their own values;
- a certain anarchy vis-à-vis the state (e.g. it is still considered legitimate by many to rob the state and not abide by its rules);
- a continuation of corruption and bribery at all levels of society;
- a political residue of apathy and impatience with politics;
- bloated bureaucracies;
- resentment at the disappearance of equality.

Jakub Karpinski claims that the post-communist period will be marked by certain legacies of the communist era, what he calls 'powerful absences':

- a lack of legal traditions;
- disrespect for the law;
- a lack of mechanisms for resolving national and social conflicts;
- non-existent professional and political experience.

Basically what is being described is a rather turbulent period of change in ECE when the continuity of the past – a history of decisions imposed from above and the lack of any tradition of active civic society from below – clashes with the adoption of Western models of liberal democracy and the free market.

Post-communism, therefore, seems to be something in-between, that is, in-between authoritarianism and democracy: something that is democratic in form, but authoritarian in substance. Elections take place and parliaments are formed, but human rights are often not respected, democratic debate is not taking place, there is no true rule of law, aspects of a normal civil society are absent, and democratic institutions can be very nationalist in content and therefore still operate in a centralised and hierarchical fashion.

As before, ECE is somewhere in-between, well behind Western Europe in terms of standards of living and levels of economic production, yet well ahead of Russia and the newly independent eastern states of the former USSR.

A repetition of the past?

This is very similar to the ECE inter-war regimes which Schöpflin has called 'failed liberalism' or 'moderate authoritarianism', where 'a fully operative civil society did not exist'. Such regimes contained elements of pluralism – there were newspapers independent of the state, trade unions did function, opposition deputies were elected, and so on – but the powers of the state could not really be limited by these independent organisations.

These inter-war regimes had very similar characteristics to ECE after 1989: political immaturity, economic backwardness, social and ethnic fragmentation, political cultures with strong elements of paternalism, nationalism as an important agent of mobilisation, often directed specifically against ethnic minorities, a very conservative role played by religion, and an apathetic international environment.

The economics of transition

In Western Europe, free-market economies developed over decades – even centuries – in a slowly evolving process. They were not created overnight. In 1989, most ECE countries were starting from a very backward position, with very outmoded production processes and extremely poor quality of goods, so a significant degree of economic restructuring was required. (After 1945 it took approximately ten years for Western Europe to resume normal production – starting with a higher overall level of economic activity, with the free-market infrastructure already in place and with the receipt of US Marshall aid.)

At the macro-level, the aims of the economic reform process were quite straightforward: the ending of government subsidies, liberalising of prices and opening up the domestic market to global competition. At the micro-level, however, this implied bankruptcies, increasing unemployment (often regionally concentrated) and declining income for the vast majority. In the end no government could allow such extremes of dislocation to take place for any length of time. Therefore, necessary widescale bankruptcies were not allowed to happen – except in Eastern Germany – and ECE countries continued to subsidise many old, defunct factories, some of which were still allowed to produce unmarketable goods.

Different approaches to economic reform

The 'third way'

Right at the beginning, in 1989 and early 1990, there was much talk of a 'third' or 'middle' way between capitalism and communism, especially among the intellectual ex-dissident elite. In fact, this was more of an ideal than a reality – an attempt to create capitalism with a human face. 'Third-wayers' used to point to the Swedish economy (free market but with a comprehensive welfare system) as their role model, and it is perhaps just bad timing that the Swedish system began to require radical reforms at the end of the 1980s. So, the flirtation with 'third way' did not last long, before there was a mad dash to imitate Western practices and copy their institutional structures.

Shock therapy

Here reforms are implemented quickly and simultaneously in a 'big bang' approach: all prices are liberalised in one go, firms are allowed to go bankrupt almost immediately, and capital is permitted to move around freely. Critics contend the dislocation is too great and the rapid changes confuse the vast majority of the population – as occurred in Poland, for example, where prices increased 100 per cent in the first three months of 1990. Clearly, there has been a backlash, with the return of the ex-communists since 1993, but Polish growth rates of 7 per cent and 7.5 per cent in 1993 and 1994 indicate that production picked up once again more quickly than elsewhere.

Gradualism

In this model of economic transformation, reforms are instigated in a gradual, piecemeal approach, allowing time for the economy and the population to adapt to the new conditions, thus avoiding massive economic and social dislocation.

Critics contend that it basically continues the old system of semi-central planning by supporting outmoded industrial capacity and practices, so that real change will take a very long time, and in the meantime the economy will stagnate. In fact, most governments have been 'gradualist' in practice, such as the government of the Czech Republic (in rhetoric the most outspoken advocate of neo-liberalism) and all Polish governments since the initial massive dosage of 'shock therapy'.

Marshall Plan mark 2

This is effectively the German approach: a massive programme of capital investment, particularly in infrastructure, overseen and financed from the West. For example, the Germans installed more telephones between 1990 and 1995 in the territory covered by the former GDR than had been installed throughout the whole of this century. Such a scheme could have been adopted for the whole of

ECE, but the political will was totally lacking among West European states and it perhaps ranks as an enormous missed opportunity as far as the EU is concerned. The restructuring of the devastated economies of ECE could have provided a stimulus to economic recession in Western Europe in the same way that the Marshall Plan helped to solve the USA's immediate post-war excessive economic capacity.

The ECE economies: the 'tigers' of Europe

Recently some commentators have suggested that the ECE economies, with their very high growth levels, of 5–7 per cent per annum – far surpassing anything in Western Europe – have the capacity to become the equivalent of the 'Far Eastern tigers' within Europe. However, three points must be remembered.

First, the growth rates reflect a dramatic increase in services – which were not registered in the official statistics before 1989, since such activity took place on the black market – mostly by barter.

Secondly, ECE countries are so far behind the West that Jeffrey Sachs estimates that they will have to grow at a rate of 7 per cent *above* the annual West European states' growth rates in order simply to catch up with the West by the year 2020 (so growth rates of 9–12 per cent are needed in ECE, not 5–7 per cent).

Lastly, there are some interesting comparisons to be made between ECE countries and the Far Eastern 'tigers':

- The tigers invested heavily in education, especially in sending their brightest students to be educated abroad, whereas ECE governments are tending to reduce expenditure on education quite dramatically.
- The tigers initially protected their infant industries with high tariffs and so did not immediately expose their domestic markets to foreign competition. This is precisely what the so-called 'Cambridge group' of economists recommended for ECE. Such advice was rejected in favour of an IMF-promoted policy of opening up ECE borders to foreign

competition, which proved much more beneficial to Western Europe – especially Germany and Austria – than it did to ECE.

• From the outset, the tigers did much to build up inter-regional trade. Likewise, after the collapse of COMECON, the ECE countries needed to cooperate with each other first before attempting to gain access to the EU on an individual basis. The ECE countries could have stimulated inter-regional trade by at least accepting each other's currencies. A few bilateral agreements have materialised (e.g. mutual 80 per cent tariff reductions between Slovenia and the Czech Republic) but they are really no substitute for institutions and practices which could promote trade over the whole region. (A Central European Free Trade Association was established in 1994, and will eventually lead to reductions in tariffs throughout the region. By mid-1996, however, its economic effect had proven almost unnoticeable, as tariff wars between ECE countries were the norm, not tariff reductions.)

Problems of successful economic transition

Basic lack of capital for infrastructural schemes

Money transfers from West to East Germany (which has a population of approximately 16 million) totalled $100 billion per annum between 1989 and 1995, whereas all foreign investment in ECE during the same period has amounted to $18 billion – almost all of which went to Hungary (50 per cent), Poland and the Czech Republic (just under 25 per cent each). In addition another $62 billion has been given in aid programmes over the five years from all international agencies and foreign governments.

The *Economist* illustrated this contrast in an interesting way: it pointed out that the Germans were spending the same amount of money in refurbishing a single street in former East Berlin – Friedrichstrasse – as the total foreign capital investment in the whole of Poland over 1990–95: $4 billion.

Lack of buyers for large state-owned industries

Older heavy industry is still in state ownership in most places, even in East Germany, where huge steel-making factories have not been bought by anyone and will continue to be owned and operated by the state well into the twenty-first century, because of the potential social problems caused by shutting down the plants.

Only 'voodoo' or 'paper' privatisation

Privatisation as the centrepiece of the economic reforms has really been what the *Economist* called 'voodoo privatisation', that is, away from the central state, but often into the hands of local authorities or other government holding companies. The magazine concluded: 'for the most part "private" industry in ECE is still short of real money and real owners'. This is because:

- very few people have enough private capital to buy firms;
- foreign buyers are attracted to only the very best and most profitable businesses, as happened in Hungary, leaving the government holding all the firms no one wants to buy;
- many East Central Europeans who have accumulated capital have done so by illicit means;
- giving away shares via voucher schemes might have made people feel part of the system (although subsequent dividends have often been derisory), but they did not raise badly needed capital;
- new capital effectively has to come from profits, which will take the private sector years to build up;
- there are moral problems with selling one's enterprises (the 'family silver') to foreigners;
- there is the problem of economic *dependencia*, whereby indigenous industries become little more than sources of cheap labour for multinational concerns, which will move elsewhere if labour costs rise too steeply.

Economic bottlenecks

Several bottlenecks are slowing down economic reform:

- a lack of purchasing power – for example in Hungary, where 10 per cent of the population account for 50 per cent of purchasing power;
- an inability to estimate the real value of industries to be sold off – for example, it was calculated in 1991 that 80–85 per cent of all Czechoslovak companies were technically bankrupt;
- overmanning and exceedingly low productivity rates – which cannot be changed without a sudden and dramatic increase in unemployment;
- the excessive consumerism is being channelled mainly into the purchase of (superior) Western goods – for example, the Czech Republic is arguably the most dynamic economy of the region, with a healthy balance of payments, yet, if it were not for invisible earnings (e.g. tourism and large speculative investments – 'hot money' – in particular), then the Czech economy would have a 4 billion crown deficit on visible trade, and all money spent on imports is effectively money lost to the economy;
- artificial exchange rates, which lead to a dangerous type of money-go-round; again to take the Czech Republic as an example –
  (i) there are high interest rates (12 per cent), so foreign investors buy Czech crowns, but they do not invest in business – these invisible earnings help the Czech Republic to maintain a balance of payments;
  (ii) if the government brings down the interest rates, then the hot money will disappear, the currency will lose value, but people will continue to buy imported goods and there will be a real trade deficit;
- there is a continuing tendency to subsidise outmoded firms rather than allow them to go bankrupt;
- there is massive, often regionally or locally concentrated, unemployment;
- there are growing regional disparities – for example, western Hungary is quite rich, while eastern Hungary is poor, western Slovakia is better off than eastern Slovakia, Silesia is wealthier than eastern Poland;

- there is a horrific legacy of environmental pollution and ecological destruction, with attendant dangers to health;
- there is the continued importance of the 'black economy' – for example, the President of Hungary's Central Bank claimed in 1995 that the black economy still accounted for 30 per cent of national output;
- the incidence of corruption is increasing, particularly by the former Communists, who constitute many of the new millionaires – 'Corruption seems almost to be accepted in Central Europe as part of the market-economy learning curve,' wrote the *Economist*.

The return to Europe

With the disintegration of the Soviet bloc, the COMECON barter-like arrangements ceased, trade within the region collapsed, as the Soviets, in particular, lacked cash to pay their debts, and the CMEA was formally abolished in January 1991. Not only did ECE lose its traditional markets in the former USSR and East Germany (through reunification), but overall inter-ECE trade decreased dramatically, as everyone turned to the West, that is, mainly to Germany and Austria.

Likewise the Warsaw Pact was ended in July 1991; the Soviet armies of occupation withdrew from the region, proper frontiers were secured and all signs of previous Soviet control were removed. Concomitantly, there was a headlong rush by ECE post-communist states to join 'Europe' (meaning the various existing West European organisations). They sought economic assistance from the IMF and the World Bank, political acceptability by joining the Council of Europe, and greater security through membership of the EU and NATO. By 1990, all ECE states except Albania had entered the IMF and had begun negotiating loans to aid economic recovery. By the end of 1995 – except for the former combatants in former Yugoslavia – they had all gained admission into the Council of Europe. But it was the EU and NATO that were the main pull within the region.

Why the headlong rush to the West?

Reasons for this pull included:

- the 'historical opportunity' of leaving the Russian sphere of influence once and for all;
- from a security viewpoint, the residual fear of Russia;
- an attempt to remedy their economies devastated by over forty years of communism and to attain Western living standards;
- a search for stability in the vacuum of the collapse of the Soviet bloc;
- a belief that membership of both NATO and the EU would increase the stability of democracy within the region.

In respect of the EU

From 1991 onwards, the EU negotiated 'Association Agreements' with each ECE country which were expected to lead to full membership within ten to fifteen years (although most ECE states thought they would be joining in two to five years). On the whole, these Agreements were more protective of the EU's own interests, as they actually restricted trade in those areas where ECE had comparative advantage, such as agriculture, steel, shoes and textiles. The Association Agreement with Hungary, for example, substantially reduced the amount of beef the country could export into the EU. There were some economic aid programmes for certain specific schemes, especially environmental, but they represented a minute fraction of the region's actual needs.

Even so, by spring 1995, Hungary, Poland, the Czech Republic, Bulgaria, Romania and Slovakia had all become EU associate members; by March 1996 the first three had all applied for full membership of the EU (Slovenia and Slovakia were to follow). In May 1995 the Commission issued details of EU laws which applicant countries had to adopt in order to attain membership, and in November 1995 it published a series of reports on the implications of membership for both the EU itself and the ECE applicants.

Negotiations were supposed to begin within six months of the conclusion of the 1996–97 intergovernmental conference. Even if negotiations began in the spring of 1998, they could take up to five or six years to complete (it took seven years in Spain). Given than all EU parliaments must then ratify the accession treaties, enlargement could hardly occur before 2005 even for the most likely candidates (Poland, Hungary and the Czech Republic).

Problems with EU membership

Membership of the EU will give ECE rapid access to a huge common market, substantial regional aid, potential economic growth, higher living standards and increased security. In the 1990–95 period, however, there were still several impediments to entry:

- With their own steady downturn in economic activity, EU countries are in no position to be generous to prospective members from ECE.
- In January 1995, Sweden, Finland and Austria all became full members of the EU – a process which detracted from ECE entry.
- The EU is at a cross-roads in terms of the proposed implementation of the Maastricht Treaty (involving political and currency union, a common defence framework, more powers to the European Parliament and greater use of qualified majority voting). Some member states – in particular Great Britain and Denmark – are opposed to such 'deeper' integration, and such institutional problems must be solved first, before any expansion eastwards.
- The ECE countries lag far behind most EU member states in terms of economic development – even within the most successful ECE economies (e.g. Slovenia and the Czech Republic) living standards are one-third the EU's average. ECE countries are much poorer than were Greece, Portugal and Spain when they joined.
- Under the existing budgetary schemes, the EU does not have the resources to absorb such backward economies with

large rural populations (e.g. Poland, Bulgaria and Romania). The present Common Agricultural Policy (CAP) still accounts for 50 per cent of EU expenditure, and this would increase by another 33 to 40 per cent if ECE farmers were allowed in (implying a 60 per cent increase in each member state's budget contributions). The CAP needs to be totally overhauled before ECE entry.

- On entry under existing rules, ECE countries would lower the EU's average income, thereby depriving other less developed countries (e.g. Ireland, Greece, Portugal and Spain) of their current benefits from the EU's structural funds. Not surprisingly, such countries oppose early admission of ECE states and could easily block their entry in the long term, as unanimity is required in the Council of Ministers for accession of other countries into the EU.

- Accession into the EU will be extremely costly for ECE with regard to adapting to EU environmental and health regulations, and so on, even over a ten-year transition period.

- The formation by the ECE countries of a regional free-trade area to stimulate inter-ECE trade first would perhaps have made accession a little easier and would have demonstrated a greater propensity to cooperate. (Unfortunately, the one partial attempt to produce a common entry plan – the so-called 'Visegrad Group' of the Czech Republic, Slovakia, Poland and Hungary – failed in 1994.)

- Entry into the EU would require a commitment to democratic practices that some countries (e.g. Slovakia or Romania) might have problems fulfilling in respect of control of the media, treatment of ethnic minorities, freedom of the press, manipulation of the constitution, and so on.

- It will take much longer than supposed to gain entry – Turkey has had an Association Agreement with the EU since 1963 and is still excluded from full membership.

- The Maastricht Treaty, if implemented in full, would almost certainly lead to a 'two-speed Europe' and could drastically alter the EU as we know it today. The ECE countries might join such an organisation in the near future, but only in the slower lane, with a watered-down or second-class membership.

At present, the EU is itself in real crisis and seems to have real problems with regard to a 'deepening' the Union. In such a climate, there is really no incentive for the member states to want ECE (in its current state of economic development) inside the EU.

In respect of NATO

Almost all ECE governments wanted to join NATO as soon as possible after 1989, because of the persistent fear of Soviet/ Russian expansionism. There was also a widespread fear that the region would find itself 'in-between' two economic, political and military blocs without belonging to either. Therefore, for some ECE states like Poland, membership of NATO is just as important as joining the EU.

In theory, it would be both easier and less costly for NATO to take in new members from ECE, particularly the Czech and Slovak Republics, Poland and Hungary. There are very different options, ranging from an upgrading of ECE's equipment and command structures to a full commitment of NATO forces on ECE territory, to guard against any potential land attack from Russia. But, with the one notable exception of former East Germany, which gained automatic entry into NATO on unification, full membership for ECE states is unlikely in the immediate future.

In October 1993, NATO defence ministers endorsed the US-led Partnership for Peace (PFP) initiative, which was invented mainly for ECE participation. This comprises individual programmes of cooperation between the particular nations concerned and NATO. It is somewhat like the EU Association Agreements, in that it allows ECE armies to participate in joint manoeuvres with Western troops, to plan joint training, and to work towards introducing common equipment and applying similar command structures.

In December 1994, the NATO Council of Ministers began a 12-month study on the why and how of enlargement. But when the study appeared, it offered no timetable for membership. Likewise, world leaders and politicians often reaffirm the West's and especially American commitment to NATO expansion into ECE, but the 'when' and 'how' still remain unanswered at the time of writing.

Problems with NATO membership

As with entry into the EU, there are also certain problems in respect of potential NATO membership.

- There is a reluctance among most NATO members to apply Article 5 (committing all members to come to the aid of any member that is attacked) to ECE countries, who, in turn, doubt that NATO forces would ever defend the region in the case of an attack from an external enemy (still potentially Russia).
- NATO countries do not wish to provoke or annoy Russia while it still possesses so many nuclear warheads and while it still has the capacity to export nuclear technology to developing countries. There are concerns about the adverse reactions inside Russia to an expansion of NATO eastwards and apprehension about a return to power of the old Russian, ex-communist elite.
- Inside Russia itself, even President Yeltsin and the democratic parties (not to mention the Communists and nationalists) are opposed to NATO expanding eastwards, because it would effectively split Europe into two blocs again, isolating Russia. In 1995 President Yeltsin warned that an expansion of NATO would 'fan the flames of war right across Europe'.
- NATO is going through a period of re-evaluating its own role in the post-Cold-War era: whether it should become an international police force, as it is in Bosnia; whether there is

still a role for the USA in Europe now the Cold War is over, and so on.

- From a technical point of view it would be difficult to incorporate the ECE armies' command structures and equipment into NATO, without a long transition period.
- It would be difficult for NATO to accept some ECE countries into the alliance and reject others. It seems to be a policy of everyone or no one, which only complicates potential entry.
- 'Partial membership' has been discounted by NATO and the ECE countries themselves, so any potential new members will be expected to take on all the obligations of membership from the beginning, which could prove too expensive for many ECE states.
- A sort of 'political' membership, rather than actual 'military' integration, has been suggested as a compromise, and even the Russians have shown interest in cooperating with NATO in this capacity. (But, this defeats the purpose of ECE seeking enhanced security against the very power they still most fear – Russia.)

Not surprisingly, ECE has been grossly disappointed with PFP (Article 5 of the NATO Treaty being the key missing ingredient). The PFP still does not give a timetable or criteria for NATO membership. Yet, the PFP is the most the ECE states can expect for the moment: a loose membership that will keep them out of a Russian sphere of influence, but which will not join them to 'Europe'.

Different alternatives for ECE

There are various alternatives facing the region:

1 integration with the Western organisations, principally NATO and the EU (with all the problems outlined above);
2 a reformed Soviet-type alliance, centred on Moscow (but Russia is still seen as an enemy, not a friend);
3 regional security and economic cooperation (but ECE

countries still seem to be too individualistic to make such
structures work, for example, Visegrad);

4   a new pan-European security arrangement, based on an
      extension of the OSCE (but this would just duplicate
      existing organisations);

5   different, shifting alliances, depending on the sphere of
      interest (but this would be most unstable and would be
      rejected by the West in any case);

6   neutrality, like Sweden and Switzerland (but it implies being
      able to defend one's own territory, as well as other countries
      respecting that neutrality, both of which are in doubt in
      ECE);

7   reliance on national defence (but this would be too costly
      and could also increase tensions with neighbours, especially
      when there are still disputes involving ethnic minorities);

8   a return to economic dominance of the region by Germany,
      which will gradually pull ECE countries into existing
      alliances (rather similar to what happened to East Germany,
      but over a much longer period).

To a certain extent, the last alternative is already happening – more
or less by default. Proximity to the West, especially Germany and
Austria, is the key to the region's future development. German
firms are already investing quite heavily in the region, especially
in the Czech Republic, Hungary and Poland, accounting for
about one-third of total foreign investment in the area and
becoming the chief trading partner of most ECE countries. It
would seem that ECE will fall into a German sphere of influence,
with their currencies tied to the Deutschmark and trade relations
centring on Berlin and Frankfurt – similar to what happened in
the region during the 1930s and like the post-war Austria case. (If
there is to be an enlargement of either the EU or NATO into ECE
in the near future, then it will certainly be German-led.)

Conclusion

The return to 'Europe' is becoming a reality for most ECE
countries, because of re-established trade links, tourists, the influx

of Western goods and Western advertising, the PFP, the Association Agreements with the EU, and so on. There is no doubt, really, that these countries will eventually join both the EU and NATO, but 'eventually' is certainly the operative word. At the moment, NATO seems an easier option, but it is really the financial benefits of being inside a widened EU that the ECE countries seek and that is very much a long-term option.

Different outcomes

Different experts and authors see the future of the ECE in very different ways.

Z. Brzezinski envisages a 'prolonged period of uneasy balance between the forces of nationalist authoritarianism, democratic pluralism and social anarchy'.

Vojtech Cedlacek has used the term 'totalitarian democracy' to describe a polity with the same sort of personalised and hierarchical decision making as under the communist regimes, but within the framework of democratic structures.

Bill Lomax points to a drift towards statist authoritarianism with continued centralisation, especially under 'strong' leaders.

Vladimir Tismaneanu still concentrates on nationalism, seeing the emergence of 'ethnocracies' rather than 'democracies'.

Vaclav Havel and Stephen Heintz identify the main problem as being the authoritarian patterns of thought and behaviour that have been ingrained over most of this century.

Charles Gati, in his study of all twenty-seven post-communist regimes from ECE and the former Soviet Union, states that 'the transition is producing a group of semi-authoritarian, semi-democratic, nationalist, populist regimes', where the vast majority 'reject the way democracy is working and long for a strong, paternalistic leader who would presumably look after their welfare'.

On a more positive note, Jacques Rupnik points out that a shrinking public sector, weak political participation, growing mistrust of parties and politicians, and falling confidence in parliamentary institutions are common problems in established democracies. 'Should we see this as a sign that ECE is at the threshold of Western democratic "normality"?' he asks.

Conclusion

Post-communism will last for some time to come – in its sense of an in-between situation, in-between the First and the Third Worlds, in-between democracy and authoritarianism, in-between East and West. It will take some time for ECE countries to overcome the many legacies of the past and emerge as fully fledged democracies and fully operational market economies, re-anchored in their European home.

In the meantime, almost anything could happen, but it is very unlikely that there would be a full-scale reversal of the economic reform process: a slowing down, maybe, but not a reversal. As far as the democratic reforms are concerned, though, there are some worrying signs – particularly in Slovakia, former Yugoslavia, Bulgaria and Romania – of a much more centralised and authoritarian style of politics emerging under post-communism.

It might be called 'crony democracy' and it might have a degree of authoritarianism, but it will certainly be more stable than the (sometimes utter) chaos of the post-communist, dissident elites. That era is over – as is illustrated most vividly by the former Polish President Lech Walesa returning to his previous job of electrician at the Gdansk shipyards. 'The time of the Great Electrician is ended,' as Adam Michnik put it so succinctly.

Further reading

Attila Agh, 'The Europeanisation of Central European Polities: The Search for a Viable Perspective' and 'The New World Order and the Young East European Democracies', *Budapest Papers on Democratic Transition*, Nos 23 and 48, Budapest University of Economics.

Andrew Cottey, *East Central Europe after the Cold War*, Macmillan, 1995.

'The Return of the Habsburgs', *The Economist: A Survey of Central Europe*, 18 November 1995.

Saul Estrin, Josef Brada, Alan Gelb and Inderjit Singh, *Restructuring and Privatisation in Central Eastern Europe*, M. E. Sharpe, 1995.

Charles Gati, 'The Mirage of Democracy', in *Four Perspectives on Post-Communism* (Michael Mandelbaum, ed.), Council of Foreign Relations, 1996.

Jakub Karpinski, 'Velvet Evolution Continues', *Transition*, 2 (6), 22 March 1996.

George Kolankiewicz, 'Consensus and Competition in the Eastern Enlargement of the European Union', *International Affairs*, 70 (3), 1994.

Marie Lavigne, *The Economics of Transition: From Socialist Economy to Market Economy*, St Martin's Press, 1995.

Adam Michnik, 'The Velvet Restoration', *Transition*, 2 (6), 22 March 1996.

George Schöpflin, 'Post-Communism: Constructing New Democracies in Central Europe', *International Affairs*, 67.

'Enlarging NATO: How? When? Why?', *Transition*, 1 (23), 15 December 1995.

'Post-Communism: A Search for Metaphor', *Transition*, 2 (6), 22 March 1996.

Appendix. Summary histories of the ECE states

The Czech and Slovak lands	Poland	Hungary	Romania

Before 1914

830 – Moravian Prince Mojmir I establishes the Great Moravian Empire of Bohemia, Slovakia and south-east Poland.

904 – Great Moravia is ended by the Magyars.

1018 – Slovakia is annexed to Hungary at the Bautzen Peace.

1347–78 – Charles IV is Czech King and Holy Roman Emperor during a time of incredible economic and cultural expansion.

1400–34 – The Czech Kingdom is dominated by the Hussite reform movement. Jan Hus criticises the wealth and power of the Catholic Church. He is accused of heresy and burnt in Constanz in July 1415.

1526 – Czech nobles elect Ferdinand Habsburg as Czech King, thereby securing Habsburg rule in Central Europe for 400 years.

1618–20 – Czech uprising led by Protestant reformist nobility against the Catholic Habsburgs at the Battle of White Mountain. The Czech

Before 1914

963 -The establishment of the Polish duchy under the rule of the Piast dynasty. Poles become Christians.

1138 – The Polish Kingdom splits into a number of duchies.

1333–70 – Cassimir III reunites Poland into one state which becomes a safe haven for Jews.

1386–1572 – Lithuania is united to Poland under the Jagellonian dynasty, which later absorbs Belarussia and the Ukraine.

1683 – The Polish army defeats the Turks and breaks the Ottoman siege of Vienna.

1772 and 1793 – First partitions of Poland between Prussia, Russia and Austria.

1794 – A Polish national uprising under T. Kosciusko to restore Poland's independence.

1795 – Final division of Poland, so that the country disappears completely from the map of Europe.

1807 – Napoleon founds the Grand Duchy of Warsaw as a French dependency.

Before 1918

Tenth century – Magyar tribes undertake destructive raids into Europe (e.g. France and Italy), and threaten Constantinople twice.

972–97 – Geyza I and his son Stephen (997–1036) integrate the Magyar tribes into a Hungarian state

29 August 1526 – After its defeat by the Turks at Mohacs, Hungary becomes part of the Ottoman Empire.

1550s – The Habsburgs gain rule over Slovakia (Upper Hungary), western Hungary and Croatia.

1687 – The Turks are repulsed from the rest Hungary and northern Serbia after another battle at Mohacs.

Early 1800s – A revival of the Hungarian language and the spread of nationalism among the peasantry.

1848–49 – The Hungarian nationalists, led by L. Kossuth, end feudal rights, free the peasants, establish civil liberties and declare an independent Hungarian state. There are armed

Before 1914

From the 4th century - Romanian lands are part of the Byzantine Empire.

Late thirteenth century - The region splits into two provinces: Wallachia and Moldavia.

Fifteenth and sixteenth centuries – The two provinces are dominions of the Ottoman Empire.

1699 – Habsburgs add (Romanian) Transylvania to their Empire.

1730–1854 – The two provinces, under Turkish rule, are constantly being occupied by the Russians or Austrians.

1821 – A nationalist revolution is brutally suppressed by the Turks.

1830 – The two provinces are granted autonomous status by the Turks.

1848 – After another revolution (pressing for union with Romanian Transylvania), the two provinces are occupied jointly by the Turks and Russians.

1856 – Most of Russian Bessarabia is annexed to Moldavia.

1859 – Moldavia and

Bulgaria

Before 1914

681–1018 – The First
Bulgarian Empire.

814–88 – The height of
the Bulgarian Kingdom,
which absorbs most of
the Balkans.

1018 – Bulgaria
becomes part of the
Byzantine Empire.

1188 – Bulgarians
regain their indepen-
dence. The Second
Bulgarian Empire lasts
until 1396.

1396 – Bulgaria is
captured by the Turks
and becomes part of the
Ottoman Empire.

1876 – Bulgarian
national revival is
crushed by Turks.

1878 – Under the
Treaty of San Stefano,
'Greater Bulgaria' is
declared, reaching from
the Danube to the
Aegean Sea. These gains
are lost six months later
in the Treaty of Berlin.

After the 1870s – The
alien Ottoman nobility
is expelled and the land
distributed to the
indigenous peasantry.

1899 – The Peasant
Party is founded as a
social (i.e. not a
political) movement.

Albania

Before 1914

In ancient times –
Albania is the home of
the ancient Illyrians.

**First to fifth
centuries** – Albania is
a Roman province,
invaded by the Goths in
the fourth to fifth
centuries.

640 – The north of the
country is overrun by
the Serbs.

861 – Bulgaria conquers
the south of the country.

**From the nineth
century** – Albania
comes under Greek,
Serbian and then
Ottoman Turkish rule.

1443–68 – Christian
revolt against the
Ottoman Turks headed
by the Albanian leader
Skanderbeg.

**From the fifteenth
century** – Albania
remains part of the
Ottoman Empire and is
converted to the Islamic
religion, although the
country remains partly
Christian. Albania
retains its clan-based
social structure and is
dominated by tribal
warfare (between the
Gheg mountaineers in
the north and the Tosk
farmers in the south).

Prussia/
Germany

Before 1914

962 – As First Holy
Roman Emperor, Otto I
rules over a loose
confederation of Central
European states centring
on Germany.

1300s – Lacking a
strong and centralised
monarchy, Germany
disintegrates into 350
warring states.

1517 – The Reform-
ation splits Germany
into a Protestant north
and a Catholic south.

1618–48 – The Thirty
Years' War devastates
Germany.

1648 – The Treaty of
Westphalia reduces the
Empire's power by
recognising the German
princedoms.

1701 – Brandenburg
becomes the Kingdom
of Prussia.

1756–63 – The Seven
Years' War: Prussia
defeats the alliance of
Austria, France and
Russia.

1806 – The Holy
Roman Empire of the
German Nation ends.

1815 – At the Congress
of Vienna, Prussia
increases its German
and Polish territory. The

Region of the
South Slavs
(Yugoslavia)

Before 1918

Ninth century –
Serbia first emerges as a
principality inside the
Byzantine Empire.
Bulgaria acquires
Macedonia.

1102 – Croatia is united
with Hungary.

**Thirteenth century
onwards** – Slovenia
comes under Habsburg
dominion, where it
remains until 1918.

1331–55 – Serbia
becomes the dominant
power in the Balkans
during the reign of
Stephen Dushan.

1389 – The Serbs are
defeated by the Ottoman
Turks at Kosovo Field.
Macedonia is acquired
by the Turks.
Montenegro remains
unconquered.

1459 – Serbia is fully
incorporated into the
Ottoman Empire.

1463 – Bosnia becomes
part of the Ottoman
Empire until 1878.

1526–1699 – Croatia is
also under Turkish rule.

1699 – Habsburgs add
northern Serbia and
Croatia to their Empire.

1794, 1804 and 1813 –
Serbian nationalists

nobles are dispossessed of their lands and their leaders are executed.

12–18 June 1848 – The Austrian army easily suppresses the Czech 'revolution' in Prague.

1867 – At the founding of the Austro-Hungarian Dual Monarchy, the Czechs are refused the equal status to the Hungarians.

1886 – Czech is given equal status to German within the Czech lands.

1918–39

28 October 1918 – A republic is proclaimed in Prague.

30 October 1918 – The Martin Declaration: the Slovak representatives declare the right of the Slovak nation to self-determination.

14 November 1918 – T. G. Masaryk is elected the first Czechoslovak President.

1919 – Ruthenia joins Czechoslovakia. The Tesin region is divided between Poland and Czechoslovakia.

1918–38 – Five major democratic political parties (Agrarians, Social Democrats, Czechoslovak National Socialists, National Democrats and People's Party) form broad coalition governments.

30 September 1938 – Great Britain, Germany, Italy and France agree at the Munich Conference that Czechoslovakia must give up its Sudeten German borderland to Germany.

5 October 1938 – President Benes

1815 – The Congress of Vienna makes some changes in territorial boundaries in Europe. The Grand Duchy is abolished and the land returned to Prussia, Austria and Russia.

1830, 1846, 1848, 1863 and 1905 – Unsuccessful revolts against the Russians to restore Poland's sovereignty. On each occasion thousands of Poles are killed, gaoled or exiled.

1914–39

1915 – During the war, the Russians are routed near Cracow in May and are pushed out of the Polish region entirely in August when the Germans take Warsaw.

1918 – The Austro-Hungarian monarchy disintegrates. Poland is restored as an independent nation, receiving large areas of Prussia, a corridor to the Baltic Sea and the port of Danzig.

1920–21 – After a war with Russia, Poland acquires large areas of Belorussia and the Ukraine. There are also border disputes with the Germans and Czechs.

1922 – Democratic elections are held, but the Premier is murdered and the one-year-old government falls. A non-party government rules over economic and political instability.

Between 1918 and 1926 – There are fourteen different governments in Poland.

May 1926 – After a coup, General J. Pilsudski leads a highly

conflicts with Slovaks, Serbs and Croats. The Austrian Emperor sends a large army led by Croats, and then seeks help from the Russian Tsar, whose army defeats the revolutionaries in Transylvania.

1867 – The Austro-Hungarian monarchy is established in which Hungary and Austria have equal status but one monarch.

1905 – Universal suffrage is introduced into Hungary.

1918–40

28 October 1918 – Austria accepts President Wilson's fourteen points (including the right of self-determination of the small nations in the Habsburg Empire).

1918 – Count M. Karolyi sets up a democratic system with free elections. He tries to keep all former territories in a federation, and resigns when the Allies oppose the idea, forcing him to withdraw all troops from Transylvania.

1919 – The Austro-Hungarian monarchy disintegrates. There is a brief attempt to establish 'Greater Hungary' after a Bolshevik-like coup, led by Bela Kun and supported by the Soviets. After initial military successes in souther Slovakia, Kun is defeated by the Romanian army in August. In the following 'white terror' in western Hungary, 5–6,000 civilians are killed.

1920 – Hungary loses 72 per cent of its pre-

Wallachia are united under Prince A. Cuza.

1866 – Prince Cuza is deposed and the crown offered to Prince Carol of the Hohenzollerns.

1878 – Independence of Romania is guaranteed by the Treaty of Berlin, but Bessarabia is returned to Russia.

1913 – After the Second Balkan War, Romania gains southern Dobrudja from Bulgaria.

1914–39

1916 – Romania joins the allies, hoping to recover Transylvania and Bessarabia, which it does in the post-war peace treaties.

1921–27 – The nominally democratic country (dominated by the National Liberal Party and the National Peasants' Party) is ruled benevolently by King Ferdinand. Under his rule there is extensive land reform, but it does not end rural poverty. Industry begins to develop, thanks mainly to German capital.

1920–28 – Effectively a period of martial law and press censorship, beginning under General Averescu in May 1920.

1920s and 1930s – Elections are basically 'arranged' by the interior minister in power.

1927 – King Ferdinand dies and his son Carol abdicates for personal reasons. A regency is set up, but Carol returns and takes over the throne again.

1912–13 – The First Balkan War: Bulgaria, Serbia and Montenegro defeat the Turks. Bulgaria regains western Thrace and access to the Macedonia.

1913 – In the Second Balkan War Bulgaria is defeated by Montenegro, Serbia and Romania, losing western Thrace to Turkey and southern Dobrudja to Romania.

Since the tribes are so tough and barbaric, Turkish rule is very weak outside the main towns. Albania becomes the poorest region of Europe.

1908–12 – There are several revolts for independence within the country.

1912–13 – First Balkan War, after which Albania attains nominal independence from the Ottoman Empire.

German Confederation is created.

1848 – The democratic revolution and Frankfurt parliament fail to unite Germany.

1864–70 – Prussia easily defeats Denmark, crushes the Habsburg army and overpowers France to become the dominant power in ECE.

18 January 1871 – The founding of a united German Empire.

revolt against Turkish and Habsburg rule.

1878 – At the Congress of Berlin, Serbia and Montenegro are granted full statehood and Austria occupies Bosnia. Turkey keeps Macedonia.

1912–13 – During the First Balkan War, the Balkan League (Serbia, Bulgaria and Montenegro) defeat the Turks. In the Second Balkan War, Bulgaria is defeated by its former allies. Serbia keeps northern Macedonia.

1914–40

1914 – Bulgaria enters the war on the side of the Germans in order to regain lost territories.

October 1918 – The 'Radomir Rebellion' (major mutiny of peasant troops) replaces Tsar Ferdinand with his son Boris, but fails to establish a republic.

1919 – In the Treaty of Neuilly, Bulgaria loses its wartime conquests.

1920s – Inter-war politics are dominated by the Peasant Union and IMRO (nationalist-revolutionary movement seeking the recovery of Macedonia from Greece and Serbia).

December 1922 – The Peasant Union's 'Orange Guard' (a para-military force) tries to kill many opposition politicians, who are then imprisoned for 'their own safety'.

9 June 1923 – Premier Stamboliski, leader of the Peasant Union, is assassinated by IMRO, after a nationalist coup involving the military, intelligentsia and IMRO.

1914–30s

1914–18 – During the First World War, Albania is occupied five times by different armies, including the Italians, Greeks and Austrians.

1917 – Italy declares Albania an independent state under Italian protection.

1920 – The Italians withdraw and Albania becomes a sovereign state after the 1919 Paris Treaties, but its borders are not finally fixed until 1921.

1920s – Fierce political competition takes place between A. Zogu, a warrior chieftain from the north, and Bishop S. Noli, from the intelligentsia in the south.

December 1923 – In elections Zogu's partisans win 40 seats to Noli's 35. Zogu's supporters assassinate a young opposition leader and Zogu flees to Yugoslavia.

June 1924 – Noli forms his only govern-ment and announces a sweeping reform

1914–39

1914–18 – Austro-Hungary and Turkey are Germany's allies during the First World War.

11 November 1918 – Germany signs the armistice.

November 1918 – The Weimar Republic is established and the Kaiser abdicates.

1919 – In the Treaty of Versailles Germany loses its colonies and Alsace and Lorraine. Germany west of the Rhine is occupied by the French, and Saarland is to be governed by the League of Nations.

1922 – Germany cannot pay its enormous war reparations, so Belgian and French troops occupy the Ruhr district.

1923 – Germany suffers from hyperinflation; its currency is worthless.

November 1923 – Hitler's 'Braukeller' putsch fails in Munich.

1931 – The Nazi Party is the strongest single party in the Reichstag.

January 1933 – A. Hitler is appointed German Chancellor.

1914–40

28 June 1914 – The assassination of Austrian Archduke Franz-Ferdinand at Sarajevo by a Serb nationalist triggers the First World War.

1917 – By the Deal of Corfu, Serbs and Croats agree to the formation of a southern Slav state, with its own Serbo-Croat language.

December 1918 – Serb King Alexander proclaims the Kingdom of Serbs, Croats and Slovenes.

1920 – A new constitution establishes a unitary state, which the Serbs dominate. The Croats boycott the constituent assembly.

1920s – Fighting begins between the Serbs and Croats almost as soon as the new state is formally established. The Croat Peasant Party under S. Radic leads a vigorous campaign for autonomy.

1928 – A Serbian nationalist shoots Croat political leaders inside the national parliament.

Between 1918 and 1929 – There are 24

abdicates and leaves the country together with many other politicians for the USA or Great Britain.

October 1938 – Slovakia and Ruthenia declare independence.

14 March 1939 – The Slovak parliament proclaims an independent Slovak (cleric-fascist) state.

15 March 1939 – The German army occupies Bohemia and Moravia. Thousands leave the country in the following months to join the Allies against the Nazis.

authoritarian regime with a parliamentary facade and multi-party elections.

1926–35 – Pilsudski's rule is marked by religious intolerance, continuing ethnic conflict and problems with Germany over the Polish corridor.

1935 – Pilsudski installs a repressive, nationalistic and very anti-Semitic presidential dictatorship. Political parties and the Polish parliament are rendered more or less powerless. After his death in 1935, Poland is ruled by a military council.

war lands and 64 per cent of its population to neighbouring states in the Treaty of Trianon.

1920–44 – Power is assumed by a mainly military government under the leadership of Admiral Horthy.

1920s and 1930s – Under Horthy elections are rigged in favour of the government. The Smallholders' Party is the largest party in parliament.

1930s – During the rise of Europe-wide anti-Semitism the fascist Arrow Cross grows dramatically, but never enters government.

1930s – There are significant German, Hungarian and Jewish minorities in inter-war Romania. This provokes increased anti-Semitism and nationalism, leading to the founding of the fascist Iron Guard.

1938 – Carol declares a royal dictatorship.

1940 – When Romania cedes territory to the USSR, Bulgaria and Hungary, the Iron Guard mount a coup and Carol is forced to abdicate in favour of his son Michael. Antonescu establishes a military, pro-Hitler, fascist dictatorship.

1939–46

16 March 1939 – Bohemia and Moravia become parts of the German Reich.

27 May 1942 – Czech resistance forces assassinate the Protector of the Reich in the Czech lands, R. Heydrich. In revenge the Germans annihilate the village of Libice, killing or deporting its entire population.

1943 – Disputes about Czechoslovakia's post-war orientation begin between the exiled government in London led by President Benes and the Communist leadership in Moscow headed by Klement Gottwald.

April 1945 – A National Front government is formed in Kosice from six pre-war parties (two are Communist). The government is headed by a former Czechoslovak ambassador to Moscow with six Communists in other key posts.

1939–46

August 1939 – The Molotov–Ribbentrop Pact, when Hitler and Stalin agree to divide Poland

1 September 1939 – The Second World War begins as Poland is invaded by Germany. The Germans and Soviets occupy Poland according to the 1939 Pact.

1939–42 – Many Nazi concentration camps are built in Poland. One million Poles are deported to the USSR.

1943 – In Warsaw the Jewish ghetto revolt is ignored by the Polish underground and is crushed by the Germans.

August 1944 – The Warsaw Uprising (led by the Polish government in London) is put down and 200,000 Poles are killed, while the Soviet army waits outside the city gates.

December 1944 – The Soviet-supported

1941–48

1941 – Hungary receives parts of Slovakia and Romania after joining the Axis powers in the war.

1942 – Hitler occupies Hungary. Admiral Horthy appoints a pro-Nazi Premier. Over 1 million Hungarian Jews and gypsies die in Nazi extermination camps.

1944–45 – The Red Army liberates Hungary.

November 1945 – The Smallholders' Party gains 57 per cent of votes in free elections (Communists gain 17 per cent). A broad coalition is formed under the Smallholders' leader F. Nagy. The Communists obtain the Interior Ministry.

1946 – Many members of the Smallholders' Party are arrested and tried for conspiracy or fascist collaboration. By December, the Communists control the government.

1940–48

14 September 1940 – The Iron Guard declares itself the guardian of the state and begins to slaughter its political opponents and massacre Jews.

21–23 January 1941 – General Antonescu suppresses the Iron Guard in brutal street fighting, with Hitler's connivance.

1944 – King Michael deposes Antonescu and forms an alliance with the Allies.

March 1945 – After a brief pro-Soviet military government, Moscow orders King Michael to appoint Communist P. Groza head of a National Democratic Front, composed of many parties but dominated by the Communists.

1946 – The Communists create the Ploughmen's Front as an alternative to the National Peasants' Party.

July 1946 – The peace

September 1923 – Another coup is staged by the Communists. The National Concord government begins a 'White Terror' campaign against both Communists and Peasantists.

1925 – The Communists' terrorist bombing of Sofia cathedral kills 128 people, including several government ministers.

1934 – Another coup establishes a brief military regime, which crushes IMRO.

1934–43 – King Boris III, supported by the army, sets up his own personal dictatorship.

1940–46

1940 – Hitler arranges the return of southern Dobrudja to Bulgaria. As a result, Bulgaria joins the Axis powers.

1941 – Nazi victories in the Balkans allow Bulgaria to annex Macedonia and western Thrace.

August 1943 – King Boris is killed, after visiting Hitler and proposing to change sides in the war.

1943 – The Communist-led resistance against the Germans and the pro-German regime grows. By December the German army pulls out of Bulgaria.

Mid-1944 – Bulgaria turns neutral, but the Russians still declare war on the country.

September 1944 – Bulgaria joins the war on the Allies' side just as Soviet troops enter the country.

Autumn 1944 – The Communist Fatherland

programme (but does not implement it).

December 1924 – One year after the elections Zogu reinvades Albania and it is Noli's turn to flee into exile.

January 1925 – Zogu is elected to the presidency by parliament.

September 1928 – Zogu turns Albania into a monarchy with himself as King Zog I.

1930s – King Zog I modernises Albania, ending its clan warfare, introducing modern civil, penal and commercial codes and building up the country's infrastructure.

1930s–46

After 1931 – Zog I refuses to renew the defence alliance set up with fascist Italy in the late 1920s.

1932–33 – Zog I also rejects Mussolini's offer of a customs union and distances himself from Italy, despite losing Italian subsidies.

1935–36 – Zog I wins great popularity by resisting Italian pressure. He even begins to liberalise his regime.

March 1939 – Mussolini demands a formal Italian protectorate over Albania. When Zog I delays his reply, Albania is bombed and occupied by the Italians in early April 1939. Zog goes into exile.

1940 – Mussolini uses Albania as a base from which to invade Greece (on the pretext of regaining Albanian territory in Epirus, northern Greece). But Italian troops are repulsed and the Greeks counter-attack into

1934 – The German army reoccupies the Rhineland and Saar regions, against League of Nations dictates.

11 July 1936 – The Austro-German treaty is signed: Austria declares itself a 'German state'.

13 March 1938 – The Anschluss of Austria to Germany.

30 September 1938 – Czechoslovakia is sacrificed by France and Britain for the sake at Munich over the German Sudeten question.

1939–48

23 August 1939 – Von Ribbentrop and V. Molotov sign the German–Soviet non-aggression pact.

1 September 1939 – Germany attacks Poland, beginning the Second World War.

1939–41 – Germany invades Denmark, Norway, the Netherlands, Belgium, Luxembourg, France, Yugoslavia, Greece, northern Africa and Russia. It is allied with Italy, Finland, Hungary, Bulgaria, Romania, Croatia and Slovakia.

22 June 1941 – Germany and its allies attack the Soviet Union unexpectedly.

July 1942 – January 1943 – A hard-fought battle at Stalingrad ends in the destruction of the German 6th army division. It is a turning-point in the war.

2 May 1945 – The Red Army invades Berlin; Hitler commits suicide three days earlier.

different governments. National extremists – IMRO (Macedonia) and Ustasi (Croatia) – seek independence through violence and terror.

1929 – Alexander ends the period of democracy, imposes dictatorship and changes the country's name to Yugoslavia.

June 1932 – Croatian Ustasi launch a revolt.

1934 – Alexander is assassinated by IMRO/ Ustasi activists in Marseille. A regency is formed in the name of his son Peter.

August 1939 – Croatia gains virtual autonomy.

1941–45

March 1941 – The Serbs break their pre-war pact with Hitler and join the Allies. Germany conquers Yugoslavia in 18 days. Serbia – particularly Belgrade – is extensively bombed.

1941 onwards – Hitler sets up a Croatian puppet state under the Ustasi. Slovenia and Serbia are annexed to the German Reich, Macedonia is occupied by Bulgaria and the Adriatic coast is overrun by the Italians.

1941–45 – The Ustasi and pro-Nazi Muslims commit horrendous acts of genocide against the Serbs in Nazi-type concentration camps. The Croatian Serbs are also forced to convert to Roman Catholicism.

1941–44 – Anti-Nazi resistance by the Serbian royalist Cetniks and J. Tito's Communist partisans breaks into a bloody civil war, with the pro-Nazi Croatian Ustasi also being

1 May 1945 – The Czech uprising begins. Eight days later the Red Army liberates Prague.

24 October 1945 – Over two-thirds of Czechoslovak businesses, including mines, grocers, banks, private insurance companies and other key industries are nationalised.

1945–46 – The property and land of the Germans, Hungarians and all former collaborators are confiscated.

1946 – According to international agreements, 2,250,000 Germans are expelled during the year.

(The above three measures are all taken by the non-communist government based in Kosice.)

Lublin Poles set up a provisional government.

July 1945 – A Polish government of national unity consists of the Lublin Poles and a few non-communists.

August 1945 – At the Potsdam conference, eastern Poland is kept within the USSR, but Poland gains territory from eastern Germany and east Prussia.

1946 – The Peasant Party is terrorised and its leaders accused of being British agents.

January 1947 – The Communists and their allies gain 86 per cent of seats in the Polish parliament after elections. The Peasant Party secures only 6 per cent of seats.

Mid-1947 – Communists emerge as the largest party after rigged elections (they still manage only 22 per cent of the vote).

June 1947 – Nagy and many non-communist politicians flee Hungary.

June 1948 – The Social Democrats are forced to merge with the Communists into the MSZMP. A one-party dictatorship is established under M. Rakosi.

May 1949 – A Communist-dominated People's Independence Front wins the third post-war elections.

1949 – Hungary becomes a People's Republic under the new constitution.

treaty with the USSR confirms the loss of territories and requires war reparations to be paid.

November 1946 – The Communist National Democratic Front claims to have won over 66 per cent of the vote in disputed general elections.

1946–47 – Potential opposition parties are persecuted, manipulated and banned, especially the National Peasants' Party. Others are forced to integrate with the Communist Party.

30 December 1947 – King Michael is coerced into abdication, the monarchy is abolished and the Romanian People's Republic proclaimed.

Under communism, 1946–89

May 1946 – The Communists win the elections with 37 per cent of votes. Gottwald becomes Premier and the Communists receive nine government seats (out of twenty-six).

20 February 1948 – Thirteen non-communist ministers resign in protest against the tightening Communist control.

25 February 1948 – After staged mass protests in support of the Communists, President Benes accepts the resignation of the thirteen ministers and Gottwald forms a totally Communist cabinet.

1948–53 – There are several political show trials directed against the democratic elements of society

Under communism, 1948–88

December 1948 – Communists merge with the Socialist Party to form the PZPR.

1950s – Resistance of the traditional Polish peasantry causes the collapse of collective farming in Poland.

1956 – After Bierut's death there is a relaxation of political purges, press censorship and police repression.

June–October 1956 – 50,000 workers riot against higher prices and increased work quotas in Poznan. The protests become anti-regime and are crushed by the army. Fifty-four are killed and hundreds wounded.

1956 onwards – Further relaxation of controls under the new leader, W. Gomulka.

Under communism, 1949–89

1949 – Stalinist Rakosi purges L. Rajk and other leading members of the MSZMP.

1950–51 – The collectivisation of agriculture and nationalisation of industry are carried out.

July 1953 – I. Nagy becomes Premier. He relaxes the police terror and releases political prisoners.

1955 – Rakosi condemns Nagy's reforms and reinstates the hard-line regime.

23 October 1956 – Student demonstrations in Budapest become a popular uprising, demanding the reinstatement of Nagy.

24–25 October 1956 – Nagy becomes Premier again. He sets about

Under communism, 1948–89

1948 – The Social Democrats and Communists merge to form the Romanian Worker's Party.

1948–50 – The collectivisation of agriculture and the nationalisation of major industries begin.

June 1952 – G. Georghiu-Dej becomes Premier and continues with Stalinist policies. Several show trials take place, but it is the hard-liners within Party who are purged. He promotes an foreign policy independent from Moscow; for example, Romania remains neutral in the Sino-Soviet dispute.

1953–54 – Leading members of the Jewish community are tried for Zionism and anti-state activities.

Front takes over power in a coup.

Autumn 1945 – Communist resistance forces, led by T. Zhivkov, quickly try to execute about 2,800 wartime political figures, claiming they were all German collaborators or foreign spies. Many other potential political opponents are arrested on false charges.

1946 – In the post-war peace conferences Bulgaria is allowed to retain southern Dobrudja, but otherwise reverts to its pre-war borders.

8 September 1946 – In a referendum Bulgaria votes for a republic and against restoring the monarchy.

southern Albania (with the intention also of annexing this region to Greece).

1941 – Germany now invades Albania, in order to rescue the Italians, and the Greeks are driven out. Albania then joins the Axis powers and helps to occupy Greece and Kosovo.

1941–43 – The Nazis complete their occupation of Albania. Then the Albanians turn against the Germans.

Summer 1944 – The Germans pull out of Albania. Communist partisans claim all the credit for the explusion of the Germans from Albanian territory

8 May 1945 – Admiral K. Donitz signs the armistice and the Second World War in Europe ends.

From 1945 – Germany and its capital Berlin are divided into four zones of occupation (Russian, American, British and French).

April 1945 – The 'Ulbricht Group' is sent from Moscow to set up a civil administration and found a Communist Party.

From 1945 – In their zone of occupation, the Soviets dismantle whole factories and ship them back to the USSR as war reparations, along with thousands of German and ECE prisoners of war.

involved. The different groups fight each other just as often as they do the Germans.

1944 – Belgrade is bombed by the Allies without explanation.

1945 – Exceptionally in ECE Yugoslavia is not liberated by the Red Army. Tito's partisans do most of the work, with 350,000 killed and 400,000 wounded.

1945 – Tito sets about installing a communist system straight away. Pre-war politicians are sometimes given posts in a coalition government. More often, they are tried as 'foreign agents'. The Cetnik leader Mihailovic is executed for being a German collaborator.

Under communism, 1946–88

October 1946 – The Communists take 277 out of 465 seats in rigged legislative elections. The ruling Fatherland Front as a whole wins 364 seats.

November 1946 – G. Dimitrov, the Communist leader, having spent twenty years in exile, forms a new government.

1947 – Members of the Peasant Union (the greatest threat to the Communists) are further persecuted.

23 September 1947 – Peasant leader N. Petkov is executed for treason after a show trial.

December 1947 – Soviet troops are taken out of Bulgaria.

August 1948 – The Social Democrats are

Under communism, 1944–90

Autumn 1944 – The Communist-led National Liberation Movement takes over power under its leader Enver Hoxha. Rivals in the pro-Western National Front are shot or escape into exile.

November 1944 – Hoxha becomes Premier of a Communist-dominated coalition government.

January 1946 – Hoxha proclaims the People's Republic of Albania after winning rigged elections.

1948 – Dramatic rift with Yugoslavia begins, as the country's leaders are clearly associated with the Albanian nationalist movement in Yugoslavia. All pro-Yugoslav factions within the Party are purged by

East Germany under communism, 1946–89

April 1946 – In the Soviet zone the Social Democrats are 'persuaded' to merge with the Communists to form the SED.

May 1946 – The SED dominates elections in the Soviet zone.

1947 – Soviet-type socialism is introduced into East Germany.

1949 – Poland officially takes over former German regions. Mass expulsions of Germans follow over the next two years.

April 1948 – May 1949 – The Soviet blockade of West Berlin and the massive airlift which keeps the city alive.

7 October 1949 – The GDR is officially

Yugoslavia under communism, 1945–87

November 1945 – The Communist-controlled People's Front 'wins' elections to a provisional assembly with 96 per cent of the vote, as no opposition candidates are allowed. The Federal People's Republic of Yugoslavia is proclaimed by Tito.

1946 – A new constitution is adopted, by which Tito becomes President. Ministries are staffed by partisan veterans, freedom of the press is ended, industries are nationalised and farms collectivised, following the Soviet model.

1948 – Because of the Yugoslav Communist Party's independence from Moscow, Tito establishes his own path to socialism.

(Church, non-communist parties etc.). In all about 230,000 citizens are victims of these trials.

September 1949 – Purges against (mostly Jewish) leading members of the Communist Party begin. Eleven are executed in 1952, including the General Secretary of the Party, R. Slansky.

1953 – A workers' protest over price rises and currency reform in Pilsen, following the death of both Gottwald and Stalin, is swiftly suppressed.

1963 – Novotny ousts the leading pro-Stalinists in the party.

March 1968 – The Prague Spring begins. A. Dubcek, Party leader, proposes an Action Programme of economic liberalisation and political reforms.

June 1968 – Czech intellectuals issue the '2,000-word statement' advocating greater liberties.

21 August 1968 – A huge invasion by Warsaw Pact troops ends the Prague Spring. Dubcek and the other reformists are 'kidnapped' to Moscow, where they agree to end the reforms.

January 1969 – Jan Palach sets fire to himself in protest against the Soviet invasion.

April 1969 – Gustav Husak replaces Dubcek and begins a process of 'normalisation' (purges of reformers and a return to hard-line Stalinist policies). One-fifth of Party members are expelled.

November 1968 – L. Brezhnev elaborates the 'Brezhnev doctrine' at a PZPR Congress in Warsaw.

December 1970 – Poland and West Germany sign a treaty recognising the Oder–Neisse borderline. The Federal Republic thereby renounces its claim to the 'German territories under Polish administration'.

December 1970 – Price increases are followed by riots in coastal cities, in which several hundred protestors are killed.

December 1970 – W. Gomulka is replaced by E. Gierek.

June–July 1976 – Huge riots force the government to rescind proposed increases in food prices.

1978 – L. Walesa and other workers found an illegal Committee of Free Trade Unions for the Baltic ports.

October 1978 – The election of Cardinal K. Wojtyla as Pope John Paul II. He makes his first visit to Poland in June 1979.

31 August 1980 – Strikes end when the government agrees to a list of twenty-one trade union demands, including the right to strike and form free trade unions. Solidarity is born, becoming a legal entity one year later.

1981 – General Jaruzelski becomes Premier and L. Walesa is elected Solidarity Chair.

1981 – Twelve million people join Solidarity. Hundreds of thousands of members resign from the PZPR.

disbanding the secret police, permits the restoration of multi-party democracy and announces Hungary is to leave the Warsaw Pact.

4 November 1956 – The Soviet Army crushes the Hungarian revolt. Some 32,000 die and over 250,000 flee to the West. Nagy is arrested and executed for treason along with three other reformists two years later. J. Kadar assumes power and returns the country to more hard-line communism.

January 1968 – The Kadar regime begins the 'New Economic Mechanism' (NEM), which attempts to combine elements of a market economy with central planning.

Late 1970s – After some half-hearted attempts at reform, the NEM is retained but is increasingly criticised.

November 1972 – The beginning of a partial retreat from the experiments of the NEM, with a return to the policy of subsidising uneconomic enterprises.

December 1981 – The first issue of the influential samizdat magazine *Beszlo* is published as martial law is declared in Poland.

15 March 1986 – Thousands attend a pro-democracy march marking the thirtieth anniversary of the 1956 revolt. Police stop the march.

November 1986 – Influential economists demand a radical change in economic policy in the document 'Turning Point and Reform'.

1986 – The samizdat

July 1958 – Soviet 'occupation' troops withdraw from Romania under a Warsaw Pact agreement.

19 March 1965 – Gheorghiu-Dej dies, and is succeeded by N. Ceausescu. The Party reverts to its pre-1948 name of Romanian Communist Party (PCR).

January 1967 – Romania further annoys Moscow by recognising West Germany.

August 1968 – Romania condemns the invasion of Czecho-slovakia and sends no troops. It then reduces its commitment to the Warsaw Pact by no longer allowing military manoeuvres on its territory.

December 1970 – Ceausescu visits the USA. His anti-Moscow foreign policy earns him respect in the West.

1971–72 – Romania becomes a member of GATT and the IMF.

March 1975 – The USA grants 'most favoured nation' trading status to Romania.

April–July 1978 – N. Ceausescu visits the USA and Great Britain.

March 1980 – Romania issues a statement criticising the Soviet invasion of Afghanistan.

December 1982 – Ceausescu's decision to pay off the country's foreign debt by the end of the decade is followed by series of harsh restrictions, including rationing of food and energy.

September 1983 – G. Bush describes Ceausescu as 'one of

merged with the ruling Communist Party. Other political opposition parties are abolished in 1949.

December 1948 – G. Dimitrov claims Bulgarian people's democracy is a model for the whole of ECE. He dies in July 1949.

April 1949 – The Party is purged of nationalists, whose leader is hanged in December.

March 1954 – T. Zhivkov becomes Party First Secretary. His long reign (1954–89) is characterised by absolute loyalty to the Soviet regime. He even suggests Bulgaria joins the USSR.

Late 1950s – Collectivisation of agriculture is achieved and a rapid industrialisation is attempted.

1961–62 – Zhivkov ousts leading rivals within the Party and becomes Premier

April 1965 – Elements of the Bulgarian army mount an unsuccessful coup to remove Zhivkov from power.

1970s – The Bulgarian economy deteriorates steadily. Zhivkov tries to hide the crisis by selling Bulgaria's oil (coming from the USSR at concessionary rates) on the world market.

1971 – Zhivkov becomes President and P. Mladenov is appointed Foreign Minister.

June 1980 – The introduction of laws to permit the creation of joint ventures with foreign firms.

January 1982 – Under the new economic reforms businesses are to operate under market

its Stalinist leader, E. Hoxha.

1950s onwards – All private property is banned, all foreign economic assistance is refused and any opponents of the regime are dealt with ruthlessly in periodic purges.

1961 – Albania criticises the Soviet policy of peaceful co-existence with the West and supports China in the developing Sino-Soviet dispute. Purges of pro-Soviet elements begin in May.

Late 1961 – Albania leaves COMECON and breaks off diplomatic relations with the USSR and all other ECE communist lands.

1960s and 1970s – Hoxha's rule develops into an all-pervasive, Stalinist personality cult. During his reign the country becomes more and more isolated from the rest of the world.

1967 – Religion is officially abolished in a country with strong Muslim, Orthodox and Roman Catholic populations.

1974–76 – Several purges are made against those supporting East–West detente. The former Defence Minister is executed in September 1974.

January 1976 – The introduction of a new constitution, ending the increasingly isolationist and inward-looking policies so typical of the past thirty years of Albania's type of socialism.

July 1978 – Albania also breaks with China, after Hoxha accuses its leaders of seeking

proclaimed in the Soviet zone, four months after the creation of the Federal Republic of Germany in the three Western zones.

1949 – East and West Germany become symbols of the Cold War. The Soviets see the borders as fixed, while the Western Allies see them as provisional, awaiting a proper peace treaty.

June 1950 – East Germany formally accepts the Oder–Neisse line as its frontier with Poland.

1950 – W. Ulbricht becomes SED General Secretary and imposes rigid Stalinism in the Party. Purges of opponents follow.

17 June 1953 – Workers' riots begin in Berlin and spread to other cities but are ruthlessly suppressed with assistance from Soviet forces.

September 1955 – Signature of a treaty with the USSR formally recognising the GDR.

13 August 1961 – The Berlin Wall goes up to halt massive emigration into West Berlin.

March–May 1970 – Negotiations between Premier W. Stoph and West German Chancellor W. Brandt lead to the recognition of the GDR by West Germany.

August 1970 – West Germany signs a treaty with the Soviet Union recognising the Oder–Neisse border.

May 1971 – E. Honecker takes over from W. Ulbricht as Party leader.

September 1971 – The Four-Power

1948 – Tito breaks with Moscow when he suggests a Balkan federation including Yugoslavia and all neighbouring countries outside the Soviet sphere of influence.

June 1948 – The Communist International meeting in Budapest denounces Titoism as a 'nationalist deviation'. Yugoslavia is expelled from communist bodies and a Soviet economic blockade is begun. (It is broken by the West.)

1950s – Leading hardline Stalinists and supporters of Moscow are purged from leadership positions in the Party.

June 1950 – Worker's councils are established in industry in order to bring about worker self-management of enterprises.

May 1951 – New measures in agriculture allow farmers to operate a free market.

May 1955 – N. Khrushchev and Tito ending the conflict between the two states.

1960s and 1970s – The USA pours millions of dollars into the country, which it sees as a bulwark against the Soviets. Tourism – aimed mainly at Westerners – booms and becomes a major foreign currency earner.

1966 – There are further purges among top Party members.

1968 – Major protests occur in Croatia and there is an armed revolt in Serbian Kosovo. These are put down by the Yugoslav army.

1971 – Tito purges all liberals from business,

1976 – Czechoslovakia signs the Helsinki Final Act, guaranteeing basic human rights and personal freedoms.

January 1977 – A small group of artists and intellectuals publish Charter 77, documenting violation of basic human rights.

April 1987 – Gorbachev is given a warm welcome during a state visit to Czechoslovakia.

17 December 1987 – Milos Jakes becomes General Secretary. G. Husak is made President.

21 August 1988 – Demonstrations in Prague by dissidents and students, twenty years after the 1968 invasion.

January 1989 – 800 protestors are arrested (V. Havel receives a nine-month prison term) after protests over human rights abuses.

May 1989 – V. Havel is freed from prison.

13 December 1981 – Martial law is declared. Solidarity's leaders, including Walesa, are arrested, trade unions suspended and strikes banned. For the next eight years Solidarity continues its activities underground.

30 October 1984 – 250,000 people attend the funeral of J. Popieluszko, a pro-Solidarity priest killed by the security forces.

1985–86 – There are over 2,000 regular samizdat publications in Poland, some printed in tens of thousands of copies.

6 November 1985 – General Jaruzelski becomes President.

1987 – The Pope and US Vice-President Bush express support for Solidarity during visits to Poland.

document 'The Social Contract' calls for Kadar's departure as the beginning of real change.

September 1987 – Reformist Communists, led by I. Pozsgay, meet with the opposition and create the MDF (formally constituted one year later).

March 1988 – FIDESZ is created as an independent student body.

May 1988 – J. Kadar is replaced as leader by reformist K. Grosz.

12 September 1988 – Environmentalists demonstrate in Budapest against the building of the Gabcikovo-Nagymaros dam.

November 1988 – SZDSZ is formed and the FKGP is reconstituted

11 January 1989 – Parliament passes a law allowing the creation of independent political parties.

Europe's good communists' on a visit to Romania.

15 November 1987 – Major riots in Brasov are brutally suppressed by the police and the Securitate.

April 1988 – Plans are announced to demolish half of Romania's villages by the year 2000, releasing land for the use of collective farms. Hungary accuses Romania of specifically targeting the 1,700,000 ethnic Hungarians in Transylvania. The plan gradually changes Western attitudes towards the Ceaucescu regime.

March 1989 – Six prominent veteran Communists accuse Ceaucescu (in an open letter) of discrediting socialism, ruining the economy and causing international condemnation over human rights issues.

The 'velvet revolution'

Mid-1989 – After a trip to Moscow, Premier L. Adamec announces certain economic reforms.

July 1989 – Gorbachev repudiates the 'Brezhnev doctrine' in Strasbourg.

Late summer 1989 – East Germans camp inside the American Embassy in Prague, before being put on special trains to Austria or West Germany.

October 1989 – The police break up a pro-democracy demonstration.

The Polish revolution/ refolution

1988 – Strikes and demonstrations caused by new price rises.

June 1989 – Solidarity urges a boycott of local elections, which achieve only 55 per cent turnout.

August 1988 – More strikes and protests. The government tells Walesa it is ready to discuss the legalisation of Solidarity if the strikers return to work.

January 1989 – The PZPR finally agrees to

The negotiated 'revolution'

28 January 1989 – An MSZMP commission spurns the official line that the 1956 uprising was a counter-revolution and describes it instead as a 'popular uprising'.

March 1989 – The MSZMP considers a coalition. Eight opposition groupings (including MDF, FIDESZ and SZDSZ) form an opposition round-table.

2 May 1989 – Hungary opens its borders with Austria and tears down the 'Iron Curtain' along

Sudden and violent revolution

15–17 December 1989 – In Timisoara protests against the removal of the Hungarian priest L. Tokes develop into an anti-regime demonstration involving several thousand people. The army and Securitate open fire and about 100 people are killed.

21 December 1989 – A large crowd, mainly of students, shouts down Ceausescu during his speech; the Securitate fire into the unarmed crowd.

forces and become financially self-supporting, with a minimum of central planning. In practice the economy remains highly centralised.

1984 – The first of Zhivkov's 'assimilation campaigns' directed against the minority Muslim Turks (22 per cent of the population). The Turks are forced to adopt Bulgarian names. This leads to the first mass emigration of Turks to Turkey.

July 1987 – Following the Gorbachev lead, Zhivkov issues the 'July Conception', advocating liberalisation and decentralisation of the economy. These reforms are never implemented.

July 1988 – Reformists are dismissed from the Politburo and other Party organs.

hegemony, just like the Soviet Union.

1981 – Hoxha is most careful not to identify himself with or support the demands made by ethnic Albanians in Yugoslav Kosovo.

December 1981 – The death of Premier M. Shehu is officially described as suicide, starting a wave of purges in the top party leadership, which lasts another three years.

April 1985 – Hoxha dies and is succeeded by Ramiz Alia.

January 1990 – After the upheavals throughout ECE in 1989, the Party insists no 'revolutionary' changes are necessary in Albania. Even so, Alia proposes some economic and political reforms.

8 May 1990 – Parliament ends the ban on 'religious propaganda'.

7–9 July 1990 – Changes in the Party leadership enhance the position of the reformists.

Agreement is finally signed on the status of Berlin.

December 1972 – A treaty is signed with West Germany to normalise relations. 'Two states of One Nation' is how W. Brandt describes the two Germanies.

September 1974 – Diplomatic relations are established with the US.

January 1982 – In the 'Berlin Appeal', thirty-five Lutheran and Evangelical activists demand the removal of all foreign troops from both Germanies and the creation of a nuclear-free zone, *inter alia*.

September 1987 – E. Honecker finally visits West Germany.

May 1989 – Church organisations protest against the rigging of local elections in favour of the SED.

politics and all universities.

1971 – A Croatian nationalist movement is crushed by Tito.

December 1973 – Croatian nationalists are purged from top Party and government posts.

February 1974 – A new constitution gives greater powers to six autonomous republics. Serbia is split into three regions, which are given republican status, Bosnia becomes an autonomous Mulsim state and the use of ethnic lanuguages is encouraged. Ethnic differences are ignored when fixing new boundaries, however.

4 May 1980 – Tito dies and the Presidency of the country is rotated among the leaders of the eight republics/regions, exacerbating nationalist differences.

Autumn 1981 – A state of emergency is declared in Kosovo after widespread unrest among ethnic Albanians.

The Bulgarian refolution

Mid-1988 – Political clubs and other groups to promote human rights are formed.

May–August 1989 – About 300,000 ethnic Turks are expelled to Turkey in Zhivkov's second assimilation campaign.

26 October 1989 – Forty Eco-glasnost activists are beaten up and arrested.

10 November 1989 – Zhivkov is 'persuaded' to resign by the Party. P. Mladenov replaces him.

Albania's refolution, 1990–91

9–13 July 1990 – Thousands of asylum-seekers taking refuge in foreign embassies are given passports and allowed to leave Albania.

November 1990 – The PSS leadership supports constitutional reform and encourages religious tolerance. The first Catholic mass is held on 16 November the first legal Muslim service on 18 January 1991.

11 December 1990 – Stalinist hard-liners are dismissed from the

The 1989 revolution in East Germany

11 September 1989 – East Germans who have left the GDR as 'tourists' in huge numbers in previous weeks are allowed to cross the border from Hungary to Austria.

7 October 1989 – On a visit to the GDR, M. Gorbachev urges the East German leaders to implement economic and political reforms.

9 October 1989 – The Monday evening protest march across Leipzig is not suppressed by the

The nationalist revolution in Yugoslavia after 1986

September 1986 – Serbian Academy of Sciences and Arts publishes a text attacking Yugoslavia's 1974 constitution and calling for unification of all Serbs into one nation.

February 1987 – Slovene intellectuals propose a national, Christian programme, claiming Slovenia would be better off with secession. Communism is blamed for the country's problems.

17 November 1989 – A large student march turns into an anti-regime protest and is attacked by riot police.

19 November 1989 – The opposition forms into the OF in Prague and the VPN in Slovakia.

24 November 1989 – The entire Communist leadership resigns. A. Dubcek joins V. Havel to speak to 400,000 people in Prague.

28–29 November 1989 – The Federal Assembly abolishes the Communist Party's leading role.

3 December 1989 – There is the threat of a general strike when Adamec proposes a Communist majority government.

10 December 1989 – Adamec resigns and M. Calfa forms a mainly non-communist government.

29 December 1989 – V. Havel is elected President (unanimously) by the Federal Assembly. Dubcek becomes leader of the Assembly.

20 April 1990 – The country becomes the Czech and Slovak Federal Republic.

those talks, only after Jaruzelski threatens to resign.

6 February 1989 – Round-table talks begin in Warsaw between the PZPR, the Catholic Church and Solidarity.

April 1989 – The talks conclude, allowing for partially free elections in June 1989. Solidarity and Rural Solidarity are both legalised.

4 and 18 June 1989 – Solidairty convincingly wins the first semi-free elections in ECE since the late 1940s. The PZPR gains only its reserved seats in the Sejm and no seats at all in the Senate.

19 July 1989 – General Jaruzelski is elected President by a very narrow margin: 50 per cent plus one vote.

24 August 1989 – Solidarity candidate T. Mazowiecki is elected Premier by the Sejm. He leads a Solidarity-dominated government (the first non-communist ECE government since 1948.

30 December 1989 – The country is renamed the Polish Republic.

its border with Austria.

June 1989 – The MSZMP agrees to negotatiate with the opposition.

16 June 1989 – The remains of I. Nagy and other 1956 leaders are given a state funeral (attended by thousands).

6 July 1989 – The death of J. Kadar.

22 July 1989 – An opposition candidate is elected in a by-election.

11 September 1989 – Thousands of East German refugees are allowed to pass through Hungary on their way to Austria.

September 1989 – The participants of the round-table agree to major constitutional changes, independent parties and elections in 1990. SZDSZ and others seek a referendum on presidential elections.

17–20 October 1989 – Parliament approves the round-table proposals.

23 October 1989 – Hungary is declared a republic.

22 December 1989 – The FSN is 'spontaneously' formed from 145 leading personalities of all walks of life, but is led and dominated by former top Communists of the Ceausescu regime. Fighting begins between pro-FSN army and the Securitate, which is still loyal to Ceausescu.

25 December 1989 – Ceausescu and his wife Elena are captured, tried and executed by an impromptu military court.

26 December 1989 – The fighting subsides. I. Iliescu is declared President of the FSN, and P. Roman forms the new government. In its first proclamation the FSN assumes complete control over the state. It is supposed to be an interim arrangement until free elections.

28–29 December 1989 – Government decrees change the country's name to Romania, guarantee national minority rights, allow freedom of religion, begin the transition to a market economy, and plan free elections for April 1990.

Post-revolutionary Czechoslovakia

8–9 June 1990 – In elections to the Federal Assembly and the Czech and Slovak parliaments, OF wins 54 per cent in the Czech Republic and VPN 33 per cent in Slovakia. A Federal KDH/OF/VPN/KDH coalition is formed under M. Calfa.

Post-revolutionary Poland

1990 – Finance Minister L. Balcerowicz initiates rapid economic reform, or 'shock therapy'.

28 January 1990 – The PZPR becomes a social democratic party and elects A. Kwasniewski as party leader.

Post-revolutionary Hungary

26 November 1989 – A referendum approves the SZDSZ/FIDESZ proposal for the President to be chosen by parliament.

21 January 1990 – The state security service is disbanded.

10 March 1990 – The USSR agrees to

Post-revolutionary Romania

24 January 1990 – Dissident D. Cornea resigns from the FSN, saying it is dominated by former Communists and Securitate officers.

20 May 1990 – Legislative elections bring a convincing victory for the FSN, which gets 66 per cent of votes. Iliescu

18 November 1989 – Large crowds celebrate the fall of Zhivkov and demand further reforms.

December 1989 – The SDS is created from seventeen opposition groups.

11 December 1989 – The Party leadership advocates free elections.

2 February 1990 – The BKP proposes a programme of political reforms.

8 February 1990 – The SDS is invited to join in a coalition but refuses.

5 March 1990 – Parliament legalises the use of Muslim names, reversing the most-hated of Zhivkov's anti-Turkish decrees.

13 April 1990 – The Bulgarian parliament (GNA) elects Mladenov interim President and sets elections for June. The BKP renames itself the BSP.

June 1990 – The BSP wins 53 per cent of seats in the new GNA but still asks the SDS (36 per cent) to join in a coalition.

Politburo and opposition parties are permitted (e.g. the Democratic Party, PD, and the Forum for the Defence of Human Rights).

9 February 1991 – Thousands of people are prevented by police units from leaving the country at the port of Durres.

February 1991 – A series of mass protests and demonstrations begin in Tirana. Many arrests and deaths occur.

February 1991 – F. Nano becomes the new Premier.

Early 1991 – Thousands of mostly young people attempt to escape to Italy by boat. At first they are given political asylum; later they are either persuaded to go back or are moved to refugee camps.

March–April 1991 – In multi-party elections, the Communist PSS wins a two-thirds parliamentary majority, but still invites the opposition PD to join a government of 'national stability'. A coalition is formed under Communist Premier Y.Bufi and R. Alia is appointed President.

security forces. Mass demonstrations occur elsewhere, in Halle, Dresden and Berlin.

23 October 1989 – In Leipzig a crowd of 300,000 calls for free elections. Some banners also support a reunited Germany.

18 October 1989 – Honecker resigns and is succeeded by E. Krenz as both Party leader and head of state.

7–8 November 1989 – The government and SED Politburo resign.

9 November 1989 – A new government under Premier H. Modrow ends all travel restrictions and opens crossing points in the Berlin Wall.

Mid-November 1989 – People storm the Stasi headquarters and destroy secret police files.

3–6 December 1989 – Krenz and the rest of the SED leadership resign.

December 1989 – G. Gysi becomes leader of the reformed SED – the PDS, which ends the Communists' 'leading role' and approves elections for March 1990.

April 1987 – S. Milosevic gives a very nationalist speech in Kosovo on the anniversary of the Serb military defeat at Kosovo Field.

May 1987 – Milosevic wins control of Serbia's League of Communists.

October 1988 – In the so-called 'Yoghurt Revolution' Milosevic installs 'his' people to the leadership of the Vojvodina region.

7 October 1988 – Milosevic manipulates protests in the capital of Monetenegro to bring a 'friendly' government to power.

17 November 1988 – Strikes and protests follow the dismissal of the Kosovo leadership.

December 1988 – The federal government of B. Mikulic falls when it is defeated in the Assembly over its budget proposals.

January 1989 – A. Markovic becomes Yugoslav Federal Premier on a programme of economic and political reforms, hoping to end hyperinflation and create a new republican union.

Post-revolutionary Bulgaria

6 July 1990 – P. Mladenov has to resign, after a video is made public showing him advocating the use of tanks against unarmed protestors in November 1989.

1 August 1990 – Z. Zhelev (SDS) is elected President by the GNA.

Post-revolutionary Albania

August 1991 – The government begins to return land to the peasants.

25 August 1991 – Anti-communist demonstrations take place in Tirana. Riots occur elsewhere.

September 1991 – S. Berisha becomes PD leader.

Post-revolutionary East Germany and the process towards German unity

1 February 1990 – Modrow makes his own proposals for the unification of Germany, including a precondition of military neutrality.

6 February 1990 – West German Chancellor H. Kohl calls for

Yugoslavia: the road to independence

February–March 1989 – The Kosovo assembly ratifies the new Serbian constitution, ending the region's political autonomy.

May 1989 – Milosevic becomes Serbian President. By now he controls four of the

5 July 1990 – V. Havel is re-elected federal President for two years.

23–25 November 1990 – In Czech and Slovak local elections OF confirms its commanding position, but VPN loses to KDH in Slovakia.

1 January 1991 – Small-scale privatisation begins.

22 March 1991 – Ten parliamentarians are publicly exposed as collaborators of the former secret police.

March–April 1991 – OF formally splits into ODS, OH and ODA.

April 1991 – V. Meciar is replaced as Slovak Premier by the leader of KDH – J. Carnogursky.

13 June 1991 – Large-scale privatisation begins under the famous 'voucher scheme'.

June 1991 – The withdrawal of all Soviet troops is completed.

4 October 1991 – The Federal Assembly passes a law banning former members of the security police and their collaborators from all public offices.

5–6 June 1992 – In elections, Klaus's ODS and Meciar's HZDS both win 34 per cent in their respective republics. But the two leaders cannot form a federal government.

July 1992 – HZDS, SNS and SPR-RSC prevent the re-election of V. Havel as Czechoslovak President.

17 July 1992 – The Slovak parliament passes a declaration of sovereignty. V. Havel resigns his post.

27 August 1992 – HZDS and ODS leaders

19–25 April 1990 – L. Walesa is re-elected leader of Solidarity.

27 May 1990 – Solidarity wins the first fully free local elections.

June 1990 – A 'war at the top' is fought over who controls the local Solidarity committees. It splits Solidarity into several groups including the UD, PC and the NZSS.

9 December 1990 – L. Walesa defeats emigrant businessman S. Tyminski and Premier T. Mazowiecki in direct presidential elections.

12 January 1991 – A new 'government of experts' is formed by J. Bielecki.

4 June 1991 – The Pope visits Poland and sparks a controversy over abortion.

27 October 1991 – In the first fully free Polish national elections the UD becomes the largest party with only 13 per cent of the vote, while the ex-communist SLD comes second with 12 per cent. (Turnout is below 40 per cent.)

23 December 1991 – A centre-right Catholic coalition forms under Premier J. Olszewski. It stresses de-communication and is highly critical of President Walesa.

June 1992 – The Interior Minister releases a confidential list of sixty-four supposed security police collaborators, including many leading figures in the UD and the President himself. (The list is of people the secret police attempted to recruit.)

July 1992 – President

withdraw its troops from Hungary by July 1991.

25 March and 8 April 1990 – Multi-party elections are won by the MDF with 42.5 per cent of seats. The SZDSZ comes second.

May 1990 – The new parliament elects A. Goncz (SZDSZ) Speaker, and thus interim President.

16 May 1990 – J. Antall, leader of the MDF, forms a centre-right coalition with the FKGP and KDNP.

October 1990 – Local elections are marked by very low turnouts (36 per cent and 27 per cent). Results are very poor for the governing parties.

28 June 1991 – COMECON is formally disbanded at a meeting in Budapest.

1 July 1991 – The Warsaw Pact is formally dissolved.

29 July 1991 – In a referendum on the direct election of the President, 85 per cent of voters favour direct elections, but the turnout, at under 14 per cent, is way below the constitutional minimum of 50 per cent.

3 August 1991 – Goncz is re-confirmed as President

5–6 October 1991 – In the 'Cracow declaration' Hungary, Czechoslovakia and Poland agree to work together to attain entry into NATO and the EU.

December 1991 – Hungary and the EU sign an Association Agreement.

1992 – The MSZP performs well in

becomes President after winning 85 per cent of the poll. But there are voting irregularities.

13 June 1990 – Student protesters in Bucharest claim the revolution has been 'stolen' by Communists inside the FSN.

Mid-June 1990 – Miners are bussed in from the provinces to quell the protests. They attack 'intellectuals' and students, and ransack opposition newspapers and party headquarters, and so on. The police do nothing and Iliescu later thanks the miners later. Six people are killed and hundreds are wounded.

27 September 1991 – P. Roman is summarily dismissed by President Ilescu without parliament's approval.

October 1991 – T. Stolojan becomes non-party Premier in a coalition government including the PNL.

November 1991 – The main opposition parties form the CDR.

December 1991 – 77 per cent of Romanians accept a new constitution in a referendum. The constitution gives parliament more control over the government, but leaves the President with wide powers. (There is no choice between a republic and a monarchy.)

February–March 1992 – The popularity of the FSN drops dramatically in local elections, to 34 per cent of votes. The CDR is second, with 24 per cent, and wins mayoral contests in Romania's largest cities, including Bucharest and Timisoara.

26 August 1990 – The BSP party centre is badly damaged by fire and looted during a wave of riots in Sofia.

15 November 1990 – The country's official name becomes the Republic of Bulgaria.

29 November 1990 – The government falls after an opposition boycott of parliament and a general strike.

December 1990 – A coalition government is finally formed under non-party D. Popov.

25 February 1991 – The GNA passes a law allowing the restitution of Communist-expropriated land and property.

12 July 1991 – The GNA approves a new constitution, which provides, *inter alia*, for direct presidential elections.

13 October 1991 – In legislative elections the SDS gains 34 per cent to the BSP's 33 per cent, winning just four seats more in the GNA.

8 November 1991 – Bulgaria's first wholly non-communist post-war government under Premier F. Dimitrov. It is an SDS minority government with consistent support from the DPS – the party of the minority ethnic Turks.

11 December 1991 – Parliament passes restitution and small-scale privatisation bills.

January 1992 – Z. Zhelev (SDS) wins direct elections for President.

April 1992 – Parliament adopts a privatisation law, covering large-scale industries.

Autumn 1991 – The Italians begin 'Operation Pelican' to deliver food and medicine to the Albanians.

6 December 1991 – Y. Bufi resigns after the PD leave the 'national stability government'.

December 1991 – V. Ahmeti forms a new government. President Alia calls new elections for March 1992.

23 March 1992 – The PD wins the second elections with 92 of the 140 Assembly seats, just missing the two-thirds majority required to amend the constitution. A. Meksi (PD) becomes Premier of a PD/PSD coalition government.

March 1992 – Just before presidential elections, changes are made to the constituion to enhance the position of the President.

9 April 1992 – PD leader S. Berisha is elected President. During his campaign he stresses protection of human rights, privatisation and a liberal democratic constitution.

1992 – Meksi's government starts Polish-type 'shock therapy' economic reforms, resulting in rising unemployment and high prices.

July 1992 – The Socialists make gains in the country's first local elections, gaining 41 per cent of the vote (to the PD's 43 per cent) and winning most of the rural councils.

September 1992 – The PD/PSD coalition loses its two-thirds majority when six deputies leave the PD to found the AD, which is

swift economic and monetary union.

18 March 1990 – The right-wing Alliance for Germany wins the East German elections. The Alliance receives considerable financial and personnel aid from the West German Free and Christian Democrats.

9 April 1990 – L. de Maiziere from the East German CDU becomes the new Premier, leading a 'Grand Coalition' of Christian, Social and Free Democrats.

1 July 1990 – German economic and monetary union occurs. East Germans exchange their marks one to one with the West German currency.

July 1990 – At the meeting in Stavropol, M. Gorbachev agrees that a united Germany could remain a member of NATO. There are to be general troop reductions within Germany as a whole and no nuclear weapons are to be sited on East German territory.

12 September 1990 – The 'two plus four' talks (France, USSR, USA and Great Britain, plus the two Germanies) produce the Treaty on the Final Settlement of Germany, confirming existing German borders, the withdrawal of Soviet troops and a united Germany's right to find its own allies.

3 October 1990 – The former GDR is absorbed into the Federal Republic of Germany, with its five regions becoming five new *Bundesländer* within the all-German federation.

2 December 1990 – The first all-German

eight votes of the Yugoslav Presidency.

28 June 1989 – One million people attend a rally addressed by Milosevic in Kosovo.

September 1989 – Slovenia adopts constitutional amendments allowing the right to secede from the Federation.

January 1990 – The SKJ votes to end its 'leading role'. It also rejects Markovic's plan and then basically disintegrates into its various republican groups.

April–May 1990 – Slovenia and Croatia hold the first multi-party elections. The DEMOS coalition wins the elections in Slovenia, with former communist M. Kucan (now reformist) becoming President. In Croatia the elections produce a crushing victory for the nationalist HDZ, with its leader F. Tudjman becoming President. The Slovene and Croatian governments are formed by L. Peterle and S. Mesic, respectively.

July 1990 – Serious unrest is reported from Kosovo, as the ethnic Albanians declare their province a separate Yugoslav republic after constitutional changes approved by referendum in Serbia.

agree to a split of the federation.

25 November 1992 – The Federal Assembly votes to end Czechoslovakia.

16 December 1992 – The Czech parliament approves the new Czech constitution.

1 January 1993 – The Czech and Slovak Republics become independent.

The Czech Republic after the split

26 January 1993 – V. Havel is elected Czech President.

February 1993 – Parliament rejects the law allowing former Czech deputies of the Federal Assembly to constitute the new Senate.

June 1993 – Parliament votes to establish the Constitutional Court.

1993–94 – Klaus's ODS refuses to establish the Senate, saying it is unnecessary.

1993–94 – Restitution of both Church and Jewish property causes tensions within the governing coalition.

November 1994 – Local elections show a small decrease in the coalition's popularity.

December 1995 – The coalition finally agrees on the formation of the Senate, fixing elections for late 1996.

June 1996 – The coalition just loses its parliamentary majority, after a dramatic rise in the vote for the Social Democrats. A right-wing government is

Walesa dismisses Olszewski and names W. Pawlak, leader of the PSL, as Premier, who is unable to form a majority government. Former Solidarity parties then unite behind H. Suchocka (UD), as Premier.

December 1992 – The 'Small Constitution' is passed, strengthening both the government and President.

1992–93 – Suchocka's government pursues economic and political reforms, but is plagued by moral and ideological issues, for example separation of Chruch and state, abortion and de-communisation.

April 1993 – A new electoral law sets a 5 per cent threshold for parliamentary elections.

28 May 1993 – Suchocka's cabinet falls.

June 1993 – The President tries to unite Solidarity into the BBWR party bloc under his own leadership.

October 1993 – The SLD and PSL win a two-thirds majority in parliament. An SLD/PSL coalition is formed under Premier W. Pawlak, PSL leader.

1994 – The PSL/SLD government slows down almost all the previous government's economic reform programmes, including large-scale privatisation.

March 1994 – The government passes its first budget and continues with the austerity programme.

July 1994 – The coalition kills the idea of any 'screening law' to punish former Communist officials.

parliamentary by-elections. FIDESZ is the most popular party in opinion polls.

February 1992 – The FKGP leaves the government coalition because of the latter's inability to return land to its former owners.

March 1992 – The Constitutional Court annuls a parliamentary law enabling former Communist officials to be prosecuted for treason and murder

1992 – The 'media war' between Premier Antall and President Goncz, who claims the right to decide on the dismissal of the television and radio directors.

August 1992 – Anti-Semitic tracts are published by I. Csurka, a populist member of MDF. He is expelled from the party in the summer of 1993.

December 1992 – The four 'Visegrad countries' (Poland, the Czech and Slovak Republics and Hungary) sign a free-trade pact.

Spring 1993 – Hungary signs an Association Agreement with EFTA.

October 1993 – The Constitutional Court approves the prosecution of former Communist officials who committed crimes in 1956.

12 December 1993 – Premier Antall dies and is succeeded by former Foreign Minister, P. Boross.

June 1994 – The MSZP wins the elections and its leader, G. Horn, becomes Premier. He heads a coalition with the SZDSZ (based on the

March 1992 – Ultranationalist G. Funar is elected mayor of Cluj, promising to restrict the activities of the Hungarian minority.

March 1992 – The FSN splits after a series of conflicts between P. Roman and I.Iliescu; Roman blocks Iliescu as FSN presidential candidate. The PD/FSN is formed to support Iliescu. Many former Communists join this 'presidential party'.

April 1992 – The PNL leaves the CDR because of the membership of UDMR. The party now takes a strong nationalistic stance.

April 1992 – Former King Michael visits Romania after forty-five years and is given an enthusiastic welcome.

27 September 1992 – Legislative and presidential elections take place. Iliescu wins the second round of the presidential elections with 61 per cent of votes against the CDR candidate. In legislative elections the FDSN emerges as the largest party, with 28 per cent of votes. The CDR is second with 20 per cent.

October 1992 – N. Vacaroiu forms a non-party government of technocrats, FDSN members and ex-ministers of the former regime. It relies on FDSN and the national-ists in parliament.

1 February 1992 – Romania signs an EU Association Agreement.

May 1993 – Thousands of workers demand the government's resig-nation because of falling living standards.

September 1992 – T. Zhivkov is sentenced to seven years' imprisonment for misappropriation of state funds and other crimes.

28 October 1992 – The DPS unites with the BSP in a vote of censure against the government. President Zhelev then appoints L. Berov to form a government of mainly non-party technocrats.

8 March 1993 – Bulgaria signs an Association Agreement with the EU.

1993 – Despite promises very little progress is made towards full-scale privatisation of either agriculture or industry.

1993 – The SDS criticises the government for reinstating former Communist officials.

1993 – A constitutional amendment bans all political parties based on race, ethnicity, religion or nationality (aimed at the DPS).

April 1994 – President Zhelev publicly withdraws his support from the Berov government.

June 1994 – Berov persuades parliament to pass a new privatisation programme in an attempt to save his government.

2 September 1994 – Berov resigns and Zhelev appoints a caretaker government.

By December 1994 – The SDS has split into many different factions.

18 December 1994 – Elections produce an absolute majority for the BSP, which gains 43.5 per cent of the vote.

Early 1995 – The

strongly critical of Berisha's 'autocratic methods'.

March 1993 – Parliament adopts a Charter of Human Rights.

April 1993 – The Pope visits Albania.

1993 – Albania seeks membership of Western alliances, but also joins the Organisation of the Islamic Conference.

Summer 1993 – Former Socialist Premier F. Nano, previous President R. Alia and almost all the former Politburo are charged with corruption and misuse of power. The Socialists demand that the government resigns.

Summer 1993 – Greece deports thousands of illegal Albanian migrant migrant workers after a Greek Orthodox cleric is expelled from Albania.

Autumn 1993 – Some right-wing deputies leave the PD.

November 1993 – Macedonian authorities arrest eight ethnic Albanians for inciting rebellion.

December 1993 – The Italians end 'Operation Pelican'.

1993 – Albania's 8 per cent growth rate is the highest in Europe.

10 April 1994 – An illegal Greek paramilitary unit kills two Albanian border guards

August 1994 – Five leaders of OMONIA (Albania's ethnic Greek organisation) are gaoled for spying and other anti-state activities.

November 1994 – In a referendum 55 per cent

elections produce a victory for H. Kohl and his CDU-led government coalition.

8 December 1990 – L. de Maiziere is accused of having been a Stasi informer.

Early 1991 – The German government introduces very rapid privatisation: 15,000 small to medium-sized companies and 900 large concerns are sold off by the end of March.

9 March 1991 – The government drops the plans for an amnesty for former Stasi agents.

25 March 1991 – A huge crowd of some 60,000 protests in Leipzig against unemployment.

May 1991 – Chancellor Kohl is forced to ask for general increases in taxation in order to pay for 'unity' and economic restructuring in the eastern regions of Germany (despite promises not to raise such taxes).

20 May 1991 – Four former GDR leaders, including the former Premier W. Stoph and State Security Minister E. Mielke, are arrested over the GDR's 'shoot to kill' policy.

Mid-1991 – The all-German Bundestag votes that Berlin will become Germany's capital city and seat of government.

1991 – The crime rate in eastern Germany soars.

1991 onwards – East Germany's economic and democratic reforms are controlled and financed by their West German compatriots ($100 billion per annum).

The beginnings of the disintegration of the Yugoslav state

August 1990 – Insurrection among the Krajinian Serbs in Knin, who proclaim the Serbian Autonomous Region of Krajina.

October 1990 – Milosevic calls for Federal Army intervention to defend the Krajinian Serbs from Croatian repression.

November–December 1990 – In region-wide multi-party elections, the nationalists claim victory in Bosnia and Macedonia, while the Communists maintain power in Serbia and Montenegro.

9 January 1991 – The federal Presidency requires the surrender of all arms within 10 days by all non-federal units. Croatian paramilitary forces comply.

25 January 1991 – The Macedonian assembly declares its sovereignty and the right to secede.

20–21 February 1991 – The Slovene and Croatian governments propose that Yugoslavia be dissolved into sovereign states.

9 March 1991 – Tanks crush an opposition rally in the centre of Belgrade. V. Draskovic, leader of the main opposition party, the SPO, is arrested.

13 March 1991 – After protests by students, V. Draskovic is released from prison. The Yugoslav army plans a military coup.

formed and the Social Democrats agree to support parts of the government programme.

The Slovak Republic after the split

15 February 1993 – M. Kovac is elected Slovak President.

April 1993 – Meciar sacks M. Knazko, his Foreign Minister, who forms a new party. The SNS ends its informal coalition with HZDS.

9 November 1993 – An official HZDS/SNS coalition is formed, but lasts only one month as the SNS splits, returning the government to minority status.

11 March 1994 – The Slovak opposition unites to oust Meciar in a vote of censure, encouraged by President Kovac.

March 1994 – Six political parties plus independents form a coalition government under J. Moravcik in advance of elections.

October 1994 – HZDS wins those elections with 34 per cent of votes. Meciar becomes Premier of a HZDS/SNS/ZRS coalition government, which begins a slow-down in the economic reform process.

November 1995 – a new 'Language Law' is passed which restricts the use of Hungarian in the public and educational sectors.

March 1996 – A 'Law Protecting the State' is passed which makes it more difficult openly to criticise the government.

1994 – There is just as much animosity between the two coalition partners as within previous Solidarity governments. The SLD wants to direct subsidies to industrial workers, pensioners and state employees, not peasant farmers, whom the PSL supports. Former Communist officials return to positions of power in the 'velvet restoration'. The PSL still favours state ownership of major industries and state intervention in the economy. The government coalition tends to blame the previous four Solidarity governments for all of Poland's problems.

Early 1995 – Walesa provokes another government crisis over the speed of the reform process. In the end, the coalition dismisses Pawlak and appoints J. Oleksy (SLD) Premier.

19 November 1995 – In the second round of the presidential elections, A. Kwasniewski (SLD) beats L. Walesa by 52 to 48 per cent. This is seen as the 'end of an era' in post-1989 Polish politics.

Early 1996 – Premier Oleksy is forced to resign over (unproved) reports that he spied for the Russians in the 1980s, and even after 1989. (The case against him is dropped in May 1996 through lack of evidence.)

similarity of their economic policies).

1994 – The MSZP/ SZDSZ government abolishes the committee examining crimes carried out under communism, slows down privatisation laws and obstructs the 'screening law'.

December 1994 – The MSZP receives the most votes in local elections. SZDSZ comes second but loses seats compared with 1990

By December 1994 – There are tensions inside the coalition as the SZDSZ complains of non-consultation and contradiction of the SZDSZ ministers by Premier Horn. The political consensus of the last four years over foreign and domestic policy is broken (e.g. Horn pledges to 're-negotiate' the terms of the EU Association Agreement and proposes a referendum on NATO without consulting with the opposition).

19 March 1995 – Hungary and Slovakia sign a treaty of 'good neighbourly relations and friendly co-operation', in particular calming concerns about the Hungarian minority in Slovakia.

19 June 1995 – President A. Goncz is re-elected for another five-year term by the Hungarian parliament.

July 1993 – The FDSN becomes the PDSR.

October 1993 – Romania is made a full member of the Council of Europe.

Late 1993 – The government reveals an abuse of power by ex-Premier Roman and other ex-ministers.

December 1993 – There is a sharp depreciation of the currency, and a revival of Romanian nationalism, anti-Semitism and racial attacks on gypsies.

1994 – The signing of a formal coalition agreement between the PDSR and the PUNR (extreme nationalists).

May 1994 – A Council of Europe report is most critical of Romania's human and minority rights record.

Mid-1994 – A motion of no confidence and the impeachment of President Iliescu nearly succeed, when the PUNR almost votes with the opposition.

December 1994 – Workers strike over unpaid wages.

January 1995 – A four-party ex-communist/nationalist (PDSR/PUNR/PRM/PSM) coalition forms.

February–March 1995 – The opposition CDR breaks up.

October 1995 – The PRM leaves the coalition government.

GNA passes an amendment to the 1992 Land Law Act, whereby farmers wishing to sell their land have to offer it to the government first. President Zhelev refers the new law to the Constitutional Court, which deems it to be against the right of private ownership.

March 1995 – The government publishes the White Book, placing all the blame for Bulgaria's economic and social problems on the 1991–92 SDS government.

May 1995 – On a visit to Sofia, Z. Brzezinski, former US Secretary of State, is critical of both the tone and content of the White Book.

June 1995 – The appointment of new BSP-sympathetic television and radio directors.

August 1995 – The Constitutional Court is arbitrarily moved to smaller offices: a political move to penalise it for supporting President Zhelev over the Land Law.

February–March 1996 – The value of the Bulgarian lev collapses. The BSP introduces an austerity economic reform programme.

June 1996 – Incumbent President Zhelev loses a primary election to choose a joint opposition candidate for the autumn presidential elections.

of voters reject Berisha's proposed constitution, which would have given the President greater powers of appointment of top officials, and so on. Three Constitutional Court judges resign as they consider the referendum illegal.

Early December 1994 – Berisha dismisses twelve ministers and appoints five.

4 December 1994 – The PR leaves te coalition due to the government's inability to fight corruption, followed by the PSD two days later.

24 December 1994 – President Berisha pardons one of the OMONIA prisoners and reduces the sentences of the others.

Early 1995 – A new screening law is passed banning many leading members of the opposition PSD and PSS from participating in any elections before 2005, because of their links with the communist past.

June 1996 – The PD wins an overwhelming parliamentary majority after rigged elections, which the opposition parties boycott on polling day.

1991–92 – There is increased activity by neo-Nazi groups, in all of Germany, and frequent attacks on immigrants. The right-wing, extreme Republican Party also increases its electoral support.

Autumn 1993 – Of former East German leaders brought to trial, three (E. Honecker, W. Stoph and E. Mielke) are let free on health grounds. Three others are given light sentences (four to seven years in prison) and are free pending appeal.

November 1993 – H Kohl's choice for German President, S. Heitmann from eastern Saxony, has to withdraw his name after making disparaging remarks about foreigners, homosexuals and women.

By the end of 1993 – 18 per cent of the workforce in eastern Germany is unemployed (9 per cent in western Germany). Another 20 per cent are on government-funded job programmes.

October 1994 – New parliamentary elections result in another victory for the Kohl-led CDU/CSU/FDP coalition in Bonn, but the PDS almost doubles its vote from 10 per cent in December 1990 to 18 per cent in 1994.

October 1995 – In the Berlin regional elections the PDS wins 15 per cent of the vote throughout the whole city, but 36 per cent in the districts of former East Berlin.

16 March 1991 – President Milosevic declares: 'Yugoslavia is finished'. He means to say that Serbia has decided to abandon the federal state.

The civil war in former Yugoslavia

The beginnings of the conflict

31 March 1991 – The first inter-ethnic fighting between Croats and Serbs occurs. Barricades appear everywhere in the Krajina and east Slavonia regions.

2 May 1991 – The Serb-Croat conflict begins in earnest in the village of Borovo Selo, when four Croat policemen attempt to raise the Croatian national flag.

15 May 1991 – Serbia, Montenegro, Kosovo and Vojvodina refuse to elect the Croat S. Mesic as federal President. Mesic is then elected after CSCE intervention.

29 May 1991 – Croatia unilaterally declares its sovereignty after a 93 per cent vote for independence in a referendum. The Krajina Serbs call for the union of their territory with Serbia.

25 June 1991 – Croatia and Slovenia declare their independence and request recognition from the rest of the world.

27–30 June 1991 – The federal army enters Slovenia but quickly withdraws, after unexpected resistance and EU/CSCE diplomatic intervention.

July–August 1991 – Fighting begins between the Yugoslav federal army and Croatian troops in eastern Slavonia.

September 1991 – Serbia and Montenegro reject the 'Carrington' peace plan, obstensibly because it divides Yugoslavia into independent states. The other four republics accept the plan.

Continuing disintegration and bloody warfare

15 September 1991 – Macedonia also declares its independence.

15 October 1991 – Bosnia proclaims its sovereignty. The Bosnian Serbs organise their own referendum.

8 November 1991 – The EC imposes sanctions on the rump Yugoslav Federation only.

November 1991 – The Yugoslav federal army destroys Vukovar; 15,000 die and 500,000 become refugees.

December 1991 – Germany recognises Slovenian and Croatian independence. It is said that President Tudjman purposefully sacrifices Vukovar in order to gain international recognition.

January 1992 – Bosnian Serbs, led by R. Karadzic, declare the Serb Republic of Bosnia-Hercegovina. The EU recognises Slovenian and Croatian independence and mediates a cease-fire in Croatia.

March 1992 – UN troops arrive in Krajina. They effectively protect Serbian conquests.

March 1992 – President A. Izetbegovic declares Bosnian independence, after a referendum, boycotted by the Bosnian Serbs (33 per cent of Bosnia's population).

March 1992 – Outbreak of war between Serbs and Muslims in Bosnia. A Muslim fires on a Serb wedding ceremony. Armed Serbs erect barricades all over Sarajevo (now controlled by rival militias).

April 1992 – The EU and USA recognise Bosnia's independence.

Civil war in Bosnia

Spring 1992 – Bosnian Serbs and Bosnian Croats agree to a mutually beneficial partition of Bosnia.

April 1992 – Bosnian Serbs take the city of Bijeljina and massacre the civilians at random.

5 April 1992 – People marching for peace in Sarajevo are fired upon by Bosnian Serb snipers (six die). The siege of Sarajevo begins.

April 1992 – The Federal Republic of Yugoslavia (FRY) (Serbia and Montenegro) is declared, but remains unrecognised by the West.

23 April 1992 – Lord Carrington comes to Bosnia as EU peace envoy. He proposes partitioning Bosnia into ethnic provinces.

May 1992 – UN economic embargo begins against FRY only. Bosnia, Croatia and Slovenia (not FRY) are admitted into the UN.

May 1992 – Bosnian Serbs start ethnic cleansing in Zvornik: 49,000 Bosnian Muslims are expelled, sent to concentration camps or executed (about 2,000) by Bosnian Serb troops and Serb paramilitary forces.

5 May 1992 – The Serbs launch an attack on Sarajevo, but are repulsed by the Muslims.

6 May 1992 – Karadzic and the Bosnian Croat leaders meet at Graz airport, Austria, and agree to divide Bosnia between them.

May 1992 – The federal army kidnaps President Izetbegovic and his daughter, when they return from an EU meeting in Lisbon.

The war drags on

July 1992 – In western Bosnia, Bosnian Croats declare their own state of Bosnia-Herceg, with Mostar as its capital.

August 1992 – At a London conference it is agreed that ethnic cleansing should end and borders should not be altered by force.

October 1992 – Bosnian Serbs control 70 per cent of Bosnia.

September 1992 – D. Owen and C. Vance become EU and UN envoys, respectively, charged with solving the Bosnian crisis.

October 1992 – UN Security Council establishes 'no-fly' zone over Bosnia.

December 1992 – Milosevic wins Serb elections.

20 January 1993 – New US President Bill Clinton advocates more involvement of the USA in Bosnia. But he still refuses to send US ground troops to Bosnia.

January 1993 – Outbreak of conflict between Bosnian Croats and Muslims.

February 1993 – The Clinton administration opposes the Vance–Owen plan, saying it supports ethnic cleansing and Serb territorial gains.

11 March 1993 – General Morillon, Commander of the UN forces, is stopped from leaving Srebrenica by the besieged Muslim population. He 'decides to stay' and give the Muslims moral support. In the end, he persuades the Muslims to comply with General Mladic's demands to lay down their arms.

More Western involvement

April 1993 – NATO begins to enforce a 'no-fly' zone over Bosnia.

16 April 1993 – The UN declares Srebrenica a 'safe haven'.

17 April 1993 – Bosnian Croats commit atrocities in Muslim villages. Muslims in the Bosnian Croat army are sent to concentration camps.

April 1993 – Milosevic accepts the Vance–Owen plan in its entirety.

1 May 1993 – All the major combatants, including Karadzic, sign the plan at a special session in Athens.

1 May 1993 – The Clinton administration abandons the Vance–Owen plan in favour of lifting the arms embargo and bombing the Serbs.

May 1993 – The Bosnian Serb parliament rejects the Vance–Owen plan, after General Mladic illustrates how much territory Bosnian Serbs would lose.

June 1993 – UN peace-keepers are deployed along the Macedonian–Serb border.

August 1993 – NATO agrees to air strikes.

November 1993 – Muslims stop the Croat advance. In revenge, the Croats bomb the ancient bridge of Mostar, joining the Muslim and Croat parts of the town.

December 1993 – Milosevic wins Serbian parliamentary elections.

February 1994 – The Sarajevo marketplace massacre: 69 die. All evidence points to the Muslims themselves being responsible, in order to ensure Western help.

The beginnings of peace

8 February 1994 – The Bosnian Serbs are given ten days to move all their weapons from the hills around Sarajevo or else suffer air strikes. The Russians are angry not to have been told in advance.

17 February 1994 – The Russians persuade the Serbs to remove the guns and then put their own troops in the area, making air strikes impossible.

Spring 1994 – Encouraged by the USA and under threat of economic sanctions, Croatia and Bosnia end their war and establish a federation.

April 1994 – The USA, Great Britain, France, Germany and Russia form the so-called Contact Group.

April 1994 – NATO's first air strikes on Bosnian Serb strategic targets after the Serbs attack Gorazde. General Mladic surrounds 150 UN troops, who come under fire. The UN calls off the air strikes.

July 1994 – The Contact Group's peace plan is supported by everyone except the Bosnian Serbs.

August 1994 – Milosevic ends all types of aid to the Bosnian Serbs.

By the end of 1994 – It is clear that the USA is supplying the Bosnian Muslims with arms, against the embargo still in force. The 'safe havens' are also becoming a trap for both Muslims and UN peace-keepers.

January 1995 – Ex-President J. Carter brokers a four-month cease-fire.

Yet another attempt at peace

May 1995 – NATO bombs military targets in the Bosnian Serb capital (a pale response to another attack on the Sarajevo market).

26 May 1995 – In revenge the Serbs take 350 UN peace-keepers hostage. Milosevic negotiates their release.

May 1995 – The Croats recapture western Slavonia.

July 1995 – Bosnian Serbs attack Zepa and Srebrenica. They then engage in mass murder of the civilian populations. NATO threatens 'massive' air strikes. R. Mladic and R. Karazdic are indicted by the UN war-crimes tribunal.

July 1995 – Croats launch a sudden attack on Serbian Krajina and retake the region within a few days. 150,000–200,000 Serbs flee into Serbian Bosnia. The Yugoslav army keeps out of the conflict.

July 1995 – Serbs begin a new round of ethnic cleansing in both Serbia and northern Bosnia in order to rehouse the displaced Krajinian Serbs.

August 1995 – With 'Operation Deliberate Force', NATO bombs Bosnian Serb strategic targets in order to lift the siege of Sarajevo.

September 1995 – The Bosnian Serbs move all their heavy weaponry from around Sarajevo.

September 1995 – A joint Muslim–Croat offensive takes most of north-western Bosnia; 40,000 Serb refugees flee to Banja Luka. There is extensive ethnic cleansing of Croats and Muslims.

The Dayton Peace process

12 October 1995 – A permanent cease-fire is agreed by all sides, after negotiations with US Assistant Secretary of State, R. Holbrooke.

1 November 1995 – Peace negotiations begin at the US airforce base in Dayton, Ohio.

12 November 1995 – The Serbs agree to return eastern Slavonia to Croatia within two years, after Tudjman makes it clear he will take the region by force anyway.

21 November 1995 – The Presidents of Croatia, Bosnia and Serbia (on behalf of the Bosnian Serbs) sign an initial peace treaty ending all conflict. S. Milosevic needs the peace process to succeed (in order to lift economic sanctions) and seems ready to bully the Bosnian Serbs into acceptance. The Dayton plan keeps Bosnia as one country but divides it into two quasi-republics (51 per cent to the Croat–Muslim Federation, 49 per cent to the Serbs). There is a central government (responsible for foreign, monetary, trade and immigration policy). Free elections are set for autumn 1996 and free movement of people throughout Bosnia is guaranteed.

Late November 1995 – UN and EU economic sanctions against FRY are lifted. The arms embargo against former Yugoslavia ends.

Early December 1995 – The first 60,000 UN troops arrive from all over the world (Russia and the USA included) to implement the peace settlement.

14 December 1995 – The peace plan is formally signed by all previous combatants in Paris.

Index